Living the French Revolution, 178

# Living the French Revolution, 1789–99

Peter McPhee

First published in hardback 2006
This paperback edition published 2009 by
PALGRAVE MACMILLAN

Palgrave Macmillan in the UK is an imprint of Macmillan Publishers Limited, registered in England, company number 785998, of Houndmills, Basingstoke, Hampshire RG21 6XS.

Palgrave Macmillan in the US is a division of St Martin's Press LLC, 175 Fifth Avenue, New York, NY 10010.

Palgrave Macmillan is the global academic imprint of the above companies and has companies and representatives throughout the world.

Palgrave® and Macmillan® are registered trademarks in the United States, the United Kingdom, Europe and other countries.

ISBN-13: 978–0–333–99739–0 hardback
ISBN-10: 0–333–99739–5 hardback
ISBN-13: 978–0–230–57475–5 paperback
ISBN-10: 0–230–57475–0 paperback

This book is printed on paper suitable for recycling and made from fully managed and sustained forest sources. Logging, pulping and manufacturing processes are expected to conform to the environmental regulations of the country of origin.

A catalogue record for this book is available from the British Library.

Library of Congress Cataloging-in-Publication Data
McPhee, Peter, 1948–
    Living the French Revolution, 1789–99 / Peter McPhee.
        p. cm.
    Includes bibliographical references and index.
    ISBN 0–333–99739–5 (cloth) 0–230–57475–0 (pbk)
        1. France—History—Revolution, 1789–1799. 2. France—Politics and government—1789–1799. I. Title.
DC148.M454 2007
944.04—dc22                                                      2006044833

10  9  8  7  6  5  4  3  2  1
18  17  16  15  14  13  12  11  10  09

Transferred to Digital Printing in 2012

*For Tom and Kit, Anton and Suzy*

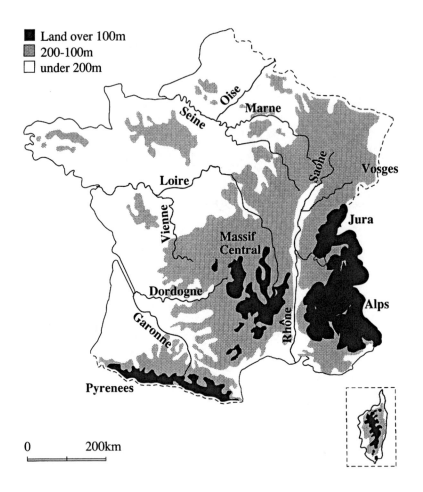

*Map 1*  France – physical

# Contents

# List of Figures and Maps

## Figures

## Maps

# Acknowledgements

## Illustrations

Cover – École française. Portrait de femme, *dit* La Maraîchère. Vers 1795. Musée des Beaux-Arts de Lyon. Photo Alain Basset.

1 Châteaux incendiés au moment de la Grande Peur. Juillet-Août 1789. Gravure. Paris, musée Carnavalet. FA-13288B © Collection Roger-Viollet.

2 Attaque de la voiture d'un aristocrate, août 1789. Gravure, B.N. FA-12466 © Collection Roger-Viollet.

3 'La chasse aux corbeaux'. Gravure antireligieuse. Paris, musée Carnavalet. FA-26084 © Collection Roger-Viollet.

4 Stone carving of the Bastille above the doorway of a house in Camps-sur-l'Agly (Aude). Photograph by Fronza Woods-Pleasance.

5 Arrestation de Louis XVI (1754–93), roi de France, et de la famille royale à Varennes le 21 juin 1791. Gravure, Musée Carnavalet, Paris. FA-13323 © Collection Roger-Viollet.

6 L'Entrée Franche: Je me suis ruiné pour l'engraisser, la fin du compte je ne sait qu'en faire. PMVP/Cliché: Habouzit. Musée Carnavalet HIST PC 016 C-G 25670.

7 Assignats. 1789–99. RVB-06884 © Collection Roger-Viollet.

8 Plat: Je suis bougrement patriote. PMVP/Cliché: Svartz, Denis. Musée Carnavalet C 0451.

9 Cocarde, carte au nom de la Société Amis de la Constitution de 1793 Commune de Dax. PMVP/ Cliché: Andreani. Musée Carnavalet OM 0176.

10 Société populaire de Mont Égalité, ci-devant Faremoutier: Unité-indivisibilité, fraternité ou la mort. [Meaux: s.n. 1793 ou 1794] . Bibliothèque Nationale de France. Hennin 11831.

11 Marie Royer, vivandière de la 51ᵉ demi-Brigade. 22 ventôse an 5. Labrousse del et sculp [Paris: sn, entre 1796 et 1805] Extrait de Grasset Saint-Sauveur. Bibliothèque Nationale de France. QB1-1797.

12 Jaque Guillon. Bibliothèque Nationale de France. LF-9C 4o.

Parts of Chapter 1 were published as ' "The misguided greed of peasants"? Popular attitudes to the environment in the Revolution of 1789', *French Historical Studies* 24 (2001), 247–269.

# List of Abbreviations

Abbreviated titles have been used for some periodicals cited in notes more than once:

| | |
|---|---|
| AHR | *American Historical Review* |
| AHRF | *Annales historiques de la Révolution française* |
| AJFS | *Australian Journal of French Studies* |
| Annales | *Annales: économies, sociétés, civilisations* |
| EHQ | *European History Quarterly* |
| FH | *French History* |
| FHS | *French Historical Studies* |
| JFH | *Journal of Family History* |
| JMH | *Journal of Modern History* |
| P&P | *Past & Present* |
| RHMC | *Revue d'histoire moderne et contemporaine* |
| SH | *Social History* |

# Introduction

The St Jean de Bouisse family was seigneur of the tiny communities of Fraïsse and Montjoi, southwest of Narbonne. In April 1790, Montjoi complained to the revolutionary National Assembly that it had been 'enslaved by the tyranny of self-styled seigneurs without titles'; indeed, Bouisse had just made a visit to houses in the village to take the best portions of a recently butchered pig. The mayor of Fraïsse in turn described the Bouisse men: 'Four big bodies, uncles and nephews, possessors of imposing physique walking around with four-pound batons, that was the sight which followed us into our houses ... M de Bouisse, following his old habits, has sworn to plague us to our deaths.' For his defence, the baron could only despair:

> I have cherished and I still cherish the people of Fraïsse as I have cherished my own children; they were so sweet and so honest in their way, but what a sudden change has taken place among them. All I hear now is *corvée, lanternes, démocrates, aristocrates*, words which for me are barbaric and which I can't use. ... the former vassals believe themselves to be more powerful than Kings.[1]

There are several layers of meanings which may be teased out of this story. On the most immediate level it is, of course, an example of an outraged noble fulminating against the revolutionary madness which had engulfed his 'vassals', who in turn presented themselves as victims of longstanding oppression. The Revolution of 1789 had given them unprecedented opportunity to confront the man who had dominated their lives, even to harass him. But was their use of the language of the Revolution – 'lanternes, démocrates, aristocrates' – only a weapon of their own with which to beat the baron in turn? Or did it have a greater resonance? In which ways might a radically altered language of power have spoken of a changed actuality? What was it to 'live' the French Revolution?

These are questions for which we will never have simple, confident answers. Like the less powerful in all societies, the peasants of Montjoi and

Fraïsse had little occasion to make unsolicited statements about their world in a form which has survived for us. Their voices have mostly been preserved for us when they came into contact with institutions which controlled their lives, such as courts of law or, as in this case, when they wished to defend themselves to authorities.[2] Because of the nature of the materials with which historians work, whether printed or manuscript, they have inevitably examined the impact of the Revolution on 'the people' through the words of others. Ever since the Vendéen insurrection of 1793, for example, combatants and then historians have argued heatedly over its causes, purposes, and the scale of its killing; we know surprisingly little, nevertheless, of how those who participated voiced the reasons for which they were prepare to kill or be killed.[3]

The French Revolution was, however, one of those rare periods in history when 'ordinary' people – peasants, labourers, trades people, the indigent – felt sufficiently confident to express themselves directly to the authorities. At times this was through the medium of the records of local government – village councils or neighbourhood meetings – and at others through legal actions they initiated, or through the language of protest. This book seeks to use such evidence, and much else besides, to reflect on the experience of the Revolution for the people who lived in mainland France's country towns and villages. It investigates the ways in which the Revolution affected daily life, both in terms of the impact of legislation and of the ways in which people made and experienced changes to their own lives. In particular, it examines whether and how the lived experience of the Revolution, war and sweeping legislative change in France 1789–99 transformed cultures and society, even daily life itself.

On one level, the aim of writing such a history is a logical impossibility. This was a land of some 28 million people – and there were hundreds of thousands of slaves in its colonies – and, for each of them, the Revolution was experienced individually as well as collectively. As Alain Corbin has demonstrated, no matter what the level of the skills the historian may bring, even an entire book devoted to 'the life of an unknown' may only take us a few steps closer. His story of Louis-François Pinagot (born in 1798) reminds us, too, that biographical details of interest to the State – in tax schedules, civil registers and conscription records – are usually all we have. The mental universe of working people in the past is the most difficult for the historian to penetrate.[4]

Perhaps no historian has come closer to glimpsing that universe than Richard Cobb. Cobb relished putting names and stories to faces in urban crowds in a distinctive, *pointilliste* and often exquisite style. His passion was to recapture individual lives, with their moments of drama, their prejudices and dreams. His distaste was for ideologues – historians as much as revolutionary politicians – who claimed to speak for the masses and their supposed interests. First published in French in 1961–63, his study of the *armées révolutionnaires*, the civilian armies of urban militants or *sans-culottes* established in the second half of 1793, is one of the seminal studies of the revolutionary period.[5] In it, Cobb documented the activities of about 40,000 *sans-culottes* in makeshift revolutionary battalions sent to the countryside to requisition supplies, to seek out deserters from the republican armies, to purge unpatriotic priests and other counter-revolutionaries and even to 'dechristianize' the provinces.

Across the next 15 years Cobb produced a series of captivating books drawing on decades spent in French archives since 1935.[6] The first of his great themes was the irrelevance of high politics to the concerns of most people. He evidently enjoyed recounting the story of Marguerite Barrois, a country girl seduced on her second night in Paris, 10 Thermidor Year II (28 July 1794), the day of Robespierre's execution, 'a date as memorable for her no doubt as for history'.[7] Most famously, Cobb wrote of the 'irrelevance' of the Revolution to the lives of masses of people who – before, during and after the Revolution – inhabited a world of unremitting poverty, uncertainty, violence and despair.[8] The targets of his thesis, that the Revolution was irrelevant to the masses of French people when it was not being made against them, were in particular his former colleagues Georges Lefebvre, Albert Soboul and George Rudé, seen to have reified the chaotic world of a revolution into peasant and *sans-culottes* 'movements'.[9]

Cobb's second theme was the increasing divide between town and country: 'The events of the Revolution constantly accentuated the economic, religious and political gulf between town and country, especially after the outbreak of war.'[10] Since Cobb was primarily interested in Paris and other cities rather than in the countryside, which he saw as locked in a bitter struggle to keep safe its foodstuffs and saints from the dechristianizing *sans-culottes*, he was sure that the Revolution was 'increasingly a townsman's affair ... it is not surprising that many countrymen turned against a revolution from the benefits of which they were apparently to be excluded'.[11] In so far as Cobb wrote about the countryside at all, it was as the source of migrants to Paris or as the terrain for *sans-culottes'* missionary zeal. The politics of its inhabitants were those of survival, against dearth, conscription and religious reform.

Perhaps because my own family background is that of country towns and farming, I have always been more intrigued by how rural people lived and worked. Although I work in an élite institution and inhabit a large city, the most interesting questions about history for me have long been to do with how rural people make their own histories. This is not a history of the people of great cities or substantial towns,[12] or of social élites, about whom so much more is known because of their literacy. Of course, any study of rural communities cannot ignore large towns and cities but, rather than following the urban–rural paradigm of laws, news, influence and change being diffused from the capital, of regions as 'provincial', this book seeks to place the inhabitants of rural France at centre stage, to examine how they lived through a Revolution they variously accepted and supported or resented and opposed.

The meaning of the Revolution for the inhabitants of rural France has long been the subject of debate. Georges Lefevbre long ago convinced historians that peasants were not passive participants in the French Revolution, arguing that there was a distinct peasant revolution within the Revolution as a whole, with its own pulse and projects.[13] More recently, other historians – such as Anatoli Ado, Peter Jones and John Markoff – have reasserted the importance of initiatives taken by rural communities across much of the country in pressuring successive assemblies to finally abolish seigneurialism in 1792–93.[14] By seeking to place rural people at the forefront of their stories, they have offered a reading of the Revolution as in part an ongoing dialogue between the capital and the countryside.

But, while the importance of popular participation is evident, was this sporadic and in some sense peripheral to everyday concerns? Was the French Revolution 'a magnificent irrelevance' to the poorer groups in French society, as Cobb claimed? Donald Sutherland agreed: it was 'largely an urban phenomenon', which drew on a narrow base of support in the countryside and left a legacy of 'perhaps even greater misery for the poor'. 'One great and unpleasant reality about the Revolution', he concluded, is that 'the revolutionaries drove very large numbers of women and men to a profound revulsion against them and all their works when they stripped away the markers that gave their lives meaning'.[15] Like Sutherland, Eugen Weber has pointed to the low participation rates in elections as evidence that the Revolution was irrelevant to most people, or even anathema. 'If a poll of French countryfolk could have been taken in 1799', asserts T.J.A. Le Goff, 'a clear majority would have qualified the Revolution as a disaster'.[16] David Andress, too, has concluded a recent overview of French society and the Revolution by asserting that it was a revolution made 'against the people'.[17]

These and other historians have asserted that the French Revolution may have begun with a peasant upheaval but that rural people quickly became disillusioned by the Revolution's religious policies, lack of reforms to tenancy arrangements, and incessant demands for taxes and conscripts. Indeed, Sutherland has argued that, if there was a popular movement in the revolutionary period, it was the royalist and Catholic provincial counter-revolution. While he has argued his case persuasively, this book will investigate the ways in which, even in communities hostile to the Revolution, the patterned rituals of daily life were transformed by the very experience of resisting revolutionary upheaval.

This is not another history of the French Revolution, nor a history of popular participation in the Revolution in the French countryside, which has been undertaken many times in every region of France and at a more general level in recent years by Sutherland, Anatoli Ado, David Andress, Peter Jones, John Markoff, Michel Vovelle and many others.[18] Writing on the rural dimension of the French Revolution has assumed that the lived experience of rural people may be equated with their popular participation in the Revolution, whether for it or against it. For almost a century – notably since the work of Georges Lefebvre on the peasants of the Nord – historians have studied the popular Revolution by analysing the behaviour of revolutionary crowds in town and country, the emergence of a *sans-culottes* 'movement', or the impact of the Revolution on society and the economy. Such an approach inevitably privileges those rare moments when working people actively participated in the Revolution. For example, David Andress has recently produced an informative synthesis of what we know about popular participation which essentially highlights moments of violent intervention in the course of the Revolution.[19]

Histories of the French Revolution have followed a familiar chronological structure in line with major political turning points. In a general way social history has questioned this conventional 'periodization' of history as privileging the world of élite politics, arguing instead that the rhythms of daily life, economic and social change move far more slowly and cut across such divisions. Do 'public and private calendars' – the linear progression of political life and the rhythms of the private and familial world – ever move to the same impulses? In the case of the French Revolution, however, not to follow a narrative structure would be to weaken the power of an unfolding drama. The French Revolution was a political and social upheaval which involved and affected all French people, though in sharply contrasting ways.[20]

This book is premised on the approach that the local experience of the Revolution is best understood as a process of negotiation and confrontation with distant governments rather than simply one of more-or-less recalcitrant provincial communities being acted upon, and only occasionally lashing out in violent retribution. The book seeks to capture something of what it meant to live through a great revolution for the mass of the population, the nine-tenths of the population who lived on the farms and in the villages and small towns of rural France. Of particular importance will be the evocation of the ways in which revolutionary changes altered the textures of daily life or were adapted as people sought to resist such change. How did rural and small-town men and women adopt, adapt and resist change from Paris? In what ways was life different by the end of that decade, and what had been the major experiences of the Revolution along the way?

Never had there been more people living in the French countryside than there were in 1789. Largely because of a protracted series of fair to good harvests in the years after 1750, by 1780 the population of France had increased by 3.5 million from perhaps 24.5 million. Using the later French measure of the 'urban threshold' being 2,000 people, perhaps two persons in ten lived in an urban centre. But most towns of up to 10,000 people (for example, Nevers, Bourg or Laon) essentially served the surrounding agrarian economy: half the 'urban' population lived in country towns like these which were essentially rural in orientation. The rest inhabited 38,000 rural communities or parishes with on average about 730 residents.[21] Ten times as many people inhabited France's villages and farms as do today: the countryside was crowded with people and livestock in a way that has today been forgotten.

These people were and are commonly referred to as 'paysans'. But this simple term disguises the complexities of rural society which were to be revealed in the varied behaviour of rural people during the Revolution. In most regions, the bulk of the agricultural population was either smallholders, tenant-farmers or sharecroppers, many of whom were also reliant on practising a craft or on wage-work. The peasantry made up about four-fifths of the 'Third Estate' or 'commoners' but across the country it owned only about 40 per cent of the land outright. This varied from about 17 per cent in the Mauges region of western France to 64 per cent in the Auvergne. Farm labourers were as much as half the population in areas of large-scale agriculture such as the Ile-de-France around Paris and in Picardy. In all rural communities there was a minority of larger farmers, often dubbed the *coqs du village*, who were large tenant-farmers (*fermiers*) or independent landowners (*laboureurs*). Depending on the region, there were those who specialized in winegrowing, charcoal burning, weaving, timber-cutting, fishing and livestock. Larger villages also had a minority of people – priests, lawyers, artisans, textile-workers and so on – who were not peasants at all, but who commonly owned some land, such as the vegetable garden belonging to the priest.

The peasant population lived in a diverse and contrasting habitat, varying from the large, clustered villages and *bourgs* of a thousand people and more in parts of the south and east to the dispersed farms and hamlets of the southern Massif Central, Limousin and western *bocage*. Everywhere, their relationship with local small towns was close and constant; indeed, central to any consideration of the revolutionary experience of the working people of town and country is the relationship between them. Georges Lefebvre, while highlighting the specificities of the peasant Revolution, saw it as having in common with towns a mistrust of capitalist commerce and production. Was Alfred Cobban correct to stress instead the town–country divide as a key element in the driving force of the Revolution? Or, rather, should one follow Richard Cobb in stressing the diversity and interplay of urban centres and their rural hinterlands?[22]

\* \* \*

Historians have tried many ways to capture the meaning of the Revolution for the mass of French people. Most commonly this has been through the use of case studies, ranging from studies of an entire region or, following the revolutionary reorganization of administration, a department, to closer analyses of a micro-region or a single community. More imaginatively, Peter Jones has written a comparative study of six very different communities.[23] Whatever the contribution these case studies have made to the overall richness of the historiography, the combined effect has been to highlight diversity. This difficulty has been compounded by the extreme difficulty of capturing the experience and perceptions of the masses of working people, most of whom were not literate in the written word. Despite the attempts by revolutionary governments to create the bases for national unity, culminating in the *République une et indivisible* after 1792, the village and its immediate *pays* remained the fundamental spatial reference point for the great mass of new citizens. The Revolution created the departmental structures of administration which have largely endured to the present, but only rarely did these coincide with people's self-identities or with a cohesive geographic and economic character.

Despite these limitations, some distance may be made in constructing a history of the lived experience of the Revolution. For we know an enormous amount about that extraordinary decade – indeed, there have been few periods in history which have been so extensively or so well studied – even if surprisingly little has been written with a view to capturing what it might have been like to live through such a revolutionary upheaval.

The richness of French archives – for which the Revolution is in large measure responsible – has made it possible for a history of the Revolution to be written about any community. Not only is there a danger in reading these sources as unproblematic records of a past reality, however; there is another danger in assuming that they represent what it was like to live through this Revolution. Put simply, the archives do not record silences. It is one thing to order extant records into a village or regional history, but what does it mean when nothing is deemed worthy of record? Should this be read as signifying that support for the Revolution was so solid as to be uncontested and therefore without trace in the records? Or that the Revolution was simply irrelevant?

Most of France's 38,000 or more villages have had a history written. With a few splendid exceptions, these have been the work of an *érudit local*, an industrious local who has returned to the extant sources of a loved village's past. These have catalogued the information recorded in local council or departmental records: very few have pondered the meaning of the Revolution for the village's inhabitants. The Bicentenary of the Revolution in 1989 was the occasion of a veritable flood of several thousands of these local histories, continuing a long tradition of local, commemorative scholarship. These monographs vary sharply in quality: from antiquarian collections of undigested detail (often, however, including valuable transcriptions of manuscript documents) to the genuinely analytical. Almost always, however, they suffer from a lack of any evocation of a dynamic between the local community and national governments. At the other extreme are outstanding local and regional monographs, such as those of the northernmost region of France by Jean-Pierre Jessenne and Liana Vardi.[24]

These difficulties serve to remind us of another dimension of the special nature of the historical dialogue into which this project enters. Those at the centre of this project are prevented from speaking directly to the historian not only because the great majority of them were illiterate; this is also a study of rural people through the filter of a French language few understood readily and fewer still spoke. As the Amis de la Constitution of Carcassonne, in the Occitan-speaking south, put it early in the Revolution, 'In the town and surrounding villages, the people understand French; but the majority speaks *patois*. In more distant places, only *patois* is spoken, and French is less understood.' Their Catalan neighbours to the south had been incorporated in the French State for only 130 years; there, too, linguistic particularity was obvious. The Abbé Chambon responded to a national enquiry in 1790 that 'Country people do not know how to speak French ... To destroy [the Catalan language] it would be necessary to destroy the sun, the cool of the evenings, the type of food, the quality of water, in the end the whole person.'[25] The enquiry estimated that only three of the 28 million people used French as their sole language: for most it was a second language used with great difficulty and for several million it was not used at all. Did this lack of facility in French accentuate the likelihood of misunderstanding and mistrust? Did it prevent provincial people from entering into their own dialogue with successive, distant French governments?

Previous attempts to reconstruct the lived experience of the French Revolution have been restricted either by their perspective or by the deliberately selective thematic approach of their authors. There have been attempts to write the history of 'daily life' during the Revolution. The first, by the director of the Musée Carnavalet, Jean Robiquet, was essentially restricted to Paris and is further limited by the paucity of published social history at the time it was written in the late 1930s.[26] Fifty years later, Jean-Paul Bertaud, a distinguished historian of the 'people in arms', published a history of daily life packed with information and insights, but with disproportionate emphasis on Paris, the culture of the literate and the army. Michel Vovelle has probed brilliantly the 'revolutionary mentality', but also largely concentrated on changes in urban popular political culture.[27] An ambitious attempt by Serge Bianchi to study the 'cultural Revolution' of the most radical period of the Revolution is restricted by its focus on – indeed, celebration of – examples of revolutionary change in daily life rather than resistance to them. Other historians have focused instead on the construction of a new civic order in Paris and its transmission to or rejection by the provinces. An outstanding overview by Isser Woloch is deliberately 'the view from the center', although replete with local examples reported to Paris; in contrast, Alan Forrest has successfully synthesized the outlines of the Revolution from a genuinely national perspective.[28]

More recent attempts to study the impact of the Revolution on daily life have resulted in illuminating specific aspects of the revolutionary experience. Surveys by Alan Forrest and Jean-Paul Bertaud of the relationship between civil society and the military have paid due attention to the ways in which conscription and requisitioning were experienced and resisted.[29] The impact of the Revolution on collective political practice has been carefully studied by Malcolm Crook, and Mona Ozouf has analysed official and, to some extent, popular festivals.[30] In contrast, historians have had little to say about the environment during the revolutionary period, and even less about whether and how contemporaries debated its protection.

This book extends these analyses into a wider, synthetic interpretation of the ways in which the challenges, opportunities and threats of the revolutionary decade were experienced by the working people of town and country. Most important, rather than proceeding on the assumption that change initiated by revolutionary governments in Paris transformed daily life, it will investigate the ways in which such changes need to be understood also as the result of a decade-long process of negotiation and confrontation between men and women in the provinces and distant governments in Paris.

Local archives, petitions, parliamentary debates and official reports have formed an important body of research materials for exploring these issues. The major pieces of legislation pertaining to daily life and of the parliamentary and Committee debates preceding them were studied through the *Réimpression de l'ancien Moniteur*. Valuable also in this regard was the rich documentation from the records of key committees of successive governments, in particular the Comité des Droits Féodaux and the Comité des Rapports. Of particular use were three major holdings in the Baillieu Library, University of Melbourne: *The Maclure Collection of French Revolutionary Materials*; the Pergamon Press *French Revolution Research Collection*; and a remarkable collection of pamphlets from the Revolution. There are, of course, limitations to the use of all such materials. First, the parliamentary debates and official reports have to be read within a framework of political structures and as articulations of particular attitudes with specific audiences in mind. Second, comparatively little of this material articulated the attitudes of the mass of working people – and was very rarely in their own words – and it has to be read as prescriptive as well as descriptive. Often, it is in examining the ideology of political and administrative élites that the attitudes may be discerned of those they condemned. One exception to this paucity of direct evidence from one side of the debate is that the committees of successive assemblies received both solicited and unsolicited letters and petitions from rural people on specific issues, for example, proposals to authorize or even encourage the sale or distribution of common lands. It has been essential to draw on local records such as family courts and the deliberations of village and small-town municipal councils. The latter are a rich source of relatively untrammelled expressions of popular attitudes, especially in 1789–93, for the men elected to these bodies. Case studies were undertaken of the regions in and around Alençon (department of the Orne), Bourg-en-Bresse (Ain), Carcassonne (Aude), Laon (Aisne) and La Rochelle (Charente-Maritime). These were complemented by earlier, more specific studies of, for example, Collioure and St-Laurent-de-Cerdans (Pyrénées-Orientales) and Gabian (Hérault).

This book has been greatly facilitated by grants from the Australian Research Council. The project was made the richer by direct contributions from research assistants, graduate students and colleagues: above all, Juliet Flesch and Emily McCaffrey, and on particular topics Greg Burgess, Suzy Emison, Elizabeth Graham, Julie Kalman, Anthony King, Jonathon Marshall, Kate Mustafa, Carine Renoux, Megan Utter and Jeremy Whiteman. It would not have been possible without the willing assistance of librarians and archivists in Alençon, Bourg-en-Bresse, Laon, La Rochelle, Montpellier, Paris, and, over many years, Carcassonne and Perpignan. Finally, Charlotte Allen has been a constant source of comment and encouragement.

# 1
# Describing the Old Regime

Thirty kilometres from Reims in northeastern France is the imposing Benedictine abbey of Vauclair, founded in the twelfth century. On 8 March 1789 some of the inhabitants of one of its dependent villages, La Vallée-Foulon, met together to respond to a royal decree of 24 January requesting parishes to produce their lists of grievances (*cahiers de doléances*) for the consideration of the looming Estates-General in May. Those present expressed their boundless gratitude to the abbey for the land and houses it made available for rent: 'they declare that they have no complaint to make'. Perhaps, they suggested, the King might consider reducing taxes; whatever the case, they put 'their full confidence in the paternal goodness of His Majesty'.[1] The reasons for the quiescence of La Vallée-Foulon were perhaps that the *cahier* was drawn up by the better-off inhabitants (it was signed by only 10 men from the 32 households in the village) and that it was composed in the intimidating presence of Charles-Louis Dequin, the abbey's own legal officer. Certainly, however, it was a highly unusual document in expressing the community's apparently passive acceptance of its lot.

In the spring of 1789, people in villages and towns all over France met like those in La Vallée-Foulon to formulate proposals for the regeneration of public life and to elect deputies to the Estates-General. Parish and guild assemblies, and meetings of clergy and nobles, were engaged in compiling their 'lists of grievances' to guide their deputies in the advice they would offer the King. The drawing up of these *cahiers* in the context of political uncertainty, fiscal emergency and subsistence crisis was for most people the first episode in a decade of revolution. They would know that only in retrospect, of course, just as it is only from hindsight that it strikes historians as the decisive moment in the mass politicization of social friction.

Country folk and townspeople had for centuries been accustomed to parish assemblies – both formal and informal – which governed local affairs. In June 1787 the Controller-General Calonne had issued an edict which imposed uniformity across much of the country on the diverse forms in which parishes had formerly met to decide matters of local concern. From now on those paying more than ten *livres* in direct taxes, in most areas a majority of adult men, were to form a parish Assembly to elect a municipal council composed of six 'conseillers' and two or three 'consuls' which would include as *ex officio* members the priest and the seigneur, the latter of whom had the right to chair meetings.[2] But the electoral provisions for the Estates-General announced on 24 January were far broader: all adult male taxpayers in the countryside were eligible to attend special parish meetings which were to agree on the terms of the *cahiers* and to appoint delegates, usually two or four depending on the size of the parish, to represent the parish at the district (*bailliage* or *sénéchaussée*) level.

The parish and craft meetings convened to draw up these *cahiers* were an outcome of a long-term political and financial crisis. France's involvement in the war of independence waged by Britain's North American colonies in 1775–83 had partially revenged the humiliations that Britain had inflicted on France in India, Canada and the Caribbean; however, the war cost France over 1 billion *livres*, more than twice the usual annual revenue of the state. As the royal state sank into financial crisis after 1783, the costs of servicing this massive debt impelled the monarchy to seek ways of ending noble taxation immunity and the capacity of noble-dominated high courts (Parlements) to resist royal decrees to that end.

In 1787–88 royal ministers made successive attempts to persuade meetings of the most prominent aristocrats to agree to lift the fiscal privileges of the nobility or Second Estate. In February 1787, Calonne sought to convince an Assembly of 144 'Notables', only 10 of whom were non-noble, by offering concessions such as the establishment of regional assemblies in all provinces in return for the introduction of a universal land tax, the reduction of other taxes such as the *taille* and *gabelle* and the abolition of internal customs barriers. His proposals were rebuffed, in particular that of the land tax: he was dismissed in April. Further attempts at reform foundered on the nobility's insistence that only a gathering of representatives of the three orders as an Estates-General could agree to such innovation. Tension between crown and nobility came to a head in August 1788, with the Parlements insisting that the measures that the King's ministry sought to impose amounted to 'royal despotism'.

In such a situation, both sides looked to an Estates-General to provide legitimacy for their claims. They were both mistaken. Instead, the calling of the Estates-General in May 1789 facilitated the expression of tensions at every level of French society. The remarkable vibrancy of debate in the months before May was facilitated by the suspension of press censorship and the publication of several thousand political pamphlets. This war of words was further fuelled by Louis' indecision about the procedures to be followed at Versailles. Would representatives of the three orders meet separately, as at the previous meeting of the Estates-General in 1614 or in a single chamber? Louis' decision in December to double the size of Third Estate representation without resolving this matter served only to highlight further this crucial issue of political power.

The calling of the Estates-General and the convocation of assemblies to frame the *cahiers* was a shock which reverberated at every level of society. Millions of rural and urban households which had hitherto experienced the structures of power and privilege as controls to be obeyed, sidestepped or occasionally contested were now authorized, even enjoined, to reflect on their efficacy and legitimacy. This was unprecedented in the lives of working people.

The *cahiers* of the Third Estate ranged in length from many pages of detailed criticisms and suggestions to the three sentences written in a mixture of French and Catalan from the tiny village of Serrabone in the stony foothills of the Pyrenees. Despite this diversity, there is no better source for understanding popular attitudes in early 1789. They also offer the historian the opportunity to sketch the outlines of the way communities described the world in which they lived, and how they felt it could be made more just.

There are three important limits to the veracity and transparency of the *cahiers* as direct statements of the views of the commoners of the countryside. A first limitation to their usefulness is that many of the *cahiers* of rural parishes in particular were influenced by a model document, usually emanating from a nearby town.[3] For example, many of the *cahiers* of parishes between Narbonne and Carcassonne in Languedoc were influenced by a *cahier* probably emanating from the former. Even so, however, the parish assemblies almost always added some articles of their own. At Moux, for example, the *cahier* reproduced 26 articles from the model, only to break abruptly into a less grammatically correct but more forceful tone for eight of its own. Parish assemblies commonly deleted articles from the model *cahier* as well as adding to it.[4] Further around the Mediterranean, half of the 346 *cahiers* in the *sénéchausée* of Nîmes used clauses in circulated *cahiers*, but none was a simple copy.[5] In the *bailliage* of Amont in eastern France, scores of parishes reproduced a statement demanding that 'all forges, furnaces and factories established in the province of Franche-Comté within the past thirty years be destroyed as well as older ones whose proprietors do not personally possess a forest large enough to power them for six months per year'.[6] Rather than reflecting unthinking peasant acquiescence in a model *cahier*, however, the common reiteration of clauses underscores the particular resonance of the issue.

A second constraint is that, at times, the *cahiers* were compiled under direct pressure or indirect forms of intimidation from *curés* and seigneurs or their agents, as in La Vallée-Foulon. In rural communities, the economically dependent were acutely aware of the potential costs of outspoken opposition to noble privilege. Even where the influence of *curés* and seigneurial agents was benign, it may have prevented the *cahiers* from being transparent representations of peasant attitudes, for example, when the *curé* or local bourgeois acted as an intermediary.[7] In the impoverished little village of Erceville, north of Orléans, for example, the Third Estate meeting was presided over by the local judge employed by the seigneur, a prominent member of the Parlement of Paris whose holdings covered most of the parish. Not surprisingly, his tenants stayed away from the meeting. Nevertheless, in this case the peasants, labourers and artisans who drew up Erceville's *cahier* were remarkably blunt, urging that 'without any distinction of title or rank, the said seigneur be taxed like them', that 'the tithe and *champart* be abolished, or at least converted into an annual payment in money', and – clearly aware of the looming issue of the locus of political power – that all taxes should require 'the consent of the whole Nation assembled in Estates-General'.

A final constraint on the transparency of the *cahiers* is that, although in theory all male taxpayers over twenty-five years of age were eligible to participate in the process of drawing up *cahiers*, their compilation was likely to be – whether or not by general consent – in the hands of the better-off minority of villagers. This does not mean that others were neither present nor involved. The 12 (of 129) extant Third Estate *cahiers* from the Corbières region of Languedoc concluded with the formula that 'the literate members have signed', but the numbers of those who did (some 165 men from the 613 households in the 12 parishes, or just 27 per cent) tell us more about literacy rates than numbers at the assemblies. For many more men, in fact, participated than indicated by the numbers of those who could sign the final document, the proportion of households which were actually represented at these parish meetings ranged from 28 per cent at Bizanet to 85 per cent at Cruscades. Similarly, we do not know whether the 10 signatures at the foot of the *cahier* from La Vallée-Foulon, with which this chapter began, were those of all present, or whether others were present who were unable to sign.[8]

Historians have commonly doubted the veracity of the *cahiers* because of these limitations or have used them as a way of indicating the fissures running through French society. They can be used in a third way: as a window into the Ancien Régime. While ostensibly a list of the grievances of all groups in French society, they can also be used to tell us much of how commoners in town and country understood the world around them and how they expressed their own identity within that world.

\*    \*    \*

Every parish and urban corporation expressed grievances which tell us something of the specifics of a local community; what is most remarkable is the similarity of grievances across the country. The *cahiers* reveal that the fundamental issue across most of France was that of control of resources and the claims of the privileged over those resources. The interaction between rural people and their environments was mediated through a complex mix of social relationships which had evolved across eight centuries. All land worked by peasants – whether or not they owned it – was subject to the claims of others: the King, the Catholic Church, seigneurs and others in the community. Few peasants owned enough land for their household's survival, and even when they did their labours had also to meet royal taxes, the Church tithe, and a maze of seigneurial and other exactions. Nor could they ignore the usage rights of others in their community. That is why any attempt to describe the experience of French people during the revolutionary decade after 1789 has to begin with an understanding of the fundamental concerns of most people: how the household could meet its own needs and the demands to which it was subject.

The world described by rural communities in 1789 was one in which control over landed property and the people who worked it was at its core. Rural people were not only vulnerable to the climate, but also underwrote the culture, lifestyles and expenditure of the three pillars of power and privilege: the nobility, the Church and the monarchical State. All three extracted 'surplus' (though the peasantry would never have described it as such), ranging from as little as 14 per cent of what a peasant household might produce in Brittany (8 per cent as tithe, 4 per cent as taxes and 2 per cent as seigneurial dues) to as much as 40 per cent elsewhere.[9] But dues were a central concern in the *cahiers* everywhere, even in Brittany. The main harvest due – variously known as the *champart, tasque, censive* or *tierce* – varied from one-twentieth in the Dauphiné to one-third in the Limousin: an average figure for the whole country would be one-sixth, but rates varied even on lands within the same parish.

The silence of most noble *cahiers* on the issue of seigneurial dues speaks volumes about their importance. Robert Forster has emphasized the role of some nobles in the introduction of market-oriented agricultural practices on their own land,[10] but noble wealth more commonly relied upon restrictive contracts on rented land and regular payment of dues in cash or kind. The importance to nobles of seigneurial dues varied sharply – in the south, from 71 per cent of noble income in the Rouergue to 34 per cent in upper Auvergne and just 8 per cent in the Lauragais – but was significant everywhere. Harvest dues were bolstered by other significant 'rights', such as a monopoly (*banalité*) over the village oven, grape and olivepress, and mill; irregular payments on land transfers and even marriages; obligatory unpaid labour by the community on the lord's lands; and important 'honorific' prerogatives recognizing pre-eminence in the parish.[11]

John Markoff and Gilbert Shapiro have analysed 1,112 of the 40,000 or more *cahiers*, 748 of them from village communities.[12] Their monumental analysis has offered the clearest understanding thus far of the range and incidence of rural grievances. The most common parish complaints concerned taxation exemptions, the structure and powers of the Estates-General and indirect taxes. It is clear from the *cahiers* that although feudalism in its 'pure' form, if it ever existed fully, no longer controlled the countryside, the economic power and seigneurial 'rights' fiercely guarded by the nobility and religious orders were a constant dimension of rural life. Their analysis demonstrates that peasants were far more concerned in 1789 with material rather than symbolic burdens, that they largely ignored all those trappings of seigneurial status which weighed little in terms of controls on produce, such as the public display of arms and reserved pews in Churches.

In the districts of Troyes, Auxerre and Sens, an analysis of 389 parish *cahiers* by Peter Jones has shown that seigneurial dues and *banalités* were explicitly criticized in 40 per cent, 36 per cent and 27 per cent, respectively, leaving aside other common complaints about hunting rights and seigneurial courts. Inevitably, the composite *cahiers* drawn up by urban bourgeois at the district (*bailliage*) level excised many rural grievances deemed too parochial; nevertheless, 64 per cent of the 666 *cahiers* at this level across France called for the abolition of seigneurial dues. In stark contrast, 84 per cent of noble *cahiers* were simply silent on the whole matter.[13]

Despite the intimidation which seigneurs and their agents were able to exert, the boldness of vulnerable rural people was a times startling. In the midst of a series of very specific complaints in the *cahier* of Silly-en-Multien, a village of 580 people near Senlis, 50 km northeast of Paris, was inserted an article from which two nervous village notables promptly disassociated themselves: 'What advantage for the public good if the hunting codes and feudal dues were abolished, that there were no *banalités*, in a word that the French regained their liberty.'[14] From the village of Pont-sur-Seine in Champagne a seigneur's agent wrote to his master:

> In vain I've done everything I can to exclude from the *cahier* the articles on the abolition of *banalités*, of the right to hunt, and other seigneurial dues ... The intention and the tenacity of the people are immovable on this question and it is impossible to dissuade them, because they have been given the right to express their grievances.[15]

Peasants took the opportunity to highlight what seemed to be humiliating 'rights', for example, that requiring the inhabitants of Moimay, near Vesoul in the east, to beat the seigneur's ponds at night when frogs' croaks were too loud.[16] In the southernmost corner of the kingdom, the few lines submitted from the hamlet of Périllos were startlingly hostile to the seigneurial system: 'This community is very poor because we don't have the same rights and privileges as do others; the Seigneur treats us like slaves.'[17]

Although more than three-quarters of the village *cahiers* criticized seigneurialism (especially dues, monopolies and periodical levies), the more common target of peasant anger in 1789 was State taxation.[18] The issues were closely linked, however, for what rankled most with commoners was the privileged fiscal treatment of the noble élite, whether seigneurs or as bishops and abbots within the Church. Typical in this regard was the *cahier* of the parish of Sagy in the Vexin region to the north of Paris, situated between

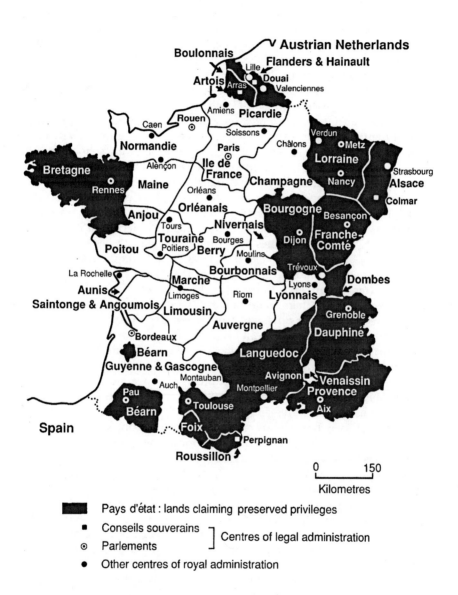

*Map 2* Provinces in the 1780s

bends in the Seine and Oise rivers. Its targets were the burden of State taxes on commoners, and noble hunting and other privileges: they wanted 'to pay taxes in proportion to their capacity, with the clergy and nobility, and to enjoy in freedom the cultivation of their land without being troubled by any form of servitude'.[19] Similarly, the *cahier* of the *bailliage* of Salers, north of Aurillac, was drawn up by professional men and substantial farmers who targeted the tax system of the monarchy and, as if in anticipation of the events of the summer, described one noble prerogative as 'a monument remaining from the *Ancien Régime féodal*'.[20]

Two rural parish *cahiers* from the province of Berry, in central France, share some essential characteristics with others across the country. Levet, 18 km south of Bourges, was a village of about 500 people in 77 households in 1789. Four *laboureurs* (farmers) and thirty *manoeuvres* (rural labourers) gathered on 1 March to draw up this *cahier*; only four of them were able to sign it. Levet was remarkable for the number of privileged persons – 17 ecclesiastics or orders and 9 lay persons – who extracted revenue from its territory. Among the former were the parish priest and several religious orders from Bourges: the Benedictines, Ursulines, Carmes and Visitandines. Marcilly, a similar distance to the east of Bourges, was smaller than Levet, with fewer than 300 people in its 43 households. Among the 40 men at the Assembly on 1 March were 3 *fermiers* (tenant-farmers), 3 *laboureurs*, 13 *manoeuvres*, a blacksmith and a longsawyer; only 8 of them could sign their names. Three nobles and a priest had seigneurial rights or privileged land in Marcilly. The two *cahiers* were in accord on the critical issue of political power and dealt with it straight away: they insisted 'that the Third Estate vote by head at the Assembly of the Estates-General' (Levet). Similarly, they agreed 'that all financial privileges be abolished; consequently, that the three orders no longer be exempt from any of the public responsibilities and taxes that the most unfortunate class of the Third Estate alone endures and pays' (Marcilly). The same *cahier* recommended 'that there be only one custom, one law, and one system of weights and measures'.[21] On religious matters the critical tone of the *cahiers* was not so typical, Levet insisting that no priest should leave his parish for more than a day without appointing a replacement, and Marcilly that the salary of some priests be reduced and 'that the Chartreuse communities be abolished, the monks secularised and each given eight hundred *livres*; the surplus of their income to belong to his Majesty'. The dominance of the gathering by the better-off peasantry in each village was attested to by the concerns voiced in Levet 'that a regulation will be created for farm workers requiring them to continue their service instead of abandoning it at the moment they are most needed' (a reference to strikes by labourers at harvest time) and in Marcilly that beggars be more tightly policed.[22]

Some parishes used *cahiers* to focus strategically on a particular issue. This was the case in the Occitan-speaking village of Gabian, 20 km north of Béziers. Among the dues payable to the bishop of Béziers, its seigneur since 988, were

100 *setiers* (a *setier* was about 85 l) of barley, 28 *setiers* of wheat, 880 bottles of olive oil, 18 chickens, 4 pounds of beeswax, 4 partridges and a rabbit. Reflecting Gabian's ancient role as a marketing centre between mountains and coast, it also had to pay 1 pound of pepper, 2 ounces of nutmeg and 2 ounces of cloves.[23] Despite the weight of these dues – and those paid to two other seigneurs – the meeting to draw up the *cahier* was instead used as the occasion for bitter complaint that a royal court had been relocated a decade earlier, leading to the departure of those it employed and a claimed breakdown of social order. As the last village of the plain before the wooded hills towards Bédarieux, it was claimed that the village was particularly prey to 'brigands' from the hills and from the village itself, so much so that travellers were forced to cross its land in groups for their own safety and the villagers themselves lived in a state of terror. Like many of the *cahiers*, that of Gabian revealed a potent sense of its own history, contrasting its situation with a flourishing past in the 1440s; since the ravages of the wars of religion had ended in 1709, its population had fallen by two-thirds. Like many other *cahiers*, too, the village had exaggerated for effect: the population had in fact increased from about 600 in 1706 to about 770 in 1780.

The role of seigneurs in administering justice was a particular concern in the province of Berry, where the parish of Levet (like many others) simply asked that 'seigneurial justice be abolished and those called to justice instead plead before the closest royal judge'. Rural folk were under no illusions that the primary purpose of the seigneurial courts was to maintain the property and privileges of the nobility and Church. Anthony Crubaugh has shown that, at least in Aunis and Saintonge, and probably elsewhere, the system of seigneurial justice was far from moribund or atrophied, as many historians have assumed it to be. The royal *sénéchaussée* of St Jean d'Angély had no fewer than 171 seigneurial courts for its 146 parishes. They were a real presence in the life of the rural communities of this region, and seigneurial justice was deeply resented as costly, slow and preoccupied with the protection of noble privilege and status. Moreover, despite a royal reform of 1772 that sought to ensure the greater presence of the courts in the maintenance of the rule of law, the courts failed in that most fundamental function of any judicial system, to offer individuals security and a regular process to redress grievances. A peasant maxim of the day was that 'a bad arrangement is better than a good trial'; the *cahier* from Landraye agreed: 'it's the fable of the wolf and the lamb'. The 24 cases that Crubaugh studied at Tonnay-Boutonne took an average of 32 months to resolve, with average costs of 106 *livres*. This was a region where harvest dues were commonly levied at one-sixth or one-seventh of produce and constituted about half of the revenues of seigneurs – in one case 87 per cent. Seigneurialism mattered: at least 39 seigneuries in Aunis and Saintonge revised their registers of dues payable (*terriers*) in the period 1750–89.[24]

While seigneurial justice seems to have been regarded as expensive and oppressive in both Languedoc and Aunis-Saintonge, in Northern Burgundy and Upper Brittany it was a respected element of village life which considered far more than the lord's interests. About 60 per cent of the parish *cahiers* in Northern Burgundy referred to needed reforms to the justice system, but few of these involved seigneurial courts and those that did focused primarily on the inconveniences of distance. In the region around Sarlat, the courts were increasing their activities, while at Pont-St-Pierre, southeast of Rouen, the court had simply withered away: from the late-sixteenth century to the 1780s the number of sessions annually declined from 48 to 15 and the number of cases considered at each from 40 to 9.[25]

Hostility to seigneurial exactions tended to go together with criticism of the tithes, fees and practices of the Church; that is, they were seen as interdependent within the seigneurial regime. In some regions, such as the countryside around Auch in Gascony or in the mountainous lands around Amont in Franche-Comté the tithe was particularly heavy and omnipresent in the *cahiers*. Across the country it ranged from as little as 3 per cent in Provence and Dauphiné in the southeast, in the Auvergne and around Vannes in Brittany to about one-sixth in parts of the Franche-Comté. On average, the tithe took one-twelfth of local produce.[26]

As members of a corporate, privileged body, parish priests envisaged a rejuvenated feudal order under the auspices of a Catholic monopoly of worship and morality. As commoners by birth, however, they were also ominously sympathetic to the needs of the poor, the opening of positions – including the Church hierarchy – to 'men of talent', and to calls for universal taxation. Unlike the Third Estate, however, the clergy were consistently hostile to surrendering their monopoly of religious worship or public morality. The First Estate of Bourges called on 'His Majesty'

> to order that all those who, through their writings, seek to spread the poison of incredulity, attack religion and its mysteries, discipline and dogmas, be seen as enemies of the Church and the State and severely punished; that printers be once again forbidden to print books contrary to religion.

It asserted that '[t]he apostolic and Roman Catholic religion is the only true religion'. Whereas the noble *cahiers* were agreed upon by consensus, those of the clergy reveal a genuine tension between the parish clergy and the cathedral chapters and monasteries of the towns. The rural clergy who flooded into Troyes insisted on the traditional distinction of the three orders meeting separately, but made a crucial exception on the matter of taxation; on this issue they urged a common Assembly to adopt a tax 'proportionately borne by all individuals of the three orders'.[27]

While the upper clergy and religious orders, particularly monasteries, were commonly seen as part of the seigneurial system, parish clergy like these men were instead described by peasants as part of the fabric of rural life.

Typical of such views was that expressed by the Third Estate of Montirat, near Carcassonne, which reminded Louis of 'the distressing situation of the second-rank pastors who alone support the weight of the day and the heat, are the fathers, friends, consolers, supports of the people'.[28] Indeed, rural *cahiers* rarely made a distinction between secular and religious matters in their reflections on the state of the parish and the nation.

A precious recording of similar concerns in one parish was compiled by Pierre-Louis-Nicolas Delahaye (born in 1745), the schoolteacher and parish clerk of Silly-en-Multien, near Senlis. From 1771 Delahaye kept a record of 'remarkable and curious events'; it was he who wrote down the *cahier* on 25 February 1789. The seigneur of Silly was the Prince de Conti, and the village was subject to the requirements of the prince's hunting estate. The *cahier* was a long complaint against the vulnerability of the crops to the prince's game and of villagers to his guards' whims: the villagers still remembered that in June 1768 a woman who took a pheasant's egg had been thrown into prison. The *cahier* of Silly underlines how central were grievances pertaining to control over resources and protection of the environment, for across the country parish assemblies focused on grievances about common lands, pasturing rights, access to and ownership of forests, land clearances, erosion and flooding. In terms of their frequency, these were of a similar order of concern to rural parishes as were the income of upper clergy, gambling, *mainmorte* and seigneurial monopolies over winepresses.[29]

Everywhere, the way rural communities described their world was a function of their understanding of the best use of physical resources. Certainly there are a few examples in the *cahiers* of a *mentalité* within which misconceptions about agriculture were matched by instrumentalism towards the environment. The Third Estate of Biécourt in the *bailliage* of Mirecourt demanded a law against sheep being allowed to graze with horses, it being necessary for horses to have a 'healthy fodder not infected by the bad breath of sheep and lambs'.[30] The *cahier* of Bossancourt (*bailliage* of Troyes) insisted 'that plantations of all types of trees on main roads be cut down, especially walnut-trees, poplars and elms, which do a lot of damage with their shade'.[31] Other communities in the area fulminated against seigneurs who planted trees along boundaries with peasants' plots, ruining them with their shade and roots. Similarly, at St-Launeuc (*sénéchaussée* of Rennes), Léthuin (*bailliage* of Orléans) and Villiers-en-Bois (*sénéchaussée* of Niort), people complained that there were too many trees and that crops would not grow because of the shade.[32]

Such complaints were rare. Far more commonly parish assemblies expressed a concern to preserve resources, and targeted as enemies of the local environment the excessive demands of local industry and seigneurs.[33] In eastern France, in particular, the proliferation of wood-fuelled extractive industries was the focus of peasant ire such as that demonstrated in the widely repeated article of the *cahiers* of the *bailliage* of Amont, that forges and furnaces only be permitted where the proprietor owned sufficient private supplies of wood. Calmoutier, Jussey and other villages were also angered by effluent from mines, 'whose cesspit (*cloaque*) and drain empty into the rivers which water the fields or in which the stock drink', causing sickness in stock and killing fish.[34] They were supported in this by the Third Estate of country towns such as Gray and Vesoul and by the nobility of the *bailliage* of Amont. Immediately to the north, in the *bailliage* of Mirecourt, it was a similar story. Here, claimed the *cahier* of Bettoncourt, the demands of forges, glassworks and other wood-fired factories, as well as saltworks, were responsible for forcing peasants to burn their fruit-trees for firewood.[35]

Around Châlons-sur-Marne, similarly, the proliferation of glass- and brick-works was the object of indignation. The forest near Beaulieu-en-Argonne supplied 18 of these enterprises, six of them situated 'at only a rifle-shot from our church-steeple'.[36] In the *bailliage* of Vic, near Metz, the village of Altwiller complained that there were 'in German Lorraine too many wood-fuelled factories'; here, as in the *cahiers* from scores of surrounding villages, the royal saltworks at Dieuze, Moyenvic and Château-Salins were especially singled out for criticism because they consumed vast quantities of wood to produce salt which was in any case more expensive than sea salt.[37] At Baronville, the high price of wood which had resulted from this had forced the poor to burn straw for heating and cooking: 'from this comes a lack of manure; and, the soil, not being manured, simply does not produce'.[38] In this area, the *cahiers* were virtually unanimous in their condemnation both of the impact of rural industries and of the complicity of forest owners and royal administrators in supplying wood to industry at the expense of the poor. It was this, argued the commoners of Guébestroff, which forced the poor to damage forests further by illegal cutting of trees.[39] The parish of Brouville claimed that 'these wood-fired factories have caused a great devastation in the forests which mostly belong to the bishop of Metz, and whose guards scarcely observe the laws concerning forests.'[40] Such attitudes were most common in the east, but recurred wherever private industry was perceived as responsible for the shortage and high price of wood. People in St-Doulchard (*bailliage* of Bourges) complained that the price of wood had doubled since the construction of a forge at Vierzon and that it was becoming scarce: 'where will we be in 20 or 30 years? The finest wood from the forest of Mehun is dragged out in logs, battens and quarters', and sold to a small group of merchants.[41] In the west, too, as at Nyoiseau near Angers, it was a local entrepreneur who was held responsible for the wood shortage because of his brickworks.[42]

Antipathy to allegedly rapacious industrialists was often linked to anti-seigneuralism, as local seigneurs were charged with having abdicated their community responsibilities in order to furnish fuel to the new industries. Around Quimper and Tréguier in Brittany, seigneurs and large landowners were singled out as primarily responsible for a shortage of wood. The parish *cahiers* of Lower Brittany targeted for criticism the regime of *domaine congéable*, whereby the landlord owned the land while the tenant owned not only the crops but also the buildings. Since many of these tenants were very long term, they had come to see themselves as owners rather than renters of the property.[43] As proprietors under the régime of 'domaine congéable', the trees belonged to the landlords rather than to their long-term tenants, but they allegedly neglected the imperative to replant. Peumérit-Cap complained that 'our countryside is almost bare; forests are visibly receding; seigneurs and landowners totally neglect to plant'.[44] Plozévet expressed a very common point of view:

> The poor vassal who has the misfortune to cut a foot off a tree of little value, but of which he has great need for a house or a cart or a plough, is plagued and crushed by his seigneur for the value of a whole tree. If everybody had the right to plant and to cut for oneself, without being able to sell, there would not be so much loss of wood.[45]

Such resentments were further irritated by the nobility's perceived taste for luxury consumption. The Third Estate of Dosches (*bailliage* of Troyes) commented that 'the poor person is rightly alarmed; he sees with indignation the wastefulness of the rich who, by the multitude of their fires, consume a terrifying amount of wood'.[46] From Juvaincourt, it was argued that the seigneur's taste for luxury was the worst example: apart from the kitchen, there were 'five or six fires that *monsieur* needs, as many for *madame*, the children's fires (one for each of course), those for the servants of both sexes'.[47] For their part, of course, the forge owners attributed the high price and shortage of wood to longstanding depredation by local communities and even, at Herserange, near Longwy, to a greater 'taste' for open fires across society.[48]

The institutions of the royal state were frequently charged with complicity in the degradation of collective resources.[49] Many communities near Châlons-sur-Marne were convinced that royal officials from the Eaux et Forêts based in the region ostensibly to ensure sustainable tree-felling were in fact protecting 'the greed of the beneficiaries' of the new glass- and brickworks.[50] Some communities wanted completely free access to the forests for their livestock. Most commonly, however, *cahiers* sought access within sustainable limits, urging the King that forests, including his own, should be open to grazing 5–7 years after a coupe, as at Vennecy (*bailliage* of Orléans), La Bouëxière (*sénéchaussée* of Rennes) and Dixmont (*bailliage* of Sens).[51] The *cahier* of Ste-Anne in the *bailliage* of Metz called for the domains belonging to the Church and the King to be sold 'or at least rented in small lots; an individual would know well how to conserve a forest near his home'.[52] 'If the province governed itself', reflected Forcelles-sous-Gugney, 'it would be better able to act effectively' to conserve the forests.[53]

This insistence of rural folk that forest resources be sustainable was not commonly matched by sympathy to the fauna which inhabited them. Seigneurial privileges in hunting and fishing, and the maintenance of dove-cotes and rabbit-warrens, were among the most common grievances of rural parishes. Across the country, too, fauna seems to have been understood as either 'useful' or 'noxious': the issue was who had the right to kill animals and fish, not whether there were some species to be protected despite being 'wild'.[54]

Rural communities were well aware of the links between land clearance and erosion. From the *sénéchaussée* of Cahors came a chorus of similar – but not repetitive – complaints about the decline in soil fertility across the previous 40 years. Such had been the extent of clearances on the hillsides that the best land along the Lot was now carried off in storms rushing down ravines caused by erosion; even vines were regularly washed away. As it was put by the parish of Ségos, 'erosion has already taken half our crops, and there is no hope for the future, for the soil has been completely stripped from the mountains and so there is nothing but rocks and huge ditches'.[55] Often, as at Douelle and Cessac, detailed description of land degradation was silent on its possible causes: the Lot 'has already taken more than 50 *quarterées* and continues to wash away the banks with every flood'.[56] At Bouziès, pastoralists were concerned by the spread of vineyards and worried that 'daily clearances are depriving landowners of feed for flocks of all kinds, and from that have come the shortage of fabric and the high price of meat'. But elsewhere the common complaint about the impact of erosion on good soil was explicitly linked to earlier clearances. At Cénac, the community described its infertile soil, 'formerly covered with woods whose clearance by our ancestors has left but a pile of stones, because the soil is of such a pliable and sandy quality ... and our best land so degraded that it produces barely twice the seed sown and at best three or four'.[57] At Le Montat, too, the causes were obvious:

> Formerly the farmer had a surplus [*superflu*], and with this surplus he paid his taxes; but today, the population having increased with the greater extent of cleared land and crops having diminished in proportion to the deterioration of the soil, there is no longer any surplus. ... there used to be immense forests where were fed a large number of flocks, the basis of fertility; most of these forests have been cleared, there are far fewer flocks, most land has gradually lost its fertility, whether because of lack of manure, or by the nature of things, or from the storms which have desolated and ravaged our mountains and valleys.[58]

The parish of St-Cirq-Lapopie asked the King for permission to divide its communal forest between the inhabitants in order to ensure that it was properly conserved, and on condition that

> it be forbidden to clear one's portion under pain of losing it and having it acquired by the first to denounce him; because if the woods on the mountain sides were cleared, they would soon suffer the fate of other hillsides which erosion (*ravines*) has reduced to rock.

At St-Martin-Labouval, too, the equal division of all commons under threat of expropriation if they were cleared was seen to be the answer: if not, the soil 'will be carried off by erosion; there will be nothing left afterwards but stones ... facts that we have observed in our neighbourhood'.[59]

The parish of Luz (*sénéchaussée* of Bigorre) expressed a widely held view that 'formerly the mountains of Barèges were covered in forests from the summit to two-thirds down: today they are almost bare'.[60] But they and others adduced various causes: the ravages of charcoal-burning, judges who were weak or incompetent, seigneurs who failed to replant, their fellow villagers. Everywhere the particular view of resources in the *cahiers* reflected not only the views of the compilers but also of their community. Attitudes to the ever-present issue of access to pastures depended on relationships with the seigneur and neighbouring villages as well as on the size of one's herd or flock. But the consequences were evident. Ordizan and Pouzac urged a more rigorous control of forests: coupes were leaving forests too thin 'for rocky and abrupt mountains, for pines which do not regrow, for beeches too exposed to the rigours of the seasons'.[61] Communities were aware, too, of the consequences of altering riverbeds. In the *sénéchaussée* of Bigorre, the villages of Barry and Bénac southwest of Tarbes urged the Estates-General to ban outright the removal of sand from the bed of the river Echez, however necessary it might be to repair houses after storms.[62]

The solution was most commonly seen in replanting. Common across much of the northwest was the demand that uncultivated land of various types be replanted in forest, often linked to a proposal for division of the wastelands with the requirement that sections be set aside for new forests.[63] Typical in the *bailliage* of Cotentin was the request from Villebaudon:

> Given that forests are almost exhausted and are becoming rarer and rarer, that part of the said the wastelands (*terres vagues*) be planted in woods and that even the most notable landowners be obliged to replant on their own lands, especially on those which are uncultivated.[64]

Indeed, in this region of France, the *cahiers* of the Third Estate consistently asserted that it was the lack of foresight of the seigneurs which was the real cause of wood shortage and high prices.

The small-town bourgeois who dominated the drawing up of the Third Estate *cahier* for the *sénéchausée* of Limoux similarly called for the development of schemes to encourage reforestation. Only by closing down 'unnecessary' forges and other charcoal-based industries, they argued, would the survival be guaranteed of the 15,000 or 20,000 families in the district who added to their income by fashioning the wooden combs used in carding wool.[65] Similarly, from Quincé and other parishes near Angers came the demand that large proprietors and seigneurs be required to replant sections of *landes* with trees; from nearby St-Barthélemy the *cahier* insisted that all who cut trees be required to replace them 'following the prudent example of the English'. A frequently reproduced article in this *sénéchaussée* called for division of *landes* between seigneur and community, but with the stipulation that seigneurs be obliged to plant their portion in forest.[66] Elsewhere, as at Fossé (*bailliage* of Blois), the answer to wood shortages was seen to lie in the cession to the community of 'wasteland' belonging to seigneurs on the condition that it was planted with trees for the general profit of the community and seigneur (who would provide the guard).[67] Near Dieppe, too, parishes such as Angreville and Wanchy demanded that felled trees be replaced as a matter of course.[68] Similar calls were heard throughout the west. In a remarkable *cahier* from St-Martin-lès-Melle, in the *sénéchaussée* of Civray, the author singled out for caustic criticism 'the consuming hunger of large-scale farming which, like Pantagruel's mare, destroys forests' and 'our parsimonious agronomists' who, with their encouragement of clearances, 'will prove to us that a Laplander's shanty, dug into the earth and covered with soil, is the most noble as well as the most solid architecture, that its design is based on the immortal works of the mole and not of the beaver, for whom wood is necessary'.[69]

The targets of many of these criticisms were Louis XV's decrees encouraging land clearing.[70] An influential 1760 *Mémoire sur les défrichemens* by the Marquis de Turbilly had recommended that land clearing be encouraged, and was reflected in royal *arrêts* of 1 March and 16 August 1761.[71] Royal decrees of 1764 and 1766 then offered fiscal inducements to those who cleared land which had not been cultivated for at least forty years. Finally, Louis XV's edict of 5 July 1770 offered tax concessions on all State taxes and tithes for 15 years for land cleared and duly reported to the authorities. The decree stipulated, however, that the forest code of 1669 remained in force, outlawing the clearing of wooded terrain, river banks and hillsides.[72]

Rural people in 1789 interpreted their physical world through their experience of the implementation of these decrees. In the decades after 1750, some 600,000 *arpents* (an *arpent* was approximately one acre) of France was cleared, some 3 per cent of the surface. Nowhere was this clearing as extensive as in Languedoc, especially in the dioceses of Carcassonne and Narbonne, and the official figures in these dioceses do not take account of land cleared illegally or of communities where officials failed to complete formal reports (one parish in 12).[73] The consequences of these clearances led the flock owners of

Montlaur, near Carcassonne, to complain in their *cahier* that

> [b]y digging up the ground ... to make it arable, the woods are being destroyed so much that in a few years there will no longer be an oak-tree in this part of the Corbières; the tanneries and the lime kilns contribute a good deal to these depradations. ... we have no hesitation in stating that the wool that [the sheep] produces in this region is as fine as that of Spain or England. The ruin of the forests is making the production of this commodity impossible.[74]

Cornillon was one of scores of communes in the neighbouring *sénéchaussée* of Nîmes which identified the ecological effects of Louis' encouragement of clearances: these 'deprive us for ever of the wood which would have grown there and of pastures for livestock which produce the manure for other cleared land; in addition, these same cleared lands are situated on the slopes of mountains and hills; rainstorms carry off the good soil and leave only gravel'.[75] In other provinces of France, too, the calling of the Estates-General offered the chance for angry pastoralists to single out the impact of the clearances of pastures. From Polisy (*bailliage* of Troyes) it was claimed that 'uncultivated land has been planted or degraded and dug up to remove soil, in such a way that there is no longer any possibility of grazing livestock'.[76] Nearby Chessy requested that

> all clearing of communal lands or other wastelands belonging to communities be forbidden, under whatever pretext, and that communities be authorized to retake possession of what has been usurped, it being well known that the lack of pastures lessens the possibility of feeding animals and of having manure for the soil, without which it becomes sterile.[77]

The suspicion that, however general the attendance at the parish assemblies, they were dominated by the better-off peasantry is reinforced by the explicit concern evinced that special attention be paid to the reinforcement and standardization of rural policing. Of particular concern was the practice of the poor illegally felling trees and clearing scrub on hillsides in defiance of the forest code of 1669, a practice encouraged, according to many parish assemblies, by Louis XV's decrees on land clearance. Those who committed infractions in the forests should not be spared: the Third Estate of Mattaincourt in the *bailliage* of Mirecourt was only the most punitive of many in suggesting that 'mauvais sujets' should be condemned, 'for the first offence, to one month in prison, on bread and water; to the iron collar (*carcan*) for the second; to the galleys for the third'.[78] The *cahier* of Portel, near Narbonne, called for stronger, immediate powers for municipal police against those

> who uproot with picks or pull out, in spite of the orders of Eaux et Forêts and decrees of the municipal council, the shrubs and bushes in the

common *garrigues* which are the staple for the sheep and the nutrition for the bees which produce such fine and precious honey.[79]

\* \* \*

The grievances of the working people of small country towns were expressed through meetings of master craftsmen and parish assemblies. Most urban working people were, however, too poor to meet the minimal property requirements necessary to participate: the sharpest limitation to the value of the *cahiers* as an insight into French society is the absence of the urban poor. Many of the artisan *cahiers* reveal a deep-seated anxiety about the exposure of craft-based work to the pressures of profit-oriented production, mechanization and the erosion of vertical bonds of occupational solidarity.[80] In August 1776, a major reform of guilds by Jacques Necker had undermined the autonomy of masters and transferred regulatory power to the government. Henceforth the *chef d'oeuvre* was no longer strictly necessary and trades were opened to those with the necessary capital, including women, who previously had been restricted to continuing a dead husband's business. The world of artisanal labour was increasingly fractured by the wage–labour relations of the workshop and the difficulty journeymen had in establishing their own businesses, but it nevertheless remained united by the culture, subsistence needs and shared labour skills and routines of the trade and *quartier*.

On 5 March, no fewer than 32 'corporations' of Limoux (population 5,000) held their meetings to draw up their *cahiers*, variously in private houses, the town hall and religious buildings. There were tailors, ironmongers, wigmakers, tanners, weavers, carpenters, bakers, innkeepers, pastry-cooks, wool carders, shoemakers, millers, locksmiths, hatmakers, harnessmakers and cloth merchants, including a woman. The largest gathering in fact was of those without a 'corporation': between 5 and 8 March, 199 gardeners, farm labourers and farm managers (called 'les gens mécanique') met. The Limoux *cahiers* are revealing of the world view of these urban artisans and labourers. The structures of local power and privilege were unquestioned: the problems of poverty and vulnerability were to be solved by a benevolent King judiciously alleviating local taxes and facilitating the trade of local cloth elsewhere in the kingdom while simultaneously protecting corporations from competition. The gardeners and farm labourers spoke powerfully of 'the sad state of our miseries to which we are exposed in all sorts of contrary (*ridiculeté*) weather in order to earn our miserable living from morning to night with a ten-pound spade and just as much earth on it!'[81]

Hundreds of kilometres away in eastern France, 23 'corporations' met in the town of Bourg (population 7,350). Among them were 14 butchers and *charcutiers* who gathered in an inn called 'Aux Armes de France'. Like their Occitan compatriots, the butchers described a world where they were taxed at every turn: for bringing animals into town, for taking them out to fatten them, for the salt for curing their flesh, and then by seigneurs who sought to impose fines wherever possible.[82]

Artisan *cahiers*, like those of the peasantry, revealed an overlapping of interests with those of local bourgeois on fiscal, legal and political questions, but a clear divergence on economic regulation, calling instead for protection against mechanization and competition and for controls on the grain trade. Bitterness was expressed about the collapse of the textile industry following the free trade treaty with England in 1786. The language of artisan *cahiers* was couched in an idiom of vertically segregated trades, each with elaborate forms of brotherhoods (*compagnonnages*), ritual and controls as defences against mechanization and competition.[83] Artisan demands were underscored by subsistence crisis and inflation: in early 1789, Abbeville weavers were spending an estimated 94 per cent of household income on bread. There and in Amiens, there had been more than 5,600 cotton looms working in 1785: in 1789 there were only 2,000, and 36,000 people had lost work.[84] The *cahier* of the Norman village of Vatimesnil, too, called on 'His Majesty for the good of the people to abolish spinning machines because they do great wrong to all poor people'.[85]

The perspective voiced on machines was, of course, a function of social background. In contrast to Vatimesnil, in the small Norman textile town of Elbeuf (population about 5,000), the manufacturers, merchants and professional men who formulated the *cahier* on 28 March were specific and blunt in their condemnation of

the inefficient administration of finances ... these constraints, these impediments to commerce: barriers reaching to the very heart of the kingdom; endless obstacles to the circulation of commodities ... representatives of manufacturing industries and Chambers of Commerce totally ignored and despised; an indifference on the part of the government towards manufacturers.[86]

As in the *cahiers* drafted by small-town merchants, officials and landowners at the *bailliage* level, here there was an insistence on individual liberties and that Third Estate deputies should refuse to meet separately. In the words of the bourgeois of the small market town of Dourdan south of Paris, they must rebuff 'any distinction which might dishonour them'.[87]

This was an urban world which bristled with resentment at the wealth and prerogatives of local élites, but one which remained dependent on the goodwill and expenditure of bourgeois, nobles and clergy. The masters were necessarily anxious about order and the reliability of supplies, and their *cahiers* were punitive towards those living on the margins. But such *cahiers* are an imperfect guide to the state of mind of those who compiled them: in general they were careful to voice their grievances only to the point where fear of likely consequences stilled their pens. It would become evident within 6 weeks in Limoux, for example, that hunger and anxiety had created an explosive situation. But the *cahiers* do reveal the deepest assumptions about the structures of hierarchy and power.

A few rare *cahiers* by urban women requested specific representation for women at the Estates-General to protect their interests. Among these were the need for improved education for girls, for protection for women's areas of work (particularly in the clothing trades), and an end to inheritance laws favouring sons. One hoped 'to leave our ignorance behind, to give our children a healthy and reasonable education, to raise subjects worthy of serving the king, and to cherish the good name of France'.[88] A women's *cahier* from the Pays de Caux region north of Paris posed the question of women's rights more bluntly:

> Whether from reason or necessity men permit women to share their work, to till the soil, to plough, to run the postal service; others undertake long and difficult travel for commercial reasons ...
>
> We are told there is talk of freeing the Negroes; the people, almost as enslaved as them, is recovering its rights ...
>
> Will men persist in wanting to make us victims of their pride or injustice?[89]

In both town and country, the family economy was sustained by what Olwen Hufton has described as a 'precarious balancing act'. Most peasants owned some land, but needed to rent more, or seek wage–labour, or engage in 'outwork' for urban-based textile manufacturers. This was also a family economy in that rural people assumed that they would contribute to their household from the time they were old enough to weed vegetables or feed chickens until their strength finally ebbed in old age. In this, the work of women was of unquestioned importance, even though women's wages were set at a level which presupposed that they were living with a father or husband and needed only to be paid enough for their sustenance.[90] We do not know, however, whether the place of women in this family economy meant that the sentiments expressed by these educated women from the Pays de Caux would have had a resonance, or whether they would have seemed irrelevant or even incomprehensible to women for whom the imperative was the well-being of the household.

\* \* \*

The repeated references in the *cahiers* to the land clearances allowed by Louis XV's decrees points to the conflicts of interest which divided rural communities internally as well as uniting them against entrepreneurs and the agents of seigneur and King. The *cahiers* also have much to tell us about self-definition in areas far from the capital or only recently incorporated into the kingdom. They are statements of identity.

Despite a lively sense of regional difference, rural *cahiers* expressed an assumption of French citizenship within a regenerated nation.[91] In the Occitan-speaking Corbières region of Lower Languedoc, for example, there were frequent hopes expressed for reformed and permanent provincial Estates, following the model of the Dauphiné, but none of the *cahiers* asserted that Languedoc should enjoy a measure of special autonomy. Instead, words like 'patrie', 'nation' and 'citoyen' were studded throughout the *cahiers*, and assumptions of a secular citizenship as the basis of a regenerated public realm informed the *cahiers* at every turn. The peasants of the Corbières had developed an understanding of society as composed of people of equal dignity, articulated in the repeated call from practising Catholics that the King accord his 'non-Catholic subjects the civic status and prerogatives of French citizens', which was based on 'civil and individual liberty for all citizens'.[92]

The *cahiers* have much to tell us about collective identity in regions such as this where French was a foreign language to most people. Occitans were conscious of the ancient linguistic and territorial division which separated them from the Catalan communities just across the linguistic border in the Roussillon, and occasionally still described themselves as living on a frontier, which they had until 1659. The southernmost Occitan parish, Leucate, fulminated against the inhabitants of the nearby Catalan village of St-Laurent-de-la-Salanque and asked why they had to pay to fish in the *étang* of Salses while the privileged Catalans did not.

But, if Occitans were ambiguous about whether their neighbours in the Roussillon were really French, they had no doubts about the Catalans south of the territorial border, seen both as part of a different nation and as an economic threat to the textile industry. The *cahier* of Montlaur insisted that local wool was as good as that of England or Spain, and that of Montolieu stressed that it should be required to be used in local textile factories rather than that from Spain. This reflected a deep unease, expressed by the people of Portel-des-Corbières, who claimed that 'the Spanish are involved in a trade which is ruinous for France'.

While the *cahiers* of the Corbières reveal an acceptance of the French State, this after all was a region which had been part of the kingdom for over five centuries. To the south their Catalan neighbours had been incorporated in the French State for only 130 years, but there too the monarchy had succeeded before 1789 in laying the groundwork for the acceptance of the idea of the French polity. Ever since 1700, for example, all public acts in the Roussillon had to be written in French. As in Languedoc, there was an engrained assumption of belonging to a French polity. This was revealed in the economic demands of the parish *cahiers* of the Roussillon. That of St-Michel-de-Llotes demanded '[t]hat trade should be free throughout the kingdom'; [t]hat of Mont-Louis asked '[t]hat obstacles to commerce and trade in the interior of the kingdom should be removed, that every subject should have full and complete freedom to transport or have transported merchandise from one province to another'. One of the communities on the very frontier with Languedoc – Vingrau – insisted both that the two provinces be divided by 'visible and permanent' markers but that all taxes and charges be uniform throughout the kingdom.[93]

The *cahiers* also reveal, like those from Languedoc, a sense of otherness towards Catalans south of the border, of belonging to a kingdom with natural borders. The community of St-Laurent-de-Cerdans requested a ban of the export of iron ore to Spain: 'while our community is becoming impoverished, Spain is rising up and becoming rich'.[94] The parish of l'Écluse complained that 'straw continues to go to Spain. It's only six months ago that the export of wheat was banned ... and that only when there was almost none left'. In the process, these communities were defining their fellow Catalans as Spaniards and therefore as 'other'. The same point may be made about the way that Flamands, Basques, Provençaux and Alsaciens defined those who spoke their language but who lived across the border.

*   *   *

At least on the surface, the *cahiers* of all three orders show a remarkable level of agreement: they assumed that the meeting of the Estates-General in May 1789 would be but the first of a regular cycle, and they saw the need for sweeping reform to taxation, the judiciary, the Catholic Church and administration. On fundamental matters of social order and political power, however, entrenched divisions were to undermine the possibilities of consensual reform. Rural communities and the nobility were in sharp disagreement about seigneurial dues, and bourgeois across the country challenged the nobility by advocating 'careers open to talent', equality of taxation and the ending of privilege. Many parish priests agreed with the commons about taxation reform in particular, while insisting on the prerogatives of their own order.

Urban *cahiers* were much more likely to use 'require', 'claim' and 'demand' than the 'pray', 'solicit' and 'beg' of rural people.[95] To the insistence of even small-town bourgeois on a new society characterized by 'careers open to talent', encouragement of enterprise, equality of taxation, liberal freedoms and the ending of privilege, the nobility responded with a utopian vision of a reinforced hierarchy of social orders and obligations, protection of noble exemptions and renewed political autonomy. To most nobles, seigneurial rights and noble privileges were too important to be negotiable, and most of the noble deputies elected to Versailles were intransigent in their defence. To self-respecting officials, professional men and property owners, such pretensions were simply offensive and demoralizing, reflected in the repeated insistence in *cahiers* at the *bailliage* level that Third Estate deputies should refuse to meet separately.

These were men who read 'enlightened' literature, but the lively world of literature in the 1780s was essentially an urban phenomenon: most men and women in towns could read. There is little sign of an Enlightenment in the countryside, whether in terms of reading patterns or other, more ambiguous evidence such as that from the Cambrésis village of Montigny, where its historian has found a proliferation of new urban names like Désirée, Rose, Sophie, Constant, Clément and Benoît in the 1780s instead of traditional saints' names such as Marie, Pierre and Joseph.[96]

Well before 1789, a language of 'citizen', 'nation', 'social contract' and 'general will' was being articulated across urban society, clashing with an older discourse of 'orders', 'estates' and 'corporations'. There is certainly evidence, too, of a greater willingness to contest authority in the countryside. Olwen Hufton and Georges Fournier have found, particularly on the lowlands of Languedoc, evidence of young men more commonly contesting the authority of seigneur, *curé* and local officials, exhibiting a fractiousness denounced as a 'republican spirit' by the authorities. Southeast of Carcassonne, a day labourer from Albas commented to others as the seigneur passed: 'If you would do as I do we'd soon put to rights this young—of a seigneur'. Later he had continued to the local blacksmith, 'If you would all do as I do, not only would you not raise your hats when you pass in front of them, but you wouldn't even recognize them as seigneurs, because as for me I've never and will never in my life raise my hat, they're a huge load of scum, thieves, young—.' At nearby Termes a man took his brother-in-law to court in the years before the Revolution for having said 'that he carried on like a seigneur, with his arrogant tone'.[97]

To be sure, there had always been moments when resentful youths had vented their anger at those in authority. In the spring of 1789, however, compilation of the *cahiers* gave every member of rural communities explicit permission to comment directly on the world in which they lived. Evident in their formulation – and all the more telling given the presence of seigneurial judges or stewards at parish assemblies – was the assuredness of the village élites who dominated the drawing up of the *cahiers*. These élites, of well-to-do farmers and, in larger villages, professional men and officials, assumed that their social influence was matched by their right to speak directly on local matters and not through a seigneurial or ecclesiastical cipher.[98]

Indeed, only on two general matters was there widespread agreement across French society. First, there was consensus that the Church was in urgent need of reform to check abuses within its hierarchy and to improve the lot of its parish clergy. Second, whatever the undoubtedly sincere protestations of gratitude and loyalty towards the King, his ministers were castigated for their fiscal inefficiency and arbitrary powers. The calling of the Estates-General was everywhere envisaged as a regular, periodic innovation: in a word, it was assumed, albeit implicitly, that absolute monarchy was at an end.

Where nobles and commoners could not agree was about how power was to be expressed within this Estates-General, and to what social and political ends. Whatever the shared commitment of all three orders to the need for change, and general agreement on a plethora of specific abuses within the Church and State apparatus, the divisions over fundamental issues of political power, seigneurialism and claims to corporate privilege were fundamental. The government had expressed its hope that representatives of the three orders should meet to draw up a common *cahier* for their province or district. The province of Bresse was one of only five *bailliages* where, in a genuine spirit of cooperation and desire for reform, this was undertaken. The result was a detailed document of 45 pages, in which the attitudes of the three orders to every issue were tabulated. As in other *cahiers*, there was greatest agreement on the need for reforms to State institutions. While there was agreement on most issues, in fact, there were four matters where it was recognized that there was such division that it would simply have to be left to the Estates-General: the question of voting by head or order, how extensive reform to religious orders should be, whether taxes should be uniform across society, and whether compensation should be paid for any seigneurial dues and rights which were abolished. The last two of these were, of course, at the heart of the system, and the first was the crucial matter of political power.[99]

The rural and small-town people of France were unaware of the consequences of such divisions, but the invitation to involvement in political life in the spring of 1789 had reverberated across the country. Participation in the process of setting out the views in these *cahiers* was an extraordinary experience, even though the signs of change had been evident from the time of Calonne's reforms in 1787. It is true that much of what may be deduced about daily life from the *cahiers* was not to change greatly across the next 10 years. Most people in town and country would continue to work in similar ways and to employ a tried and tested household strategy to meet their needs. But their mental universe and every dimension of social interaction was to be shocked to the core.

# 2
# Elation and Anxiety: The Revolutionary Year

The first experience of revolutionary behaviour in 1789 is to be found in the formulation and content of the *cahiers de doléances*. To be sure, of themselves the *cahiers* were not revolutionary: they had also been produced as part of the process of the Estates-General of 1614, and people were responding to a request for advice on the state of the kingdom, not to a question about whether they wanted revolutionary change. Again and again, however, the *cahiers* of the Third Estate had made demands for a regular meeting of a representative body such as the Estates-General, equality of taxation and the end of seigneurialism. Whether or not consciously, together these demands presupposed the end of a particular social and political order.

Some of the rural *cahiers* voiced views which are startling in their boldness, but no one in France in the early spring of 1789 knew that they were about to live through what became in hindsight 'the Revolution of 1789'. Instead, this for them was a world of confusion and anxiety. Historians have the benefit of a longer-term perspective to explain the way people responded to the world around them, knowing in broad outline what would happen next; contemporaries, of course, had no such luxury. The most difficult task for the historian is to convey an understanding of a past which people at the time experienced as the present.

The terrifying immediate challenge for most French people as 1789 began was survival in the face of a crisis in the food supply, due to the impact on the 1788 harvest of drought followed by wild summer storms. The following winter was unusually severe across the whole country, and the high price of firewood further compromised the capacity of most urban and rural people to procure sufficient food. In the tiny southern village of Rouffiac, for example, hail and rain swelled the river Verdouble to a level where it carried away part of the bridge, ruined 100 ha of millet and beans, and washed away 1,200 hay-ricks, in all about half the year's produce. In the diocese of Narbonne, an estimated 100,000 olive trees died from severe frosts; the Canal du Midi froze to a depth of 10 cm.[1]

The formulation of the *cahiers de doléances* at the end of winter 1789 occurred at the worst possible time for most rural people, and the writing of the *cahiers* was paralleled by recourse to direct action to ensure survival. Such direct action was neither unprecedented nor inherently revolutionary. The history of rural France had been studded with protest; indeed, one survey has calculated that there were no fewer than 4,400 documented collective protests in the years 1720–88. The level of friction in the countryside may be gauged from the fact that some three-quarters of them occurred after 1765.[2] These protests typically were of three types: food riots, and riots against taxation and seigneurialism. All three types were designed to put pressure on threats to the rural community when a weak spot was discerned: a merchant or large farmer taking a wagon of grain to market, a seigneur's agent making claims that were novel or had fallen into disuse, a tax official without sufficient protection. In small towns, too, there were protests of all three types, except that the food riot was most commonly against a miller, a baker or a merchant. Town and country necessarily had different ways of meeting subsistence needs, and herein lay a source of incipient and occasionally open friction between those in town and country who needed to purchase grain or bread.

These were all protests within a system which people assumed would never end. In the spring of 1789, however, people in small towns and villages began behaving in ways which challenged the structures of their world in unprecedented ways, through deliberate confrontation with local seigneurs. The sharp edge of hunger and anxiety as winter dragged into spring coincided with the elation and expectation occasioned by Louis XVI's calling of the Estates-General. Uncertain about the future, rural folk at least knew that the sudden vulnerability of seigneurs had opened up a moment in which the boundaries could be tested. The uncertainty of early 1789 encouraged peasants to abandon their traditional tactics of dissembling and manoeuvring against their seigneurs and instead to be transparent about what James Scott calls their 'hidden transcript' in confronting them directly.[3] Had not the king declared that he wished to listen to his people's grievances? Peasants had the perfect pretext and excuse for bold actions.

Since December 1788, peasants had refused to pay taxes or dues or had seized food supplies in parts of the Cambrésis and Hainaut regions in the northeast, the Franche-Comté, and the Paris basin, partly in expectation of royal recognition of their plight. Food rioting in Cambrai spread to the surrounding countryside early in May 1789, where a dozen communities around Oisy slaughtered a lord's game. In Provence, too, there was widespread food rioting in villages in the hinterland of Marseille, Toulon and Aix; peasants from around Draguignan drove their cattle onto the estate of the Count de Gallifet to ruin his crops.[4] In contrast, in the small Breton town of Vannes (population 9,000), a crowd of artisans and labourers attacked the middle-class merchants they blamed for food shortages, shouting – ominously – 'Long live the king, long live the nobility, to the devil with the Third Estate!'[5]

In the Périgord, there was a full-scale attack on the château of St-Léon-d'
Issigeac.[6] In this region a series of violent incidents in 1789 involved a
cross-section of rural communities: substantial landowners, sharecroppers,
winegrowers, rural labourers and artisans, with occasionally a country
*chirurgien-barbier* or *avocat*. Their enemies were not only primarily seigneurs
and their agents but also well-to-do bourgeois proprietors. As one peasant
from Alassac put it: 'We don't need bourgeois or gentlemen any more.' The
violence of the winter of 1788–89 also tells us something of assumptions
about masculinity. Two-thirds of those later imprisoned for these riots were
men of 15–34 years of age: there were no women. While women were often
predominant in food rioting, as before 1789 young men were more commonly present when the authority of seigneur, *curé* and consuls was being
contested, as if this was civil disobedience on a more 'serious' level.[7]

Such actions were localized. The early spring of 1789 was for most people an
exhilarating but anxious time, as the preparedness of the hardy to confront
those they blamed for the sharp edge of their hunger coincided with unprecedented opportunities to participate in political life. After drawing up their
*cahiers de doléances*, men all over France were required to elect deputies to the
Estates-General. In small rural parishes and country towns meetings male
taxpayers over 25 years of age were to elect two delegates for the first one hundred households and one more for each extra hundred; the delegates in turn
were to elect deputies for each of the 234 constituencies. Participation was
significant everywhere, but varied sharply, ranging in Upper Normandy from
10 to 88 per cent between parishes, near Vitré in Brittany from 6 to 96 per
cent, around Béziers from 5 to 83 per cent, and in Artois from 14 to 97 per
cent. In what was to become a common feature of the revolutionary period, it
was often in smaller communities with a stronger sense of solidarity that participation levels were highest. The parishes tended to elect as delegates those
whom they felt would both make a good impression and understand what was
going on, such as the larger landowners, skilled artisans, professional men and
teachers. In general, the men chosen were those elected two years earlier as
members of village councils under Calonne's law: 70 per cent in Touraine, 61
per cent around Rouen.[8]

The delegates were required to deliberate about what should go in the
*cahier* of the *bailliage*, and many urban bourgeois dismissed rural complaints
about dues, seigneurial monopolies and other specific grievances as private
matters between them and the seigneur. Despite the administrative experience of these delegates, at the *bailliage* level there was lack of clarity about
what was being decided and what those decisions represented. Desmé de
Daubuisson, lieutenant-général of the *bailliage* of Saumur on the Loire River,
complained that

[w]hat is really tiresome is that these assemblies that have been summoned
have generally believed themselves to be invested with some sovereign

authority and that when they came to an end the peasants went home with the idea that henceforward they were free from tithes, hunting prohibitions and the payment of seigneurial dues.[9]

The two-stage voting process for Third Estate deputies ensured that virtually all of the 646 deputies were lawyers, officials and men of property, men of substance and repute in their town or region. Only 85 of them were from trade and industry. A rare exception in the ranks of middle-class men was Michel Gérard, a peasant from near Rennes who would appear at Versailles in his working clothes.

The electoral process also had a galvanizing effect on parish priests, who rushed to make the most of Louis' decision to favour the parish clergy in the election of First Estate delegates. Priests were to vote individually in the assemblies to elect deputies, while monasteries would have only one representative, and cathedral chapters one for every ten canons. This was done as a way of further pressuring the nobility to make concessions on their tax exemptions, and as a mark of Louis' own religious convictions. 'As *curés* we have rights', exclaimed a parish priest from Lorraine, Henri Grégoire, son of a tailor: 'such a favourable opportunity to enforce them has not occurred, perhaps, for twelve centuries … Let us take it'. His plea was heard: when the clergy gathered to elect their deputies early in 1789, 208 of the 303 chosen were lower clergy; only 51 of the 176 bishops were delegates. Most of the 322 noble deputies were from old noble families (there were 207 princes, dukes, Marquis and counts), a world away from those like Lafayette, Condorcet, Mirabeau, Talleyrand and others active in the reformist Society of Thirty in Paris who were worldly enough to accept the importance of surrendering at least some fiscal privileges.[10]

The Estates-General opened in Versailles on 4 May. That same day, the working people of Limoux, 800 km to the southwest, staged their own revolution.[11] Like communities across the country, this little town of some 5,000 people had endured a harsh winter of critical food shortage: at the time the *cahiers* were composed in March, the price of bread was 5 *sous* compared with 1 *sous* 6 *deniers* the previous July. Then on 28 April news had spread that a merchant, Jacques Pons, had sold 400 *setiers* (in all about 35,000 l) to a merchant from Carcassonne, the local capital 25 km to the north. For a week popular intimidation prevented Pons from moving his carts from Limoux as the council debated whether to pacify the crowd by buying back his wheat. By the morning of Monday, 4 May, a crowd of about one thousand people finally forced their way into the town hall, demanding that no wheat leave the town, that it be sold at 16 *livres* per *setier* (Pons had sold it at 21 *livres* 10 *sous*), that the price of bread be pegged at 2 *sous* 6 *deniers*, and that local taxes on foodstuffs bought in through the town gates be abolished. This had been the labourers' first demand in their *cahier* [see Chapter 1]. The council agreed only to provide cheap bread to the poor. The crowd then moved to the tax office where they smashed their way in with clubs and iron bars. Scales, furniture and records were hurled into the river. The tax office director was dragged from his house but left unharmed; crowds instead forced the local well-to-do to give them money. Only one leader – Paga, nickname Pededague – was arrested, for having attempted to force the mayor to hand over the keys to the town. The others simply melted back into the anonymity of the crowd.

The Limouxins were probably well aware of the opening of the Estates-General, although there is no evidence that they made the link between the gathering of the élite of the three orders at Versailles and their own actions the same day. In their own way, these local actions were revolutionary in their boldness: food riots characterized by popular price fixing were a common feature of the eighteenth century, but the destruction of the property of the royal tax collectors, including registers, was not.

At Versailles the Third Estate deputies rapidly developed a common outlook, insistent on their dignity and responsibility to 'the Nation': they refused to meet in a separate chamber, and on 17 June proclaimed themselves the National Assembly. This was their first revolutionary challenge to absolutism and privilege. Louis appeared to capitulate, ordering all deputies to meet in a common Assembly, but at the same time Paris, 18 km away, was invested with 20,000 mercenaries. The Assembly was only saved from probable dissolution by a collective action by Parisian working people, angry at an escalation in the price of bread, and certain that the Assembly was under military threat. Arms and ammunition were seized from gunsmiths and the Invalides military hospital. Their seizure of the Bastille on 14 July not only saved the National Assembly: it also sent waves of alarm and shock across a countryside seething with conflict, fear and hope.

The desperate hopes invested in the National Assembly were captured brilliantly by the English agronomist Arthur Young, then on his third tour of France. On 12 July Young was walking his horse up a hill near Verdun in Lorraine, when

> I was joined by a poor woman, who complained of the times, and that it was a sad country; demanding her reasons, she said her husband had but a morsel of land, one cow, and a poor little horse, yet they had a *franchar* (42 pounds) of wheat, and three chickens, to pay as a quit-rent to one Seigneur; and four *franchar* of oats, one chicken and one livre to pay to another, besides very heavy tailles and other taxes ... It was said, at present, *that something was to be done by some great folks for such poor ones, but she did not know who nor how, but God send us better, car les tailles et les droits nous écrasent.* This woman, at no great distance, might have been taken for sixty or seventy, her figure was so bent, and her face so furrowed and hardened by labour, – but she said she was only twenty-eight.

At the same time Young was scathing about the lack of newspapers and clear information in the provinces: her hopes were based on rumour rather than reportage.[12]

No one in Paris could have imagined the rural response to the news of the taking of the Bastille. Rural people such as Young's interlocutor had placed their hopes in the meeting of the Estates-General; now news of the seizure of the fortress tempered such hopes with fears that the nobility would take revenge on the Third Estate and that there would be a breakdown in law and order. During the second half of July villages formed up popular militias. The bands of destitute people roaming country roads were the focus of suspicion as anxious peasants waited for crops to ripen. Panics fanned out almost simultaneously from five separate sparks as bushfires of angry rumours, travelling from village to village at several kilometres an hour, affected every region except Brittany and the east. When noble revenge failed to eventuate, village militias instead turned their weapons on the seigneurial system itself, invading châteaux in the search for foodstuffs and sometimes compelling seigneurs or their agents to hand over feudal registers to be burned in public.

This extraordinary revolt came to be known as the 'Great Fear'. After the drawing up of the *cahiers de doléances*, this was the second great act of revolution in which rural people were involved. While much of the collective protest took the traditional form of compelling vulnerable members of the privileged orders or their agents to surrender food, there were also two new elements: the seizure and destruction of feudal registers, and the public humiliation of seigneurs or their agents. Unlike the meetings which had produced the *cahiers*, this time those involved in this frontal assault on the seigneurial system were well aware of what they were doing and of the consequences of failure.

Rural communities in the regions of Bresse and Bugey east of Lyon were already menacing châteaux before news of the taking of the Bastille reached the local capital Bourg on 19 July. Once the threat of noble revenge had passed, peasants in many rural communities of Bresse seized and burned feudal registers on the basis of the popular belief that *il n'y a nul seigneur sans titre* ('Without titles there is no seigneur'). The region became an epicentre of the fears and rumours sweeping across the country. On the twenty-fourth, the inhabitants of Pont-de-Veyle, just south of Mâcon, besieged the local château and seized the seigneurial registers and other papers, which they deposited at the town hall. The scene was repeated the next day, at nearby Vonnas. At Châtillon, efforts to organize a national guard effectively put an end to any likelihood of parallel events, but up to eight hundred peasants from twelve villages attacked the abbey at St-Sulpice, forcing the monks to burn the registers and plundering the abbey's cellar. The next day they erected a gibbet in the middle of the cloister, ostensibly to hang the monks, who were allowed finally to run off in terror into the woods before the insurgents set fire to the buildings.[13]

The region of Bugey was swept by rumours of 'brigands' descending from the Alps, with villagers rushing to prepare defences. On the mountain slopes known as the Michaille, on the upper Rhône, reported a contemporary:

> everybody took up arms because of the rumours of brigands pillaging the seigneurs' châteaux. People were said to be blocking or closing wells for fear that they would be poisoned. Bells were rung throughout the Michaille as were fires to warn everybody to be alert for the brigands.[14]

In this region, it was particularly the vast seigneuries of religious orders that were targeted. This was by no means an indiscriminate attack, for peasant bands were careful not to destroy the documents which stipulated their rights to enter the forests belonging to the orders.

The valley of the Saône near Mâcon was also swept by a different type of fear, for here peasant insurrection was so violent that the middle-class patriots of Mâcon believed that the 'brigands' had indeed arrived. In late July châteaux were pillaged and burned at Igé, Lugny and Senozan (belonging to the Marquis de Talleyrand, bishop of Autun and already a prominent figure in the National Assembly), levies of food, drink and money were exacted from the wealthy and clergy, and feudal registers were burned. The abbey of Cluny, a major landowner and holder of seigneurial rights, was a particular target. Some 160 'brigands' – winegrowers, labourers, village artisans, beggars – were later arrested. Most insisted that they were 'swept up' by the crowd and meant no harm; a few admitted that the intention was 'to burn and raze the abbey', 'to destroy the abbey and the town' or to ensure 'the end of tithes and seigneurial dues'. So frightened were the 'patriots' and so determined were they to re-impose order that emergency committees were established to mete out justice: in the end, 27 men were hanged in Cluny, Mâcon and Tournus, only one of whom seems in fact to have played an active role in the uprising.[15]

To the northeast, in the Soissonnais, the epicentre of two of the panics, there was a long tradition of food rioting and popular price fixing in a region which exported grain. What was quite different in the summer of 1789 was the element of fear of outsiders, of beggars and 'brigands' likely to damage crops. The two panics in the Soissonnais began where arable land met forests, ideal hiding places for 'brigands'.[16] Here and elsewhere, there were individual actions within the currents of the Great Fear that resulted from local circumstances. As fear of 'brigands' swirled through villages around Noyon, the inhabitants of five other villages marched on and pillaged the château of Frétoy, taking a large quantity of grain. As in the food riots of 1775, the rioters took the precaution of arguing that they believed they were acting on orders of the king against hoarders.[17]

In Saintes in western France – where the price of one pound of bread was 4 *sous* 4 *deniers* in July (compared with 3 *sous* 5 *deniers* in Paris) – and other

Figures 1 and 2: There are few visual representations of the Great Fear of July–August 1789. In fact, physical intimidation (here shown as a popular 'arrest') of seigneurs was far more common than the burning of châteaux.

*Lat.*

small towns of the Saintonge, such as Rochefort, Cognac and Barbezieux, rumours spread on the twenty-ninth that several thousand 'brigands' were sweeping southwest from Ruffec, and 'milices nationales' were rapidly formed and armed. At Saintes, a band of peasants 'of all ages' armed with axes and pitchforks who had come to defend the town was sent home, perhaps in fear that they might instead be the brigands' frontline.[18] Further away to the south a current of the Fear which travelled from Revel along the valley of the Aude petered out in Bugarach, where the seigneur's agent complained to him of illegal tree felling for sales to forges: 'these forests are being pillaged, none of your guards is taking care of them'.[19]

Pierre Delahaye, the schoolteacher at Silly-en-Multien near Senlis, described vividly a winter of snow, rain and hunger in his journal. In late June 1789 he recorded that 'we are in frightful distress, all we hear is talk of revolts and massacres everywhere. There is no more wheat to be found.' On 27 July, the Great Fear reached Silly. In Delahaye's words, the inhabitants believed the rumour that harvesters guarded by soldiers were cutting the crops prematurely:

> the alarm was sounded and the priest ran through the village to gather all the men and boys, all armed, a few with rifles, the others with forks, spits, axes, pitchforks, with whatever they could, then left with the priest at their head, wearing his cockade.[20]

In other places, specific targets of local hatred were attacked, such as grain merchants. In Alsace, Jews were singled out: in Durmenach, Hagenthal and Hegenheim Jewish houses were pillaged.[21] In Flanders and the Cambrésis, there were 185 monasteries and convents. Seven of them were attacked in the last week of July, and two completely pillaged. Hundreds of peasants from Taisnières descended on the Benedictine abbey of Maroilles, which had won expensive court cases against the village in 1757 and 1775 and where early in 1789 the abbot had erected a pillory surmounted by a 'carcan' on the village square as a warning.[22] In the small town of Péronne in Picardy, it was reported that 'a large number of country people and some workers and apprentices from town' had responded to the arrival of the news from Paris by forcing the tax office employees to flee and then wrecking their office.[23]

Like the *menu peuple* of Paris, peasants adopted the language of bourgeois revolt to their own ends. From Montmartin, to the northeast of Paris, the steward of the estate of the Duke of Montmorency wrote to his master on 2 August:

> Brigandage and pillage are practised everywhere. The populace, attributing to the lords of the kingdom the high price of grain, is fiercely against all that belongs to them. All reasoning fails: this unrestrained populace listens only to its own fury and, in all our province, the vassals are so

outraged that they are prepared to commit the greatest excesses ... Just as I was going to finish my letter, I learnt ... that approximately three hundred brigands from all the lands associated with the vassals of Mme the Marquise de Longaunay have stolen the titles of rents and allowances of the seigneurie, and demolished her dovecotes: they then gave her a receipt for the theft signed *The Nation*.[24]

As Clay Ramsay has argued, the Great Fear was driven by 'conservative' impulses to protect local communities against outsiders, but its outcomes were radical, particularly in the creation of popular militias which were far more than appendages of established authority.[25] There is no over-arching reason why particular regions were receptive or deaf to rumour. Georges Lefebvre found that the Great Fear did not affect regions which had had tax revolts in the spring, and the greater alertness of local authorities in such regions may be part of an explanation. Another reason, suggests Ramsay on the basis of his study of the Fear in the Soissonnais, is that regions were more receptive to rumour where agriculture occurred within a community framework rather than through individualistic farming.[26]

Even in some areas untouched by the Great Fear the dominant reaction to the news of the storming of the Bastille was a contradictory mixture of elation and anxiety. This was certainly the case in the village of Gabian, north of Béziers, which had used its *cahier* to express its longstanding fear of the 'brigands' who descended from the wooded hills towards Bédarieux to the north and stole from travellers and villagers alike. During the summer of 1789 the municipality had to barricade the doors of the village every night. Once the news arrived of the taking of the Bastille a general assembly was held on 4 August to seek permission – which was accorded – that a 'milice bourgeoise' of 'people of good will' be formed to confront '*gens sans aveu* who are committing all sorts of brigandage'.[27]

The same night, in Versailles, the National Assembly was also taking steps to respond to rural insurrection. In an atmosphere of panic, self-sacrifice and exhilaration, a series of nobles mounted the rostrum of the Assembly to respond to the Great Fear by renouncing their privileges and abolishing feudal dues. The legislators' original intention – to respond to reports of peasant insurrection by abolishing seigneurial dues in return for monetary compensation – was overwhelmed by the surrender of a maze of other privileges. In the succeeding week, however, they made a distinction between instances of 'personal servitude', which were abolished outright, and 'property rights' (seigneurial dues payable on harvests) for which peasants had to pay compensation before ceasing payment:

Article 1. The National Assembly completely destroys the feudal regime. It decrees that rights and duties, both feudal and *censuel*, deriving from real or personal mortmain, and personal servitude, and those who symbolise them, are abolished without compensation; all the others are declared redeemable, and the price and the manner of the redemption will be set by the National Assembly. Those of the said rights that are not abolished by this decree will continue nonetheless to be collected until settlement.[28]

Accordingly, the Assembly abolished serfdom, dovecotes, seigneurial and royal hunting privileges and unpaid labour. Also ended was *mainmorte*, under which significant numbers of peasants – perhaps half a million in all – in the Franche-Comté had been subject to laws by which peasant holdings reverted to the seigneur at death, in recognition of the precept that all land was ultimately the lord's. Seigneurial courts were abolished: in future justice was to be provided free of charge according to a uniform set of laws. Tithes, like existing State taxes, were to be replaced by more equitable ways of funding Church and State; in the meantime, however, they were to be continued to be paid.

Later in August the Assembly approved the Declaration of the Rights of Man and of the Citizen. The Declaration was predicated on the key tenet of liberalism, that 'liberty consists of the power to do whatever is not injurious to others'. Accordingly, it guaranteed rights of free speech and association, of religion and opinion. This was to be a land in which all were to be equal in legal status, and subject to the same public responsibilities: it was an invitation to become citizens of a nation instead of subjects of a king. Together the August decrees and the Declaration of the Rights of Man marked the end of the absolutist, seigneurial and corporate structure of eighteenth-century France. They were also a revolutionary proclamation of the principles of a new golden age. But, while the Declaration proclaimed the universality of rights and the civic equality of all citizens, it was ambiguous on whether women and those without property would have political as well as legal equality, and was silent on how the means to exercise one's talents could be secured by those without the education or property necessary to do so. With the Assembly's prevarication on the full abolition of seigneurial dues, these ambiguities and silences were to underpin ongoing uncertainty and confrontation in rural France.

Shortly after the taking of the Bastille, the entrepreneur Palloy won the right to dismantle it, selling its bricks sculpted to resemble the fortress. This was the most apposite symbol of what had been achieved in 1789, but a more common representation of recent history took graphic form, as cheaply reproduced lithographs of 'le jeu' (in which a peasant bore a noble and a bishop piggy-back), of Louis XVI as the people's friend, or of pictorial narratives.[29] It was the taking of the Bastille above all that struck contemporaries. Just four days later, on 18 July, the liberal Marquis de Villette wrote of the need to organize a national festival to mark 'a revolution without precedent'.[30] Elsewhere, people acted to improvise festivals of their own. In the southwest, for example, peasants picnicked in the courtyard of the château of Manesgre in a manner that was both exuberant and menacing: they shot at pigeons and hens while warmly embracing the lord and insisting that 'they were all equal'.[31]

Both the August Decrees and the Declaration of the Rights of Man met with refusal from Louis. The Estates-General had been summoned to offer him advice on the state of his kingdom: did his acceptance of the existence of a 'National Assembly' require him to accept its decisions? Once again the standing of the Assembly seemed in question. This time it was the market women of Paris who took the initiative, convinced that the King had to sanction the decrees and return to Paris: in this way they believed that the noble conspiracy to starve Paris would be broken. Louis capitulated on 6 October. Later he married the white of the Bourbon family to the blue and red of Paris to symbolize the unity of King and nation. The Revolution seemed secure and complete, but Louis' reluctant consent to change was only thinly disguised by the fiction that his obstinacy was solely due to the malign influence of his court.

People in the small towns and villages of rural France were stunned to hear and read about the Declaration of the Rights of Man and the astonishing events in Paris and Versailles. Just as news of the storming of the Bastille was to trigger a distinctive response in the countryside, so the later news was the occasion of a variety of unforeseen responses. Most commonly of all, however, the months from mid-August to the end of the year in rural France were a time when the world was turned upside down, where the exhilaration of freedom was expressed through the targeting of those now seen as enemies of the new order of things.

John Markoff and Gilbert Shapiro have found that, although more than three-quarters of the village *cahiers* had criticized seigneurialism, the most common target of peasant anger was state taxation.[32] Within months, however, 'feudalism' – an umbrella term for seigneurialism, privilege and status – became and remained the prime target. One reason is that there was a widespread acceptance of the validity of the State and its demands, and that open hostility to taxes dissipated once the National Assembly announced its intention to impose uniform taxes on all citizens, including the former privileged.

Eric Hobsbawm once quipped about peasant rebellions that 'the refusal to understand is a form of class struggle'.[33] Certainly, peasants across much of France only accepted without question the opening phrase of the August decrees, and refused to believe that the Assembly had decided to require compensation. As the harvest came in, many rural communities simply refused to pay, or offered a lower cash payment. Already in August 1789 the parish priest of Sulignat in Bresse warned Garron de La Bévière, a prominent noble who had been one of those who had formulated the common *cahier* for the region, that 'the peasants, despite the explanations made to them of the articles [of the August decrees] want to be free of all levies, that's to say that they do not want to hear anything about the buying back of feudal dues'.[34]

Further south, as he traveled near Aix, Arthur Young noted that 'an unruly ungovernable multitude seize the benefit of the abolition, and laugh at the obligations or recompense'.[35]

One of the most common subjects of complaint in the *cahiers de doléances* formulated earlier in the year had been the alleged expropriation of common land by seigneurs, who levied a charge on its use for grazing livestock. In some parts of the country the poorest members of the rural community rushed to seize the opportunity to clear and cultivate a plot. The news of the seizure of such land, often with the full support of local councils, outraged the Assembly and administration. On 11 December the Assembly issued a decree forbidding communities to appropriate commons not in their possession before 4 August: it was soon apparent that the decree had not been heard.

In many areas, anti-seigneurialism meshed with hostility to restrictions on entry into royal and ecclesiastical forests and sparked widespread incursions into them. On 2 November the National Assembly placed forests under the protection of 'the Nation', but in general this too was simply ignored. On 11 December Barère de Vieuzac claimed to the Assembly that 'the devastation of forests has reached its limit everywhere in the kingdom. These precious resources of the navy, of construction, of workshops, of manufactures and of all the necessary arts, are almost annihilated.' Barère's hyperbole succeeded in having his proposed decree passed, placing forests under the protection of the law and public authorities, but this decree was to receive as little respect as the others.[36]

The new refusal to obey extended to the treatment of animals. The abolition of hunting monopolies in the August 1789 decree would unleash a massacre of wild life, and birds belonging to the former privileged orders were not spared. As Arthur Young travelled between Avignon and Aix, he recorded that

> I have been pestered with all the mob of the country shooting; one would think that every rusty gun in Provence is at work, killing all sorts of birds; the shot has fallen five or six times in my chaise and about my ears. ... [and] has, I am everywhere informed, filled all the fields of France with sportsmen to an utter nuisance.[37]

The startled *curé* of Tournissan near Carcassonne inquired whether the law allowed 'brigands' to open dovecotes and to shoot at pigeons at random, including one of his which had alighted on his window sill.[38]

The August decrees ended seigneurial hunting privileges and hunting estates such as that belonging to the Prince de Conti near Silly-en-Multien. In his journal the schoolteacher Delahaye detailed with glee the unchecked killing of the prince's game and the delight of his fellow villagers that they could hunt as they wished, 'just as the Prince used to'. The Prince de Conti fled France after 14 July disguised, to the schoolteacher's obvious pleasure, 'with the cockade of the Third Estate on a battered hat ... Everything terrified him. He was always thinking that there were assassins ready to kill him'.[39] Well into winter Delahaye was recording that 'hunting is still going on; we're hunting everywhere.' On 21 November 'we hunted the whole day in the Chaalis forest. We had four beaters with us. I killed a female deer at 150 paces and Louis Beuve killed its fawn almost as far away. I brought home 18 pounds of meat'.[40]

The elderly and acerbic Marquise de Créquy was scathing about the damage done to one of her ponds on her estate in the Gâtinais near Orléans whose produce was shared with a religious order. On the pretext that the Assembly had abolished the hunting privileges of the nobility and the feudal rights of the Church, instead of buying the fish 'four or five bands of people from roundabout, led by their mayors in their tricolour sashes' forced her guards to take refuge and 'everyone helped themselves to our fine fish and carted off what they could. It had been sixty years since this pond had been drained. ... All of them went off gaily, shouting ... '*Vive la nation! Vive Necker! Vive l'Assemblée nationale!* '[41]

In Collioure, a small Mediterranean fishing town and port just north of the Spanish border, news of the Revolution offered the chance for revenge of a different kind. Already in May two fishermen in Collioure had interpreted the calling of the Estates-General as meaning that they no longer had to pay the seigneurial levy to the Spanish noble the Duke d'Hijar for fish taken off the coast of Canet to the north. Then, in October 1789, two boats from Majorca en route to Genoa with a cargo of salt were forced to shelter from a storm in Port-Vendres, 2 km away. The opportunity was too good for Colliourencs to miss. A group of boats surrounded the vessels and a crowd imposed *taxation populaire*, that is, the forced sale of the goods at a 'just' price. The captains later claimed that this price had left them 4,000 *livres* short. It was probably fear that such popular action could be directed at them, as foreigners fishing Collioure's waters, that prompted all but two of the Genoans resident at Port-Vendres to leave during 1789.[42]

Many of the collective actions of the summer and autumn of 1789 took on a celebratory, carnivalistic element, with overtones of menace. In the small southwestern village of Paulin, between Sarlat and Brive, a group of young men approached Joseph de Bar, a disliked local seigneur, for a contribution towards the costs of celebrating the creation of the village militia. His abrupt refusal fuelled rancour and in November another group marched to the gate of his château led by Jean Faucher, a farm labourer who reportedly said that 'there were no more gentlemen and that he would certainly like to make the Sieur de Bar dance'. The crowd forced the gate and, after a shot was fired from the château, broke into the cellar for timber to light a fire. As a large crowd gathered to dance around the fire, de Bar sent out food and wine as a sign of goodwill. The next day the priest of Paulin acted as a mediator, with de Bar agreeing to repay fines levied by his court, and to return confiscated firearms. The crowd was unsuccessful in convincing him to renounce his seigneurial dues.[43]

This was to be the first of scores of attacks on châteaux in the Périgord over the next few months.[44] In the four months after December 1789 peasants from 330 parishes in the triangle between Montauban, Rodez and Périgueux invaded over one hundred châteaux to protest against the requisite payment of harvest dues, among the highest in France. Mona Ozouf has described the 'wild federations' which seemed to appear spontaneously during the winter as bands of villagers armed themselves after Church and go to neighbouring villages to join in the destruction of weathercocks and other symbols of the Ancien Régime before lighting a bonfire with pews from the Church and erecting and dancing around a maypole ('mai'). Often the pole would be decorated with a slogan, such as 'Woe to him who pays his rent!' The menace that the peasant revolt was not over was coupled with evident joy that public space was now in their hands.

One characteristic of the federations was an imposed rough egalitarianism. While at times this had a celebratory favour, at others it was menacing. At St-Bonnet-la-Rivière, near Tulle in the southwest, a crowd approached the seigneur's steward in February 1790, spat in his face, shouting that 'they no longer owed them anything, that they no longer had to go hat in hand, or be barefoot'. In this region of smallholdings, sharecropping and heavy seigneurial dues, some three-quarters of châteaux were besieged and emptied of grain.[45] On the tenth of that month, some 'poor peasants' from the area wrote in phonetic French to the National Assembly, complaining of seigneurs who 'are as cruel as the wolves who eat our lambs'. If the Assembly did not punish those who had fired on peasants during an uprising in Alassac, they warned that 'we will burn our barns, our houses and go into the forests with our livestock ... we'll kill you, and you're not seigneurs.'[46]

To the north, in Saintonge, three-quarters of the peasants in the seigneurie of Beaupuis simply refused to pay dues in 1789. It was reported that 26 of the 73 communes in the district of Tonnerre were refusing to pay dues; most of the villages around the little southwestern town of Gourdon did likewise. Similar protests, whether by violent action or non-compliance, occurred in many regions around Paris, and in the Massif Central, Brittany, the Dauphiné and Lorraine.

In Picardy, demands for a more radical revolution focused on taxes and seigneurialism. For example, in the village of Hallivillers, most of the inhabitants decided that they intended to 'put an end to the payment of the *champart* and force the other landholders to unite with them to refuse the tax'. By early 1790 the Assembly was becoming preoccupied with the stream of reports from local administrations about the non-payment of seigneurial dues and tithes.[47] At times, radical priests took the lead, as in Bourgueil, on the river Loire near Saumur, where Jacques Benoît warned the rich on New Year's Day 1790 that the poor had the right to come, Bible in hand, and demand one-fifth of their wealth.[48] Despite the good harvest of 1789, the level of anxiety in the countryside was such that in some areas rural communities sought to prevent available foodstuffs from departing. In Gévaudan, reported an official of the provincial Estates, 'the circulation of grain from town to town, from *bourg* to *bourg*, is continually stopped, and the people who are disregarding every law cannot be constrained by force since they are also armed'. Further south, in and around Albi, it was reported that 'artisans and labourers lack work, towns and countryside are full of beggars'.[49] The taking of the Bastille had done nothing to alleviate the food crisis.

Members of the former privileged élite were horrified by another manifestation of rebellion, a sudden collapse of deference. The artist Elisabeth Vigée Lebrun decided to leave France for Rome with her daughter at the time of the October Days. In their coach, she recalled;

> there also sat a mad Jacobin from Grenoble, about fifty years old, with an ugly, bilious complexion, who each time we stopped at an inn for dinner or supper made violent speeches of the most fearful kind. At all of the towns a crowd of people stopped the coach to learn the news from Paris. Our Jacobin would then exclaim: 'Everything is going well, children! We have the baker and his wife safe in Paris. A constitution will be drawn up, they will be forced to accept it, and then it will be all over.' There were plenty of ninnies and fatheads who believed this man as if he had been an oracle.[50]

Alexandre de Tilly, who in his youth had been a pageboy to Marie-Antoinette, decided to travel to England in 1789. He too was startled:

> the journey from Paris to Calais ... caused me great sadness. I could decipher a sort of savage mistrust already depicted on most faces. An austere or unruly patriotism animated everybody, some people displaying it too openly, others appearing too constrained in disguising it.[51]

Rural people expressed a new boldness in appealing to authority. On 6 May 1790, Jeanne Roques of Villefloure, near Carcassonne, appealed directly to the minister of the interior, claiming that on 5 December 1789 the son of the seigneur, Jean-Baptiste Airolles – 'a young man with all the vices and none of the virtues of his age' – had shot and killed her husband as he worked his fields. Her harrowing letter spoke of 'my grievances and my pain, deprived by a cruel murder of my only support ... a beloved spouse'. The case was the culmination of protracted warfare between Villefloure and its seigneur which may explain why, whereas Jean-Baptiste's grandfather had given 400 *livres* to the church and 4,410 to the poor on his death in 1771, his father left nothing to either when he died in 1790.[52]

But it was not only members of the court and aristocracy who were unsettled and even hostile to what had transpired. Disappointment at the attenuation of the National Assembly's putative abolition of feudalism caused a surge of peasant protest in Upper Brittany in January 1790. Already in October 1789 the *recteur* of the parish of Coëtbugat in the diocese of Vannes had warned the National Assembly of 'the murmurings of discontent in our countryside', as those who had participated enthusiastically in the drawing up of *cahiers* and elections to the Estates-General saw what they took to be a deliberate manoeuvre of the bourgeoisie of the towns to monopolize all the Revolution's gains, 'becoming more oppressive towards them than the tyranny of the feudal regime'. 'Our peasants are coarse', he added, 'but sensitive as well'.[53]

Another concerned priest was Yves-Michel Marchais, aged 63 in 1789, the *curé* since 1757 of the devout parish of Lachapelle-du-Gênet, southwest of Angers in Poitou. Marchais preached a classic Tridentine Catholicism: 'Everything that might be called an act of impurity or an illicit action of the flesh, when done of one's own free will, is intrinsically evil and almost always a mortal sin, and consequently grounds for exclusion from the Kingdom of God.'[54] On Sunday, 27 September 1789, he inveighed to his flock against liberty and equality, 'the most dangerous of all evils':

> Soon [revolutionaries] will persuade you that, all men being equal, each is his own master and that the rights, privileges and exemptions accorded to certain families or dignities are nothing but abuses. ... Don't hope too much to see the end of privilege, but just of possible abuses and the heavy burden of certain taxes that burden you.

The central hope of the farmers of the west was that their long-term leases known as *domaine congéable* would be converted into private property rights. Marchais was well aware of what had been festering among his flock when he warned the faithful:

> Perhaps [revolutionaries] will go as far as to make you believe, as some like you already have, that the properties that you lease are yours personally and that you have bought them dearly enough through your troubles and preceding payments. What a pitiable exaggeration! God preserve you from such crassness, my brothers.[55]

Everywhere, from Paris to the smallest hamlet, the summer and spring of 1789 were the occasion of an unprecedented collapse of centuries of Royal state-making. The taking of the Bastille was only the most spectacular instance of popular conquest of local power. While the Assembly moved with remarkable energy and commitment to restructure every aspect of public life, the vacuum of authority caused by the collapse of the Bourbon State was temporarily filled at the local level by popular militias and councils. As we have seen, this seizure of power was accompanied by massive disobedience to the tributary claims of the State, seigneurs and Church; moreover, as royal troops openly fraternized with civilians in provincial centres, the judiciary was powerless to enforce the law.

All the evidence points to near universal participation in these extraordinary months of celebration and protest. There is, however, little extant evidence of formal, written responses to the events of 1789 in the registers of deliberations of village councils. There were many places like St-Michel-de-Lanes and Villasavary, two large villages in the Lauragais near Castelnaudary, where punctilious registers do not record any reaction at all to the momentous events.[56] This may have been from caution: both were to be pro-revolutionary villages. In some places this was because of the collapse of local authority, but more commonly it was because village councils did not know how to respond in minute books to the swirling mass of news and rumour. In many councils, the dominant reaction to the news from Paris was fear of the possible consequences and uncertainty about the meaning of events far away. How should that be recorded in the minutes?

Where evidence does survive it resonates with support and optimism. On 20 December 1789, the municipal council of Lézignan near Narbonne expressed its joy, if somewhat hyperbolically:

> Liberty is reborn in this Empire. Man, born free, long groaned in slavery; his sacred and imprescriptible rights have just been recognized perfectly and made permanent by our august and generous representatives of the Nation, and founded on the indestructible bases of reason and equity. These unalterable truths can only be eternal in the midst of the great benefits that the National Assembly has just won for us.

In nearby Fitou the council spent part of Christmas Day 1789 lauding the 'wise, unceasing labours of the National Assembly' against 'l'antique et barbare régime féodal'. The secretary went on to transcribe in full about one hundred pages of the Assembly's decrees, as the decrees themselves required.[57]

The secretary was one of many thousands of similar men who played a key role in 1789 and beyond in the written network which was to be a vital dimension of the communication of news and decrees from the capital and elsewhere. Equally important, as Jill Maciak and Vivian Gruder have stressed, were ancient networks and practices of oral communication.[58] Most people, particularly in the countryside, were unable to read or write the printed word with ease. Instead, the expression of Revolution was most commonly in forms of communication of a non-written kind: the spoken or sung word, the resonant statements made by gesture, clothing and behaviour. Such communication occurred on the street, at the laundry, after Church and, perhaps most powerfully, at the maze of small-town markets which studded the countryside, a privileged place for hearing news and rumour that purported to be news.

From early in 1789, the working people of France were to hear of, participate in and respond to a Revolution through these non-scribal modes while
their literate neighbours sought to convince them of the veracity – and
benevolence or menace – of written documents. Printed documents made
their way via the 1,320 'distribution offices' and finally reached even the
smallest of communities in about 11 days. But there were other, chiefly oral,
ways in which the Revolution was being communicated, absorbed and contested. From the outset, the greatest difficulties revolutionary legislators
would face in communicating with the new citizenry would be the length of
time that it took and the vulnerability of distant populations to rumour. For
most people, written and oral communication was in two different languages; across most of the country, bilingual municipal officers were to play
a pivotal role as translators of laws and decrees from Paris, just as they had in
expressing grievances in French in the *cahiers* of 1789. But this role would be
all the more difficult when their non-French speaking citizenry refused to
believe what was being read to them.

# 3
# Reimagining Space and Power, 1789–91

Rural people had long assumed that the affairs of the parish were theirs to decide, albeit under the tutelage of seigneur and priest. They had assumed, in contrast, that the affairs of State were in the hands of the King and his ministers, under the tutelage of God. The exercise of power at both parish and State level was to change abruptly and radically. People may have heard of the election of George Washington to the United States presidency in March 1789, but the new practice of popular sovereignty was none the less revolutionary for that.

At the same time, the euphoria of the autumn of 1789 was tempered by awareness of the magnitude of what remained to be done. The revolutionaries' declaration of the principles of the new régime presupposed that every aspect of public life would be reshaped. The 'Ancien Régime', as it was now starting to be called, had been overthrown, but what was to be put in its place?[1]

Over the next two years, the deputies threw themselves into the task of reworking every dimension of public life. The reconstruction of France was based on an assertion of the equal status of French citizens whatever their social or geographic origin.[2] In every aspect of public life – administration, the judiciary, taxation, the armed forces, the Church, policing – a system of corporate rights, appointment and hierarchy gave way to civil equality, accountability and popular sovereignty. The coincidence of the Assembly's reform project and the widespread assumptions that 'the people' now held power was profoundly revolutionary.

The institutional structures of the Ancien Régime had been characterized by extraordinary provincial diversity and control by a network of royal appointees. Now this was reversed: at every level officials were to be elected, but the institutions in which they worked were everywhere to be the same. The institutional bedrock would be the 44,000 new 'communes', mostly based on the parishes of the Ancien Régime, the base of a nested hierarchy of cantons, districts and departments. The 83 departments announced in February 1790 were also designed to facilitate the accessibility of administration, for it was anticipated that each capital would be no more than a day's ride from any commune.

Drawing in part on Calonne's attempt in 1787 to reform and make uniform local government, the National Assembly passed its municipal law on 14 December 1789. The *communautés d'habitants* were replaced by *communes* in which the *consuls* gave way to a mayor and municipal officers, and *conseillers politiques* were replaced by *notables*. These officials were to be elected on the basis of a property franchise: those paying 3 *livres* in tax were eligible to vote as 'active' citizens and 10 *livres* were enough to be eligible for election (compared with 10 and 30 *livres* under the reforms of 1787). The local government law represented a significant change in the autonomy and electorate of village councils. Now municipalities were freed, at least in law, from the control of seigneurs: no longer would the lords have the ultimate right to choose office-bearers.

By retaining parishes as the basis of the new communes, the Assembly minimized the chances of disaffection but created thousands of tiny communes which would have little chance of exercising the responsibilities given to them. There were, for example, 131 communes in the new department of the Haute-Garonne with fewer than 200 inhabitants, 292 in the Corrèze with fewer than 150, and 81 in the Calvados with fewer than 50.[3] The new law placed a huge burden of responsibility on villagers; they were now responsible for apportioning and collecting direct taxes, carrying out public works, poor relief, overseeing the material needs of Church and school, and maintaining law and order. The records of local government across the country are nevertheless redolent of the confidence of village and small-town leaders that they had the capacity to meet these responsibilities without the tutelage of seigneurs and priests.

From the outset, however, the ideals of liberty and equality were compromised by pragmatic considerations of vested interests. Neither poorer men – dubbed 'passive' citizens – nor women were judged capable of exercising sovereign rights. The Declaration of the Rights of Man and of the Citizen had asserted that this was to be a land in which all were to be equal in legal status and subject to the same public responsibilities. There was therefore a logical inconsistency between the Declaration's universalist proclamation of rights and its decision to limit formal politics to 'active' citizens: property-owning males.[4]

Across the country about three-fifths of all households had an 'active citizen'. In rural areas this was usually far higher: in the six villages studied by Peter Jones only one – the Breton market-village of Châtelaudren, with virtually no farmland – had fewer than four-fifths who were 'actives'.[5] The villagers elected mostly the same men as *officiers municipaux* and *notables* in 1790 as they had chosen under Calonne's reforms. It was as if the *consuls* and *conseillers* elected in 1787 had, in Jones' words, served an 'apprenticeship' in self-government that was to stand them in good stead.[6] In Artois, for example, many of the same rural notables who had dominated village politics before the Revolution continued to do so. Their 'fermocratie' was based on the great farms (*censes*) which dominated the region: in 1790 the large *fermiers* were 5 per cent of the population but 60 per cent of mayors.[7]

While village council elections were straightforward, those at other levels were time consuming. For example, active citizens were required to gather in their local capital in April 1790 to elect their canton's officials. The 45 of about 100 eligible voters from Silly-en-Multien had a short walk to Nanteuil, but were expected to stay several days. The schoolteacher Delahaye has given us a precious glimpse of this exercise in popular sovereignty:

> This assembly was held upstairs in the granary, which was decorated at the end near the chestnut-trees with a rostrum raised on two steps, covered with a rug on which there were an armchair and table. Behind the armchair was attached to a large cloth the list of the fourteen or fifteen parishes which make up this canton, with the names of all the active citizens, numbering 768. Beneath the rostrum was a large table covered with a rug on which were two vases to put the ballot papers, inkwells, pens, sand and so on.

The president, to take the armchair, was the oldest man, aged 83 or 84, with the three next eldest to be scrutineers of the 231 votes cast, 'most having left, some to take some air, others to do other things'.[8]

The inevitable problems created by lack of resources in poor areas and the restricted number of men with the leisure and education to make effective use of complex legislation from Paris were added to by the local contexts into which these new structures and laws were introduced. In many areas such as the west, the local government law created a puzzling separation of municipality and vestry and excluded many men and all the women used to discussing parish matters after mass.[9]

The radical decentralization of power created a situation where revolutionary legislation from Paris was interpreted and adapted to local needs. In this process, the half-million or more men who were elected to local government, the judiciary and administrative positions played the key role in the void that existed between the Assembly's national programme and the exigencies of the local situation. Jill Maciak has calculated that between 40 and 90 printed copies of new laws were reaching the countryside each month during 1791.[10] Executing laws which to most people often seemed foreign in content as well as language, and often lacking in resources, these 'active' citizens – professional men, better-off peasants, merchants and landowners – made an enormous commitment of time and energy.

Those who were among the major initial beneficiaries of the Revolution were this middle class of country towns: lawyers, merchants, officials and property owners. The dramatic reorganization of institutional structures had meant that many thousands of officials and lawyers lost their positions, venal or otherwise.[11] But the 2,700 magistrates of the *bailliage* courts who lost their positions with the radical restructuring of judicial administration in 1790 were enthusiastic supporters of the Revolution: not only did they succeed in being elected to newly created positions but were also compensated for their lost offices (perhaps because one-fifth of the Third Estate deputies were from their ranks).

The Revolution was, and long remained, overwhelmingly popular: the extent of change in public life cannot be understood except in a context of mass optimism and support. In many country towns, however, there were early signs of resentment towards the Revolution stemming from the loss of status following administrative reorganization, as in Vence (department of the Var), where a vigorous campaign failed to protect its bishopric, relocated in nearby St-Paul. As Ted Margadant has shown, the location of departmental, district and cantonal capitals (*chefs-lieux*) swamped legislators with a flood of complaints and rivalries which could call into question support for the Revolution in towns formerly sustained by the presence of the maze of courts and offices of the Ancien Régime. The battles between Marseille and Aix, Carcassonne and Narbonne, Soissons and Laon to be the capital of their new department were replicated hundreds of times at cantonal level as, for example, Montpon and Mussidan in the Dordogne, Seix and Oust in the Ariège, and Latour and Estagel in the Pyrénées-Orientales fought bitterly over the advantages that they believed would come with cantonal status.[12]

French people had been socialized into a mental landscape of administrative, judicial, fiscal and ecclesiastical structures which everywhere bore the marks of historical accretion and privilege. Flanders, where most people spoke Flemish in daily life, was separated from the rest of France by an internal customs border; it was administered from Lille, but its highest court (Parlement) was located in Douai and its archbishopric, which had extensive seigneurial rights, in a third city, Cambrai. The Corbières, at the southern extremity of the kingdom from Flanders, was a geographically well-defined area whose 129 parishes all spoke Occitan with the exception of three Catalan villages on its southern border. Yet the region was divided for administrative, ecclesiastical, judicial and taxing purposes between offices in Carcassonne, Narbonne, Limoux and Perpignan. The boundaries of these institutions were not consistent: for example, neighbouring villages administered from Perpignan were in different dioceses. And these were other people's structures: the King's justice, the seigneur's court, the Church's tribunal.

There were now new spatial images of authority to be absorbed. The creation of a new idea of France was the work of urban élites with a distinctive vision of spatial organization and institutional hierarchy. It was designed to give reality to two of their keywords: to 'regenerate' the nation while cementing its 'unity'. There was not only a valid geographic rationale to each department, but their functions also represented an important victory of the new State over the resurgent provincial identities expressed since 1787. Their very names, drawn from rivers, mountains and other natural features, undercut claims to other provincial and ethnic loyalties: the Basque country would be the 'Basses-Pyrénées', not the 'Pays Basque', nor would there be any institutional recognition whatsoever of regions such as Brittany, Alsace or Languedoc. 'They renamed my province after a stream', snorted the Marquise de Créquy.[13]

The Assembly was also concerned to accelerate 'from above' the coincidence of the new nation of French citizens with use of the French language. In August 1790 the Abbé Grégoire sent out a questionnaire on 'the *patois* and the customs of country people'. The results of the inquiry were sobering for legislators who wrongly assumed that a facility in French was indispensable to be a patriot. Only 15 departments, with 3 million people, were identified as purely French speaking; of the 40,000 people of the district of St-Geniez (Aveyron), about 10,000 could understand French, 3,000 could read it and only 2,000 could speak it. In the Gascon Lot-et-Garonne, priests complained of peasants falling asleep during the reading of decrees from the Assembly 'because they do not understand a word, even though the decrees are read in a loud and clear voice and are explained'. In consequence, successive assemblies encouraged the translation of decrees into local languages and over much of France the new elements of political life were assimilated through the medium of auto-translation.[14]

The responses to Grégoire's 1790 questionnaire varied sharply. From the Périgord, one reply noted that 'twenty years ago, it was a ridiculous thing to speak French; we used to call it *francimander*. In the towns today, all the bourgeois speak only French'. While none of his 43 respondents reported that country folk had previously read much other than the Bible and other religious texts, the Bordeaux lawyer Bernadau noted that

> since the Revolution, the peasants have substituted for these texts the newspapers of the times, which they buy when their date makes them available at a lower price. The young have also substituted patriotic songs for hymns.[15]

There is no question, however, that non-French speakers were generally enthusiastic about the Revolution, even when the imposition of uniformity was materially disadvantageous. The Provençal villagers of Lourmarin welcomed

> the sacrifices that our deputies have made of the dangerous privilege which isolated this province from the rest of France. To be called a Frenchman is the first and most beneficial of all national rights and the most fertile source of liberty, of equality and of social well-being.[16]

Across the country, the most fervent advocates of French as the language of national unity were the patriotic élites of country towns in non-French speaking areas: while southern peasants 'continually have the magic words of Revolution and Constitution on their lips', regretted an administrator from Montauban, 'they've not yet taken a step towards enlightenment'.[17]

The same imperatives of citizenship applied to Jews and Protestants. By the end of 1789 full citizenship had been granted to Protestants and, the following January, to the Sephardic Jews of Bordeaux and Avignon. Right to the latter was granted only by 374 votes to 280. It was only during the final sessions of the National Assembly in September 1791, however, that the Ashkenazim Jews of eastern France were granted full equality and were able to stand for election. A decision at the same time to initiate an enquiry into Jewish money-lending was interpreted in the east as meaning that debts owed to them were void.[18]

Historians have seen the delay in the emancipation of the larger Ashkenazi community in the east as a measure of its perceived 'backwardness' in contrast with the greater wealth, social integration and secularization of the Sephardic Jewish community in the southwest. In fact, however, the Sephardic Jews had been in as precarious a legal position before the Revolution, and over half of them lived in poverty. Ronald Schechter has calculated that only about one hundred were qualified to be 'active' citizens in 1791.[19]

Jews in particular were regarded as a 'nation'; indeed, they had referred to themselves in that way before 1789. The civic emancipation of Jews and Protestants was understood within a paradigm of French citizenship: that is, their capacity to assimilate into the French body politic. There could be no question of religious minorities – especially Jews – sustaining a separate identity while also being French citizens, any more than religious orders could swear partial loyalty to the Revolution.[20] With the abolition of corporations, they were expected to renounce their Jewishness if they were to be full citizens. In the words of Clermont-Tonnerre:

> To the Jews as a Nation, nothing; to the Jews as individuals, everything. They must renounce their judges; they must have none but ours ... They must not form a political corps or Order in the state; they must be individuals separately.[21]

Resonating through the *cahiers* of rural people had been a chorus of complaints about systems of royal, aristocratic and clerical justice often seen as time consuming, costly and harsh. The complexity of these courts and their regional variants was replaced by a national system deliberately made more accessible, humane and egalitarian. The number of capital offences was sharply reduced, and the punishment for them would be a style of decapitation perfected by a deputy, the Parisian doctor Joseph Guillotin, and accepted as humane by the Assembly.

The laws of 16–24 August 1790 established a new judicial order. The election of judges was instituted as the logical corollary of the idea that the right to sit in judgement of others came from the 'nation'. The Assembly introduced the election of magistrates with the hope of rendering judges responsible to the people. Free access to justice was a derivative of the principle that the nation constituted the source of all justice, since access to dispute resolution was a right of every member of society. Hence judges became salaried officials of the nation and received no pecuniary benefits from the prolongation or outcome of litigation.

The seigneur's court was one aspect of the seigneurial system that the National Assembly abolished definitively in August 1789. Following English and Dutch precedents, the deputies moved to set up a new system which, in line with the repeated rural grievances expressed in the *cahiers*, would be accessible to all, cheap and designed to conciliate.[22] The introduction of elected justices of the peace in every canton with the law of 14 October 1790 proved immensely popular for the provision of cheap and accessible justice. Lawyers were removed altogether from minor civil lawsuits by requiring parties to represent themselves before a justice of the peace. Regardless of their social status and wealth, rural people could now seek redress, and did so. The institution of justices of the peace was an extraordinary success in meeting a widespread rural demand for a system of mediation that was accessible, cheap, prompt and able to resolve some of the minor but nagging irritations of rural life.

A male citizen 30 years of age or older who met the eligibility requirements for any other district or departmental administrative position could become a justice of the peace. His experience in rural affairs and the confidence in his probity that he inspired among rural communities mattered more than his grasp of the science of the law. After accumulating the information surrounding a possible crime, and seeking a resolution, the justice forwarded his findings to an *accusateur public* who decided whether to proceed with an indictment, in which case the case was presented before a jury, another revolutionary innovation. Whereas the seigneurial judge of Jonzac had commonly adjudicated 7–10 cases per year, his successor as justice of the peace would make 144 judgements in 1792 alone. While perhaps two-thirds of cases could not be resolved by justices of the peace to the satisfaction of both parties, the thousands of grievances great and small that rural people took to their justice of the peace is witness to the relevance of the institution.

\*   \*   \*

The history of the years from October 1789 to October 1791 has generally been written in terms of the National Assembly's sweeping reforms to every dimension of public life. Every institution – from the administration of taxation and justice to the Catholic Church and the army – bore the mark of an Ancien Régime based on privilege, exemption and historical accretion; now the first principles were access, equality and uniformity. The members of the Assembly approached the overwhelming task with zeal and skill, and by September 1791 Louis XVI had given his consent to a constitution.

For most French people, however, the revolutionary remaking of the nation was experienced primarily as a struggle to embed the putative victory of the summer of 1789 in the actuality of social relations at the level of the urban neighbourhood or village. As legislators struggled with the colossal task of rebuilding every aspect of public life in line with the principles of 1789, the actions taken by rural communities and small towns indicated the mix of exhilaration, menace and resolve in the countryside.[23] In particular, successive assemblies' prevarications about the outright abolition of seigneurialism fuelled a complex dialogue between peasant and legislator, in which rural communities, by legal and illegal means, pressured and responded to successive assemblies and made political choices about the means to do so. The years 1789–91 are best understood as a period of negotiation – legal, extralegal or violent – about the nature of the new régime.[24]

The bloodshed of 1789 had occurred in Paris. In rural France there had been a notable absence of violence to persons, even though individual seigneurs and their agents had been harassed, menaced and humiliated. More typically, it was property which was seized or damaged. Now the Assembly's attempt to resolve the ambiguities in the feudal legislation concerning compensation by subsequent decrees fuelled violent unrest in many areas.[25] On 3 May 1790 a decree set out the value of the redemption of seigneurial rights. For *corvées*, *banalités* and those dues paid in money, the rate of redemption was set at 20 times the annual value and, for those paid in kind, at 25 times. The decree served only to strengthen resolve.

After the formal festivals of federation in July 1790, the planting of improvised maypoles (*mais sauvages*) in the Périgord and Quercy took on a new urgency, coupled with attacks on châteaux. In such a situation these *mais* served to remind the timid of gibbets. When a column of soldiers was dispatched from Gourdon (Lot) in November 1790 to destroy the *mais* in surrounding villages, the town was invaded by peasant bands and pillaged. The 'wild federations', which involved coercion of neighbouring villages and threats to individuals likely to break ranks, were also characterized by their deliberate leaderlessness. A blacksmith of Ste-Mesme asked, 'Who should lead the march?' and received the response, 'Everybody must march, young and old alike.' At other times, the bands insisted to neighbouring villages that the king had instructed his people to destroy the weathercocks and pews.[26] Commissioners from Paris spoke of seeing maypoles decorated with both 'Long live the Nation, the Law, the King' and 'No more rents': their exhaustive questioning of peasants about the significance of the *mais* led them to conclude that they represented 'the conquest of liberty'.

It soon became apparent, through agitated reports pouring in from the new departments, and from personal correspondence received by deputies, that across most of the country the compromise legislation of May had encountered stubborn and at times violent resistance. In the increasingly fraught atmosphere of 1790, as former seigneurs and their communities attempted to intimidate or outmanoeuvre each other, there were occasions when anger spilled over into physical assault, even homicide. There were violent incidents in 38 of the 500 new districts, located in 17 of the new departments. Mostly these were attacks on property; when violence was directed at persons, it was characterized by a will for collective vengeance. In October 1790 the villagers of Varaize (Charente-Inférieure) stabbed to death their mayor Latierce, the manager of the Countess d'Amelot's estates, in the streets of the nearby town of St-Jean-d'Angély. It was later claimed that Latierce was held upright so that his neighbours could all have the opportunity to join in this violent act, as if in symbolic expulsion of him from the community.[27]

Far more common than violence was the resort to time-honoured practices of legal manoeuvring and foot-dragging, and to a new willingness to refuse to cooperate. Since the 1789–90 legislation treated seigneurial exactions as a legal form of rent which peasants could only terminate by compensating the seigneur, many communities decided to pay for legal action to force seigneurs to submit their feudal titles for judicial verification. This legal challenge often overlapped with an illegal, second type of action, the refusal to pay feudal dues in the meantime. At least 86 of the 129 communities of the Corbières were involved in taking action to resolve the issues unanswered by the 1789 legislation. This took the form of either taking legal action to force their seigneur to submit feudal titles for judicial verification or the refusal to pay any feudal dues whatsoever.[28] Often it went well beyond a simple refusal to pay, as in the eight small and desperately poor hamlets ringing a valley known as the Val de Dagne. In July 1790, the brother of the seigneur of Arquettes-en-Val warned that 'we will have to expect a formal refusal to pay our rents, formerly seigneurial. People are harvesting every day without calling us in, which is the custom and conforms to their obligations'. A few days later, a huge band of villagers marched armed with rifles and pitchforks to the château at Rieux-en-Val, where they threatened the mayor with death if he tried to collect the seigneurial dues. They then set about demolishing the château and its garden, stopping only when the seigneur and the mayor gave them a 'people's levy' of 500 *livres*.

The actions of inhabitants of rural communities went well beyond the bounds of the seigneurial legislation on 1789–90, for they also seized the moment to test the resolve of authorities and élites on a range of other local questions. Like other forms of collective action, these were a mix of old and new, for example, the 'bacchanals' which were a potent combination of labour protest and charivari. In the Oise, the teacher Pierre Delahaye reported that, after a marriage in March 1790, for three days 'the boys and even the men of Silly-en-Multien conducted a wild *bacchanal* every night until one or two in the morning, with drums, barrels, scythes, oven shovels, violins, bells large and small, cow-horns, whips, and so on'. But *bacchanals* were also carnivalesque moments when farm labourers took advantage of a bountiful crop or shortage of harvesters to confront the wealthy and demand higher recompense. In August 1790 labourers refused the rates farmers had pinned to their doors, insisting on 18 *livres* plus meals for two acres of wheat-cutting instead of 16. 'All that you hear about is terrible *bacchanals* and threats of hanging on all sides.' While the national guards convinced the harvesters of Silly to go back to work, at neighbouring Oissery a scaffold erected on the village square next to a table with paper, pen and ink was enough to convince farmers to sign up to '18 *livres* the double acre and meals, and meat and cheese twice a day'.[29]

This was matched, in sharecropping and tenancy areas, by frustration at the Assembly's protection of property owners. For example, on 1 December 1790 it decreed that the value of the abolished tithe could now be added to rents. In the Gers, where about 30 per cent of the population was sharecroppers, this decree was to cause resentment and friction as landowners began to lift rents by 10 per cent. The manager of the estate of the duke de Cossé-Brissac raised the rent on a large farm near Bressuire in western France by 24 per cent. Similarly, the increased burden of State taxes was often added to rents.[30] By June 1790 calls for more direct action on property distribution were being expressed. The municipality of Corbigny (Nièvre) reported that those spreading false rumours 'are proclaiming the agrarian law and that they will impose it themselves, by force'.[31]

There were other issues at stake, particularly that of control of resources in the forests and commons owned or controlled by the former privileged orders or the State. The collapse of local authority had opened up to the poor an unprecedented opportunity to seize land or fell trees. This was especially the case in regions with extensive *vacants* or 'wastelands', much of it common land. In August 1790 the National Assembly was forced to remind municipalities that it was quite incorrect that the decrees of the previous 11 December and 18 March protecting forests had given administration of both national and Church forests over to them. This had led to guards being forcibly expelled from forests and even to municipalities leading their villagers into forests for wholesale tree-felling.[32] While promising a thoroughgoing revision of Colbert's forest code of 1669, several times in 1790 the Assembly had to respond to the urgent appeals of the forest administration by warning that forest incursions would be punished 'with the greatest rigour.'[33]

In the early years of the Revolution the Assembly received hundreds of petitions about the commons, most in 1790. The petitions varied markedly in tone, reflecting the social background and interests of their framers. Illegal seizures of commons were particularly frequent in Languedoc and parts of the centre; in the northeast insistence on division was more commonly kept in check.[34] Some municipalities responded to the damage being done to forests and commons by urging the National Assembly to allow them to divide them between the inhabitants so that individual families would take better care of them. For others it was too late. On 12 December 1790 the municipality of Grospierres (Ardèche) bemoaned the impact of the royal decree of 1766 which, it alleged, had encouraged people to clear land; its repeated requests to divide the commons had been ignored to the point where 'the woods have continued to be ravaged, to such a point that there is no longer anything to be found there'.[35] On 21 April 1791 the King's foresters of Bouzonville (Seine-Inférieure) begged the National Assembly to re-establish order in the administration of the forests and 'complained that they can no longer prevent the depredations without number which people are committing in the forests'.[36] The Grand Parc at Villepreux near Versailles had been spared the massacre of game in the summer of 1789 as the King's private possession, but a year later thousands of poachers descended on the Parc. In September 1790 a whole venison could be bought for 50 *sous* at neighbouring Rennemoulin.[37]

The alacrity with which sections of the rural community seized on the ambiguity of the revolutionary decrees or simply chose to take advantage of the collapse of authority horrified others. Landowners from the village of Grouches (Somme) complained that 'the inhabitants of their commune, by interpreting decrees as they wish, are clearing the hills on our territory, even though these slopes, very steep and dry, cannot produce anything'.[38] In December 1790 the municipal council of Bourg (Ain) received a report that 'the forests around the town of Bourg have been completely devastated by different individuals, the guards appointed to ensure the conservation of the said woods were insufficient to prevent the damage'.[39] Similar reports were being received all over the country, but were particularly agitated from Mediterranean coastal areas with huge areas of stony pastures. For example, a spectacular dispute flared on the hillsides round Feuilla (Aude) in 1790 as villagers assumed they had absolute freedom to graze livestock and cut timber on wooded lands claimed by an absentee noble.[40] The noble in question claimed that the almost total destruction of his forest had cost him 56,000 *livres* and two-thirds of his income and successfully sought the aid of the administration in bringing in troops to search for the offenders. The response of the locals was to wait for his crops to ripen the following summer, then to burn them, including 500 *setiers* of grain and 60 tonnes of hay.

As common land, and therefore the 'people's', the *vacants* were particularly vulnerable to demands from the poorest section of the community to be given land to clear and cultivate, now without the disincentive of feudal dues. While the Revolution remained massively popular, tensions emerged within many communities between the poor, desperate for a cultivable plot for growing grain and vegetables, and the larger landowners who dominated local political power and who also possessed the largest flocks of sheep. Local administrators became agitated at the acceleration of erosion as hillsides were cleared. In January 1791 Raymond Bastoulh, the *procureur-général-syndic* of the department of the Aude, reported to his departmental administration that

> people are complaining on all sides about the misguided greed of peasants who are spending every day clearing the woods and the uncultivated land on mountain-sides, without realising that this soil will only be productive for a year or two. ... This pernicious clearing has accelerated since the destruction of the feudal régime because the people of the countryside imagine that the communes have become the owners of the *vacants*, that the former seigneurs were stripped of them at the same time as they were of judicial power, and that they have no other formalities to complete other than to inform the secretary of the municipality of the land they intend to clear.

It was already obvious, he noted, that gravel and stones were being washed down into streams, congesting their beds and causing them to spill over onto the best land. The departmental authorities decided, in the interests of the hillsides and pastoralists, to ban clearances altogether, but in vain.[41]

In the Aisne, where there was a very high percentage of landless or near landless farm labourers, the division of the commons (here called *usages*) was seen as a partial solution to land hunger. North of Château-Thierry, for example, a group of villages took it upon themselves to divide their commons in 1790–91. At Mont-St-Père, the council recorded its view that 'the pastures were only of use to the *fermiers* of Cense-à-Dieu and Chanois who alone benefited from these lands by using them daily for about five hundred *bêtes blanches* (sheep) and forty *bêtes à cornes* (cattle)'. Here, too, there was a widespread assumption that trees could be felled at will in forests that were now 'the people's', although forestry officials noted that small trees were deliberately left untouched. Particularly targeted were the avenues of trees that nobles had planted along paths leading to their estates, blamed for keeping peasants' fields in the shade.[42]

In response to a plethora of reports from many regions of France, the National Assembly sought, in its decree of 22 February 1791, to resolve the issue of ownership of the *vacants*, known according to the region as *terres vaines et vagues, gastes, garrigues, landes, biens hermes, flégards* or *wareschaix*. The Assembly had difficulty in resolving the contradiction between its policy of dealing with the land according to universal principles of private ownership and ancient popular assumptions of multiple rights of usage. The legislation was clear that former seigneurs no longer had the right to appropriate the *vacants*: they were henceforth to be *biens communaux* unless the seigneur could demonstrate acquisition before 1789, either by having put them to productive use at least 40 years beforehand or 'by virtue of the laws, customs, statutes or local usages then existing.' Even where former seigneurs could justify this ownership, however, communal rights of usage – for grazing and wood in particular – were to be respected. The legislation inevitably generated further confusion and contestation over what constituted adequate proof of prior ownership.[43]

Even though 1790 was a year characterized by optimism after what had been achieved, and the new harvest promised to be abundant, the poor in many areas did not have the resources to wait for the crops to be brought in. In May 1790 an angry gathering of men and women in Bourg (Ain) seized 16 sacks of flour from a load being brought into the town from Mâcon.[44] In mid-January 1791, people from 13 villages descended on a boat bound for Paris at Liez (Aisne), on the St-Quentin canal, and removed 1,200 of the 2,000 sacks of wheat.[45]

The Constituent and Legislative assemblies were determined to reform the provision of public assistance for the poor by establishing a rational, secular and nation-wide system of social welfare to replace the piecemeal ecclesiastical relief of the Ancien Régime.[46] On 21 January 1790 the Assembly established a Comité de Mendicité. By the time its work was completed, replies from 51 departments indicated an improbably precise figure of 1,928,064 beggars, about one-eighth of the population. After noting that its poor somehow survived by growing food on the poorest land, the officials of Volognat in the east of the Ain noted that the only remedy for poverty would be to reduce taxes, then added as a footnote: 'rocks on all sides'.[47]

In September 1790, the Assembly determined that all those whose earnings were so low that they paid less than one day's wages in tax each year were eligible for immediate assistance should further misfortune befall them. Limited public assistance to rural areas was made available in 1791, usually outdoor manual work repairing roads or riverbanks, or occasionally drainage of marshes; 50,000 *livres* was given to the Isère to build dykes to protect farmland from flooding.[48] In December 1790 the Assembly allocated 15 million *livres* to the workshop programme (*ateliers de charité*) in Paris and the departments. Ultimately, however, the cost of financing the workshops meant that they were subject to rigorous review. From 1791, no new schemes were started in Paris and from 1792 the number of schemes in the countryside was severely cut back. Instead, on 25 May 1791 the Assembly decreed that municipal councils should take charge of poor relief by setting up local *commissions de bienfaisance* without delay.

The radical devolution of responsibility for the very poor placed the new communes in an invidious position, for how were they to meet these new demands? The measures they proposed, such as allocating funding to employ men to do work on roads and canals, was not popular within the Assembly and, in any case, insufficient. The Conseil Général of Belley (Ain), noting that the indigent were the most numerous group in the town,

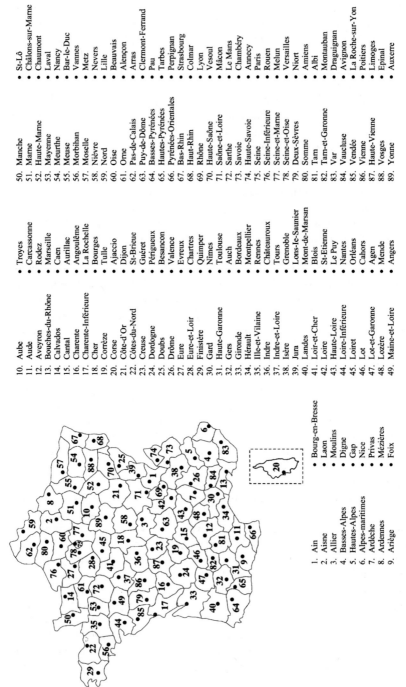

10. Aube • Troyes
11. Aude • Carcassonne
12. Aveyron • Rodez
13. Bouches-du-Rhône • Marseille
14. Calvados • Caen
15. Cantal • Aurillac
16. Charente • Angoulême
17. Charente-Inférieure • La Rochelle
18. Cher • Bourges
19. Corrèze • Tulle
20. Corse • Ajaccio
21. Côte-d'Or • Dijon
22. Côtes-du-Nord • St-Brieuc
23. Creuse • Guéret
24. Dordogne • Périgueux
25. Doubs • Besançon
26. Drôme • Valence
27. Eure • Evreux
28. Eure-et-Loir • Chartres
29. Finistère • Quimper
30. Gard • Nîmes
31. Haute-Garonne • Toulouse
32. Gers • Auch
33. Gironde • Bordeaux
34. Hérault • Montpellier
35. Ille-et-Vilaine • Rennes
36. Indre • Châteauroux
37. Indre-et-Loire • Tours
38. Isère • Grenoble
39. Jura • Lons-le-Saunier
40. Landes • Mont-de-Marsan
41. Loir-et-Cher • Blois
42. Loire • St-Etienne
43. Haute-Loire • Le Puy
44. Loire-Inférieure • Nantes
45. Loiret • Orléans
46. Lot • Cahors
47. Lot-et-Garonne • Agen
48. Lozère • Mende
49. Maine-et-Loire • Angers

50. Manche • St-Lô
51. Marne • Châlons-sur-Marne
52. Haute-Marne • Chaumont
53. Mayenne • Laval
54. Meurthe • Nancy
55. Meuse • Bar-le-Duc
56. Morbihan • Vannes
57. Moselle • Metz
58. Nièvre • Nevers
59. Nord • Lille
60. Oise • Beauvais
61. Orne • Alençon
62. Pas-de-Calais • Arras
63. Puy-de-Dôme • Clermont-Ferrand
64. Basses-Pyrénées • Pau
65. Hautes-Pyrénées • Tarbes
66. Pyrénées-Orientales • Perpignan
67. Bas-Rhin • Strasbourg
68. Haut-Rhin • Colmar
69. Rhône • Lyon
70. Haute-Saône • Vesoul
71. Saône-et-Loire • Mâcon
72. Sarthe • Le Mans
73. Savoie • Chambéry
74. Haute-Savoie • Annecy
75. Seine • Paris
76. Seine-Inférieure • Rouen
77. Seine-et-Marne • Melun
78. Seine-et-Oise • Versailles
79. Deux-Sèvres • Niort
80. Somme • Amiens
81. Tarn • Albi
82. Tarn-et-Garonne • Montauban
83. Var • Draguignan
84. Vaucluse • Avignon
85. Vendée • La Roche-sur-Yon
86. Vienne • Poitiers
87. Haute-Vienne • Limoges
88. Vosges • Epinal
89. Yonne • Auxerre

1. Ain • Bourg-en-Bresse
2. Aisne • Laon
3. Allier • Moulins
4. Basses-Alpes • Digne
5. Hautes-Alpes • Gap
6. Alpes-maritimes • Nice
7. Ardèche • Privas
8. Ardennes • Mézières
9. Ariège • Foix

*Map 3* Departments and their capitals, with nineteenth-century additions [from McPhee, *Social History of France, 1789–1914*, 2nd edition, pp. 39–40]

decided in March 1790 to create a list of the most needy and to distribute assistance according to need: 'But it will be necessary to convince a famished multitude of the same principle; it will be necessary to assume that it has enough wisdom and foresight to use the help carefully'.[49] The poor of country towns were particularly vulnerable, especially in centres such as Bayeux which had been seats of ecclesiastical administration and noble residence. A combination of harvest failure, the decline in urban domestic employment as peasants refused to pay the tithe and seigneurial dues, and the collapse of consumer demand for luxury goods such as lace placed women wage-earners in a parlous position.[50]

\* \* \*

The lived experience of thousands of rural communities was one of testing the boundaries for local advantage in the context of the new laws. In country towns, too, revolutionary legislation altered traditional forms of occupational organization. The logical consequence of the August 1789 legislation was the abolition of the nobility as a corporation (9 June 1790) and of guilds as corporate bodies which could limit membership (d'Allarde law of 2 March 1791): henceforth any individual could practice a trade through the purchase of a license (*patente*).

The removal of guild controls over entry and standards, together with the abolition of indirect taxes, threatened the livelihood of those who had been enmeshed in the maze of Ancien Régime privilege. Petitions were sent from Caen, Fougères and Vervins on behalf of 600 tobacco 'entreposeurs', wealthy wholesalers who had had a monopoly on the supply of tobacco to garrisons and tobacco retailers in return for paying an indirect tax.[51] In expanding southern textile towns like Lodève, the law represented a victory for local manufacturers over weavers who had been campaigning for guild status to prevent manufacturers outsourcing to cheaper village weavers.[52] The guilds had somehow survived the abolition of privileged and corporate bodies in August 1789, and until their abolition in 1791 there was heated debate between master craftsmen and journeyman wigmakers, tailors and others who wanted to set up on their own, not only in large cities but also in country towns such as Archiac (Charente-Inférieure), Chatellerault (Vienne), Pézenas (Hérault), Montbrison (Loire), La Flèche (Sarthe) and Loches (Indre-et-Loire).[53]

The Assembly had inherited the monarchy's bankruptcy, further aggravated by popular refusal to pay taxes, and took several measures to meet this crisis. Across the country people responded to calls for 'patriotic contributions' or donations. In November 1789, Church lands were nationalized and, from November 1790, sold at auction. These lands were also used to back the issue of *assignats*, paper currency which soon began to decline in real purchasing power. The need for a radically new and universal taxation system took far longer to meet. On 25 September 1789 the Assembly decreed that the nobility, clergy and others who so far had had fiscal immunity

Figures 3 and 4: This stone carving of the Bastille over a doorway in the tiny Occitan-speaking village of Camps-sur-l'Agly (Aude) is a very rare surviving example of the civic pride of 1790. As the antipathy of many priests for the Revolution became more evident, cheaply produced allegories of villagers hunting priests – pejoratively known as 'crows' – became more common.

would now have to pay a proportionate share of direct taxes, backdated to cover the second half of 1789. The difficulties of completing new tax registers and assessments for every community were time consuming, however, and resulted in the Assembly having to continue the Ancien Régime tax system for 1790. The formerly privileged were entreated to make an 'exact and sincere' declaration of their property and of the annual value of their tithes, dues and other rights. Across France, over 24,300 of the 41,170 municipalities still had not submitted the reassessments for 1789 by the end of May 1790.[54]

The National Assembly's prevarication about the abolition of seigneurialism and indecision about the ownership of 'wastelands' unleashed the anger of the poorest sections of the rural community. This was directed not only at the vestiges of the seigneur's power, but also at the wealthier members of their own communities. Moreover, the revolutionary nation had placed itself in an awkward position by its simultaneous partial dismantling of the seigneurial régime and nationalization of Church property, for it now found itself the proprietor of all those non-suppressed seigneurial dues belonging to former ecclesiastical seigneurs, as well as the owner of ecclesiastical and royal forests. In such a situation, the fractious relations between *privilèges* and parish rights through which access to resources were mediated before 1789 were displaced by revolutionary notions of *liberté*.[55]

The Assembly's announcement, on 14 April 1790, that the tithe was to be abolished from 1 January of the following year as part of a general reform of taxation, meant that it would be payable to the State in 1790. The decree was interpreted by communities across France as meaning that there seemed little reason to pay it in the meantime. Communes objected to paying the tithe at all, and brought in crops without waiting for the tithe collector. Finally a new system of taxation, based on the estimated value of and income from property, was introduced from the beginning of 1791.

The new taxes were considerably higher than under the Ancien Régime and, for tenant farmers, were often added to rents. The impact of the new tax rates depended on the level of taxation and seigneurial exaction under the Ancien Régime. In Brittany, hitherto exempt from the *taille*, the property tax doubled; in the Sarthe it increased by 64 per cent. In contrast, across the southern Massif Central the levels actually decreased.[56] By mid-1791 the refusal of both urban and rural people to pay taxes whenever possible had become general. In 1788 the total of indirect taxes had been 205 million *livres*: in 1790 only 32 million were collected and in 1791 21.5 million. Perhaps 150 million of the 256 million *livres* in direct taxes for 1791 were ultimately collected.[57]

Historians once believed that anything up to one-quarter of land changed hands as a result of the sale of Church property. This was largely based on Georges Lefebvre's study of parts of the Nord, where 25 per cent of land was sold, and slightly more than half (71,400 ha) was bought by the peasantry.[58]

In the Cambrésis, where 44 per cent changed hands, Lefebvre argued that a whole new class of small-holders was created. In many other areas, however, it was town-dwellers who acquired the bulk of the land, especially the most desirable, and there was less to buy: the Church owned up to 20 per cent of the Nord, Aisne and Bas-Rhin, but less than 5 per cent in the Hérault and Landes. The most detailed national estimate is that only about 6.5 per cent of land changed hands as a result of the expropriation of the Church.[59] But church land in particular was usually of prime quality, sold in large lots by auction and purchased by urban and rural bourgeois – and more than a few nobles – with the capital to thus expand pre-existing holdings. The property of the abbey of Fontfroide in the district of Narbonne alone was valued at 805,000 *livres* (one-fifth in seigneurial rights), including huge estates (and 119 beehives) at Bizanet, Boutenac and Ornaisons. In all, there were up to 700,000 purchasers: at least one family in eight bought some land.[60] In the Laonnais, 85 groups of up to 100 people formed 'associations' to buy up property. Nevertheless, here too the sales were dominated by the wealthier landowners, tenant farmers and grain merchants. The sales offered those with savings to expand their holdings: the farmer Antoine Antoine of Bruyères bought 250 *arpents* in small plots, then a farm of 255 *arpents* belonging to a convent in Laon, then some *émigré* property, in all 700 *arpents* (300 ha).[61]

Everywhere it was the well-to-do of country towns or the wealthiest peasants who dominated the purchases. In the district of Grasse, in the southeast, for example, where about 7 per cent of land changed hands, it was local bourgeois who dominated the auctions. Three-quarters of the property sold was bought by one-quarter of the buyers; 28 of the 39 largest purchasers were merchants from Grasse.[62] Ecclesiastical property in and around Angers was auctioned on the first possible day, and the eager Angevin bourgeoisie paid 8.5 million *livres* for it, 40 per cent above its estimated value. In 30 communes of the district of Villefranche (Loire), peasants were 100 of the 165 purchasers, but together bought only 27 per cent of the land.[63]

In vain members of the clergy inveighed against those who bought their property. In the old ecclesiastical town of Rieux, which had just learned that it would not be the episcopal centre of the new department of the Haute-Garonne, it was reported that two priests, 'self-styled missionaries', were reported to be touring the area threatening not to give absolution to anyone who bought Church property.[64] They were ignored.

Despite the emerging sources of friction, the popular alliance of the Third Estate and its allies among the clergy and 'patriotic' nobility continued to draw on a powerful sense of national unity and regeneration well into 1790. This unity was enacted in Paris by the great 'Fête de la Fédération', on the first anniversary of the storming of the Bastille, on the Champ de Mars. This ceremony occurred in different forms all over France, an example of the use of festivals as an element of revolutionary political culture. For the festival of the Federation in July 1790, the colliers of Montminot adapted a traditional festival by swearing 'to have the axe always raised in order to defend, at the risk of their lives, the finest edifice that ever was, the French Constitution'. At Beaufort-en-Vallée, in the Loire valley near Angers, 83 women slipped away during the festivities and returned costumed as the new departments.[65] The village schoolteacher of Silly-en-Multien recorded with evident pleasure that 54 people (presumably the 'active' citizens) had

> 54 bottles of wine, 54 1½ pound loaves of bread, 80 pounds of meat, half as roast veal and half in nine pâtés, one for each six people, 13 bottles of Burgundy wine, one for every four people, for dessert 9 salads, 13 or 14 tarts and as many cakes, 2 bottles of liqueur 'parfait amour' and eau-de-vie from Andaye … half of the dinner was given to the poor there. Afterwards, most of us went for a cup of coffee at Félix Beuve's, after which we danced under a tent and others played cards.[66]

In a society rich in religious rituals and displays of royal splendour, the initial forms of enacting revolutionary unity drew on old rituals for style if not for substance or imagery. Conversely, long-established collective displays were not immune from the spontaneous syncretism of regional culture and revolutionary politics. In 1790, following the festivals in Tarascon (Bouches-du-Rhône) in which the powers of the 'Tarasque' monster were dispelled, a local wrote in his diary,

> a long time ago, you had to be a noble to be the *abba* (captain) of the Tarasque festival, later, you had to be a *bon bourgeois*, finally it was only given to people of a certain quality. Now at last we have the first year where the rights of man have appeared in this town in the Tarasque being made to flee by peasants not specially dressed for the occasion.[67]

At Bonneuil-Matours (Vienne), the ultimate humiliation for the former seigneur César de Marans was to lose his pew with the abolition of such marks of feudalism (13 April 1791); his defeat on the issue by the mayor – a former estate manager for a neighbouring noble – was to end in Marans' emigration in January 1792.[68]

Everywhere, the birth of new systems of administration within a context of popular sovereignty and hectic legislative activity was part of the creation of a revolutionary political culture.[69] Electoral participation was only one part of that culture. The voter turnout at local elections was rarely high because municipal councillors and other officials were more likely to be chosen by public discussion in the streets and fields, at the tavern or after Church. Nationally, the protracted electoral process was one reason why participation was also generally low, perhaps 40 per cent for the Estates-General and 20–25 per cent for the Legislative Assembly in 1791 (though reaching 85 per cent in the villages of upper Normandy in 1789 and over 70 per cent around Belfort in 1791). Such figures do not imply apathy; rather, they suggest that voting was only one of the ways by which French people exercised sovereignty. Another dimension of a new political culture was the widespread appearance of new types of association, particularly among 'active' citizens. In 1789, only 19 towns and cities had Jacobin Clubs (Clubs des Amis de la Constitution); in 1790 this increased to 213 and, by June 1791, there were 833. Many departments south of a line from Bordeaux to Lyon had more than twenty clubs, mostly in small towns. The Bouches-du-Rhône, Gironde and Lot-et-Garonne each had more than thirty.[70] The new political culture was also marked by the extraordinary volume of unofficial correspondence which criss-crossed the country: both vertically, to and from constituents and their deputies in Paris, and horizontally, in particular between the Jacobin Clubs, linking patriots in a web of shared vocabulary and information.[71]

Through such vehicles of expression, millions of people learned the language and practice of popular sovereignty and, in a protracted period of State weakness, came to question the most deeply engrained assumptions about the sanctity and benevolence of monarchy. In January 1791 the Marquis de Dampmartin returned from his garrison in Strasbourg south to Uzès, his place of birth. Along the way, he was astonished by the thirst for news: 'Peasants stopped my coach in the middle of the road to ask me questions. At Autun (Saône-et-Loire), despite the cold, I had to speak from a window on the main square.' In Languedoc, too, he was struck by the level of passion, but here he was deeply troubled by the way passions had become coloured by old hatreds between Catholics and Protestants; his wife fled Uzès with their five-year-old son.[72]

We do not know what the Marquise or her son made of this, or of the new legislation which the Assembly brought to bear on family relationships. In August 1790 it abolished the *bailliage* courts and provided for the hearing of family disputes by newly established family courts called *tribunaux de famille* where matters could be settled quickly and privately. Relatives, friends or neighbours could hear and judge a dispute between husband and wife, father and son, brother and sister, nephew and uncle and so on. These family arbiters (*arbitres de famille*) constituted a *tribunal*. A new law in July 1791 provided for heavier penalties for assault on a woman than on a man: violence against a man could earn a convicted person a fine of 500 livres and 6 months' imprisonment, but the same act against a woman would result in double the penalty.

On 15 March 1790, the Legislative Assembly passed a decree abolishing primogeniture in noble families; this was primarily aimed to break the power of great noble patriarchs rather than to strengthen the economic position of women. Then, on 8 April 1791, the Assembly legislated to impose equality of inheritance between children in all families. Henceforth, no child could be disinherited as a result of parental decisions. If a farm was to be left intact to one child, other children would have to be compensated.[73]

The legislation was to have a dramatic impact in those regions (for example, areas of Roman law in most of the south and of traditional primogeniture such as Auvergne, Berry, Bourgogne, the pays de Caux, the northeast) where testamentary freedom had favoured first-born sons. In western regions (Brittany, Maine, Normandy, Poitou and Anjou), on the other hand, partible inheritance was already the norm. In the Gévaudan region of the Massif Central, notaries assisted many families to preserve customary practices by 'selling' land to the first-born son with the consent of other children; even here, however, there were many contested arrangements.[74]

Children were the object of the regenerating project. Abandoned children were now less likely to be given only a saint's name and more likely to be given a name taken from the ribbon left on them by mothers hoping one day to collect them. So in 1791 children left at the Hôtel-Dieu in Niort were called 'Prosper Red Ribbon', 'Philippe Blue Cockade', 'Jean-Marie Blue Band' and 'Unfortunate Marie White Ribbon'.[75] 'Patriotic' middle-class parents bought for their children an 'enlightened' version of the traditional snakes-and-ladders and *jeux de l'oie* board games whereby players had to work their way to the prize of the new Constitution by landing on forward squares (emancipation of Jews and Protestants) and avoiding backward steps (such as the parlements).

Legislative changes meshed with challenges to idealized patterns of deference. Already apparent in parts of the countryside well before 1789, new assumptions about the legitimate bases of local eminence were the most corrosive – and contested – cultural change of the revolutionary period. The revolutionary shift in relations of power encouraged the peasantry to make bolder demands than before. This book began with the story of the 86-year-old baron de Bouisse, horrified by the behaviour of formerly 'peaceful' peasants at Fraïsse in Languedoc. In 1790 only five people had paid the *tasque*, others were clearing land without paying feudal dues, the operator of the communal oven was refusing to pay rent, and, even though he had presented titles going back to 1569, people were pretending they did not understand them. The mayor had collected grain for the *tasque* and tithe, but then had redistributed it to the villagers.[76] Village and small-town politics was animated by friction like this over the local meaning of revolutionary decrees. In Blérancourt (Aisne), for example, the 950 inhabitants were divided over the attempts to attenuate change by the large farmers who had dominated local life. Few villages had a young man as brilliant as Louis-Antoine Saint-Just to lead the offensive against this old élite in Blérancourt, but similar battles were played out in countless other communities.[77]

# 4
# Without Christ or King, 1791

Lucy de la Tour du Pin, related to some of the most prominent noble and ecclesiastical families in France, fled the Revolution in 1790 and later recalled that, as the family passed through Dôle (Jura), there were cries of 'There go some more on the way out, those dogs of aristocrats'. Once across the border in Lausanne:

> I spent a very gay fortnight. ... There were many other *émigrés* too. I did not enjoy their company, for they were much given to exaggeration ... they mocked everything, and were everlastingly amazed that there should exist in the world anything besides themselves and their ways.

They derided those of their acquaintance who had not yet left the country, sending them white feathers or insulting drawings in the post.[1]

The first waves of *émigrés* were not always well received. The Marquis de Marcillac, a captain in the King's cavalry at 18 years of age, reached the duchy of Savoie in March 1791, only to find that 'the people of Chambéry insulted the French who wore the white cockade ... threats against those who did so were posted on every street corner'.[2] Even in exile, high aristocrats were sensitive to social slights. Alexandre de Tilly was affronted by the pretensions of non-noble *émigrés*:

> in northern countries I have seldom met a French teacher or village vicar, a pedagogue or priest of any sort, who had not in France been near to becoming a bishop ... I have never spoken to a French governess who had not been a girl from one of the best families. These bourgeois *gentil-shommes* never failed to have their mouths full of it and easily out-talked the real *émigrés*; a Montmorency with weak lungs would have cut but a pitiful figure beside them.[3]

Tilly's scorn not only speaks eloquently of the social condescension which fuelled the enthusiasm of most of the former commoners for the Revolution, but it also indicates that nobles and the élite of the Church were not the only ones who regretted the events of 1789–91. Indeed, particular groups within the old Third Estate must be counted among them. Those who had invested heavily in offices carrying noble titles or seigneurial rights regretted the demise of the Ancien Régime; so too did those whose wealth was drawn from the slave system as slave-traders or colonial planters and who now shuddered at the news that the Caribbean colonies were bubbling with unrest over the attempts of planters to preserve the status quo.

Many members of the Third Estate had also been dependent on the structures of the Ancien Régime. There were thousands of children like Marie-Victoire Monnard, 12 years old when the Revolution began, the daughter of a *laboureur* from Creil, 60 km north of Paris. Her father's situation was made difficult when it became evident that his contract from the Church to collect the tithe for the canton of Creil would be redundant, and in 1790 she was sent to Paris as an apprentice to a linen merchant.[4] The abolition of the tithe from the start of 1791 – and the refusal of thousands of rural communities to pay seigneurial dues – sharply altered the relationship between town and country, and often embittered the artisanate and the poor of old ecclesiastical centres against the Revolution after the loss of employment and charity. The Trappist monastery of Bonnecombe in the Aveyron, for example, had distributed annually 300,000 *livres* worth of bread to the destitute, paid for from the tithe collected in the countryside; after 1789, the peasantry consumed that part of their produce and the urban destitute were in an even more precarious situation.[5]

The departure of aggrieved nobles was the occasion for mockery of those unable to accept that their world had changed irrevocably. Far more concerning for people across the country was widespread disquiet at the reduced status of the Catholic Church as Protestants and Jews were accorded civic equality. In the Protestant communities of the southern Massif Central, memories of the Ancien Régime underscored support for a Revolution which had brought them civil equality, but where denominational loyalties coincided with occupational divisions, the Revolution triggered open hostilities. In parts of the Midi, a Protestant bourgeoisie had won religious freedom and civil equality, opening the way to political power, and the Assembly's refusal to proclaim Catholicism the state religion in April 1790 provided the pretext for large-scale violence in Montauban and Nîmes.

In Montauban matters came to a head over the domination of the new national guard units of 'active' citizens by Protestants, alarming the mass of poorer Catholics, and coinciding with the inventory of Catholic religious houses required by the National Assembly. After panic-stricken guards had fired on a crowd, five of them were killed in retribution; at a meeting called in a church, the mayor reminded the crowd of where they were and that God required them to pardon the troops. In the municipality's words, 'Shouts of frustration and general murmurings demonstrated the refusal of the people to forgive.'[6]

In Nîmes, however, popular Catholic hostility to the political and economic role of wealthy Protestants was bloodily crushed when bands of Protestant peasants from the nearby regions of the Cévennes and Vaunage marched on the city. The violence in Nîmes was to become known as the brawl or *bagarre de Nîmes,* a misnomer for four days of fighting in June 1790 which left 300 Catholics dead, but few Protestants. News of the killings fuelled suspicions that Protestants were manipulating the Revolution: had not a Protestant pastor, Rabaut de Saint-Étienne, been elected president of the National Assembly?

The seriousness of religious divisions was made alarmingly clear in the first instance of mass popular disaffection with the Revolution, when in August 1790 at least 20,000 Catholic peasants from 180 parishes established the short-lived 'Camp de Jalès' in the south of the Ardèche in protest at the killing of the hundreds of Catholics in Nîmes in June. The following February, about 10,000 Catholics gathered to protest at renewed violence, this time in Uzès. These two 'camps' were not so much counter-revolutionary as born of fear and hostility to the way in which Protestants now had seized power in parts of the Gard, and – with the killings in Montauban and Nîmes – were startling evidence for revolutionary administrators that old religious loyalties would colour the response of many people to 'regenerative' change.[7]

The ending of monastic vows in February 1790 and the closing of religious orders in November had already created divisions. Some of the 87 monks in the vast abbey at Prémontré (Aisne) were distraught that they were 'to be thrown into the world'. Others were delighted. Villages which had been reliant on the abbey for medical assistance and employment, for example, on its farms and in its massive forests at St-Gobain, were dismayed. From nearby Faucoucourt, reported the mayor, a band arrived to take a relic from the abbey: 'there was a cross, a banner, flag, drum and armed men in large numbers. In fact these were all children who seemed to be 16 to 18 years, not the age of prudence.'[8] When the 40 women of the abbey of Origny-Ste-Benoîte (to the east of St-Quentin in the Aisne) met in July 1790 to decide their response, only 11 declared that they wanted 'to go back into the world'. The abbey owned 3,911 ha, and its annual income from rents and nine seigneuries was evaluated in 1790 as 43,000 *livres* plus 1,440 hl of wheat and 1,032 hl of oats.[9]

The Festival of Federation, on the first anniversary of the storming of the Bastille, had celebrated the unity of Church, monarchy and Revolution. Two days earlier, however, the Assembly had voted a reform which was to shatter this unity. The widespread agreement in the *cahiers* on the need for reform guaranteed that the Assembly had been able to push through the nationalization of church lands, the closing of contemplative orders and even the granting of religious liberty to Protestants and Jews. Mounting clerical opposition to these changes ultimately focused on the Revolution's reforms to the Church.

There was no question of separating Church and State: the public functions of the Church were assumed to be integral to daily life, and the Assembly accepted that public revenues would support the Church after the abolition of the tithe. It was therefore argued that, like the monarchy before it, the government had the right to reform the Church's temporal organization. The Assembly's reform – the Civil Constitution of the Clergy voted on 12 July 1790 – was the moment which fractured support for the Revolution. Many priests were materially advantaged by the new salary scale, and only the upper clergy would have regretted that bishops' stipends were dramatically reduced. Most contentious, however, was the issue of how the clergy were to be appointed in future: in requiring the election of priests and bishops, the Assembly crossed the line separating temporal and spiritual life. Responses to reforms to the Church indicated that it would prove impossible to align a revolution based on popular sovereignty, religious tolerance, and the certainty of earthly fulfilment through the application of secular reason with a Church based on divinely revealed truth and hierarchical authority, and a certainty of one true faith.

At New Year, parish priests were required to be 'elected' by 'active' citizens – of whatever religious persuasion – and to take a civic oath in order to continue their functions. Their difficult choice – felt as one between loyalty to the Revolution and loyalty to God and the Pope – was often influenced by parishioner sentiment. Ultimately, only a handful of bishops and perhaps half the parish clergy took this oath. Many of the latter subsequently retracted when, in April 1791, the Pope, also antagonized by the absorption of his lands in and around Avignon into the new nation, condemned the Civil Constitution and the Declaration of the Rights of Man as inimical to a Christian life, for 'no one can be in the Church of Christ, unless he is unified with the visible head of the Church itself'.[10]

By mid-1791 two Frances had emerged, the pro-reform areas of the southeast, the Paris basin, and much of the centre contrasting with the west and southwest, much of the north and east, and the southern Massif Central. The sharp regional contrasts in preparedness to take the oath suggest that it was not only a matter of individual choice or of the influence of senior clergy, but also of local ecclesiastical culture and of the depth of local enthusiasm for the Revolution.[11] In broad terms, the pro-reform areas were those where priests had come to accept a role as 'citizen-priests' who provided spiritual guidance and services for their communities: they were not averse to being elected servants of villages and urban neighbourhoods in much the same way as other officials. Refractory areas, in contrast, were characterized by a religious culture which emphasized the gulf between worldly and spiritual matters, the authority of the Pope and the priests' roles as paternal guides to goodness.

Laon was one of many provincial towns which had long been ecclesiastical centres; its cathedral, religious orders and 11 churches were a major employer in this town of 7,000 people. The Church owned 28 per cent of the Laonnais region; in the surrounding diocese of Soissons, 137 of the 430 seigneurs were religious orders. The high town ('le plateau') of Laon was now to have only two parishes instead of twelve, and the six villages below two between them. Worse, Laon had won a bitter battle with Soissons to be the capital of the new department of the Aisne, but had lost its cathedral status to Soissons as compensation. The new administrators found themselves having to deal with unemployment as they closed churches and orders; professional people employed in the ecclesiastical courts and administration suffered too. The head of the administration was confronted by the brother of a gardener at the Capucin monastery who called him 'Judas': 'I used to be your friend, but today I hate you, I detest you as a wicked anti-Christian. I hate and detest equally your district and your department'.[12] The steadfastly pro-revolutionary administrators of Laon recognized that any 'great revolution' would have its attendant problems, but they were acute in this clerical town 'where religious houses and the clergy were the source of almost all wealth ... workers of all types are without work and without bread; the number of beggars used to be excessive, now it is incalculable'. The administrators wanted a proportion of the proceeds of the sales of Church property in the department, which took them 80 pages to list. The enemies of the Revolution 'are saying to the people that in the times that they dare to call happy, the worker did not lack work, and the beggar received charity'.[13]

On 13 April 1791 the constitutional bishop of the Ain visited Bourg and received a rapturous welcome, with the municipal council reporting that the bells of the Church could not be heard for shouts of 'Bravo, vive la constitution, vive la nation, vive l'évêque, vive la liberté, vive la loi, vive le roi'. Such apparent unity was not to last. In June the superior at the town's hospital refused to go to mass said by the constitutional priest and prevented the children in her care from attending. By March the following year the municipality was taking action to prevent 'a large number of citizens of both sexes' from going to the hospital to hear mass.[14]

Timothy Tackett has stressed that one of the critical determinants of the parish clergy's response to the Civil Constitution of the Clergy was the attitude of their parishioners. Of course, this was not always the case: in Ormoy le Davien (Oise), the priest refused the oath, was besieged by his parishioners in his presbytery and had to flee to Soissons.[15] In Mortagne, a town in the south of the department of the Orne, the national guard pressured parish priests to take the Revolutionary oath, arriving with guns and swords.[16] In parishes where there were gendered differences in religiosity, a non-juror could aggravate conflict within the home, as at Neuve-Maison (Aisne) where, according to the village council, the priest is causing 'divisions between husbands and wives, and children and their parents'.[17]

In general, however, anger at Church reform created a constituency of hostility to the Revolution, and not vice versa. It is only from hindsight that the pre-1791 roots of popular counter-revolution seem evident. It was the importance of religion in the daily lives of so many people which was to deflect general support for the Revolution into mixed feelings, resentment or open hostility. All over France, Church reform was an explosive issue as departmental officials, whose administrative zeal was not always matched by a sensitivity to rural practices, implemented laws requiring the election of new priests, the closing of 'surplus' churches and cemeteries, the redrawing of parish boundaries, and the emptying of contemplative religious houses. In some areas, such as the Aveyron and Ardèche, sympathetic administrators sidestepped instructions from Paris for several years, while, in Anjou, the pre-existing gulf between urban and rural cultures was widened disastrously by the alacrity with which officials in Angers upheld the letter of the law.[18] In the small southern towns of Millau (Aveyron) and Sommières (Gard), milling crowds of poor women and children aimed their anger not so much at local Protestants as at pro-revolutionary Catholic administrators deemed to be destroying established forms of religious life: at Millau, women shouted, 'We want to conserve our religion, the religion of Jesus Christ, we want our clergy!'[19] Here, as elsewhere, it was above all women who offered refractory priests support, courage and shelter.

There were many priests like Gilbert-Jacques Martinant de Préneuf, *curé* of Vaugirard on the outskirts of Paris, who had welcomed the Revolution – indeed, he would be *procureur syndic* of the commune until September 1791 – but who could not take an unqualified oath. Martinant de Préneuf wrote a 30-page explanation for his parishioners in which it is clear that his decision was strongly influenced by the attitude of his superiors and peers, 'above all those who are held in the highest regard'.[20] The retraction of the oath by a popular priest like Martinant de Préneuf could be harrowing for a community. In the foothills of the Pyrenees, in the tiny, isolated village of Missègre, municipal officers reported with palpable regret in April 1792 that their priest had retracted his oath:

M. Lacaze, our priest, did not retract in any way his oath concerning the temporal. Quite the contrary: he exhorts us to stay obedient and faithful to the law, the nation and the king and he desires nothing more than the good, the peace and the happiness of the people. And he exhorts us very strongly as well to follow the Christian religion, which causes us a profound sorrow when we think of the fine and beautiful qualities of this person we know. He renounces the tithe and says that he wants the nobles to pay taxes like any commoner, these were the very words he used on the eleventh of March last, when he retracted everything that his conscience dictated on the spiritual level. Moreover he declared that he is ready to swear to maintain the *patrie* with all his might and that he has no other desire than to stay among us for the rest of his days to continue to give us his good example and good instruction every Sunday and on feast-days.[21]

Their plea fell on deaf ears and by then many thousands of communes had found themselves without a priest and the regular routines of parish life.

Brittany was one of those regions where rejection of reform by established clergy was the norm, and meshed with peasant disappointment with the Revolution. Mother Sainte-Félicité, superior of a convent in the diocese of Rennes, did not spare her scorn towards her former novice Sister Sainte-Scholastique, who had taken the oath:

you have prostituted yourself before the demon of liberty and the furies of equality ... Oh, unfortunate child! How you make my tears flow. How you are afflicting my old age! ... You who I formed, with God's help, for the perfection of religious life! Now you've become a juror! A juror of liberty and equality!'[22]

As a petition from 105 Breton priests put it:

it is the thread of the Apostolic succession which gives life to our powers; if it is broken, our mission ceases to be divine. ... Purely spiritual things and the affairs of this world cannot be directed by the same principles or by the same laws.

This is what underpinned the conditional oath.[23]

By the time the 'active' citizens of Brittany were to elect their priests their hopes had been dashed for a prompt resolution of their grievances against both seigneurialism and long-term leases. The Revolution's reforms to local government imposed a strict separation of parish and municipality, parishioners and 'active' men. The Revolution was perceived as interfering in the lives of rural communities without bringing obvious benefits. Perhaps one-third of the men of the department of the Ille-et-Vilaine and up to one-half in the district of Vannes had been deemed 'passive' citizens, well above the national average.[24]

The strength of refractory or 'non-juring' clergy in non-French speaking areas fed Parisian suspicions that peasants who could not understand French were prey to the 'superstitions' of their 'fanatical' priests. The Basque country, Brittany, Flanders and the Roussillon had few jurors, as did the German-speaking areas of the east: in Moselle only 19 per cent of the clergy in German-speaking parishes were jurors, compared with 69 per cent in French-speaking areas.[25] The experience of German-speaking Alsace was also conditioned by the religious mixture of 450,000 Catholics, 220,000 Protestants (Anabaptists, Calvinists and Lutherans) and 20,000 Jews. Catholics in Alsace could not accept the thought that the constitutional bishops had been elected with the votes of Lutherans. Fewer than 10 per cent of clergy in the Bas-Rhin would accept the Constitution compared with 32 per cent and 45 per cent in the neighbouring departments of Moselle and Meurthe.[26]

All over France the willingness of local clergy to take the civic oath became a matter which united or divided whole communities. Gabian, north of Béziers in the Hérault, had warmly embraced the Revolution. One reason for this was that the abolition of seigneurialism had alleviated a major burden; another was that, unlike most of the priests of the district, Pierre Blanc, the *curé* of Gabian, took the oath of loyalty on New Year's Day 1791 and stayed in the village. But his decision angered some, and this erupted on 6 March 1791, the Sunday before Carnival. As young adults were dancing in front of a tavern, Rose Lasserre claimed to have been insulted by Etienne Bousquet, from a family of 'patriots'; she grabbed him by the hair and he punched her. The next day the Lasserres returned with rifles, blackened faces and wearing what seemed to be white surplices from the monastery of Cassan near the village. The resulting scuffles lasted three days, and a group of villagers became entrenched in their counter-revolutionary views. When some of them began to commit robberies with violence, the situation became much more serious.[27]

Villages like Gabian were relatively fortunate. In fewer than half of the parishes of France had the priest overcome qualms about the Civil Constitution of the Clergy and the Pope's terrible threat, thereby ensuring the continuity of religious life. Elsewhere the refusal of a *curé* to take the oath, and the need for a replacement to be elected meant that a parish had to accept the departure of an often esteemed priest, or even the absence of a priest at all. The new priest – if one was available – could be in an invidious position: condemned as a heretic by the Pope, he could also be treated as an *intrus* by his new flock and subject to contempt ranging from a Church devoid of sacramental vessels now in safekeeping to actual physical assault. Rural women in particular were most attached to the patterns of the ecclesiastical year and most visceral in their responses to an *intrus* or to the departure of the former priest, regretted by some, reviled as a coward by others. The ecclesiastical reforms disrupted traditional patterns of worship in other ways, such as in the reduction in the number of churches to what seemed to the legislators to be a suitable and rational number. The most dramatic changes were in country towns which had been ecclesiastical centres – Bayeux had had 17 parishes for its 10,000 people, Laon 12 for its 7,000, and now both had just two – but the basic principle of one parish Church for each commune caused heartbreak and anger in hamlets and urban neighbourhoods long accustomed to their own services. This was especially so in the west, Brittany and parts of the Massif Central characterized by dispersed patterns of settlement, where the Church was a physical as well as spiritual centre of community life.

But there was more than one clerical culture and more than one response to the ecclesiastical reforms. Two priests from near Troyes (Aube) had drafted a marriage contract for Rémi Vinchon, the priest of Herbisse, who, 'in addition to his priestly function, is a man and a citizen'. His marriage to Marie-Anne Puissaut was noted by the mayor and other officers on 17 April 1791. The contract stated that 'marriage is one of the natural and inviolable rights of man' and that they expected the National Assembly to act against 'the tyranny of the Roman Church in this regard'. They noted, in a printed and circulated document, that the contract might serve as a model for three other priests with or about to have children, and whom they named.[28]

Just four days before this marriage, the Pope had issued the Papal Bull *Caritas* requiring priests to retract their oaths on pain of excommunication. Large numbers obeyed, but not all. J.F. Nusse, a country *curé* at Chavignon (Aisne) asked his friend Courtonne, the *curé* at Crépy 15 km to the north,

> how can we believe that the Pope has the right to force us to disown a constitution which is so close to the Gospel, and so necessary for the happiness of the State? ... [But] we are attached to Saint Peter's chair, whatever may be the particular views of he who occupies it at present.

In the end, 78 per cent of the priests in his district maintained the oath. But Nusse was an exceptional man, also mayor of his village, who had made a special trip to Paris to present his village's *don patriotique* to the Assembly. He returned to a festive welcome in his honour, with 'the greatest display of joy and affection' from his flock.[29]

Unlike Nusse, non-juring clergy who fled the Revolution had made a choice approved of by the Pope and their former bishops. But they now often found themselves without resources and in the midst of political tension in their adopted lands. Such was the case for the senior cleric Martinant de Préneuf, from a family of *noblesse de robe*, who described the range of occupations nobles and priests were forced to undertake in Brussels:

> an abbot made crêpes for a *traiteur*. ... I knew a canon who worked in the cellar for a wine merchant ... Many refugees were very skilled in fine woodwork ... One noble *émigré* made a small fortune from a sort of aniseed cake, which was wildly successful ... all Brussells wanted to taste this *émigré's* pastry.

Martinant himself moved through various German towns, surviving by giving French lessons.[30]

The ecclesiastical reforms were everywhere controversial and meshed with wider anxieties about foreign attitudes to the Revolution. Historians have commonly written of the Revolution as if, before 1789 and after 1791, issues of foreign policy and military strategy dominated the domestic reform agenda. They have generally assumed, too, that during the two intervening years of sweeping revolutionary change, 1789–91, France enjoyed the chance to undertake internal 'regeneration' while other States looked on with some relish at the sight of Europe's leading power being immobilized by internal upheaval. This picture is flawed in several ways. It could instead be argued that a major impulse for revolutionary reform was in fact the desire to 'regenerate' as well France's capacity to act as the key military and commercial player in Europe and the Caribbean. Central to the reforming zeal of the National Assembly was the belief that the new nation would thereby return to the international status it had enjoyed before the successive foreign affairs humiliations since 1763.[31] From the outset the reactions in French slave colonies – particularly St-Domingue – were of central importance to the economy. Internally, from 1790 there was often a startlingly bellicose edge to the popular imagination of what the Revolution represented. Most important, from the time that the Pope began to anathematize the Revolution from late 1790, regions along the frontier became increasingly edgy about the likelihood of foreign intervention. Any reckoning of the revolutionary experience of Basques, Catalans, Provençaux, Flamands and other frontier populations must take into account their nagging fears from late 1790.

Following rumours that a counterrevolutionary army, commanded by the Prince de Condé, was assembling on the frontiers and preparing to invade France, a decree of 12 June 1791 calling for volunteers to present themselves to their town halls was issued. It described a system of 'voluntary conscription' and envisaged the creation of new battalions which would serve in parallel to those of the line. Volunteers were to be raised by each district in the proportion of one volunteer for every twenty national guardsmen, and the assumption was clearly made that these volunteer soldiers would spring from the ranks of the guard. In 1791, a total of 120,000 volunteers was enlisted. Many of them hoped their duty would be only short-term. Gabriel Noël, an army volunteer from the department of the Vosges in northeastern France, wrote home of his unit early in 1792 that 'I read with pleasure that leave will not be out of the question ... But many volunteers from my district who haven't had leave since its formation are claiming that they'll simply take it'.[32]

From the outset, soldiers were also expected to be involved in patriotic activity outside their regiment. A decree of May 1791 permitted and even encouraged soldiers to take part in political clubs and societies in those towns where they were stationed. In July those soldiers who qualified as 'active' citizens were allowed to exercise their rights as citizens in the communities where they served, and from August 1792 these rights were extended to all soldiers, regardless of their wealth or property, provided that they were 25 years old. On 3 February 1792 a decree sanctioned the creation of elected *conseils d'administration* to oversee the running of military battalions. Noël, a man of patriotic seriousness, wrote of the elections that

> we don't just have a corporal to elect ... we have to appoint a captain, a lieutenant, a sergeant-major, a sergeant, a corporal and four volunteers ... The officers aren't well liked; it's rare to hear anything good about them, such is the level of mistrust of them. I'm sure that, for our council, the choices will be bad; the hotheads will be chosen. The masses always allow themselves to be deceived by those who flatter them.[33]

\* \* \*

Ever since July 1789 the Assembly had had to face a double challenge: how could the Revolution be protected from its opponents? Whose Revolution was it to be? These questions came to a head in mid-1791. Louis fled Paris on 21 June, publicly repudiating the direction the Revolution had taken, especially in its reforms to the Church. On the evening of the next day, Louis was recognized in a village near the eastern frontier and arrested. He was suspended temporarily from his position as king, but the Assembly was determined to quell any popular unrest which might threaten the constitutional monarchy. On 17 July, an unarmed demonstration to demand Louis' abdication was organized on the Champ de Mars by the democratic Cordeliers Club, with some Jacobin support, at the same 'altar of the homeland' on which the Festival of Federation had been celebrated a year earlier. Lafayette, the commander of the National Guard, was ordered to disperse the petitioners; his guardsmen killed perhaps 50 of them.

The news travelled across France with unprecedented rapidity, at an average of 8–10 Km/h. At times it was faster: it was known in Saintes (Charente-Inférieure), 470 km from Paris, just 36 h later. The news of the storming of the Bastille had taken 10 days. After five days news of the King's flight had even reached Brest and Perpignan. News of his recapture the next day was flashed around the country just as quickly.[34]

The king's flight and recapture sparked a new collective panic, more limited geographically than the Great Fear of 1789 but revealing of the changes in popular attitudes over just two years. Within several days of the news much of northeastern France was gripped by rumours that tens of thousands of Austrian troops were on French soil, pillaging as they went. Early in the morning of the 23rd at Ste-Menehould (Marne),

> an unknown man, without a coat, bathed in sweat and accompanied by a gendarme, arrived on horseback. He announced in a frightened manner that Varennes has been pillaged and that the Austrians are wreaking horrible carnage on its inhabitants. This news plunged the town into terror.

Figures 5 and 6: News of the arrest of Louis at Varennes on 21 June 1791 spread rapidly across the country, triggering a short-lived panic. Once fear had subsided, rural people in many parts of the country would have agreed with the sentiments of this allegory of Louis as a pig: 'I ruined myself to fatten him up – now I don't know what to do with him'.

L'ENTRÉE-FRANCHE.

*Je me suis Ruiné pour l'engraisser —— la fin du compte je ne sai qu'en faire.*

The tocsin summoned national guards from surrounding villages, and men were sent to warn other towns. The same day, a noble who saluted the King repeatedly as the royal coach left Ste-Menehould to return to the capital was killed by peasants with whom he had been at odds for years.[35]

Timothy Tackett has charted the way in which fear gave way to indignation as people across the country reflected on the meaning of the attempted flight. At Châlons (Marne) it was reported that 'the queen could hear the offensive shouts of the citizens of Châlons and particularly from women, who said the most humiliating things to her'. Further along the road, between Dormans (Marne) and Château-Thierry (Aisne), deputies from the Assembly had difficulty in dissuading a crowd from using the wheels of the carriage to garrotte the entire royal party.[36]

News of the King's flight triggered outbreaks of panics on other frontiers, in Brittany, the southwest and the Roussillon, where there had long been anxieties that the European powers would attack the revolutionary nation, supported by the departed non-juring clergy. None of these regions had been affected by the Great Fear. Timothy Tackett has stressed how, in comparison with the 'wild panics' of 1789, that of 1791 was marked by resolve, military organization, communication across affected areas and a powerful sense of national defence against internal as well as external enemies. When news arrived in Hautefort (Dordogne) on the twenty-fifth, 'three to four hundred peasants gathered at the château', reported the seigneur's agent, 'they swore to be loyal to the Constitution ... they disarmed all the gentlemen ... and all the non-juring clergy, and searched every room in the château'. After two good harvests, however, the object of the search was not food but counter-revolutionary non-juring clergy.[37]

The Jacobins of La Bassée, southwest of Lille, insisted that they had regarded Louis as the greatest of French kings; now 'this prince has entirely lost his reputation'.[38] While the Assembly moved to reinstate the monarch, Jacobin societies and other groups all over the country made it plain that they were accepting the decision from a sense of civic duty; the language of the debate revealed how rapidly the mystique of monarchy had faded. At the celebration of 14 July 1790 the mayor of Belley (Ain) had extolled from the altar of the *patrie* 'the feelings of fraternity and the sweetness of friendship which today unite the monarch and his children. This union ... will always guarantee the safety and happiness of France'. Almost a year later, on 7 July 1791, the municipal council wrote to the Assembly that, now that

> the king of the French has deserted the post assigned to him in the constitution, a new function awaits you. ... the approaching storm will find you unshakeable and the calm firmness which presides over your deliberations is now in the hearts of all the French.

Another week later, on the second anniversary of the taking of Bastille, the tenor of celebrations was in sharp contrast with those of 1790. In the mayor's words,

> The homeland is in danger, almost abandoned, and today offers on this same altar [as in 1791] only its wishes for the victory of our arms against traitors ... we have felt the price to be paid for freedom.

The ceremony was punctuated by collective swearing of oaths of loyalty by men, women and children, and by repeated volleys of artillery fire. At the end of the ceremony all the soldiers, men, women and children took each other by the arm and danced around the altar for half an hour to military music.[39] Despite the mountains separating Belley from France's eastern frontier, the changed tone is resonant of the impact of the King's flight. Communities near all of France's borders were now uneasy, consumed by a mixture of fear and anger at the possibilities of war. These were to be the dominant characteristics of public opinion for the next four years.

Like the Great Fear of 1789, that of 1791 occurred in regions which were highly susceptible to rumour. In mid-1791, the coincidence of distress at the disruption of religious life by the reforms to the Church, the Pope's imprecations at those priests who supported the heretical principles of the Revolution and those who accepted the sacraments from them, and the edginess of frontier regions about mounting foreign invective created the context for panic to spread. Responses to the news of the King's flight and recapture were also heightened by the unresolved grievances of rural producers.

Outside France, monarchs expressed concern at Louis' safety, and fears that the Revolution might spread, in threatening declarations from Padua (5 July) and Pillnitz (27 August). Inside France, too, there were many people across the country who could not imagine a France without its King. When de Rozoi's royalist *Gazette de Paris* called for 'hostages to the King' to offer themselves in return for Louis' 'freedom', some 4,160 letters were received; over 1,400 of these were from Paris, but there were large numbers from Normandy, the northeast, Alsace and Guyenne. From Lourmarin, on the other hand, the council petitioned the Assembly to hasten to 'banish the monster of feudalism' from what they already called 'the Republic'.[40]

Underpinning increasing uncertainty and division were key pieces of economic legislation. A free market in labour was imposed by the Le Chapelier law of 14 June 1791 outlawing associations of employers and employees. Le Chapelier, an ennobled lawyer, had presided over the session of 4 August 1789 in the National Assembly, and was one of the radical Breton deputies who had founded the Jacobin Club. The law which bore his name decreed that 'Citizens of the same trade or profession, entrepreneurs, those who have shops, workers and craftsmen of whatever art, may not ... form regulations on their supposed common interests.' While these laws were decisive in the creation of a laissez-faire economy, they were also aimed at the 'counter-revolutionary' practices and privileges of the Ancien Régime. No longer were there specific orders of clergy or nobility, or guilds, provinces and towns which could claim particular monopolies, privileges and rights. The old world of corporations was dead.

The Le Chapelier law was not only chiefly aimed at 'coalitions' of urban wage-earners, but it was also targeted at the waves of strikes by harvesters working on the large commercial wheat farms in the Paris basin, where *fermiers* hired up to 80 harvesters at a time. These often violent strikes or 'bacchanals' occurred at times, as in the summer of 1791, when harvests were plentiful and labour in demand. In June–August the administrators of the Aisne had to outlaw strikes of up to 700 harvesters on farms around Château-Thierry, and ultimately set Maximum rates of pay (in wheat, which the harvesters customarily sold). In early August, in the canton of Baron (Oise) groups of harvesters numbering up to 1,500 went on strike for higher wages and attacked gendarmes with sticks and volleys of stones.[41] On 20 July 1791 there was a similar stand-off near the village of Totes north of Rouen when 200 soldiers and national guardsmen from the city were confronted by up to 4,000 people, armed with rifles, led by members of municipal councils wearing their sashes and a canon bearing the flags of national guard units from 22 villages, insisting on controls on the grain-trade. Five hundred more soldiers were necessary to disperse them.[42]

Jean-Baptiste Bourget, the priest of Silly-en-Multien, had taken the oath (like three-quarters of priests in the Oise) on 16 January,

> offering his plaudits for the civic-mindedness of his parishioners who have declared themselves to be defenders of liberty without confusing it with license, and congratulating them on the union and harmony which is so apparent among them at public festivals.[43]

This was not to last. The wealthiest man in the village was Charles-Léonard Carriat, with over 330 acres, in a region of large-scale farming where more than two-thirds of the land belonged to ecclesiastical orders and seigneurs. Carriat was a dominant figure on the Church vestry and local council, of which he had been elected mayor. He was also the prime focus of the resentments of impoverished rural labourers, and in August 1790 they had threatened to hang him if he refused to increase payments at harvest time. During the night of 28–29 October 1791 his barn burned to the ground and with it 11,000 sheaves of wheat. A week later he resigned as mayor.[44]

Elsewhere, a village unity was sustained by ongoing antipathy to former seigneurs insisting on their rights to harvest dues. In declaring in May 1791 that his community would pay no more dues unless the seigneur produced the evidence of his titles, the mayor of Villesèque-des-Corbières (Aude), the blacksmith François Séguy, insisted to the village council that

> it is wrong to give blindly and immediately the subsistence of a miserable family, the work of our arms, and even our sweat, to someone to whom we don't know we are obliged. Our ancestors, too simple and ignorant, would have given everything and would have submitted to anything these gentlemen required of them, but in the present century this simpleness and this ignorance no longer exist, wickedness has been destroyed, justice punishes it.[45]

It was a remarkable statement, not only because of its boldness, but because of the historical narrative Séguy had constructed. Villesèque was a small, impoverished and isolated village in the hard *garrigues* of the Corbières, but there was plainly a shared notion among his fellows of historical progress and justice.

Despite the strength of support for its work, however, the National Assembly appeared increasingly to rural people as both hesitant in its attitude towards the abolition of the last traces of seigneurialism and unwilling to restrict the individual exercise of property rights. A law of 5 June 1791 explicitly supported the right of landowners 'to change their land-use as they see fit' against deeply rooted assumptions by communities that there was a sense in which all property and its uses were subject to public use. The next day a new law maintained the regime of *domaine congéable* in parts of the northwest. For most peasants, the 15–20 per cent increase in taxes was more than offset by the ending of tithes and, ultimately, of dues. In Brittany, on the other hand, where the seigneurial régime and taxes had been relatively light and tenants had enjoyed considerable security of lease through the *domaine congéable*, the Revolution substantially increased the burden of taxation and made tenants more vulnerable to expulsion.[46] Despite a protracted pattern of protest across the three departments of Lower Brittany (Côtes-du-Nord, Finistère, Morbihan), the regime of *domaine congéable* was spared by the legislation following the session of 4 August and then further maintained by a law of 6 August 1791.[47]

Just like the large landholders, the Revolutionary authorities were at pains not to antagonize the nursing orders, despite their religious calling and devotion. The Civil Constitution specifically excluded them from the oath of obedience to the State; then the law of 17 April 1791 extended the right of exclusion to those nuns involved in education and public instruction. (Only in October 1793 would the National Convention finally accept that this concession was irrational and insist that nuns, like all other public servants, be brought within the terms of the Civil Constitution.) Legislators were less tolerant of non-juring parish clergy. In August 1791 the activities of refractory priests, such as clandestine masses, were denounced by the Assembly, and citizens were encouraged to engage in the surveillance of non-jurors. Finally, on 29 November 1791 the Legislative Assembly decreed that all priests, whether or not salaried by the State, were obliged to take the oath if they wished to continue to say mass.

While revolutionary administrators made a point of having laws translated into local languages in the early years of the Revolution, there was always an assumption, shared by politicians from non-French speaking areas, that there should be a single language of liberty in the regenerated nation. The reality was far more complex, and the ecclesiastical reforms in particular commonly perplexed communities of ethnic minorities otherwise enthusiastic about their membership of the new nation. The little Catalan port and fishing town of Collioure was one such place, both solidly behind a revolution which had removed entrenched privilege and practising with the fervour of fishing populations vulnerable to sudden storms at sea. Collioure's ten religious were solidly 'refractory', and the town would now have just one priest, an Occitan, for its 2,300 inhabitants. On 30 June, at 7 am, 'almost all the citizens' gathered in the Church: the names of 255 of them were recorded – then crossed out at some later date – in the council's minute book. The meeting unanimously protested against the Civil Constitution of the Clergy and, in particular, against the decrees enforcing an oath of loyalty. Despite the abolition of the tithe and of the privileges enjoyed by Collioure's religious under the Ancien Régime, the community as a whole resented the changes imposed on their religious life – and Catalan identity – by the National Assembly. This resentment was particularly intense among the fishermen, women and sailors of the *faubourg*, used to worshipping in the chapel of a Dominican monastery in their neighbourhood, now up for sale. But if the clergy had thus made a choice between Revolution and counter-revolution, the great majority of Colliourencs did not want to have to make such a choice: their attitudes towards the Revolution were henceforth to be somewhat ambivalent, but not hostile. Moreover, the anti-revolutionary attitudes of the priests were to alienate a growing number of their parishioners.[48]

Those most antipathetic to the strength of local languages were commonly the bilingual educated élites in non-French speaking areas. On 5 January 1792, the administrators of the district of Sauveterre-d'Aveyron claimed that greater use of the 'national language' was their most pressing need and described their own Languedocien as an 'unfortunate jargon which smothers the development of our ideas'. From Salins (Cantal), too, it was claimed that the local *patois* 'places the poor beneath the rich ... To destroy it would be to work towards the establishment of equality'.[49] While members of ethnic minorities continued to make their own translations, they were not to have official recognition of their double identity, that they were Basques or Bretons as well as French citizens.

But here, as everywhere in France, the birth of new systems of administration within a context of popular sovereignty and hectic legislative activity was part of the creation of a revolutionary political culture in 1789–91. The work of the Assembly was vast in scope and energy. The foundations of a new social order were laid, underpinned by an assumption of the national unity of a fraternity of citizens. This was a revolutionary transformation of public life.

Until 1791 the Revolution was overwhelmingly popular: sweeping changes in public life occurred within a context of mass optimism and support. At the same time, the Assembly was walking a tightrope. On one side lay a growing hostility from nobles and the élite of the Church angered by the loss of status, wealth and privilege, and bolstered in many areas by a disillusioned parish clergy and their parishioners. On the other side, the Assembly was alienating itself from the popular base of the Revolution by its compromise on seigneurial dues, its exclusion of the 'passive' citizens from the political process, and its implementation of economic liberalism in town and country. The King's flight and capture had focused these anxieties and enmities; now the Assembly hoped that his agreement in September 1791 to proclaim the new Constitution on which it had laboured since 1789 would serve to stabilize the Revolution and to quieten uncertainty. It did neither.

# 5

# Deadly Divisions, 1791–92

On 14 September 1791 an apparently sincere Louis XVI promulgated the Constitution which embodied the Assembly's work since 1789. France was to be a constitutional monarchy in which power would be shared between the King, as head of the executive, and an assembly elected by a restrictive property franchise. A new Legislative Assembly was elected by 'active' citizens and convened in Paris in October. At the outset most of its members sought to consolidate the state of the Revolution as expressed in the Constitution. The scission in the Church and the attempted flight of the King had, however, changed everything. Threatening statements by the Pope and Europe's crowned heads vindicated the fears that had been endemic in border areas since the spring of 1790 that old Europe would not accept revolutionary change in its midst. At the same time, the emergence of a more militant activism in Paris and other cities and towns was paralleled by a resurgence of protest in the countryside insistent on the abolition of remaining seigneurial claims.

The legislators in the National Assembly had been caught between their commitment to the sanctity of private property, their uneasy awareness of the strength of peasant attachment to customary practices and their horror at environmental damage in many parts of France. These contending forces were evident in two long-awaited pieces of legislation passed in late September 1791. First, on the twenty-eighth, the Assembly voted its Rural Code. In this decree 'on rural property and practices, and their policing', the deputies, in one of the final acts of the National Assembly, made a statement endorsing agrarian individualism. It decreed that collective practices of *droit de parcours* (allowing livestock access to pastures across private land) and *vaine pâture* (sending livestock onto private fallow land) could not prevent individuals from enclosing their land for their private use:

Section 1, article 1. ... Property owners are free to vary at their will the cultivation and management of their lands, to manage their harvests as they wish, and to dispose of all the products of their property within the kingdom and outside of it, without harming the rights of others, and while conforming with the law.

Yet it also acknowledged the continued existence of collective practices in cases of 'usage immémorial'. The Rural Code merely removed the legal basis for these practices.

> Section V, article 1. All property owners are free to have on their property the quantity and type of livestock that they believe useful to the cultivation and management of their land, and to have them graze there exclusively, with the exception of the following ruling, with regard to pathways (*droit de parcours*) and to infertile pastures (*vaine pâture*).
>
> Article II. The reciprocal service between parishes, known as the *droit de parcours*, and which has as a corollary the right of *vaine pâture*, will continue provisionally within the restrictions of the present section.

While proclaiming the right of landowners to harvest when and how they wished, it recognized too that 'in those areas where it is the custom to announce the beginning of the grape harvest, with regard to this a ruling may be made each year by the general council of the commune'.[1]

Also at stake were wider questions about the ownership, control and use of other rural resources. The day after the passing of the Rural Code, in a decree sanctioned with the Rural Code by the King on 6 October, the Assembly voted its Forest Code. This amounted essentially to a restatement of the major provisions of Colbert's 1669 code, with an administrative reorganization to match the new departments. True to the principles enunciated since 1789, however, the Assembly insisted that privately owned forests were fully at the owners' disposition, to use 'as he sees fit'.[2]

The decrees strengthened the hand of the embattled administrators of forests and of large landowners, but the Assembly's hopes that they would put an end to law-breaking in forests and friction over the exercise of customary rights were soon dashed. Local authorities were similarly unsuccessful in their attempts to halt extensive felling in forests and occupation of the *vacants*. Despite regular missives from Paris reminding municipalities of laws protecting forests dating from 1669 and 1754 and now reinforced, illegal wood-cutting went on unchecked. Half of all the *bailliages* and districts in France experienced conflict over forests by 1793; 30 per cent did so over common lands.[3]

Fuelling the intensity of unresolved issues in the countryside was anxiety about the possibility of war. The impact of the Revolution on the experiences of country people is evident from those few lengthy accounts of army volunteering which survive from them. These reveal a mix of male sexual bravado, a thirst for adventure and a potent sense that this would be a new type of conflict. Xavier Vernière was just 16 when he enrolled in

October 1791 as a volunteer in the Anjou regiment: 'I cannot describe the elation with which this filled me, comparable to that felt by a passionate lover, consumed by long and burning desire, when he finally comes to receive in his mistress' arms the prize for his perseverance.'[4] Jean-Claude Vaxelaire, born in 1770 and raised on a farm in the parish of Vagney (Vosges), volunteered in August 1791, one of 120,000 who responded to the Assembly's call in June. His own department would provide 14,500 volunteers from a population of 227,000. In later life Vaxelaire recalled his sense of adventure: 'as I had never seen a town and had seen nothing but our parish church steeple, I was as delighted to leave as if I was going to my marriage'.[5]

Gabriel Noël was two months younger than Vaxelaire. Like him born into a peasant family in eastern France, he had been entrusted to the care of his godmother, in the village of Sommerviller, 30 km from Nancy. Like Vaxelaire, too, he volunteered in August 1791. Noël, who had received secondary education, was more explicit than Vaxelaire in his commitment to the Revolution, writing home on hearing of the Assembly's January 1792 decree threatening *émigrés* that 'in fighting for our country's cause, we will at the same time be fighting for that of all peoples'. But Noël despaired of the lack of a zealous spirit of self-sacrifice among the volunteers:

> [A] large number of villagers amongst us want only to go back home to till their soil: there are some who have resigned. They do not see, the fools, that in order to till their land peacefully and profitably, it is essential that the *patrie* is not at risk: their self-interest blinds them. And yet it is the people of the countryside who have benefited most from the Constitution.[6]

He was shocked, too, by a brawl that broke out on New Year's Day between professional soldiers dressed in white and the blue-uniformed volunteers in his garrison town of Sierck (Moselle), leaving 4 dead and 16 injured. Conditions in the army were hard: Noël wrote home from the border near Givet (Ardennes) that

> I won't invite you, dear family, to come and eat the soldier's food ... the raw meat is divided, cut up and sliced on the ground that is used as a cutting board. This meat is sometimes so covered with filth and soil that I don't think that dogs would eat it; but hunger makes you close your eyes and open your mouth.

But he was delighted with the countryside of the Thiérarche: 'Everywhere you look you can see only wheat suggesting a very fine harvest, oats, barley, tilled fields ready for autumn crops ... No painter, no author could give an idea of the beauty of the rural surroundings.'[7]

The rebellion of mulattoes and slaves in St-Domingue in August 1791 further convinced the deputies of the insidious intentions of its rivals, England and Spain. The revolt was to have dramatic economic effects. St-Domingue was the key colony in the West Indies, attracting 550–600 ships per year for the purchase of cotton, sugar, tobacco, coffee and indigo in return for food and manufactured goods from France and an average of 28,000 new slaves per year. Some 71,000 of the 95,000 tons of sugar imported annually into France came from the colony. Certainly, the great ports of the coasts, from Le Havre on the Channel to Nantes, La Rochelle and Bordeaux on the Atlantic and Marseille and Toulon on the Mediterranean, were hardest hit. They had long lived not only on their privileged trading relationship with St-Domingue, commerce with northern Europe and the coast and the sale of African slaves, but also on exports of salt, wine and wheat from their rural hinterlands.[8] Finally, most sectors of the urban economy would be hit: Bordeaux had exported to the colonies textiles from as far away as Troyes, Sedan, Le Puy and St-Étienne.[9] It was the rebellion which was responsible for pressuring the Legislative Assembly in April 1792 into extending civil equality to all 'free persons of colour'.[10]

The growing anxiety about the opposing threats of popular radicalism and counter-revolution, on the one hand, and bellicose posturing from European rulers, on the other, were to convince the Legislative Assembly that the Revolution and France itself were in danger. On 14 January 1792 a new law proclaimed that any French citizen who took part in a gathering designed to challenge or modify the Constitution, or who engaged in helping the *émigrés* or foreign princes, would be considered a traitor and charged with treason. In its decree of 22 May 1790 placing the power to declare war and make peace in the hands of the Assembly rather than the King, the National Assembly had declared that 'the French nation renounces the undertaking of any war with a view to making conquests, and that it will never use its forces against the freedom of any people'. After October 1791, however, the Jacobin followers of Jacques Brissot argued that the Revolution would not be safe until the foreign threat was destroyed and the loyalty of French citizens to the Constitution demonstrated by a patriotic war against internal and external enemies. By early in 1792, most deputies in the Legislative Assembly had convinced themselves that the rulers of Austria and Prussia in particular were engaged in naked aggression towards the Revolution. On 20 April 1792 the Assembly declared war on Austria, insisting that 'the war that it is obliged to support is in no way a nation to nation war, but the rightful defense of a free people against the unjust aggression of a king'.[11]

The war declared on Austria exposed internal opposition, as the 'Brissotins' hoped, but it was neither limited nor brief. With the Civil Constitution of the Clergy, it was to prove one of the major turning points of the revolutionary period, influencing the internal history of France until Napoleon's defeat in 1815. Every family in France was to experience its impact at first hand; hundreds of thousands of them would lose fathers, husbands and sons in battle. The divisions between those who welcomed or opposed the changes wrought since 1789 were now deadly.

The French armies were initially in disarray after the emigration of many noble officers and internal political dissension within garrisons, and lost a series of battles in the summer of 1792. The towns and villages along the eastern frontier rapidly became devastated by both armies. A Prussian soldier, Frédéric-Christian Laukhard, the son of a Lutheran pastor, whose sympathies for the French Revolution were matched only by his appetites for debauchery, was horrified by his comrades' pillage, noting how around Bréhain-la-Ville (Meurthe-et-Moselle) 'wheat was cut, pulled out, trampled, and in an hour a countryside which was to give subsistence to eight or ten villages was reduced to a desert'.[12] A decree of July 1792 clarified the areas in which the government would accept some measure of responsibility for these problems of devastation and destruction occasioned by war and civil conflict. Those who had suffered could apply for compensation to their local councils. The Convention agreed that compensation should cover three major areas of loss: the destruction of crops; houses and farms burned down or wrecked in the course of fighting; and all property, including furniture, personal effects, livestock, woods and vineyards, destroyed as a result of enemy action.

The *émigrés* with Laukhard's army had assured him that there was such anarchy in France that the peasants had stopped cultivating the soil, but in Champagne 'agriculture was obviously flourishing'. In the summer of 1792 Laukhard spoke with many peasants in Lorraine who enthused about the benefits of the Revolution, especially with the end of seigneurialism: 'now they were able to think, work, help each other, enjoy in peace their lives and the fruits of their labours and to save a little … in brief, they felt that they were now men and no longer slaves at the mercy of nobles and priests'.[13]

Certainly Laukhard was correct about the economic suffering. In the winter of 1791–92 subsistence became more difficult for all those dependent on buying grain or bread as an extremely wet winter threatened the planting of winter crops and drove up prices. Inflation was both aggravated by and in turn aggravated the continued erosion of the purchasing power of the *assignats*: from about 85 per cent in late 1791, their purchasing power declined to 60 per cent by spring 1792. Even in garrison towns such as Sierck butchers and bakers were refusing to accept *assignats* in early 1792. According to one volunteer: 'You can't even exchange them now by taking a loss of 30 sous on 5 livres. People say to us: no money, no meat or bread'.[14] There were massive food riots in the Aisne during the winter of 1791–92.[15] The response of rural communities sometimes went beyond hostility to the vestiges of seigneurialism and also contested the power that the large farmers of Picardy had over prices. In February 1792 people from about 40 parishes around Noyon (Oise) organized a huge public granary in the former abbey of Ourscamps.[16] Most famously, in

March 1792 Simonneau, the mayor of Étampes south of Paris, was killed by his townsfolk when he opposed demands to fix the price of bread: the Assembly accorded him a State funeral.

The wars which began in April 1792 and which lasted across the rest of the revolutionary decade were to dominate life in the towns and villages of France. The war was a disaster for the slave trade: there were only two slave 'expeditions' from La Rochelle in 1792, for example, compared with 22 in 1786. This not only shattered the businesses of the intensely pro-revolutionary Protestant traders, but also directly affected the rural and small-town economy for 100 km around. In inland towns and cities, the effects were felt less directly but every sector of the economy was ultimately affected by the collapse in colonial trade, which had been the boom sector of the French economy, increasing ten-fold in 1716–87. Everywhere, the war would mean insecurity about employment, increasing prices as inflation sapped the purchasing power of the *assignat*, and the imperatives of conscription and requisitioning. All along the borders and coastlines it meant the threat or actuality of occupation, privation and death.[17]

The war raised the stakes abruptly for those who opposed the Revolution. While the first two 'camps de Jalès', organized on the plain around Berrias at the junction of the departments of the Gard and the Ardèche, were above all anti-Protestant in motivation, the third – in July 1792 – was self-consciously counter-revolutionary. The 'guerre des châteaux' in the Vivarais and Gard in the spring had reinforced the resolve of the Revolution's enemies. This time as well, however, the 10,000 or so people who gathered were quickly dispersed.[18]

After the declaration of war a threatening decree was immediately issued against *émigrés* who did not return, and a law passed on 27 July 1792 confiscated *émigré* property, to be sold off in small lots. Non-juring clergy still in the country faced an ultimatum in August to take a new oath – 'I swear to be faithful to the Nation and to maintain Liberty and Equality or to die defending them' – and those priests who refused to swear the oath were imprisoned. By this time there were, for example, no fewer than 90 non-juring priests living in Laon.[19] Many non-jurors chose to stay and faced the deadly consequences of capture; more fortunate were those, like the priest François-Pierre Julliot of Troyes, who decided in September 1792 to 'flee far from a country consumed by anarchy, irreligion, blood and carnage'. Julliot and 80 others were, however, searched, insulted, threatened and obliged to pay bribes to reach the Swiss border.[20] Priests who emigrated sought out others from their region: there were 109 priests resident in the Swiss town of Einsiedeln in early 1794, and 47 of them were from Alsace.[21]

Large numbers of villages divided readily into supporters of the elected priest and those who, as in Airoux (Aude), said to municipal officers in April 1792 that 'there is nothing wrong with vomiting on those who go to services said by the *curé constitutionnel*'.[22] With the departure of so many non-juring clergy and the collapse in the authority of the pulpit one of the most ancient and trusted ways of receiving news disappeared from villages and small towns. Most communities across the country now had to face privation and uncertainty without the spiritual solace of a priest. In a world where the vast majority of French people had taken the meaning of time, of the seasons and of life itself from the rituals of the Church year and their interpretation by a priest, this absence would be a source of despair for many, of anger and resentment for others, but everywhere a profound shock. It is this which was at the core of the visceral responses of French people towards priests they blamed for betraying the Revolution or, in contrast, towards those blamed for shattering the certainties of earthly existence by attacking the Church.

The pace of emigration quickened dramatically after the declaration of war. *Émigrés* later delighted in recounting narrow escapes, as did Étiennette Lâge de Volude, aged 28 and a former member of the court at Versailles, who left Paris on 1 August 1792. At Châtellerault (Vienne) she was questioned as a suspect, as she had a Russian maid. She succeeded in winning over one of the guards, dressed in a liberty cap and revolutionary sash, by trading her tobacco. After asking if she could try some of his tobacco, which was 'detestable',

> I told him that I had some from Paris which was very good. ... he came back an hour later, without his sash and simply as a citizen. I gave him a pound of my tobacco, which delighted him. He returned my passport and saved me from further questioning.[23]

More numerous, but far less voluble, were the thousands of commoners who now emigrated, outnumbering aristocrats by a factor of five. These were people for whom the collapse of the Ancien Régime had brought unemployment and uncertainty, who were loyal to a particular noble family or priest, or who were convinced that the war would be catastrophic.

Many noble *émigrés* resolved – some with vengeful delight – to join with Austrian and Prussian forces to take revenge on the *canaille* of the towns and the insolent of the countryside. Gabriel-Isidore Blondin d'Abancourt was a career soldier of 25 at the time of the outbreak of the Revolution. His father had been a royal counsellor, and Abancourt did not hesitate to emigrate when commanded by his superior in September 1791. The gaiety of the newly created French community in Coblenz soon palled, however, and Abancourt was only too pleased when he heard in July 1792 of the bellicose manifesto of Brunswick, the commander of the Prussian army, threatening the total destruction of Paris: 'it was war, and joy was written on all our faces'.[24] Blaise de Fournas de la Brosse, the brother of four other *émigrés*, who had emigrated in 1791 and would never return from Spain, expressed in a poem in 1792 the vengeful resentment which the actions of peasants now inspired in royalists:

People, may suffering break you and consume you
Ungrateful people, you have worn out God's good will
This day full of bitterness has finally arrived
Attracted by your impiety.[25]

Reciprocal hatred was unleashed on those blamed for refusing to accept revolutionary change and being in league with counter-revolutionary armies slaughtering patriots on French soil. Following a call-up of volunteers in Aurillac (Cantal) on 11 March 1792 they celebrated by throwing rocks and firebrands at the house of a notorious aristocrat, Colinet de Naucelles, and firing rifle shots. The rumour swept through Arpajon, just 2 km away, that 'patriots' were being massacred; up to 700 people armed with rifles, axes, pikes, pitchforks and swords descended on Aurillac, decapitated Naucelles and paraded his head through the town on a pitchfork. In the following weeks the Cantal was swept by a wave of arson attacks on châteaux, and assaults of non-juring clergy and others suspected of being counter-revolutionary.[26] The level of vengeful violence and menace in the Soissonnais terrified office-holders in small towns such as Villers-Cotterêts. At a ceremony for the planting of a liberty tree on 29 June 1792, the mayor expressed his fears that a Revolution for liberty was under attack from 'license':

Liberty requires submission to the Laws, personal safety, respect for property and the maintenance of order; license, in contrast, brutal and ferocious, does what it wants with the Law, maintains disorder, thrives on crime, drinks blood, troubles endlessly the honour and peace of the Citizen, makes life and society detestable with the affliction of its perpetual terror and recurring calamities.[27]

\* \* \*

This prolonged battle over the consequences of the Revolution of 1789 had called into question the ways in which the inhabitants of the countryside and its small towns had been socialized into the meanings implicit in a landscape and language of power. Resonant statements of the meaning of earthly life and the authority of King and seigneur, bishop and priest emanated from every church, château, cathedral and palace. There were three major sources of Challenge to these assumptions about power and authority in the daily life of French people after 1789. Certainly, the most important of these were the attempts by successive governments after 1789 to respond to the collapse of the Ancien Régime by 'regenerating' public life on the basis of principles of popular sovereignty and the 'career open to talents', however limited by wealth, colour and sex these principles were in practice. A second major challenge occurred as the impact of such legislative changes meshed with challenges to idealized patterns of deference with the rural assault on every dimension of seigneurialism and the collapse of the Church in many areas. The third, linked source of challenge to older assumptions about power and authority was mass mobilization for war.

War also fuelled non-compliance and rebellion against those seigneurial practices which the Assembly still seemed hesitant to abolish. In April 1792 alone, at least one hundred peasant attacks on châteaux were recorded in the department of the Gard. John Markoff has analysed 4,689 protests or 'incidents' between 1788 and 1793, 1,687 of them in some detail, charting them according to the type of protest, location, frequency and timing (whereas before the Revolution incidents were twice as likely to occur on a Sunday as on any other day, thereafter Monday was the most common day). Anti-seigneurial protests were 36 per cent of the total, and subsistence 'troubles' 26 per cent; anti-tax rebellions just 3 per cent. Counter-revolutionary incidents made up 9 per cent. Some 83 per cent of *bailliages* and districts experienced at least one incident: indeed, 49 per cent experienced at least one anti-seigneurial protest, and 67 per cent at least one subsistence incident.[28] Those who continued to collect or attempt to collect harvest dues did not surrender meekly. The Monnet family had lost many of the seigneurial rights on their huge estates around Chavagné east of Niort (Deux-Sèvres), although they had also bought swathes of Church land for 110,000 livres. But now the talk of the abolition of all dues without compensation was seen by the family patriarch in April as

> the birth of the most horrible anarchy, the flame of civil war burning on all sides, the weak oppressed by the strong, the seeds and development in a people without property and still unenlightened, the evil principles of the agrarian law.[29]

In referring to the 'agrarian law', Monnet was expressing the most profound fear of rural property owners, the mutterings of the rural poor that all resources should be shared out equally.

Peasant communities effectively pressured successive assemblies towards complete abolition. The months of March–June 1792 were the pinnacle of peasant rebellion after 1789 and ultimately explain the decision of the Legislative Assembly to all but end the seigneurial regime.[30] On 25 August seigneurial dues were abolished without compensation, unless they could be proven to be derived from a legally valid contract.

> The National Assembly, seeing the feudal regime as having been abolished, but that nonetheless its effects continue, ... decrees the following:
> Article 1. All outcomes that may be a product of the maxim, 'no land without its lord' [*nulle terre sans seigneur*], of that of enclaves, of statute-customs and rules, be they general or specific, will remain null and void.

All landed ownership is henceforth to be unequivocal and free of all dues, be they feudal or monetary, if those who lay claim to them cannot prove the opposite.[31]

Forms of restrictive claims over peasant holdings or rents, such as *bordelage* in the Bourbonnais and Nivernais and *quevaise* in Brittany, were abolished with the legislation of 25 August 1792. A law of 27 August abolished *domaine congéable* in return for financial compensation of the landowner, but this was too little and too late to recapture support for the Revolution among the *domainiers* of the west, seething at what they saw as the forced departure of their clergy.[32] Finally, on 28 August 1792 villagers were authorized to seek restitution of common land believed to have been unjustly taken from them by former seigneurs.

The issue of ownership and control of common lands was more complex than that of leases. When the Legislative Assembly initiated a survey of commons in 1791 it unleashed a torrent of demands about their future, ranging from spirited defence of their continuity to pleas that they be divided. 'What a joy it would be to offer our children, when they return to their countryside, a bread produced in their own fields!', enthused the inhabitants of Louhans (Saône-et-Loire). The better-off from St-Jory (Haute-Garonne) snorted instead at the pretensions of 'the citizens who have nothing, because they do not like to work'.[33] The Legislative Assembly finally acted on 14 August 1792 with a brief, radical decree directing communes to divide non-forested common land. However, the precise details concerning its implementation were never forthcoming, and on 11 October the law was repealed.

The law of 25 August did not end hostility to former seigneurs. At Coucy-le-Château (Aisne), up to two thousand peasants from 17 villages who had been attending a recruitment gathering on 4 September threatened a well-known noble and pillaged two of his houses, leaving nothing standing but the walls. The noble, Desfossés de Vauschetin, was an intransigent former Second Estate deputy who had consistently refused to recognize revolutionary legislation; his refusal to supply horses for a military convoy was the final straw.[34] In Provence, there was a wave of violent attacks on the property of former seigneurs. Relations between the Marquis de Sade and his seigneurie of Lacoste on the slopes of the Lubéron deteriorated from a certain level of local sympathy with a man perceived in 1789 as a victim of despotism to the pillaging of his château on 17 September 1792. Sade had drawn considerable wealth (17,500 *livres* annually) from his seigneurie, but he had been content to leave it in the hands of a notary from Apt instructed to run the estate as profitably as possible.[35]

It was here in Provence that Michel Vovelle located the presence of a whole system of traditional festivals ranging from religious festivals to popular rituals, already undergoing change after 1750, and now affected by a radically different calendar of revolutionary commemoration after 1790. In

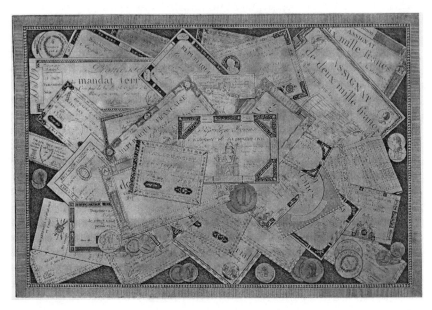

Figures 7 and 8: The Revolution changed the material objects of daily life in the provinces. The flood of *assignats* and consequent inflation was resented across much of the country. Revolutionaries nevertheless celebrated their resolve, as in the proclamation that 'I'm a damn good patriot' on this plate.

a society rich in religious rituals and displays of royal splendour, Vovelle found that the initial forms of enacting revolutionary unity drew on old rituals for style if not for substance or imagery. Conversely, long-established collective displays were not immune from the spontaneous syncretism of regional culture and revolutionary politics. In these years, collective display also went through what Vovelle describes as a 'creative explosion', as popular initiatives in organizing festivals and in remodelling ancient rituals meshed with the Convention's encouragement of civic commemoration. When news arrived, for example, of a military victory, whole villages improvised celebrations. Anti-clerical ceremonies in particular had a carnival and cathartic atmosphere, often utilizing the 'promenade des ânes', or promenade of asses, used in the Ancien Régime to censure violators of community norms of behaviour.[36]

In November 1790 the radical Paris newspaper *Lettres bougrement patriotiques du véritable père Duchêne* had compared 'poor buggers without knee-breeches (*sans-culottes*) or shoes' with '*Messieurs les foutriquets* aristocrats with their tight knee-breeches, their large neck-ties, their small cockades'. In 1791 active democrats among the *menu peuple* in Paris commonly became known by this new term *sans-culottes*, which was both a political label for a militant patriot and a social description signifying men of the people who did not wear the knee-breeches and stockings of the upper classes. The sexual *double entendre* was not lost to the masculine sensibilities of working men.[37] Nor was the term confined to working men of the cities: the Jacobin administrator of the district of Lagrasse (Aude), Jean-Baptiste Ciceron, responded to a request for information about common land by retorting that 'all the land which could produce anything has been cleared for a long time now. The *sans-culottes* of these mountains didn't bother to wait for the publication of the law concerning the division of the commons'.[38]

One element of the new political culture was the thousands of political clubs established in the early years of the Revolution, the most famous of which was the Paris Jacobin Club, but which were found across the country, particularly in the southeast and northeast. In larger villages popular societies played a similar role. With the abolition of guilds through the d'Allarde law, and the prohibition of wage-earners' associations by the Le Chapelier law, the neighbourhood section meeting came to be the place where artisans could express their grievances and experience the sort of solidarity of workplace and neighbourhood they had once – at least in theory – enjoyed.[39]

Sitting uneasily alongside the new associational activities of men were those of women. The unhappy experiences of feminists and of militant *sans-jupons* in Paris have often been recounted, but there were at least 60 Jacobin women's clubs in the provinces, and not all of them in cities such as Bordeaux and Lyon. Among the clubs in small country towns were that comprising 22 girls in Civray (Vienne) to more substantial ones in Cognac (Charente), Avallon

(Yonne), Casteljaloux (Lot-et-Garonne), St Junien (Haute-Vienne), Meulan (Seine-et-Oise) and the 'Constitutional Amazons' of Grasse (Basses-Alpes). A few large villages also had one, such as Damazan (Lot-et-Garonne), Beaumont (Dordogne), Gevrey (Côte-d'Or), Éguilles (Bouches-du-Rhône), Plombières (Vosges) and St-Zacharie (Var). These were gatherings of 'patriot' women whose activities drew not only on old assumptions about women and charitable works but also on an evident desire to participate as fully as possible in the act of regenerating and defending France. In 1791–92, at least, they were applauded by their male peers. The women of Castellane (Basses-Alpes) formed their own 'Amies de la Révolution' in June 1792, before agreeing to join with their menfolk.[40] The 236 'Amies des vrais amis de la Constitution' in Ruffec (Charente) included seamstresses and laundresses as well as the priest's sister and two bar owners. Its president Chedaneau began her inaugural speech in August 1791 by stating that '[a]lthough women seem to take little part in public affairs, at all times their feeble hands have held the destiny of the universe; their wishes, desires and caprices have made war and peace'. While their activities were mainly born of a self-consciously serious desire to support the Revolution, they were at times insistent on women's political rights. In 1791, a 22-year-old mother of four named Élisabeth Lafaurie spoke to the men's club in St-Sever (Landes), arguing that the denial of the vote was 'unjust, because the mass of women is subject to laws which they have not been able to refuse or approve, which is contrary to their liberty and to the idea that we should have of social conventions'.[41]

The vast majority of male revolutionaries, including the Jacobins, favoured the withdrawal of women from the public arena into the home. The Revolution had made a place for women in the public forum (as evidenced by their active participation in food riots and their gathering to listen as posters, brochures and penny broadsheets were read aloud on village squares), and it was because of this that the reaction against 'civic woman' was as vehement as it was. To admit female citizens into the body politic was to entertain the possibility that they might make decisions and become active subjects of the Revolution on a footing of equality with men.

In newspapers, songs, plays and broadsheets, the period 1789–92 was an age of savage satire, distinguished by a mix of obscene mockery, anti-clericalism and political slander. In this world of lampooning and pornographic attack, the King and queen were the most vulnerable of targets. In particular, Marie-Antoinette was relentlessly attacked for her alleged sexual depravities and a maleficent political power which was seen to have emasculated the monarchy. These attacks were the most startling manifestation of the articulation of a new politics of gender. In contrast, the new man of the Revolution was imagined to be politically and physically virile, the opposite of the mocking stereotype of the aristocracy as physically and morally decadent.[42] These ribald attacks on the moral stature of the King and queen sapped the monarchy's symbolic standing, confirmed by Louis' 'desertion' of his people in June 1791.

The vitriol of counter-revolutionary rhetoric fuelled the popular conviction that Louis was complicit in the defeats being suffered by the army. In response to violent menace from Brunswick, the commander of the Prussian army, the 48 neighbourhood 'sections' of Paris voted to form a Commune of Paris to organize insurrection and an army of 20,000 *sans-culottes* from the newly democratized National Guard. Among those who participated in the overthrow of the monarchy on 10 August were soldiers from Marseille and its department of the Bouches-du-Rhône en route to the battlefront. They brought with them a song popular among republicans in the south – the 'Marseillaise' – composed by the army officer Rouget de Lisle as the 'Chant de guerre pour l'armée du Rhin'.

The most startling feature of the overthrow of the monarchy was the relative lack of anger or shock in most parts of the country: it was as if the aura of monarchy had evaporated with the King's attempt to flee 14 months earlier. There were no doubt many rural people who were aghast at what had happened to the King, but their voices are largely silent in the historical record. The declaration of war and now the overthrow of the monarchy radicalized the Revolution. The political exclusion of 'passive' citizens called to defend the Republic was now untenable. Moreover, by overthrowing the monarchy on 10 August, Parisian working people and their provincial supporters had issued the ultimate challenge to the whole of Europe. The Revolution was now armed, democratic and republican.

On 2 September, news reached Paris that the great fortress at Verdun, just 250 km from the capital, had fallen to the Prussians. The news generated an immediate, dramatic surge in popular fear and resolve. Convinced that 'counter-revolutionaries' (whether nobles, priests or common law criminals) in prisons were waiting to break out and welcome the invaders once the volunteers had left for the front, hastily convened popular courts sentenced to death about 1,200 of the 2,700 prisoners brought before them, including 240 priests.[43]

The 'September massacres' are commonly understood to refer to the hundreds tried by these street courts in Paris and often killed in horrific circumstances. But the killings were not confined to the capital. In his study of the massacres, Pierre Caron identified in all some 65 'settlings of scores' by murder in 32 departments, all but 15 of them in towns. Anatoli Ado has placed the latter among 45 peasant 'interventions' in July–October 1792, most being attacks on nobles, their châteaux or the last vestiges of seigneurialism. All of them smacked of deeply entrenched social hatred, a desire to punish those alleged to be in league with the enemy now advancing through eastern France.[44]

The September killings were the third wave of popular panic which swept parts of the country, following those of July–August 1789 and June 1791. This time, however, the panic found its outlet in violent retribution and deliberately cruel death. Once war had broken out in April, those who were deemed to be in league with the enemy – as counter-revolutionaries, intransigent nobles, non-juring clergy or even certain types of criminals – were dealt with in advance of the invading armies.

The massacres occurred in many parts of the country. As well as five collective murders in Soissons in this bloody fortnight in September, for example, in and around Alençon, capital of the Department of the Orne 190 km west of Paris, two nobles and nine priests were killed. Only three of 53 prisoners being escorted from Paris to Saumur for their own safety escaped from popular justice at Versailles. At Pamiers and Mirepoix in the department of the Ariège, rumours that officials had made off with funding destined for volunteers led to several murders and arson attacks. When news arrived in Reims of the fall of Verdun, two 'suspects' were immediately put to death.[45]

In 18 of the 32 departments in which there were killings in September there was but a single incident. In the department of the Orne, in contrast, there were eight killings, claiming 11 lives, between 15 August and 10 September. The first four of these murders occurred prior to the Paris Massacres. On 15 August a noble was bludgeoned to death accompanied by cries of 'Vive la Nation'; his head was cut off and his body displayed on the public square in Le Sap; the next day another noble was murdered at Chapelle-le-Moche. On the nineteenth, a non-juring noble *vicaire* was murdered at Putanges and a non-juring *curé* was murdered at Bellême.[46] On 9 September, four priests were murdered at Gacé; 61 men were ultimately charged, most of whom were *journaliers* (day labourers).[47]

The most exhaustive judicial enquiry into one of the killings has much to tell us about the motivations of the crowd. After the murder on 6 September of the 27-year-old Capucin monk Valframbert on the Place d'Armes in Alençon, the tribunal overseeing the case interviewed 224 witnesses about the 23 arrested, of whom seven were women. Those arrested were typical of urban working people, including tailors, a shoemaker, a gardener and a candlemaker. Witnesses described the anger of the public after Valframbert had been sentenced to deportation for 'incivisme'; incensed at such a light sentence, some began to call for the capucin's head: 'sa tête, sa tête'. The crowd had attacked Valframbert, ripping off his wig, throwing it out a window, and then dragged him out from under a table. As assailants attacked him with sticks, knives and feet, they shouted 'Vive la Nation'. Shouts were heard of 'We'll see if the twelve good lords (icons) that he carries in his pocket will save him!' and, from a woman, 'He's the reason why our men are leaving (for the war)'. After Valframbert's murder, his severed head was paraded around Alençon; a restaurant owner testified that several people asked if they could bring the dead man's head into his restaurant in order to have a drink.[48]

In Meaux, 50 km to the east of the capital, a large crowd went to the prison and demanded the registers of prisoners: seven priests and seven criminals were killed, the former by being stabbed, kicked and beaten. Another 14 prisoners, including seven beggars, were released. None of the seven criminals killed was from Meaux, and this may indicate a greater sympathy for the local poor who were spared.[49] The killings shocked the sturdy patriot Pierre Louis Nicolas Delahaye, schoolteacher of Silly-en-Multien in the Oise, just 20 km from Meaux:

> I have even heard here some young of Silly living in Meaux boast of having participated in these massacres. ... As for me, I believe that the day will come when they themselves are horrified to have said such things ... Today everyone has gone mad: there is talk only of massacring, of guillotining, of hanging from lamp-posts, and so on.[50]

Another who was shocked to his core was Nicolas-Joseph Grain, who had worked as a stonemason, book-binder and land-surveyor before becoming involved full-time in politics as secretary to the municipal council of Vadencourt, near Guise in the department of the Aisne. In August 1792, aged 42, he was one of the electors of his canton chosen to go to Soissons to elect the department's deputies to the National Convention. When he arrived early in September, the town was in the grip of panic about the rapidly approaching Austrian soldiers. About 25,000 soldiers and volunteers were camped outside the town, their numbers regularly swollen by new arrivals from all over the country. The word spread that one of these new arrivals was in fact enrolling volunteers to cross to the enemy. Other soldiers dragged him through the streets, stabbing him with their bayonets to cries of 'Long live the homeland! Death to the traitor!' He was taken to the town hall where the council tried in vain to convince the volunteers to release him. Almost dead, the individual was forced to kneel, ask forgiveness from the nation and then decapitated. His head was presented to the town council on the end of a bayonet, where Grain recalled how,

> I recoiled in horror from this sight because there is nothing more horrible to see ('Il n'y a rien d'aussi horrible à voir'). I shuddered to the tips of my fingers. The sight followed me everywhere and I just couldn't forget it.

The cadaver was then hacked into pieces and paraded through the streets.[51]

A fortnight later, a lieutenant-colonel was killed on the public square in Soissons, for having allegedly said to his volunteers from the Côte-d'Or 'that it would be good enough for them to wear only their nightshirts *[toile]* to go to the butchery' that they would undergo the next day. The officer had been arrested, but soldiers had broken into the prison and led him to the public square where, like his predecessor, he was decapitated, then cut to pieces, the sections of his body paraded through the town.[52]

To historians such as Simon Schama, J.F. Bosher and François Furet, such punitive violence was the result of a revolutionary intolerance already discernible in 1789: the counter-revolution was essentially a creation of revolutionary paranoia and popular bloodlust. Schama, for example, argued that violence was at the heart of the Revolution from the very first, and that the middle-class leadership was complicit in its barbarity. Indeed, the September massacres have been described by him as 'the central truth of the Revolution'.[53] This argument is based on the premise that this was a society in which the masses were as violent as they were ignorant. It fails to acknowledge the disgust and shame felt by people such as Delahaye and Grain; nor can it account for the specific acts of violence, which were both discriminating and spectacularly cruel.

Summarily dispatching counter-revolutionaries would have been far too simple and lenient: the need for collective punishment, cruelty and, at Soissons and elsewhere, the exaction of a confession of guilt recall the ritualized cruelty of the public execution or *supplice* of the Ancien Régime.[54] The September massacres and other instances of collective killing during the Revolution bear the imprint of both the practices of punishment under the Ancien Régime and of carnivalesque inversion of established legal processes.[55] The rage expressed towards the alleged traitors was a form of popular justice, a final, dehumanizing act of contempt, representing, in the words of Colin Lucas, a 'symbolic extrusion [from the community] beyond death'. The mutilation of the bodies represented a chance to express a loathing which was to be manifested in exemplary and communitarian fashion. The most potent forms of vengeful violence had to be in public.[56]

Several weeks after these 'September massacres', revolutionary armies won their first great victory, at Valmy, 200 km east of the capital. Gabriel Noël, one of the victors of Valmy, wrote to his family from Ste-Menehould on 26 September that the starving troops were reduced to eating horses which had died of hunger.[57] As news arrived of the victory, the new National Convention, elected by universal manhood suffrage, but in a two-stage process, was convening in Paris. The men of the Convention were mostly middle class and provincial by social background, by now experienced in revolutionary administration and politics. They were also democrats and republicans: immediately on convening, they abolished the monarchy and proclaimed France a republic. The awesome challenge that confronted them was how to unify a country teetering on the edge of a civil war, and how to provision soldiers such as Noël.

# 6

# In the Fires of War, 1792–93

French people had been born into a world where the pre-eminence of a king responsible to God was unquestioned. Four years after Louis had decided to ask his people for advice on steering his kingdom through a financial crisis the monarchy itself had been abolished. The Revolution had also abolished the titles of nobility and the very notion of 'seigneurie' which had been the universal temporal expression of the origins, powers and privilege of the nobility. The other major source of certainty in pre-revolutionary France had been the Catholic Church, under the spiritual authority of the Pope. With most of the French clergy, the Pope had now decided that the war to overthrow the Republic was a crusade against godlessness: those killing French volunteers on the borders were doing God's will. The central markers of power in the mental universe of French people were no longer in place.

Across much of the country the news of the proclamation of the Republic on 21 September was the occasion of celebration, tempered always by the knowledge of the nation's parlous military position. At Villardebelle, in the foothills of the eastern Pyrenees, the constitutional priest Marcou celebrated the proclamation of the Republic by planting a liberty tree which is still standing today.[1] Other rural people – and not just non-juring clergy and former nobles – were horrified by the news of the fall of the monarchy. Gabriel Noël, an army volunteer from the Vosges, was shocked by the news of the actions of 'la vile canaille' in Paris on 10 August:

> I swore to live free or to die, and to that end to fight the external enemy ... But how can one live free in a land which is falling back into slavery by tearing itself apart? ... We no longer have a Constitution; the maddest anarchy has taken its place.

He advised his family that England would be the most congenial refuge. In the end, however, Noël decided to become a professional soldier and took up an officer's commission, and his letters henceforth avoided politics.[2] What was most striking, in any case, was how widely and readily accepted was the end of a monarchy which had lasted a millennium: Louis' attempted flight 14 months earlier had sapped popular faith in the benevolence of his intentions.

Once the Legislative Assembly had decreed 'la patrie en danger' in July 1792, army officers and national guards began recruiting volunteers. In all, some 200,000 came forward, especially from frontier departments. They were young men: three-quarters were 25 years of age or younger, and 10 per cent were under 18. Their average height (one-third were shorter than 1m 63) points to their humbler origins compared with those who had already volunteered in 1791: most were farm labourers, unskilled workers and domestic servants. This may also be explained by the financial inducements offered to volunteers by some departments: 100–120 *livres* in Brittany, 260–600 in the Massif Central. But there is abundant evidence of the circulation of ideas about the nation and the Revolution. As one mother wrote to her son, a volunteer from Saône-et-Loire, his country 'is certainly the most beautiful and honourable that you could ever choose, as it stands for humanity and the Rights of Man'; he should 'pray to the Almighty and obey all your superiors'.[3]

The legislation of July and August 1792 had quietened the anti-seigneurial actions – legal and otherwise – which had been common across much of the countryside for three years. This was far from the end of rural revolution. The flash-points in the south in particular concerned not only seigneurial rights, but also access to land. From the outset of the Revolution, the friction over the incomplete legislation of 1789 on seigneurialism had been one aspect of a more general conflict over access to, ownership and control of the *vacants*, poorer or marginal land often used for grazing livestock. Some of this land was seized and cleared by the rural poor, desperate for an arable plot. In response to these reports the National Assembly had sought, in its decree of 22 February 1791, to resolve the issue of ownership of the 'wastelands': but neither it nor that of subsequent assemblies had any tangible success.

From 1789 governments issued a maze of legislation pertaining to land use, including a reformed Forest Code and a general Rural Code, laws on the subdivision of commons and on illegal land clearances. Of particular importance were decrees seeking to protect forests, decrees outlawing unauthorized clearing of common and State-owned land, and others authorizing the subdivision and sale of Church and common land. Much of this legislation was predicated on the assumption that individual owners enjoyed unqualified rights to use their property as they wished, leading to tensions between, on the one hand, rural people too poor to fear penalties and who believed that clearing forests improved the land and, on the other, officials and landholders for whom the forests were a precious commercial or national resource.

At the local level, too, there was an impassioned and intelligent debate in the years after 1789 about the impact of the revolutionary years on the environment. The concerns expressed in many *cahiers* about erosion in particular became more agitated with the intensification of land clearance. Administrators in the south, for example, were well aware of the acceleration of cultivation and wine-growing on newly cleared hillsides, but the means by which it was achieved alarmed them. Their main opponents in this debate were small peasants and the rural poor, whose rationale for land clearance has, of course, left far fewer traces in the records.

From 1789 a plethora of reports had poured in to Paris of seizures of land belonging to the State and to seigneurs, and of unchecked felling of trees in State and private forests. Where noble *émigrés* had been proprietors of forests, local populations assumed that they now had the right to cut wood and graze their livestock as they wished. In 1792–93, for example, the municipality of Neauphes-sous-Essai, north of Alençon, had to arrest repeatedly people cutting wood and grazing animals in the forest belonging to the *émigré* Oilliamson. Even his tenants were behaving 'more as if they had acquired the properties than were renters of them'. This was a story common across much of the country.[4] In the process a *légende noire* developed of a destructive peasant 'atavism' unleashed by revolutionary licence.

In the aftermath of the Great Fear of 1789, the unity of rural communities against seigneurs and royal officials had fractured as the conflicting interests within rural communities became more exposed. The four motors of the peasant revolution of 1789–93 – anti-seigneurialism, control of resources, subsistence issues and taxation – varied in their power depending on the specific structures of regions and individual communities.[5] The rural revolution had its own rhythms and inner dynamic, generated by the specific nature of the locality. Certainly it cannot be reduced to levels of participation in elections, as historians have tended to. The local orientation of rural politics was a function of perceptions of the benefits and hardships brought by the Revolution, attitudes to the Church and local social structures. But, while political attitudes varied across the countryside, underpinning attitudes everywhere was hostility both to the Ancien Régime and to bourgeois concepts of untramelled rights of private property: the communitarian impulse was dominant.[6]

In much of Normandy, responses to the Revolution were mediated through the web of confraternities, religious associations of lay people, men, women and children, which oversaw charitable activities and parish life, and acted as both a type of parish welfare agency and a centre of sociability. The little town of Vire (Calvados), with 8,000 inhabitants, had more than 50 of them; three-fifths of all villages in the surrounding diocese of Lisieux had at least one. Fearful that they would be closed as being illegal 'corporations', these confraternities petitioned the Convention that they were good republicans who should be free to follow their religion. When a law of 18 August 1792 required that their property be inventoried, most municipalities simply failed to respond; in many places the confraternities went underground as 'sociétés d'humanité'.[7] In Provence, on the other hand, a similar density of confraternities co-existed – sometimes peacefully, at others violently – with a remarkable density of *sociétés populaires*.[8]

In small rural communities, the years 1792–94 were a time of social levelling in political power, with peasants and even labourers represented for the first time on councils. In northeastern France in particular, social hatreds were now turned increasingly against the wealthy families of the former Third Estate, particularly large landowners and tenant farmers. In 1792–94, the longstanding political – as well as economic and social – power of the *fermiers* was contested in Artois. Village councils and the surveillance committees established to monitor suspicious behaviour were the means by which smallholders, village artisans and labourers contested and often took control of local affairs. The surveillance committees had a similar composition: a study of 20 committees in the Vosges, for example, has found that half the members were peasants and rural labourers; there was a disproportionate presence (30 per cent) of village artisans.[9]

In Annay (Pas-de-Calais), where there had been a violent conflict over seigneurial rights in 1789–90, the popular society declared that 'permanent membership of public office has been banished in the sacred code of our laws, our lawmakers have clearly felt the negative effects which may step from a continuity of power-holders'.[10] This was expressed more bluntly by an official from Blérancourt (Aisne) in February 1793: 'The large landowner or farmer is a despot who has no scruples about doing down his neighbour and friend and does not care at all about what might become of a family he has plunged into misery'. The municipality of Neuves-Maisons (Meurthe) agreed that the 'hoarders of wheat and the farmers ... are at present more to be feared than despotism; they are more to be feared than the cruelest aristocracy'. At Courville, near Chartres, a crowd estimated at 6,000 strong forced republican officials to sign a document fixing prices on grain, candles, meat, shoes and other essentials.[11]

It was from these resentments that sprang the desire for the division of the commons, or even for a division of all resources. From the little town of Nantua (Ain) came a petition to the Assembly that

> there is no liberty without equality, and no equality while there are landed properties belonging to individuals ... the community of wealth (*communauté des biens*), in making the nation richer, will destroy forever all seeds of discord, all humiliating distinctions between rich and poor.[12]

On 18 March 1793 the National Convention declared the death penalty for such proposals for the 'agrarian law'. From 1789 the Revolution had been studded with examples of collective protest and occasional popular violence; from early in 1793 state institutions became far more effective in repressing such behaviour. Across the country, most municipalities were in the hands of experienced men resolved to ensure, at a time of war, that the fractious reluctance of young men to go to war did not spill over into sedition. Instead, opposition to particular laws or levies of men and supplies more commonly took their pre-revolutionary forms of foot-dragging and silent non-compliance.

Everywhere the experience of Revolution was mediated through the institutions and social practices of village and urban neighbourhoods. The Savoyard communities hitherto subject to Sardinian regulation and annexed by France in 1792 quickly applied the law of 14 December 1789 on local government. In the 35 months from the beginning of 1793 until November 1795 the municipal council of Viry met 122 times on a total of 187 matters, from religious, military and administrative issues to local policing, roads and bridges, schooling and, increasingly, food supply. The enthusiasm for the Revolution was quickly attenuated by the departure of the priest and his curate.[13] Elsewhere, religious issues were a reason why local politics became more radical. The schoolteacher Delahaye noted that in his village in the Oise, where the constitutional priest became the mayor, 'many people no longer go to mass or vespers; I don't know whether people will be better and more just, and personally I don't believe so'.[14]

All over the country the new language of politics was overlaid on ancient forms of communication, whether to express community attitudes or to circulate news. Pedlars continued to be a source of news for populations desperate for information. They were also vulnerable: the pedlar Tilliet was arrested in Mirecourt (Vosges) in 1792 for spreading news about a well-known local *émigré* noble, protesting in his defence that he had been pestered for news.[15] No less than under the Ancien Régime, republican authorities were hostile to some aspects of popular culture, in particular the wearing of masks during Carnival, when these were used to express opposition to or mock republican authorities.[16]

The politics of new popular festivals were particularly confrontational in towns. Gabrielle Gauchat, born in St-Domingue in 1744, had become a Visitandine nun in the priory of St-Gengoux (Saône-et-Loire) at the age of ten. In September 1792, the convent was closed and converted into a store for hay. In memoirs she wrote for her brother, she explained how she refused to swear an oath to the Revolution, and thereby had to forego a pension: 'To take an oath to liberty and equality seems to me to be a monstrous thing in a century in which liberty and equality have ravaged everything.' In November she described the 'fêtes diaboliques' in St-Gengoux:

> Names, objects, everything is profaned; there are, it is said, five chapels where people will go in a procession to make five stations and to sing the Marseillaise, to worship goddesses, trees, bonnets, etc. ... is that not the purest idolatry?[17]

Some of her sisters did not agree. On 12 September, during the electoral assembly for the National Convention at Rieux (Haute-Garonne), one of those present announced that 'the citizenesses of Carbonne marching armed with pikes under a banner of Liberty were demanding to be allowed to take the civic oath like those of Montesquieu-Volvestre'.[18]

We cannot know whether one of the elements in this dramatic statement of women's rights was an awareness of radical shifts in the nature of marriage and women's rights within the family. Among the final acts of the Legislative Assembly on 20 September 1792 was the secularization of the registration of births, deaths and marriages, prefigured in the Constitution of 1791. This new law replaced the sacrament of marriage with a civil contract that did not require the services of a priest. Only civil marriage would be recognized by the State. Hitherto the preserve of parish clergy, the nature of the marriage ceremony now changed, with the priest performing only an optional blessing if indeed a priest was available at all. Religious strictures against marriage in Advent, in Lent, on Fridays and Sundays were now commonly ignored.[19]

Responses to the radical change in the nature of private ceremonies varied. Early in November 1792 the son and daughter of two people of Collioure known for their opposition to the priests' lack of patriotism appeared before the officer of the civil registry:

> Citizen Jean Nomdedeu, aged 30 years, farmer, son of another Jean Nomdedeu, farmer, and of Catherine Ostalrich his living wife, on the one hand, and Angelique Calvet, aged 29 years, daughter of Joseph Calvet, carpenter, and of Angélique Ramone, his wife when she was alive ... the said parties thus united deliberately declare that they have a child in common, named Jean Joseph François, born on the ninth of June 1791.[20]

Elsewhere, people often turned to the clergy to sanctify a marriage that they assumed would only have validity before God. On 16 January 1793, for example, the priest Grillet of Bourg-en-Bresse married two wine-growers 'to satisfy their religion and their consciences and regarding the ceremony they had to fulfill at the town hall as a purely civil act which did nothing to prevent the freedom of following their beliefs'.[21]

The repudiation of the most fundamental sources of authority in the Ancien Régime inevitably called into question the position of women within the family and society.[22] A number of pieces of legislation were designed to improve family life, deemed hitherto to have been cruel and immoral, like the Ancien Régime itself. Family tribunals were instituted to deal with personal conflict, and penalties for wife-beating were introduced which were twice as heavy as for assaulting a man. The law of 20 September increased the age at which boys and girls could marry with parental consent from 14 and 12 to 15 and 13; the age at which parental consent was no longer needed was lowered from 30 for men and 25 for women to 21 for both.

It is doubtful whether patterns of male violence changed, despite the exhortations of revolutionary legislators to a peaceful, harmonious family life as the basis of the new political order. What did change was the possibility of women protecting their rights within the household. Of greatest importance was a divorce law voted at the last session of the Legislative Assembly, on 20 September 1792, at the same time as the law secularizing private ceremonies. This gave women remarkably broad grounds for leaving an unhappy or violent marriage:

II. The divorce may occur through the mutual consent of the spouses.

III. One of the spouses may have the divorce issued on the simple allegation of incompatibility of temperament or character.

IV. Each of the spouses may equally have the divorce issued on specific grounds, that is:

> the dementia, madness or violence of one of the spouses;
> the condemnation of one of them to corporal or serious punishment;
> the crime, cruelty or serious affront of one toward the other;
> the acknowledged dissoluteness of morals;
> the abandonment of the wife by the husband, or of the husband by the wife for at least two years;
> the absence of one of them, without news, for at least five years.[23]

In effect this law abolished the pre-Revolutionary law of *séparation de corps et d'habitation* (which did not dissolve a marriage but did permit the spouses to live in separate dwellings and to have control of their own property) and made divorce, the total dissolution of marriage, the remedy for marital breakdown. It recognized both the breakdown of marriage without the attribution of fault and the concept of matrimonial offence. The law specified that in some cases divorced persons had to wait a certain period before contracting a new marriage: a year in the case of mutual consent or incompatibility, although the couple could remarry each other at any time. Where divorce was granted on the grounds of one of the specific matrimonial offences, the husband could remarry as soon as he wished. A divorced woman, on the other hand, was unable to remarry for one year after the divorce except when the divorce was for reasons of her husband's absence for more than five years. The required delay was founded on the concern that there should be no confusion over the paternity of a child born to a divorcée. The law also stipulated that, with respect to material goods and rights, divorced persons were to be returned to their position before marriage. The law treated men and women equally, with the exception that if a husband divorced his wife on any of the specific grounds, except madness, the wife was to be deprived of all her rights and benefits in the joint estate, although she was to recover the property which came from her family.

Perhaps 30,000 divorces were decreed under this legislation, disproportionately in towns: in Paris, there were nearly 6,000 in 1793–95. In the rural canton of Mont-aux-Malades around Rouen, there were only 31 divorces in 1792–1803 in a population of 12,500, about one-fifth of the rate in the city.[24] There were only 7 divorces in Bourg in 1793, compared with 110 marriages.[25] In Collioure, a town of 2,300 people, there were just two divorces, and in Gabian, a village of 800 people, just one. In small communities such as these, however, these divorces would have been common knowledge, so the impact of the law on domestic relationships would have been far broader. Similarly, although violence was a common cause cited by women who initiated proceedings, the customary power of men to humble their wives by physical abuse (called *correction modérée* under the Ancien Régime) would have been debated by women on the streets and at markets, and called into question in every household.

Many of the divorces were based on long-term separation. Others revealed unhappy, violent marriages, as when Marie-Jeanne Bernié from the village of Marchais (Aisne) sought a divorce from the farmer Jean-Claude Cointe on the grounds of his violent assaults on her: she had had to have a finger amputated after he twisted it as she tried to scratch his face to fight him off. The tribunal rebuffed Cointe's defence that 'several times she had refused to live with him out of spite' and had not looked after their economic affairs, for which she was responsible.[26]

On 7 March 1793 the Convention strengthened the 1791 legislation on partible inheritance by passing a law which forbade a parent to favour one child over another. The family arbitration tribunals established in 1791 considered applications for divorce as well as disputes over the application of the new inheritance laws, especially where there were children from previous marriages. But debates about the limits to active citizenship and the ideal nature of the family necessarily involved the rights of children born outside marriage, and on 4 June 1793 inheritance rights were extended to children born outside wedlock (but not those from adulterous relationships).

The precise impact of the inheritance law varied according to the specific cultural and legal bases of prior practice in particular regions. In the Quercy region around Montauban, parents had had the 'faculté de tester', by which they could leave their property to whomever they wished by written will. The inter-generational 'pot-and-hearth' extended families had essentially been a way of property being transferred from father to son. From 1775 to 1793, about half of all peasant marriage contracts established such communities; from 1793, the practice declined and by the 1820s was present in only one-fifth of contracts. Where it continued among land-holding peasants, a range of legal fictions had to be agreed to by children, or the property had to be left undivided between heirs but worked by a son. It became more difficult for this to occur while parents were still alive. Before 1793, the fathers of two-thirds of bridegrooms were alive; after 1793 two-thirds of grooms married only after their fathers had died and, in the six years of strict equality after 1793, this was the case for 86 per cent of grooms. Wives were, however, expected to be complicit in strategies: they were named as heirs in only one-tenth of cases, but daughters did end up receiving significantly more than previously.[27]

\* \* \*

While some historians have been content to take the examples of collective violence as symptomatic of the people's Revolution, others have instead seen the popular violence of the Revolution as sporadic, discriminate and limited. Instead, the Revolution 'from below' was characterized rather by mass participation in democratic politics. In the months between August 1792 and the end of 1793, the political participation of urban and rural working people reached its peak. By mid-1793 there were probably as many as 1,500 Jacobin clubs across the country, particularly in the southeast and northeast, and thousands of formal and informal 'sociétés populaires'.[28] Whereas urban elites had tended to remain in power in the early years of the Revolution, by the time of the municipal elections of December 1792–January 1793 a far wider cross-section of the population was on town councils. In the small northern textile town of Elbeuf (Seine-Inférieure), for example, there were not only seven manufacturers and four merchants, but also four carders, three tailors and other artisans and petits bourgeois: among them an innkeeper, a locksmith, a joiner, a glazier and a wool shearer.[29]

Four years of revolutionary experience, of boundless hopes, sacrifices and anxieties, of living within a revolutionary political culture, generated a distinctive *sans-culottes* ideology in many country towns, as well as in cities. This discourse drew on pre-revolutionary symbolism, was often expressed in messianic terms and drew on idealized collective practices of the workplace to visualize a new society free of aristocrats, priests and rich men. The vision was of a regenerated France of artisans and smallholders rewarded for the dignity and usefulness of their labour, free from religion, the condescension of the high born, and the competition of merchants and manufacturers. More formal meetings of popular societies and neighbourhood sections drew on religious rituals for their format and on revolutionary experience for their content. Meetings often began with the singing of the 'Marseillaise' or the 'Ça ira' and the reading of letters from the front, followed by discussions of forthcoming anniversaries and processions, the collection of patriotic donations, the denunciation of 'suspects' and orations on the republican virtues. To break from a lifetime of induction into the vocabulary of inequality, meetings sought to impose the familiar use of 'tu' in all social dealings, dismissing the 'vous' formerly required towards their superiors as intrinsically aristocratic. By this time, too, the use of *Citoyen* and *Citoyenne* instead of *Monsieur* and *Madame* had become general, the key discursive sign of changed public relationships.

The proliferation of popular clubs was dubbed 'clubinomanie'; those who frequented them were said to 'clubiner'. The Prussian soldier

Frédéric-Christian Laukhard recalled that 'clubbiste' meant not only a member of a pro-revolutionary club but also more generally a supporter of the Revolution. Laukhard, who deserted to the French at Landau in September 1793, was struck that a good republican addressed all without exception with the familiar 'tu', and was expected to sprinkle his conversation with profanities such as 'sacrée garce, 'sacrée merderie' and 'sacristi'.[30] If he is to be believed, the troops fighting on the eastern frontier were motivated by a powerful sense of commitment to the Republic and disdain for old Europe.

There were many villages where the distinctive politics of small, face-to-face communities resulted in generalized support or rejection of the Revolution. This unity was not the case in country towns, particularly those which had been in some way dependent on the Ancien Régime through the expenditure of resident clerics and nobles, as administrative centres for the Church, through luxury goods trades or as administrative centres whose functions had been moved elsewhere. There were many town-dwellers who bitterly resented the dramatic upheaval the Revolution had brought into their lives. Among the casualties of the Revolution were the 'imagists', those businesses – such as Pellerin of Épinal (Vosges) – which had made their profits from mass production of religious and royal images sold in shops or by pedlars. The Barc business in Chartres had produced half a million images in the decade 1777–87. By 1792 the imagists had been ordered to destroy their printing blocks, but few were prepared or able to make the transition to revolutionary imagery. A rare exception was Letourmy of Orléans, who now made a living printing images of the storming of the Bastille or the evils of the non-juring clergy.[31]

The difficulties of towns directly or indirectly dependent on overseas trade, and the polarization of urban politics, were intensified by the trial of Louis XVI. The Jacobins within the Convention, also known as the 'Mountain', argued that 'Louis Capet' was a citizen guilty of treason; their opposition, the 'Girondins', whose label denoted men closer in sympathy to the concern for political and economic stability among the upper bourgeoisie of Bordeaux, capital of the Gironde, sought to placate the rest of Europe by considering a sentence of exile or mercy. The Convention narrowly agreed with the Jacobin argument, and Louis went to the guillotine on 21 January 1793. One effect of this regicide was the expansion of the enemy coalition to include Britain and Spain.[32] News of the execution of Louis XVI created deep divisions across the country, even among Frenchmen far away. Bruny d'Entrecasteaux's expedition had been sent to Australia in 1791 in search of the missing explorer La Pérouse. Its leader dead, the malnourished and homesick expedition straggled into Java in October 1793 to learn of events earlier in the year. A violent division emerged between the expedition's new leader, the royalist d'Auribeau, and the naturalist Labillardière, in the 1760s a classmate in Alençon of Jacques Hébert, now a prominent Enragé militant in Paris.[33]

As the military situation deteriorated in the early months of 1793 it was the frontier regions of ethnic and linguistic minorities – Flamands, Basques, Catalans, Provençaux, Alsaciens – who bore the brunt of foreign invasion. From Bayonne to Lille, frontier populations faced deadly choices about which side was likely to win. Nor was depredation the exclusive preserve of invading troops given licence to exact a heavy toll on republican France. In devout frontier areas such as Lorraine and the Roussillon, the anti-clerical behaviour of urban French troops was as destructive as that of those from whom they were supposedly defending them.[34]

The deteriorating military situation created a less tolerant and inclusive attitude to ethnic and linguistic difference. The willingness of the National Assembly to have decrees translated into minority languages, indeed, the heart of the revolutionary principle that people from whatever part of the nation were fellow citizens, dissipated before the certainty of legislators and army officers that minority languages were those of 'backward' peoples. Some went so far as to call for a national uniform: in 1792 an imaginary voyage across France expressed the hope that

> sooner or later the Revolution will lead to the benefit of a national cos-
> tume, and that the traveler, in passing from one department to another,
> will no longer believe that he is among different people ... This variety of
> dress is truly unconstitutional ... With regard to clothing, the first thing
> that is said is 'there is a Cauchois', 'there is a Basque'.[35]

Before 1789, naturalization of foreigners had been both costly and rare, less than fifty per year. After the outbreak of war in 1792, the prospect of citizenship for foreigners not only became more attractive and easy, but it also became more dangerous for foreigners to be in France at all. Along the borders, tens of thousands of French, Spanish, Italians and others had regularly moved across territorial lines as part of ancient economic itineraries: these shepherds, harvesters, traders and smugglers were now more likely to be under surveillance.[36] On the borders of the east and south, the ebb and flow of the battles between revolutionary and coalition armies exposed people to the necessity of a choice which could be fatal. In Verdun (Meuse), a group of young women, dressed in white and bedecked with flowers, presented the keys of the town to the Prussians in 1792; when republican troops retook the city later that year they were found and guillotined.[37]

While principles of popular sovereignty were never applied in the professional army, the detachments of volunteers chose their own officers of all levels in ceremonies of exuberant patriotism. Their revolutionary zeal was not always a substitute for military training. In the south of the department of the Aude, from where the fighting with the Spanish army around Perpignan could be seen and heard, the former seigneur turned 'patriot' Antoine Viguier was unimpressed by the volunteers: 'The officers who have been chosen by their companies know no more about military matters than they do the Koran. The soldiers have no experience, they spend the whole day scouting the river-banks for frogs.'[38] Like that of volunteers across the country, the enthusiasm of these volunteers from the Aude was to be sorely tested after the declaration of war on Spain on 7 March 1793. The new Committee of Public Safety ordered the formation of a legion of 'Braconniers montagnards' (literally 'poachers from the mountains') from the districts of Quillan and Lagrasse. Resplendent in brown and green uniforms, these 1,800 men were specifically charged with guarding the gorges leading from the Cerdagne and Capcir down the valley of the Aude. As the military situation in the Roussillon rapidly deteriorated, this 'Légion des Corbières' was dispatched south, much to the chagrin of most of its soldiers, who had assumed they would never be too far away from home to help with the coming harvest.[39] Across the country, volunteers exhibited a similar preparedness to enrol in the army which was equally matched by a desire to defend their own *pays*.

By March 1793 revolutionary France was at war with Austria, Prussia and Spain, and Britain was preparing a naval blockade. As the external military crisis worsened with the widening of the war in early 1793, most of the Convention swung behind the Jacobins' emergency proposals. The imperatives of creating mass support for the defence of the Republic pushed the Convention into egalitarian legislation concerning the armed forces. In February 1793 the Convention voted the law of *amalgame*, a merging of the old line regiments with new volunteer units, to resolve problems between 'professional soldiers' (from old line regiments) and the new 'volunteers' which had often resulted in confrontations. Generals and commanding officers would henceforth be directly chosen by government and for under-officers, the principle of election was enthusiastically adopted.

On 24 February the *levée des 300,000* was decreed of all males between the ages of 18 and 40 who were unmarried or were widowers without children. While in March a decree accorded soldiers the right to marry without the express permission of their commanding officer, this did not then exempt them from service. By the following July, the recruitment had produced around 150,000 men, well short of the target. In practice the *levée* was not equitable. The Convention had authorized the use of *remplaçants* whereby a man who was designated for service could buy someone else to serve in his stead. There were widespread allegations that the sons of the wealthy thereby evaded recruitment. Through 1793, the government was forced to turn again and again to the civilian population with repeated demands for recruits.[40]

Between March and May 1793 the Convention placed executive powers in a Committee of Public Safety and policing powers with a Committee of General Security, and acted to supervise the army through 'deputies on mission'. It passed decrees declaring *émigrés* 'civilly dead', provided for public relief and placed controls on grain and bread prices. An ambitious decree of 19 March 1793 set out the parameters of a new policy for poor relief. Assistance payments were henceforth to be treated as 'a national debt', money was to be disbursed at a rate related to the daily wage level in the department, and cantonal agencies were to be set up to supervise its distribution. On 28 June this was extended by a decree detailing the pensions to be paid to abandoned children, the children of the poor and to *vieillards* and *indigents*, a natural extension of the previous measure which laid out the basis of the Revolutionary welfare state. Neither law was ever put fully into effect; they may be seen as a statement of intent but not as practical measures that brought relief to the poor.

On 14 March 1793, the Convention decreed that for the duration of war those bakers, carters and drivers who could provide evidence that they were engaged in servicing or provisioning the armies should be exempted from service. Then the law of 2 April 1793 extended the privilege of exemption to another group of workers whose aptitudes were desperately needed elsewhere: those making guns and powder for the war effort. Not surprisingly, specific amendments to eligibility for military service provided the would-be conscript with useful loopholes (for example, marriage, self-mutilation) and local officialdom with the temptation of corruption (for example, the issuing of fake medical or birth certificates).

In other places there was outrage that other categories of citizens – particularly constitutional clergy and local officials – were exempt, or that there was a ballot at all. In Neulise (Loire), for example, armed youths who gathered for the conscription ballot conducted their own choice for the 15 men the commune had to supply: the constitutional priest and 14 bourgeois 'patriots' who were seen to have profited most from the Revolution.[41] In Labécède-Lauragais (Aude), the proceedings had to be suspended on 26 April when 'a great tumult erupted with some shouting that everyone had to go or no-one'.[42] In Seysses, south of Toulouse, a man waiting to have his confession heard on 8 April, the day of the ballot, reported that a large crowd had appeared of

> citizens armed with sabres, guns and other weapons who were shouting that they should kill all the patriots. When the *curé* went outside to send them away, they continued, shouting even louder that, since by means of conscription [the government] was exposing citizens to the risk of death, people should exterminate the patriots.

The departmental administration responded by sending 200 national guardsmen to restore order.[43] At the other end of the country, in Hesdin (Pas-de-Calais), where anxiety about looming war with Austria was acute, the government official was almost lynched by villagers.[44]

Even where there was general support for the Revolution, as in the village of Gabian (Hérault), conscription and the expansion of the war translated other conflicts into counter-revolution. In 1791–93 a group of local men and women from families opposed to the reforms to the Church committed 30 thefts, often with violence, as they lived on the run. They enjoyed taunting the revolutionary officials who attempted to arrest them. After the execution of Louis XVI and the invasion of the south by the Spanish army in 1793 they openly threatened that the latter 'would make the patriots of Gabian dance ... that they would join the Spaniards to help them make them dance and cut their throats ... things are going well in the Vendée'.[45]

In the region of 'the Vendée' in western France to which they referred the levy of 300,000 was the pretext for massive armed rebellion and civil war. The Revolution had brought the peasants of the Vendée no obvious benefits. Heavier State taxes were collected more rigorously by local bourgeois who also monopolized new offices and municipal councils, and bought up Church lands in 1791.[46] Successive Assemblies failed to reform the distinctive long-term tenancies of the west, treating them as just another form of property. Above all, the Revolution's secular reforms to the Church antagonized the devout. The rural community had responded to these accumulating grievances in 1790–92 by humiliating constitutional clergy elected by 'active' citizens, by boycotting local and national elections, and by repeated instances of hostility to local office-holders. The conscription decree of March 1793 served to focus their hatreds, for the 'patriot' officials who enforced it were exempt from the ballot.

The first targets of the insurgents were local officials, who were assaulted and humiliated, and small urban centres such as Machecoul (Loire-Inférieure), where more than 150 'patriots' were killed, mostly on the twenty-fourth in a day of vengeful killing, but also after popular 'trials' which dragged out over more than a month. Here was a case where rebels and patriots lived side by side: the killers knew their victims. The two sides were a broadly similar cross-section of this small town of about 4,000 people – artisans, professional people, merchants, officials – but they had been increasingly at odds since 1789, particularly over the ecclesiastical reforms.[47] In general, as shown by Claude Petitfrère's analysis of some 5,000 rebels who later applied for pensions under the Restoration government, the Vendéan rebels were rural and small-town people: 63 per cent were peasants, 15 per cent were textile workers and 19 per cent small traders and artisans. Bourgeois were virtually absent.[48]

The groups of rebels which formed in the regions in revolt were significant from a military point of view, numbering between 20,000 and 40,000. The terrain of the *bocage* suited sporadic ambushes and retreat, and exacerbated a vicious cycle of killing and reprisals by both sides convinced of the perfidiousness of the other. General Turreau de Garambouville was commander in chief of the Army of the West, and became notorious for his *colonnes infernales*. In his memoirs, published in 1794, he outlined how the rebels, highly adept with guns, used the terrain to their advantage:

> they only fight when they want, and where they want. Their skill in the use of guns is such that no other known people, no matter how warlike or clever they might be, fires so many shots as the hunter of Loroux or the poacher of the woodlands. ... Their battle formation is the form of a crescent, and their flanks thus pointed are made up of their best sharpshooters, of soldiers who never fire a shot without first aiming, and who almost never miss a target at a reasonable distance. ... they withdraw so rapidly that it is very difficult to reach them, especially since the terrain almost never allows for the use of cavalry. They scatter, they escape over the fields, woods, bushes, knowing all the paths, byways, glens, passes, knowing all the obstacles that oppose their flight and how to avoid them.[49]

A central reason for the merciless repression of the Vendéan insurgents was that they were seen to have stabbed the Republic in the back at the very moment when it was most vulnerable. A more deliberate act of collaboration occurred at the other end of the country when on 17 April the Spanish army crossed into France, guided by men from the little town of St-Laurent-de-Cerdans, high in the Pyrenees. Until the battle of Peyrestortes on 17 September 1793, the Spanish invasion was virtually unchecked through the south of the department of the Pyrénées-Orientales. In the chaotic year which followed, when the fate of the Revolution was fought out in the region, virtually all of the 450 able-bodied men of St-Laurent, with hundreds of others from nearby villages, fought alongside Spanish troops in the 'Légion du Vallespir'. The Spanish advanced with the active collaboration of much of the population of the district of Céret, which stretches along the border: municipal councils were formed in 36 of the district's 42 communes during the occupation.[50]

Despite bitter grievances expressed against the privileged in their own community in the *cahier* of 1789, the distinctive economic and social structures of St-Laurent meant that there were few obvious material gains for most people from the legislation of the early revolutionary years. Only a small minority of non-privileged Laurentins owned more than a house and perhaps a small garden and, in any case, seigneurial exactions had been very light, except for a heavy *lods et ventes* of one-sixth on land sales. Tenant farmers were especially vulnerable to their landlords, from whom they rented directly on short-term leases, usually four years, paid in kind. The Revolution left these contracts untouched. The hostility of St-Laurent to revolutionary Church reform stemmed from the general nature of the diocese and its clergy. The diocese retained its special relationship with the Papacy in place long before the annexation of the Roussillon in 1659; the articles of the Gallican Church proclaimed in 1682 had never been taught. The constitutional priest was referred to as 'Démon, Diable, Schismatique'. There were cries of 'To the devil with the Nation!': 'our *curé* said to us from the pulpit that those who recognize the new bishop and the new priests would be schismatics. Those who have the least communication with them must therefore be massacred'. In 1793 most in the community now looked to Spain to restore old religious structures and, importantly in this centre of metallurgy, allow them access to desperately needed Spanish charcoal.

*   *   *

The nation was in grave danger of internal collapse and external defeat. The military challenge was met by an extraordinary mobilization of the nation's resources and repression of opponents. The Convention passed emergency decrees, such as those declaring *émigrés* 'civilly dead', and placed controls on grain and bread prices. The Convention was confronted with a general crisis brought to a head with the expansion of the war after Louis' execution. In March it introduced a more elaborate system of sending 'représentants en mission' to the army than had occasionally been the case up until then. They were chosen for their reliability and resoluteness: of the more than 400 chosen across the next two years, almost half were Montagnards; three-quarters were regicides.[51]

Despite these measures, by mid-summer 1793 the Revolution faced its greatest crisis, which was at the same time military, social and political. Enemy troops were on French soil in the northeast, southeast and southwest and, internally, the great revolt in the Vendée absorbed a major part of the Republic's army. These threats were aggravated by the hostile response of departmental administrations to the purge of a number of Girondin deputies in June.

In May the Paris Commune ordered the formation of a paid militia of 20,000 *sans-culottes* which surrounded the Convention and compelled the reluctant deputies to meet its wishes for leading Girondin deputies to be arrested.[52] In much of the country the intimidation and purging of the Convention was seen as an inexcusable affront to the principle of national sovereignty. While perhaps 60 of the 83 departmental administrations protested formally, and some went as far as joining forces in what came to be known as 'federalist' rebel movements against the authority of the Convention, in countless villages and country towns there was a similar sense of outrage. The 'federalist' revolts were united only by the coincidence of their timing; however, they all drew on strong regional traditions, as in the hinterland of Marseille, where villages such as Lourmarin (Vaucluse) followed the example of their local metropolis.[53] Typical were the sentiments expressed on 29 June in a special general Assembly held in Tuchan (Aude) to consider a circular from Paris. It then declared that

> a small section of the Republic has threatened liberty in general and has dared to dictate laws to those from whom it should receive them; that this town of Paris, formerly the capital of despotism, cannot make up its mind to release from its grip a domination which has become second nature to it; that this same town of Paris ... gathers into itself the enormous taxes with which the other departments are burdened ... the Republic being united must act as one to force this superb city to do its duty, and to punish it when it rebels.

The deliberation was passed by 'un murmure général' and signed.[54] After the movement collapsed, both communities found ways to exculpate themselves from the charge of complicity, although in Lourmarin the price paid was a purge of the local officials who had thus compromised themselves.

The Convention acquiesced in draconian measures – such as surveillance committees, preventive detention and controls on civil liberties – necessary to secure the Republic to a point where a new democratic, republican and libertarian Constitution, voted in June 1793, could be implemented. The Constitution was remarkable for its guarantees of social rights and popular control over an Assembly elected by direct, universal male suffrage:

> Article 21. Public aid is a sacred debt. Society owes subsistence to unfortunate citizens, either by obtaining work for them, or by providing means of existence to those who are unable to work.
>
> Article 22. Instruction is the necessity of all men. Society must further the progress of public reason with all its power, and make instruction available to all citizens ...
>
> Article 35. When the government violates the rights of the people, insurrection is the most sacred of rights and the most indispensable of duties for the people and for each portion of the people.[55]

The referendum on the Constitution was the first direct vote in French history. The results (1.8 million 'yes' votes to 17,000) were announced at the 'Fête de l'Unité' on 10 August, the first anniversary of the overthrow of the monarchy. The final figure for 'yes' votes was probably closer to 2 million of the approximately 6 million eligible males. Between 34 and 38 per cent of eligible men voted; however, rates ranged from fewer than 10 per cent in much of Brittany to 33 per cent in Paris and 40–50 per cent along the Rhine and in parts of the Massif Central.[56]

The referendum was conducted in July–August, in former churches, meeting halls and covered markets. Occurring as it did at much the same time as the votes on division of common land – in which landowning widows were eligible to vote – there were many occasions where women assumed that for this too they were eligible. As the first occasion in which there was a direct expression of will, many of the meetings took on the guise of deliberative assemblies, in which the referendum was translated if necessary, discussed, even modified, before voting. In some areas the voting took the form of a festival: at St-Nicholas-de-la-Grave (Haute-Garonne), at the confluence of the Tarn and Garonne rivers, some of those present were moved by a speech into 'transports of the most sublime enthusiasm ... their eyes swimming with tears of joy, threw themselves into each others' arms to share a fraternal kiss'. Women insisted on being able to take the civic oath and vote, and the men agreed:

> all citizens and citizenesses intermingled, holding each other by the hand, as a sign of unity forming a single chain, and to the sound of drums, fifes and bells danced a farandole as they went through all the streets of the town, mixing with the sound of the instruments the singing of the holy hymns of Liberty.[57]

At Lamballe (Côtes-du-Nord), similarly, 'women swarmed into the assembly to offer their assent to the Constitution'. Elsewhere, 343 women voted at Laon and 175 women and 163 children at Pontoise. In Collioure, a gathering of 135 citizens (about 30 per cent of adult men) voted, unanimously, to approve the Constitution after it had been translated into Catalan.[58]

The referendum on the Constitution of 1793 resembled the gatherings that had drawn up the *cahiers de doléances* in 1789 in that the voting occurred in the midst of collective gatherings in which men, and often women, discussed the text of a document, in many cases after it had been translated from French into the local language or dialect.[59] The presence of women at the referendum, as in the elections to the Estates-General in 1789, suggests widespread assumptions that the right to vote represented a household rather than individual vote, a reflection of the Ancien Régime practice of censuses by *feu* or household.[60]

Such was the degree of individual freedom guaranteed in the Constitution, however, that the National Convention suspended its implementation until the peace, lest counter-revolutionaries abuse its freedoms. Once the euphoria of the celebratory vote had dissipated, people in communities across the nation were again confronted by the hard realities of conscription and requisitioning, the absence of priests and the likelihood of death in a war whose duration they could not know. What did seem likely, terrifyingly so, was that the combined weight of the European coalition would prevail, and with it the opportunity for revenge by its *émigré* battalions.

# 7
# The Experience of Terror, 1793–94

There are few crises in modern history comparable to that of the summer of 1793, when a revolutionary nation wracked by civil war and dissent was evidently about to be overrun by a coalition of its neighbours. The prime objective of the Jacobin Committee of Public Safety elected by the Convention on 27 July was to implement the laws and controls deemed necessary to win the war and to strike 'Terror' into the hearts of counter-revolutionaries. This period of draconian martial law always had another aim, however: the 'regeneration' of a citizenry worthy of the new Republic. The degree of success the government would have in both of these projects has often been recounted. Less accessible but equally dramatic, however, was the lived experience of working people during this year.

To mark the epochal significance of the new age the proclamation of the Republic on 22 September 1792 was retrospectively dated the first day of the Year I of the republican era. The new calendar introduced on 5 October 1793 combined the rationality of decimal measurement (12 months of 30 days, each with 3 *décadi* of 10 days, plus 5 *sans-culottides*) with a repudiation of the Gregorian calendar. Saints-days and religious festivals were replaced by names drawn from plants, the seasons, Greek and Roman history, work implements and the virtues. The calendar was imposed across the country, but would always co-exist uneasily with the ancient rhythm of Sunday worship, the calendar of the church year and weekly markets. At times it was simply scorned. In the village of St-Vincent, north of Le Puy (Haute-Loire), the patriot priest rose on a *décadi* to read a paean to the goddess of reason when the women present rose as one, turned their backs on the altar of liberty and the priest, lifted their skirts and exposed their buttocks as a sign of contempt. The priest complained bitterly to the authorities of these 'gestes gigantesques et obscènes', but the practice spread to other villages.[1] Across most of the country people commonly used both calendars, for different purposes; it was the replacement of Sundays by the *décadi* which was most resented.

First and foremost among the Convention's priorities, however, was how to build and provision a large enough army to save the Republic. A common grievance in the *cahiers* had been the 'blood tax' of regular ballots conscripting militia for six years. The social inequities in the system – for nobles were among those exempted – led to its abolition early in the Revolution. By 1792, however, it was apparent that calls for volunteers were insufficient. The decree of 23 August 1793 proclaimed a *levée en masse*:

> Henceforth, until the enemies have been driven from the territory of the Republic, all the French are in permanent requisition for army service. The young men shall go to battle; the married men shall forge arms and transport provisions; the women shall make tents and clothes, and shall serve in the hospitals; the children shall turn old linen into lint; the old men shall repair to the public places, to stimulate the courage of the warriors and preach the unity of the Republic and the hatred of kings.

While the decree's language was fulsome, the Convention intended to raise a huge army and to call for unity rather than conscript every available man. The *levée en masse* in effect returned to the conscription ballot, with exemptions for those in administrative positions.[2] This time there would be no possibility of those wealthy enough being able to buy a *remplaçant*. No limit was stipulated to the length of service. There were thus good reasons – the exemption of married men from conscription – for *de facto* couples to marry and for people to marry younger: compared with a pre-revolutionary annual average of 240,000 marriages, there were over 325,000 in both 1793 and 1794.

As a corollary, the Committee and its thousands of agents across the country were preoccupied by the need to provision and pay for an army of hundreds of thousands of men. This necessarily placed the administration in the position of requisitioning foodstuffs and war materials in every department. The law of 28 August 1793 placed at the government's disposal all the soil in the country which might contain deposits of saltpetre. Army commanders were authorized to procure the food stocks they needed, as well as supplies of clothing, arms, equipment and transport, from the peoples of occupied territories. Besides these seizures, French agents were to impose taxes and war contributions and to force local communities to contribute towards French military levies.

In October the Convention ordered the requisitioning of 40,000 military horses, holding village and town councils responsible for finding animals of adequate size and strength. Attempts to requisition horses (or carts, mules or oxen) were often met with recalcitrance from peasants who deeply resented having to part with their most treasured possessions. In the canton of Ribiers (Hautes-Alpes) a census reported 'thirty-nine horses or mares and 201 mules used for work in the countryside and usually also for ploughing, 322 donkeys for transporting manure, wood and soil, and thirteen carts used for the same purposes'.[3] In general, however, the villagers complied. The municipality of Fabrezan (Aude) was astonished that even tiny handcarts were being taken from them, as well as all its young men, but accepted this 'new requisition that the municipality will execute as much as is within its power'. Less palatable were the levies of grain. In nearby Villesèque, after noting that all its young men had volunteered for the army except three, who were now enrolled in the coast guard at Leucate, the council added that 'despite the many house visits we have made, we have only found fourteen cooking-pots, which we will send you'.[4]

A realization of the urgency of mobilizing people across the country renewed temporarily the earlier practice of translating key decrees into local languages.[5] Conscripts from the same region were given basic instruction in French and scattered through the army to reduce the temptation of collective flight. Soldiering aroused cases among young men far from home of what army doctors described as 'nostalgie'. This homesickness or *mal du pays* had well-known symptoms: sad appearance, apathy, lack of appetite or sleep and solitariness. While Bretons were notoriously vulnerable, no one was immune. It was the one medical condition for which the commander of the Armée du Nord was prepared to countenance leave.[6]

Mass propaganda, such as the *Le Père Duchesne*, was distributed to the army, and 'deputies on mission' from the Convention guaranteed swift retribution to hesitant officers and unwilling rank-and-file. This did not prevent endless complaints about disgusting food, ill-fitting uniforms and poor weaponry. During the winter of 1793–94 a soldier wrote from the southeast that his battalion 'is in the greatest need, just like real *sans-culottes*, since from first to last we are without shoes, tormented by scabies, and eaten by vermin'. A nearby battalion reported that it was surviving by eating roots.[7] Soldiers' letters home were also full of remarks about revolutionary zeal and their commitment to the *patrie*. The political culture of the Republic implied new relationships with authority. In August 1793, Laurent Peyrot, a peasant from Vermenton (Yonne) wrote to the departmental administration asking for financial help because of a wound he had suffered at the battle of Neerwinden on 18 March: this 'defender of liberty' felt 'justly entitled' to aid, and assured the administration that 'the laurel which he has reaped by pouring his blood for liberty will shed its leaves upon your heads'. The language of the officials is similarly revealing, their positive response referring to 'justice' and their 'most sacred duty' towards those 'who have shed their blood for the defence of the *patrie*'. The creation of mass republican armies, with 'line' and volunteer units now fused, had engendered a new military culture which was a microcosm of the 'regenerated' society the Convention anticipated.[8]

The basis on which war pensions were calculated was dramatically reformed in 1793. The amount paid to a wounded soldier, unable to continue his service and severely incapacitated in civilian life, was now made proportionate to the gravity of his wound, and not to the rank he held in the army: those soldiers who were rendered unfit for further action were to receive 15 *sous* per day; those who had lost a hand or an arm 20 *sous*; and those who had lost the use of two of their limbs 500 *livres* per year. In this, the rank-and-file were accorded equality of status with officers: a law of 6 June 1793 provided that, because serious wounds necessarily ended all possibility of a man's promotion in the army, all seriously wounded soldiers should automatically be promoted to the rank of *sous-lieutenant honoraire* and be rewarded with a lieutenant's pension. Pensions for war widows were also made more generous and guaranteed at a level determined by the length of their husband's service. Further, late in 1793, the same benefits due to volunteers and their dependents were extended to those who worked for the armies in an ancillary capacity, such as carters, grooms, blacksmiths and gunsmiths. Finally, by the law of 13 Prairial Year II/2 June 1794, pensions for war widows and their dependents were to be given at a flat rate that would guarantee a basic level of well-being to all.

The Convention had to overcome the odds of fighting on numerous fronts at a time of internal division and civil war, and a good deal of despair: perhaps 35,000 soldiers (6 per cent of the total) had deserted in the first half of 1793, and many others reacted to deficiencies in supplies by theft of local produce. The March 1793 levy of 300,000 men had resulted in the department of the Puy-de-Dôme furnishing 95 per cent of its share; but while only 12 per cent of those conscripted under the *levée en masse* in August failed to register, it is estimated that only 60 per cent finally joined their regiments. Young men either failed to show up for the draft, deserted en route after being conscripted, or deserted while in camp.[9] Common was the complaint in September 1793 from Labécède-Lauragais (Aude), on the western flank of the Montagne Noire, of deserters hiding in forests during the day and making exactions on locals at night.[10] By early in 1794, nevertheless, there was an army of at least 600,000 men, supported by a thorough-going attempt to mass produce arms and munitions, and, whatever the desire of volunteers and conscripts to return home once they had had their fill of army life, the ranks were imbued with a sense of service to the *patrie*.[11]

The referendum on the Constitution of 1793 coincided with a series of Jacobin measures designed to win over the rural masses, a necessary condition for military success. The decree of 25 August 1792 was now pushed further in the direction of a complete abolition of seigneurialism. From 17 July 1793, former seigneurs were left with only those 'rents and charges which are purely on land and non-feudal'. The definitive resolution of the fate of the seigneurial régime had taken 4 years of revolt, legal action, foot-dragging and refusal to pay. It was the most significant change in the lives of French people during the Revolution, and one which changed forever the economic structures and social and political relationships of the countryside.

There were occasional cases where seigneurial dues were paid after this date – in the district of Arbois (Jura) as late as the following January – but in most places the autumn of 1793 was a time for celebration, often by *auto-da-fé* of feudal titles and other symbols. In the heart of the region of the 'wild federations' of 1789–90, at Salviac (Lot), for example, the feudal registers were burnt near a liberty tree with the inscription: 'It is here that, on 1 November of the Year II of the one and indivisible French Republic, the People cleared itself of dues and all feudal rights by setting alight the usurpations and tyrannical acts of the former seigneurs'.[12] The requirement that seigneurial titles be destroyed gave surveillance committees and municipalities the pretext for searching the houses of former seigneurs at will.

The Jacobin legislation sought to make a distinction between seigneurial dues and commercial rents which was not so sharp in reality: there were to be protracted issues in some areas over whether particular clauses in leases were one or the other. Nor did the decrees address the grievances of share-croppers and tenant farmers, for it was assumed that the value of seigneurial levies and the tithe were now retained by the landowner, who now entered a purely commercial relationship with the lessee. Most controversially, where the tithe had been paid by the tenant as part of a lease, the proprietor was permitted to add its value to the rent. Among a chorus of complaints, that from the justice of the peace of Charroux (Vienne) was typical:

> the owners of lands on which dues used to be paid are claiming half their value from their tenants; the latter refuse on the basis that the suppression of the former nobles' dues is to their benefit … it is only the rich, say the tenants, for whom the Constitution is advantageous – everything for the rich, nothing for us, we are still poor.[13]

Subsequent consideration by the Convention did nothing to satisfy such grievances.

During the autumn of 1793 deputies on mission in the southwest were quickly made aware of the sharp disappointment experienced by sharecroppers that landlords had been able to increase rents by adding the value of the former tithe. The deputy Roux-Fazillac, sent to the Dordogne and the Charente, reported of an 'infinity of complaints' and noted that the share-croppers were 'the only French citizens who had gained nothing from the Revolution, even though they and their children fought to defend it like other citizens'. A decree of 1 Brumaire Year II/22 October 1793 sought to meet the sharecroppers' grievances by decreeing that those with verbal leases were no longer required to pay the 'neo-tithe' or any form of seigneurial due, but uncertainty remained over whether this included cases where rents had simply been increased.[14]

Other measures taken by the Convention to alleviate land-hunger proved inconsequential in practice. On 3 June and 25 July the Convention had passed laws seizing *émigré* property, and had then resolved to pass further legislation to make it more accessible to the poor. The law of 13 September 1793, giving the poor interest-free loans of 500 *livres* for 20 years, seems to have been stringently applied only where popular pressure for sales coincided with official determination, for even small lots were usually sold for more than anticipated and officials had to be prepared to further subdivide. In the district of Tours, there were 112 sales; in the Ardèche an estimated 109.[15] By the end of 1793 some 1,546 landless families around Versailles had been allotted an *arpent* (about one acre) of land from the former royal domain. Never large enough to be viable, these plots were almost all to be sold within a few years.[16] There were extensive discussions in September on the possible limitation of the size of tenant farmer holdings to 400 *arpents* (about 165 ha); nothing seems to have come of them.

On 14 August 1792 the Legislative Assembly had issued a brief decree directing communes to divide non-forested common land. On 10 June 1793 the Convention replaced this law with one which was more radical and contentious, one of the most ambitious attempts of the revolutionary government to meet the needs of the rural poor. The legislation empowered a municipality to convene a general Assembly of all inhabitants in order to debate the division of non-wooded common land into equal plots. It required communes to proceed to a division if this was the wish of one-third of adult men; the land was then to be divided on the basis of an equal share to every man, woman and child. Because the law on commons directly involved women as heads of household, they sometimes assumed that they were among those eligible to vote. Hence, for example, in the Creuse, there were 65 women among the 360 voters at Pionnat and 21 of 60 at Cressat, and there are many other examples elsewhere.[17] On the other hand, former seigneurs who had previously invoked their 'right' of *triage* were excluded from the proceedings and a separate measure stipulated that common land might only be divided among the inhabitants of the village or section to which it belonged.

The law resolved some of the ambiguities inherent in the decree of 14 August 1792 and is often regarded as the corner stone of revolutionary agrarian legislation, remaining in force until 20 Thermidor Year X/8 August 1802. But would the interests of the rural poor best be secured by dividing common lands or by preserving them?[18] Debates about the substance of the decree polarized many communities. The commune of Seynes, east of Alès in the Gard, petitioned the Convention that, while

> monarchy, the clergy and the nobility have been abolished for ever, there are still large landowners to destroy (*abattre*), because it is at this very moment that their hands are becoming heavier on the poor people of the countryside. You have allowed the division of the commons, and these big landowners are making every effort to oppose it. Why won't you put a stop to their audacity?[19]

From St-Jory, north of Toulouse, in contrast, a group of farmers denounced to the Convention 'the illegal division of the grasslands of the commune, the crimes committed on the possessions of the former seigneurs, and the devastation of their forests'.[20]

The objectives of the decree were sharply attenuated by the fact that only a minority of communities possessed commons, that where they did exist many of the poor did not want them divided, and by the cost of surveyors' fees; many of the tiny portions quickly passed into the hands of better-off locals. Surveys of sales show that, for example, 29 of the 107 communes in the district of Châtillon (Côte-d'Or) had commons and perhaps 15 divided them. In the Somme, only 31 communes out of 958 finally divided their commons, in the Oise 149 of 734; in the Ardèche just 5 of 334 and in the Gard 18 of 385.[21] In general, the law had little application outside the areas north and northeast of Paris and parts of the south. In the district of Nancy, 34 of the 79 communes with commons were in favour of division, but ultimately only 12 divisions occurred. In the Gers, in contrast, only 27 of 286 were in favour; 135 communes did not even bother to respond. Sometimes the areas involved were tiny, even when all members of a family combined their shares: in Rousies (Nord), the 215 families each received 0.22 ha. In the Corbières, where land seizures had been endemic, it seems that the flock owners succeeded in keeping much of what remained of the commons as pastures: Ornaisons decided to keep about 275 ha for pasture and to divide the remaining 95.[22] Upland areas were largely untouched because of the requirements of pasturing, except in communal forests where a further decree of 25 Nivôse Year II/15 January 1794 extended the egalitarian principle of 'par tête d'habitant' to *affouages* (wood-cutting rights).[23]

Everywhere, debates on the commons revealed the anger of local administrations as well as revolutionary legislators at the environmental damage in many parts of France as the poor cleared and cultivated these 'wastelands', especially on hillsides. On 4 June 1793 the National Convention decreed that 'communes may not fell or sell any trees on land belonging to it without authorization', following a detailed description and justification.[24] On 15 July 1793 *commissaire* Bedegis wrote to the Minister of the Interior from Dieppe (Seine-Inférieure) that

> during the trip I've just made, I heard a general outrage expressed against the depredations which are occurring daily in the national forests, particularly those of Arques and Eawy, and in the forests of *émigrés*. … The administration has issued strict decrees about this, but as the execution of these decrees is in the hands of municipalities which are almost all composed of labourers, and as it is labourers who are doing the damage, one can see that their implementation is not all it might be.[25]

From Condé-sur-Sarthe (Orne) came the complaint on 10 Frimaire/ 1 December that a battalion of volunteers from Argentan, 45 km to the north, was camped on the property of the *émigré* Vaucelles and 'every day cutting huge quantities of all kinds of trees, walnuts, oaks, elms, alders, plums'.[26]

Despite the Jacobins' preparedness to restrict individual freedoms in the national interest, in the end they had had no more success on this matter than their predecessors. In a report from the southern department of the Aude on 17 Frimaire Year II/8 December 1793, the Jacobin official Cailhava fulminated in his distinctively blunt fashion:

> The shortage of wood is felt all along the coastline, and especially in Narbonne, due either to the drying up of the soil, or to the disdain that the inhabitants of Narbonne show for all those trees that produce only shade ... It is enough to drive you into a holy rage when, under a burning sky, you see destroyed in one minute the parasol that nature has spent fifty years perfecting. ...
>
> The terrain of the municipalities that make up the district of Lagrasse were once covered with wood thickets, mostly holm oak; but, in the Revolution, each individual used them up as though they were cabbages from his garden. Moreover, coal having become highly expensive, the charcoal-burners used their neighbours' possessions all the less sparingly for that; the villagers who remove the bark from the holm oak in order to sell it to the tanners were no more sparing; add to that the shepherds who prefer to take their herds to the youngest thickets, and who fell the tall trees so that their animals can enjoy the tender leaves that grow on the stalks, and you will agree that it takes much less than this to destroy the largest forests.[27]

The Ancien Régime monarchy had long encouraged the draining of marshes as a way of increasing the land available for cereal production (as it had the clearing of so-called wastelands). Now a decree of 14 Frimaire Year II/5 December 1793 declared that not only marshes, but also all *étangs* (lagoons and ponds) would be drained. The measure appealed to the government as a part of the *levée en masse* of the nation's resources; moreover, most *étangs* had been Church or noble property. Local populations, more aware of the benefits of the ponds than the government, objected to what the measure would mean for fishing, irrigation, the milling of grain and the availability of reeds for roof-thatching, but close to Paris many ponds were indeed drained.[28]

On 5–6 September *sans-culottes* invaded the National Convention demanding price controls. The Convention acted to meet *sans-culottes* demands by decreeing the 'Maximum Général' of 29 September which pegged wages and the prices of 39 commodities.[29] It was the Maximum more than any other law which created a divide between the urban population and farmers, especially in the grain-producing areas in the north. Many rural producers, particularly those who produced for the market, refused to sell their produce at set prices: as the Société des Amis du Peuple of Chartres complained in Floréal Year II, 'even though the Revolution has made the fortunes of seven out of eight large tenants and farmers, most of them ... act only like true aristocrats and egotists'.

One farmer from Lozère exclaimed under interrogation that 'he would rather give his wheat to the pigs and other animals than to sell it under the Maximum'. The bloodiest conflict erupted in the hamlet of Les Loges (Yonne) where a family of farmers engaged in a protracted gunfight with troops and national guards, killing five and wounding 25, before being burned to death in their farmhouse. Troops found a ton of grain and a ton of flour buried on the farm. Poorer members of the rural community, dependent for work on large farmers such as these, were often united with them by despair over the absence of priests and the threat to food supplies: on 8–9 Ventôse Year II/27–28 February 1794, a huge crowd led by two large farmers in Rabastens (Tarn) shouted 'Bread and religion, down with cockades, down with the patriots!' before seizing the granaries and returning the grain to the farmers.[30]

The demands of war, a modest harvest and the unwillingness of many large farmers to make produce readily available at set prices made the position of urban and rural wage-earners precarious. In Floréal Year II/April 1794 a letter from St-Quentin (Aisne) to the Jacobin Club in Paris described the destroyed villages and farms, and 'the pain we feel every day seeing our streets full of poor unfortunates asking us for bread, bread, bread'.[31] Like the department capital, Laon, the experience of St-Quentin during the military crisis was one of fear and hunger: these were towns whose wealth had collapsed with the end of clerical orders and Church wealth, leaving behind chronic unemployment and food shortages. At the same time it was caught between an encroaching enemy army and incessant demands to supply food for Paris. Laon buried 112 women and 1,151 men in the Year II, most of the latter wounded soldiers who had died in hospital.[32]

Some of the deputies on mission, such as Paganel in the Aveyron and Romme in the Dordogne, established food stores and rationing as a way of avoiding the worst consequences of food shortages. In the towns of the southwest the bread ration declined from 24 to 16 ounces for men between 1 March and 1 June, for women from 16 to 8 (except for pregnant women), and for children from 16 to 4.[33] The Committee of Public Safety was particularly aware of the desperate shortage of food in Paris, reminding the departmental administration of the Orne on 25 ventôse Year II/16 March 1794 that 'while Paris fights internal and external enemies with as much courage as constancy', they should respond by sending butter, eggs and vegetables.[34] That departmental administration had other concerns as well: 204 of the 2,610 men requisitioned in the Orne had failed to appear.[35]

The shortage of foodstuffs created pressures for extraordinary measures. In February 1794, the seizure of a quantity of eggs and butter that the wife of an Ancien Régime judge had procured in the countryside rather than on the open market led the town council of Bourg to decree that in future half the profit of sales of such seizures would go to the informer and the other half to the poor.[36] The records of the councils of country towns like Bourg are a litany of measures to ensure that foodstuffs were sold publicly rather than on the black market, that the Maximum was respected, that groups did not mill around market stalls.

Jacobin social welfare policy was as bold as it was impossible to implement in a context of war and emergency controls. On 22 Floréal Year II/12 May 1794 a *Grand Livre de Bienfaisance Nationale* was proposed as a means of ending destitution in the countryside (it was felt by many deputies that it was in the countryside that hardship and neglect were greatest) and sharing out more equitably the funds available for assistance. It was proposed that each department open a book containing the names of those who fell into certain categories of *pauvres* and for whom assistance was urgent; as a corollary, begging would become an offence. How the book might be resourced and implemented was not addressed.

A change in social practice was that, whereas children born outside marriage (about one in seven throughout the period) had commonly been left at the Charité or baptized as 'of an unknown father', under the Terror fewer were left at what was now the Humanité and such children were more likely to be recognized as 'issu des inclinations volontaires' of a particular man.[37] Social policy necessarily centred on the question of these *enfants trouvés*. Again, the collapse of Ancien Régime institutions forced the hand of the government, and responsibility for *enfants trouvés* reverted to the State: henceforth they were to be cared for by local authorities who agreed to recognize them as *les enfants naturels de la patrie*. There were increasing numbers of children being taken into care after 1792, partly as a result of larger numbers of widows and orphans as a consequence of revolutionary wars and of the effects of inflation on food prices.

Hospitals to care for the thousands of war wounded were established in towns near the frontiers. On 15 Vendémiaire Year II/7 October 1793 it was declared that the task of nursing in hospitals undertaken hitherto by nuns should now be performed by the laity, 'des citoyennes connues pour leur attachement à la République'. Those nuns who had previously been exempted from taking the oath of obedience to the State were now declared refractory and faced dismissal or imprisonment. Hospitals and governments alike had not made any contingency plans for caring for patients during the weeks that followed their departure. A few days later, the decree of 24 Vendémiaire/16 October prohibited almsgiving, a major source of income for hospitals under the Ancien Régime. On 23 Messidor/12 July 1794 all hospital property was nationalized and put up for sale in exactly the same way as lands confiscated from *émigrés*, making hospitals totally dependent on the State for resources.

\* \* \*

The image of the Terror as an authoritarian and doctrinaire régime unable to provide many of its citizens with personal security or the essentials of life is a common one. It is also doubly misleading. First, it misses all those villages and towns across the country where local officials were able to implement the controls necessary to meet military requisitions and to ensure an equitable distribution of scarce foodstuffs. Second, it ignores the ways in which men and women were able to manoeuvre for advantage, or even to disobey. Even though the Maximum was imposed on wages as well as consumer goods, farm labourers in many areas took advantage of the absence of able-bodied men in the armies to press for higher wages. Typical was the complaint from the district of Montpellier in Ventôse that 'the workers involved in agricultural labour form themselves into groups ('se coalisent'), threaten, aggress and force the landowner to pay a day's labour at a rate far above that fixed by the law'.

At critical moments of the harvest employers were highly vulnerable, while dock-workers and loggers on rivers could readily go slow. In Heudi-court and other communes of the Somme, labourers confronted farmers with demands that bags of wheat be added to their salaries. They were holding a placard reading: 'Unity is strength – to the harvester of good will – to harvest at that price – republicans have had enough. All citizens will come at two o'clock for a festival ... to dance around the tree of fraternity'.[38] In mid-June the justice of the peace of Durban (Aude) was complaining similarly of the parlous state of agriculture: 'because of the lack or exorbitant price of labour, the law of the *Maximum* of 29 September last (old style) is ignored by labourers, merchants and tradesmen'. Labourers once paid a *livre* or two for a day's work were now expecting five or six, or sitting back and letting crops spoil. As Jean-Louis Cros, now calling himself 'Rosemary' in line with the Jacobin cult of nature, put it, 'they would prefer to do nothing rather than work for the Maximum'.[39]

These labour movements were a continuation of ancient forms of collective action known as 'bacchanals', and they were still marked by a carnivalesque tone. Their incidence led the Convention to pass two decrees before the 1794 harvests: the Law of 11 Prairial Year II/30 May 1794 requisitioning citizens for harvests and setting wages and conditions, and the amnesty of 21 Messidor Year II/9 July 1794 freeing labourers held as suspects. In the district of St-Flour (Cantal), authorities conscripted a workforce of 1,000 harvesters and their families.[40]

Popular initiatives in organizing festivals and remodelling ancient rituals meshed with the Convention's encouragement of civic commemoration, although not always in the direction the Convention would have wished. Communes were expected to use the *fête décadaire* to celebrate the civic virtues in parallel fashion to the way the Church had previously celebrated mass. Some were elaborate affairs, as in Bourg in February 1794 where it was announced that, after cannon-fire at dawn, bells would summon the populace at 7 am. Young citizenesses dressed in white would bear a slogan ('Flowers which victory will merit'); they would be followed by a young couple representing liberty and the genius of the Revolution. Then would come other groups with banners: a carriage containing pregnant women ('Respect, care and assistance for pregnant women'), young married couples ('Down with all fortresses, our children are our ramparts'), people dressed as the Pope and his acolytes ('There are no more prejudices, I'm done for'), young schoolchildren ('Tremble tyrants, we are growing up'), a group of deserters from foreign armies ('It's not enough to be on the soil of liberty, it must be worked for'), a group of priests who had abdicated ('No more priests, no more imposters') and finally a group of former prisoners ('In future we will put the homeland first'). Then would appear the local authorities with detachments from the army of the Basses-Alpes. At the temple of reason in the former cathedral, laws would be read, patriotic hymns sung, speeches delivered and a free piece of theatre performed. A few days later, the council proposed the establishment of a library in the town and the expulsion of a theatre troupe which had performed a play containing the words 'princess' and 'queen'.[41]

On 20 Nivôse Year II/10 January 1794, the recapture of Toulon was celebrated in Belley (Ain) by members of the *conseil général*, members of the committee of surveillance, members of the district *conseil général*, justices of the peace and a deputation from the *société populaire* carrying a pike with a liberty cap and portraits of Marat and Chalier, a prominent Jacobin from Lyon assassinated in July. A day of dancing, speeches and toasts was punctuated by the marriage of an ex-priest, Jean-Baptiste Oriol, and Anne Bardet in the former cathedral, their wedding party followed by an ass carrying a mannequin of the English Prime Minister William Pitt escorted by four sword-bearing citizens.[42] While Saint-Just may have regretted what he saw as the lack of popular enthusiasm in Paris for the Festival of the Supreme Being, rural festivals were sometimes lively celebrations of nature and locality. In the little village of Theys, high in the valley of the Isère, three ploughmen bearing a harrow were to be followed by six women as harvesters, 'all of whom will hold a sickle in one hand, a small bunch of cornflowers under the other, tied with mixed fresh herbs and they will have straw hats tied to their backs'. Finally a group of men would carry their tools of trade, such as a shuttle, an axe and a saw.[43]

Popular festivals expressed hostility to the Church by mockery of priests and other counter-revolutionaries. At Dormans (Marne), through which Louis had passed to and from Varennes in 1791, the figure of William Pitt was perched backwards on a donkey and paraded through the town. At Tulle (Corrèze), there was a burial of a coffin containing the remains of 'superstition' and crowned with a pair of asses' ears and a missal; saints' statues were flogged. 'Dechristianization' ceremonies in the autumn of 1793 had a carnival and cathartic atmosphere, often utilizing the 'promenade des ânes', used in the Ancien Régime to censure violators of community norms of behaviour, but now with someone dressed as a priest sitting backwards on the donkey.

Such festivals were boycotted by those most aggrieved by the regime. Pierre Delahaye, the village schoolteacher in Silly-en-Multien (Oise), noted that the ceremony for the planting of the liberty tree on 30 Pluviôse Year II/18 February 1794, conducted by the mayor and former priest Bourget, had been followed by 'a frugal but fraternal meal, at which no farmer was present'.[44] The *agent national* of the district of Loudéac (Côtes-du-Nord) on 24 Ventôse Year II/ 15 March 1794 wrote to his municipalities urging them not only 'to rid themselves of their priests' but to 'hand over the furnishings of their churches, ornaments, sacramental vessels and linen' before turning them into temples of reason. It would seem that few complied.[45]

Elsewhere, popular initiative, at times encouraged by 'deputies on mission', closed churches and pressured the constitutional clergy to abdicate and marry as a sign of patriotism. In the Nièvre, where the deputy on mission Fouché led one of the most vigorous 'dechristianization' campaigns, the attack on 'superstition' was experienced as imposed and unwelcome. Local Jacobins in small towns such as Clamecy were as militant as they were outnumbered.[46] In anti-clerical areas just south of Paris, however, the practice of dechristianization found fertile soil. At Corbeil bones were taken from the Church ossuary, burned on the public square, and the cinders were thrown in the Seine.[47] It was a wave of similar actions violently attacking and destroying physical remains of the Ancien Régime that impelled the Abbé Grégoire to denounce 'vandalism' to the Convention on 20 Nivôse Year II/10 January 1794.

For those parish clergy still in the country, living through 1793–94 was a dreadful experience which most resolved by formally or informally abdicating their calling. In St-Michel-de-Lanes (Aude), the priest declared on 19 Germinal Year II/8 April 1794 that 'animated by deeply republican feelings ... I have given my resignation from my position and have renounced my priestly functions ... and promise to no longer exercise them'.[48] There were wide variations in the number of such abdications, from only 12 in the Alpes-Maritimes and 20 in the Lozère to 498 in the Saône-et-Loire; in the 21 departments of the southeast, there were up to 4,500. In all about 20,000 priests abdicated their calling and up to 6,000 of them married.[49] In the Allier, only 58 of 426 priests did not abdicate, and nationally perhaps only 150 parishes out of 40,000 were openly celebrating mass in spring 1794.[50] However, for many other priests – and their parishioners – these were desperate times, in which the institutional forms of religion collapsed almost completely.

Non-juring clergy were the common focus of rage. The deacon Jean Michel was one of 48 religious marched across France from Nancy to Rochefort, to be imprisoned on the île d'Aix, in the spring of 1794. In almost every town large and small through which they passed, he recalled, they were assailed 'by the crudest words and tone, with the most impious and at times obscene remarks, the most frightening shouts and threats, on the faces and in the movements and gestures of a crowd out of control'.[51]

Every town, every village, every hamlet was for us a type of arena where we had to fight against sarcasm, offensive behaviour, blasphemy and attempted murder from a furious populace which was often on the point of taking our lives.

Along the Loire, the local population wanted to 'give them a drink' in the river in the same way as many other priests. These prisoners were fortunate, for they finally reached the island, where there was little to do but kill fleas and fight pigs for their food.[52]

By 1794 France was a land almost devoid of officiating priests. Among the 3,000 violent clerical deaths in these years were at least 920 clergy who were publicly executed as counter-revolutionaries, and probably 30,000–40,000 (up to 25 per cent) of all clergy emigrated. The former First Estate was thereby more directly affected than the nobility: the number of noble *émigrés* (16,431) was about 15 per cent of the Second Estate.[53] The rituals of mass, confession and absolution, administering the last rites and catechism for children all became clandestine. Even the absence of the pealing of a parish bell to summon the faithful to mass, or to call the community together for some other religious or civil reason affected the rhythm of daily life. The spatial universe of rural communities could change forever, as around the massive former abbey of Prémontré (Aisne) which was sold off to a glass manufacturer for more than 223,000 *livres* and converted into a potassium and saltpetre factory; the sanctuary was cleared and used as part of the factory.[54]

The dechristianization campaign in the autumn of 1793 coincided with and was often identified with the activities of 45 *armées révolutionnaires* (in all, about 40,000 men) active in 66 departments. These bands of *sans-culottes* militants were mixed with men on the run from justice and others who simply enjoyed the camaraderie. Their size ranged from small groups of 10 to democratically run armies of up to 7,000 in the Lot, Aveyron and Lozère. The smaller departmental and municipal *armées* drew on local populations, especially the very poor and wage-earners. The 64 men in the Avallon (Yonne) *armée* included 54 from the countryside, among them 15 day-labourers, 6 farm servants, 2 wine-growers, and rural artisans such as clogmakers and blacksmiths. They had as their mission the requisitioning of food for cities and the armies, the payment of taxes, the purging of counter-revolutionaries, the search for deserters from the military, the seizure of metals from churches for the war effort and the maintenance of revolutionary zeal. Their tactics ranged from careful, judicially correct and consensual activities to large-scale intimidation and violence.[55]

Relations between these civilian armies and the rural and small-town populations was a function of the political situation in the particular area in which they were situated as much as of the degree of discipline and militancy of the army itself. In about one-quarter of the country, estimated Richard Cobb, they were involved in violent incidents, and those at Nantes and Lyon were to colour the reputation of the *armées* forever. Just as common, however, were expressions of regret from rural communities that they were departing.[56] They were often welcomed by the populations of small towns already at odds with farmers unwilling to meet requisitioning targets or to sell produce for *assignats* on the open market. In Écouis (Eure) the *société populaire* praised the *armée* 'in our struggle against the farming and mercantile aristocracy, and those offenders in the national forests which surround us'. Municipalities rich in grain, and where the local authorities were supportive of their farmers – such as Compiègne, Noyon, Provins and Pontoise in the Paris basin – were more likely to be outraged by their presence.

Where the *armées* turned their attention to rooting out 'superstition' then their welcome rapidly soured. In about 11 departments – Loire, Nièvre, Allier, Bas-Rhin, Loire, Nord, Morbihan, Haute-Garonne, Gironde, Ariège, Isère – the *armées* undertook thoroughgoing dechristianization. At Seix (Ariège) an *armée* member lectured the local *société populaire* that

> Jesus Christ was a bastard, a useless bugger, a man with no power, who, by consorting with the Madgalene, had hit the jackpot, that the Virgin was a whore, Christ a bastard ... if there was a bloody God, he only had to show his power by crushing him.

Often this behaviour outraged devout locals, whatever their politics. A Protestant from Anduze (Gard) wrote to Paris that

> the ultra-revolutionary patriots are more dangerous than the aristocrats; at St-Jean-du-Gard, they are trying to force the people to observe the *décadi* and work on Sundays, they ripped and burnt the Huguenot minister's vestments ... I fear now that this most patriotic of areas might become the most fanatical.[57]

Rural producers with produce to sell were the major target of the *armées*. They were not always intimidated. A wine-grower of Clairoix (Oise) retorted to the leader of the Compiègne detachment: 'I have some [wine], and it is not for sale at the price of the Maximum ... bugger the Maximum ... those who have made the Maximum made it so they could take what belonged to the country people.' It was not only people such as him who were targeted for arrest, along with former nobles and priests, but also deserters. At St-Marcel (Isère), the locksmith Contamin, after arresting a wealthy farmer, announced that it was 'high time these buggers were taken up and their goods distributed to the poor'; in Moulins (Allier) the former priest Boissay urged: 'Brave *sans-culottes* who want for everything, throw yourselves on the rich, the merchants, the financiers, the *notaires*, etc. Let them, too, eat black bread and onion soup.'[58]

The law of 18 Frimaire Year II/8 December 1793 reasserting the freedom of religious practice was seized upon in many rural areas. Despite the paucity of clergy, many of the parishes such as Stains, Nanterre and Villetaneuse within walking distance of Paris had well-attended services on the Sundays before Christmas 1793 and at midnight mass on Christmas Eve. Augustin Roussel, the former *curé* of Colombes just to the north of Paris, had closed his Church and abdicated the priesthood, but women from his parish and other villages obliged him to open his Church and celebrate mass. The following Easter, people from around Moissy, near Melun, poured into the Church, according to the *comité de surveillance* of Brie-Comte-Robert, to hear mass said by Claude-Lazare Larue, who admitted that he 'had dressed himself in a surplice and cassock ... had sung mass at the altar, imitating the former *curé* ... and that on that day the mayor of Moissy had been the first to ask him to perform the role'. There were many similar cases in the Somme and Aisne.[59] Even a priest imprisoned in the former Carmelite convent in Caen could take pleasure that the government 'has just crushed with one of its decrees the monsters who wished to deny God and establish in the republic the horrible system of atheism'.[60] Attempts at dechristianization did not quite end with the decree of Frimaire. In the district of Compiègne (Oise), a concerted effort was made to convince communities to formally renounce Catholicism in April 1794, but only the town itself did so with alacrity. Of the three villages which did so (out of 65), only Estrées-St-Denis did so spontaneously, and that as the result of a bitter dispute between priest and parish.[61]

Nationally there were perhaps 6,000 Jacobin clubs and popular societies – one for every seven communes – created during the Terror, short-lived and ephemeral though many of them were. In the southeast, for example, 75–90 per cent of communes had clubs. They were far less common in the north, but there were 358 in Upper Normandy (the departments of Seine-Inférieure and Eure), of which 87 per cent were founded under the Terror, the concrete manifestation of the rural support for the Revolution in this region.[62] In the mountainous region of the Auvergne, in contrast, only about 10 per cent of communities had clubs, again mostly creations of the Year II.[63] The proliferation of clubs was often the result of cajoling or intimidation by a *représentant en mission* like Javogues in the department of the Loire, where 42 of the 59 clubs were founded after his arrival in September 1793.[64]

Regions with very small villages had few societies: for example, only 6 of 129 communes in the Corbières had *sociétés populaires* during this period, all of them in the larger villages.[65] There were so few hostile clergy or *émigrés* in the Corbières that there must have seemed little point in creating a new institution in a tiny village to express solidarity against non-existent local enemies. Despite their proximity to Paris, there were *sociétés populaires* in few of the villages and small towns of Seine-et-Oise and Seine-et-Marne: there were clubs in just 10 of the 116 communes of the district of Melun.[66] In contrast, the Gard, Vaucluse, Bouches-du-Rhône and Var were also centres of counter-revolution, and popular societies served as centres of republican political solidarity.[67] In the district of Béthune (Nord), three-quarters of the communes had a club; in smaller communities, they were so common as to have become a new type of village Assembly.[68]

From local societies came urgings to the Convention, as from Montmeillant (Ardennes):

> The strength of Hercules with which you are armed and the buckle of Minerva which defends you should not leave your hands until the hydra of aristocracy has been reduced to ashes and there is no more trace of its blood on the globe.

Every rural district had its share of ardent Jacobins like these, who read Parisian and local papers or belonged to Jacobin clubs and popular societies. Cerutti's *La Feuille villageoise*, aimed specifically at a rural audience, sold up to 16,000 copies (with an estimated readership of 250,000) in 1793; the administration of the Gers subscribed to a copy for each of its 599 communes.[69]

*Comités révolutionnaires* had sprung up in many municipalities, districts and departments in response to war, the revolt in the Vendée and the federalist insurrection. On 21 March 1793, these *comités* became responsible for the surveillance of all foreigners and suspects. The 'Law of Suspects' of 17 September 1793 established these surveillance committees in every commune and gave them the authority to arrest all suspects. This same law defined 'suspect' in very vague terms as anyone who was a supporter of federalism or the monarchy, who was an enemy of liberty, who could not produce a *certificat de civisme*, or who was related to an *émigré*. The social composition of the surveillance Committee of Bourg Régénéré was typical of those in small towns: several merchants (of locks, glass, iron), a cabinet-maker, a bailiff, a notary, a cartwright, two carpenters, a wigmaker, a stonemason and a former soldier.[70] In the context of protracted military crisis and civil war, the practice of denunciation became endemic in public life and, indeed, was encouraged by the Convention. This was particularly the case in towns: in smaller communities, it seems that closer knowledge of individuals acted as a brake on the preparedness to impute malevolence.[71] Here the arrest of 'suspects' was by no means indiscriminate and was directed at those who, by word, action or status, were associated with the Ancien Régime.

There were other ways in which citizens of both sexes could show their support for the war effort. Towards the end of 1793 the *société populaire* of Montpellier had the idea of launching a public subscription towards the cost of a boat to be called 'Le Sans-culotte de l'Hérault', and appealed to other *sociétés populaires* to contribute. It was successful: by the following summer it had raised 172,259 *livres* from 116 of the 334 communes of the department. While on average the donors made up 10–15 per cent of the population of a village, in some it was over 20 per cent: 51 of the 230 inhabitants of Montouliers, 31 of 114 in Candillargues and 21 of 92 in the tiny Cévenol village of Agonès.[72]

The period of the Terror, according to David Andress, combined the rhetoric of popular revolution with repression of its expression, and amounted to a cultural war on the countryside, the 'savage' use of State resources. 'The Terror sought to impose a cultural revolution on the countryside', but succeeded only in driving nails into 'the coffin of urban–rural relations'. This urban–rural divide was not so clear-cut in actuality, and the Revolution continued to enjoy mass support in some areas. Many of the changes of name given to communities, streets and children were in fact initiatives taken by ordinary people rather than being, as he asserts, an 'orgy of onomastic innovation' imposed by Paris.[73] The invention and use of new names for familiar faces and people was one way in which was expressed the sense of living through a period that was both heroic and terrifying.

Supporters of the Revolution marked their repudiation of the old world by attempting to eradicate all of its traces. Apart from name changes imposed by Jacobin armies after the defeat of counter-revolution, some 3,000 communes themselves acted to erase Christian connotations: in the district of La Rochelle villages named after saints were renamed to remove traces of the Church: St-Ouen became Marat, St-Rogatien was changed to Egalité, St-Soule to Rousseau and St-Vivien to Sans-Culottes. Elsewhere St-Izague became Vin-Bon, St-Péray became Péray-Vin-Blanc, St-Bonnet-Elvert became Liberté-Bonnet-Rouge, St-Tropez and Montmartre were renamed Héraclée and Mont-Marat, while Villedieu took the name La Carmagnole, and Saintes became Xantes. In the Aisne, St-Gobain renamed itself Mont-Libre, Guise became Réunion-sur-Oise, Château-Thierry Égalité-sur-Marne, St-Quentin became variously Sommarobrive, Somme-Libre and Linon-sur-Somme; at Chauny, the cemetery became 'the garden of sleep'. In the Aisne, as elsewhere, royal and aristocratic connections were removed.[74] Communes in the district of Alençon with the prefix of 'saint' also had their names changed: for example, St-Denis became Sarthon-sous-Chaumont.[75] Not all suggested changes were made: Bourg retained its name rather than Blédvin, although once it had been purged of 'federalist' elements, it became for a time Bourg Régénéré. Major public spaces in the town were renamed Place Jemappes, Rue Brutus, Rue de la République, Rue de la Fraternité, Rue Mably, rue de la Révolution, Place Marat, Rue de la Fédération et Champ de la Fédération.[76]

It is impossible to estimate how many parents gave revolutionary names to babies in these years instead of naming them after saints in the Ancien Régime manner. Revolutionary names reflected the contrasting sources of political inspiration: a study of 430 names adopted in the Seine-et-Marne shows that 55 per cent drew on nature or the new calendar (Rose, Laurier, Floréal), 24 per cent on republican virtues (Liberté, Victoire, La Montagne), 12 per cent on antiquity (Brutus, Mucius Scaevola) and 9 per cent on new

Figures 9 and 10: Members of the Jacobin Club (Société des amis de la constitution) in the small southwestern town of Dax (Landes) celebrated the Revolution's credo on their membership cards. So did patriots in Mont-Égalité, 50 km east of Paris, formerly Faremoutier and known chiefly for its seventh-century Benedictine abbey founded by Ethelburga.

heroes (Le Peletier, Marat). One little boy was called Travail, another Fumier. In the Hautes-Alpes the Lacau parents gave their daughter the names Phytogynéantrope, Greek for a woman giving birth only to warrior sons.

The practice of giving revolutionary names varied enormously across the country, however, and, in any case, is difficult to ascertain precisely. For example, in the districts immediately south of Paris, Rose accounted for 226 of the 783 first names drawn from 'nature' in the Year II, but how deliberately political was such a choice? Some leave us in no doubt, such as the little girl from Laon called Rose Prairial Poisson. Some names were trenchant, such as Faisceau Pique Terreur from Châlons-sur-Marne and Scipion l'Africain from Laon. In many rural areas the phenomenon was infrequent: only 20 per cent of the 133 communes of the district of Villefranche-en-Beaujolais had any such first names at all.[77]

Even in the same region the practice varied enormously and is a gauge of popular attitudes. Notre-Dame-de-Liesse (Aisne), northeast of Laon, kept its name throughout the Revolution and its civil registers (kept in Gregorian style as well as using revolutionary dates) record only three revolutionary names among the 47 births in January–September 1794. In contrast, 7 of the 16 babies born in Coucy-la-Montagne (formerly Coucy-le-Château) in those months were given names such as Octave Floréalle and Hyacinte Pelletier. Significantly, there were 25 marriages but no divorces in Notre-Dame-de-Liesse between January 1793 and September 1795, compared with 22 marriages and four divorces in Coucy.[78] In Gabian (Hérault), most people were in support of the changes wrought by the Revolution, but were sufficiently judicious to give revolutionary names to the newborn only as second names. Hence the état civil lists François Abricot Alengri, Marguerite Myrthe Colrat, Jean-Pierre Abeille Canac, Rose Eléonore Jonquille Couderc, André Aubergine Foulquier, Rose Tubéreuse Jougla and Catherine Laurier Thim Latreille. There was also a Marie Étain Salasc.[79]

In Bourg, the first child to have been given a revolutionary name was Conrad Liberté, born to the single mother Louise-Adelaide Cherbourg, a 'citoyenne comédienne', in December 1792. There were 331 children born in the town in 1793 and 250 in 1794; of these 581, only 16 (3 per cent) had what may readily be identified as revolutionary names. Apart from four called César, four Brutus and two Liberté, the son of the public prosecutor was named Ambroise-Scipion-Émmanuel-Républicain, the son of a municipal officer Républicain-Jean-Jacques-Marie-Matthieu-Brutus and the daughter of a gendarme and a servant was named La Vertu (she survived only 11 days). There was also a Germinal and a Camomile. The son of the judge in the district tribunal was registered as Bâton d'Or (his parents had renamed themselves Apossien and Noisette). The occupations of the parents who followed this new fashion suggest that it had caught on only among those most directly involved with the new institutions.

The practice of popular sovereignty in the context of war and counter-revolution generated a spate of neologisms and changes to the meanings of existing vocabulary. One study has charted more than 1,350 such innovations in the decade after 1789, and most of these originated in 1792–94. The most famous neologisms, of course, were 'sans-culottes', 'enragé' and 'terroriste'; names drawn from individuals were more short-lived: 'chaumettiste', 'robespierriste', 'pittiste', 'maratiste'. Words were used ironically: 'prince' was used for beggar, 'madame' for prostitute. Some new words expressed vindictive mockery of the victims of the Terror, who would 'boire à la grande tasse' ('drink a large cup') and be subject to 'déportation verticale', in reference to the mass drowning of priests at Nantes. Vendéens were commonly known as 'les Corneurs' because of their cattle-based economy.[80]

Of course, such neologisms, like the decision by local patriots to represent revolutionary change in the names they gave themselves, their children and their communities did little to alleviate the weight they were expected to bear through this period of extraordinary demands. Nor, unlike historians, did they know when or how it might end. For the vast majority of people, the Terror was experienced as an anxious time of emergency exaction of property and young men in a world devoid of the markers of power and certainty once inherent in daily life.

For most children, it was a time of harder farm and shop work, unbroken by attendance at school. While a majority of urban children had been functionally literate before the Revolution, this was the case for only a small minority of rural people. School for them was an intermittent experience in winter, when labour was less needed by the family. Only more substantial villages had a lay teacher rather than a priest whose task it was to ensure that children could at least read the catechism. By 1793 the primary school system was reliant on the minority of constitutional priests still in the country and the government had recourse to employing lay teachers with little ability. Districts and municipalities could make recommendations for the nomination of a teacher but ultimate decisions were made on the basis of *civisme* by the *comités de surveillance*. But few children attended school during the Terror: for example, just 5 of the enrolled 220 children in Wissembourg (Bas-Rhin).[81]

The curriculum was modified to eradicate teaching about religion, monarchy, 'superstition' and to emphasize civic instruction through studying the Constitution, the rights of man, republican feast days and republican martyrs. Teachers were encouraged to take their students on excursions (*études du milieu*) to observe and participate in the daily lives of workers, republican festivities and even the meetings of popular societies. Physical education was promoted: in 5 Brumaire Year II/26 October 1793, the Convention decided that 'to develop agility, stature and strength, children will undertake walks, military exercises and swimming'. After the outbreak of war, the revolt in the Vendée and the federalist insurrection, the authorities were less tolerant of the use of what they called *patois* in schools. In July 1793 the Convention decreed that a French language teacher should be employed in each commune of each department and that these teachers should also be skilled in teaching the laws of the Republic.

Bouquier's law in December 1793 defined 'a truly republican education' as characterized by 'bearing arms, taking part in the exercises of the National Guard, by becoming accustomed to work in the exercise of an art or craft'. This law proclaimed that all primary schools were to be free and that attendance should be compulsory from the age of five or six.[82] Between January and July 1794 five issues were published of *Recueil des actions héröiques et civiques des républicains français*, and 150,000 copies were printed of the second of them. In these children could read of edifying examples to emulate, such as that of seven-year-old Émilien Fréville who, before expiring from a fall, had said to his mother, 'What pains me most is to leave you, mother, and not to be able to be of use to the Republic'.[83] School texts such as these poured off the presses during the Terror, but the Jacobins never had the time or money to implement their education policy, let alone train lay teachers to replace priests.

Except in those regions where partible inheritance between all children had been the norm, children now faced a very different future in terms of what they might expect to inherit. On 5 Brumaire Year II/26 October 1793, the Convention strengthened the June decree extending equal succession to collateral heirs: brothers and sisters born outside wedlock. But on 12 Brumaire/ 2 November it was stipulated that this did not apply to offspring 'which were the fruit of debauchery and prostitution'.[84] The decree of 4 June 1793 extending inheritance rights to children born outside marriage, and with it the principle of the right of women and children to initiate paternity suits had been unnerving for men until the law of 12 Brumaire, which was to limit the rights of single mothers to initiate paternity suits until 1912.

According to a decree of 17–21 Nivôse Year II/6–10 January 1794 only a small portion of the estate (10 per cent if there were heirs), known as the *portion disponible*, was left free to be assigned by will, and it could be left only to non-heirs such as a charity. Further, this law made equal inheritance retroactive to 14 July 1789, the date on which the new regime was supposed to have commenced, resulting in thousands of court cases as siblings sought redress. Equal inheritance was now the law of the land.[85] The laws enabled children who had been cajoled into accepting unequal arrangements to contest wills. Pierre Lassalt of Montory (Pyrénées-Atlantiques) complained on 16 Floréal Year II/6 May 1794 that his older brother 'had exploited the dominance that he had always had over his spirit'. It took 15 legal sessions to reach a conclusion, but Pierre ended with 8,342 *livres* instead of 460. Just as commonly, however, children agreed to keep contested property in joint ownership: in the districts of Oloron (Pyrénées-Atlantiques) and Rieux (Haute-Garonne) there were respectively only 78 and 40 retrospective judicial cases across the next year.[86]

The Convention made a series of changes to the divorce law passed in September 1792. On 28 Vendémiaire Year II/19 October 1793 a new law was passed which encouraged women with *émigré* husbands to sue for divorce on the grounds of their husband's absence by enabling them to resume his property: 'any French woman who divorces an *émigré* must be treated like other citizens in the application of the law of 17 September' on suspects. On 8 Nivôse Year II/28 December 1793 an amendment to the 1792 law permitted a man to remarry immediately after his divorce. With respect to women the delay was reduced from 12 to 10 months. Finally, on 4 Floréal Year II/23 April 1794, divorce was allowed on the basis of *de facto* separation for 6 months or longer, and where the *de facto* separation had been longer than 10 months the woman could remarry immediately.

Certainly, women continued to use the divorce law. The civil registers of most communities, particularly of towns, are studded with occasional examples such as that in Bourg Régenérée on 4 Nivôse Year II/24 December 1793, when Hélène Alexis Noyel obtained hers from Antoine Marie Victor Villette on the grounds of 'the incompatibility of character and opinions which has been continual and notorious between her and her husband; and his emigration, which has left her in grave difficulty in her affairs and the education of her children'. On 3 Prairial Year II/22 May 1794, however, the court decided not to hear the claims by the carter Claude Girary against his wife, the cotton-spinner Françoise Genaud, that she had had two children by other men on the grounds that he had been seen in his village only three times in the past 5 years.[87]

There was, however, mounting hostility to women's political clubs in contrast to the more easy-going acceptance in 1791–92. Citizen Boileau of Avallon (Yonne), where there was an active Jacobin women's club, warned that the presence of women in mixed popular societies and assemblies was corrupting men: 'the podium is becoming a musk-scented area; the women are seated in the front, the speakers aim only to win them over'. While it was the politics of the capital which gave Robespierre and others the pretext to move against the Société des Citoyennes Républicaines Révolutionnaires in Paris, the decree of 8 Brumaire Year II/30 October 1793 closed all women's clubs – including up to 60 in the provinces.[88]

For women across the country, the Terror was a time of penury and heavier work covering for the labour of men now in the armies. In frontier and counter-revolutionary areas, they were not only vulnerable to requisitioning and privation, but also exposed to deadly risks though military occupation and the temptations of collaboration, and possible recapture and revenge. The measures taken by deputies on mission were often draconian. Although the Terror was aimed at individuals, when there was mass desertion from the army in the Basque country in early 1794, the inhabitants of the border villages of Ascain, Itxassou, Sare and elsewhere – perhaps 4,000 people in all – were deported 100 km or more from the border.[89]

The devout inhabitants of the Mediterranean village of Canet were outraged when the deputy on mission Milhaud (a leader of the 1792 'guerre aux châteaux' in the Cantal) and an army officer mocked 'superstition' by sitting on the altar and drinking wine from the sacramental vessels before making a bonfire of the wooden furnishings in the Church.[90] Further south, for the people of Collioure, the Spanish occupation for five months from late 1793 was the most appalling experience of the entire period. The civil register is chilling. Though only the register of deaths for 71 of the 157 days of the occupation is still extant, there were 161 burials on those 71 days: twice the annual average in just two months. Milhaud later recalled that, when Jacobin armies recaptured Collioure, 'a large number of men and women and many *émigrés*' who were escaping with the Spanish 'were swallowed up by the waves'.[91]

Like the people of other frontier regions, those of Alsace lived the French Revolution through the medium of their own language. Like other ethnic minorities, too, Alsaciens bore the brunt of the military campaigns; here, however, reactions and experiences were complicated by the uneasy co-existence of Catholics, Protestants and Jews. While Protestants and Jews in general had supported a Revolution which had brought them civil equality, a majority of Catholic clergy repudiated it. Those who had accepted it struggled to maintain Catholic practice. On 21 Prairial Year II/9 June 1794 the constitutional priest of Hirsingue celebrated the festival of Saint Fortuné on the Monday of Pentecost; but when some of those present cut down the liberty tree and deposited its upper branches in front of the house of the *agent general*, the administration proceeded to arrest 285 priests in the department. Not all Protestants remained pro-revolutionary, particularly after the closure of all places of worship in Alsace in the autumn of 1793. On 4 Frimaire/ 24 November the pastor Jean-Jacques Fischer of Dorlisheim was guillotined for having expressed his joy when the allies arrived that he would no longer have to shout 'Vive la Nation!' Nor did patriotism ensure that Jews would be untroubled in those practices which made them distinct: on 24 Nivôse Year II/13 January 1794 the municipality of Hagenthal-le-Bas decreed that 'Jews must cut off their beards, no longer carry their commandments in public, no longer wear a handkerchief on their heads, and in general avoid all external symbols of their religion'. All religions were mistrusted in Alsace by this point, but it was Jews in particular whose appearance was seen to denote difference and hence danger.[92]

Once again, the counter-revolution strengthened Jacobin mistrust of minority languages. In January 1794, Barère (though himself from the Occitan-speaking Pyrenees) inveighed against the 'ignorance and fanaticism' which the foreign coalition manipulated in 'people who are badly instructed or who speak a different idiom from that of public education'. Forgetting the extraordinary sacrifices being made on the borders as he spoke, by patriotic Basques, Catalans, Flamands and Provençaux, Barère assumed that republicanism, civilization and the French language were synonymous. In fact, responses to the Revolution were mediated through the use of minority languages, but not determined by them. Nor were such responses intimidated by the apparatus of the Terror: the mayor of Monbalen (Lot-et-Garonne) was arrested early in 1794 for describing the Convention as composed of 'idiots who did not know what they were doing', and as far as he was concerned they could 'wipe their arses with their decrees'.[93]

In Flemish-speaking areas of the north coast, part of France only since 1662, the imposed changes to place names (Dunkerque – the Church of the Dunes – became Dune Libre), the conversion of churches to temples of reason and the imposition of the calendar were overlaid on a culture which used its bilingualism as a defensive shield for its religiosity (95 per cent of clergy in the district of Hazebrouck were non-jurors). Markets were still held every Friday because Flemish speakers feigned not to understand the new calendar. The frustrated deputy on mission concluded in December 1793 that, 'If the people of the coast of Flanders are not in step with the Revolution, then the language cultivated in secret must be blamed'. As the fortunes of war turned, Jacobins organized a festival in Dunkerque with members of the *société populaire* 'arm-in-arm with Americans and with Batavian patriots in a gesture of fraternity. The procession ended with puppets representing the kings and emperors being dragged in chains on an open cart'.[94] We do not know what the Flemish speakers made of this.

Nowhere was the loss of life greater than in areas of the Vendée which had rebelled against the Convention in March 1793. On 1 October 1793, the Convention solemnly proclaimed to the army it sent to the west: 'Soldiers of liberty, the brigands of the Vendée must be exterminated; the soldier of the nation demands it, the impatience of the French people commands it, its courage must accomplish it'. The major battles were fought between the Vendéen victory at Torfou on 22 September and the defeat of the 'Catholic and Royal Army' at Savenay on 3 Nivôse An II/23 December 1793. A key turning point was the battle at Cholet in mid-October, which put an army of up to 80,000 in disarray. Then the repression commenced. On 30 Vendémiaire/ 21 October four deputies on mission reported that 'the Convention wanted the war to be finished before the end of October and we can today announce to it that [in words they underlined] the Vendée no longer exists'. A general reported the Vendée 'steaming with blood, strewn with corpses, burning for the most part'. The diary of a soldier from the Corrèze noted on 23 Frimaire/ 13 December 'a massacre of women and children'; on New Year's Day 1794 an order was received 'to kill all peasants and others who are not carrying a certificate from their council, counter-signed by that of Cholet'.[95]

Yves-Michel Marchais, the *curé* of Lachapelle-du-Gênet in the heart of the Vendée, had refused the oath on 1 January 1791 and, after having declined to leave his parish and take up residence in Angers, was arrested and imprisoned there on 17 June 1792. In his absence, on 12 March 1793, 69 men from his parish – weavers and spinners, day labourers, servants, farmers and artisans – joined others to assault the national guard recruitment at St-Florent-le-Vieil as the region erupted. A year later, on 18 June 1793, he was freed by the

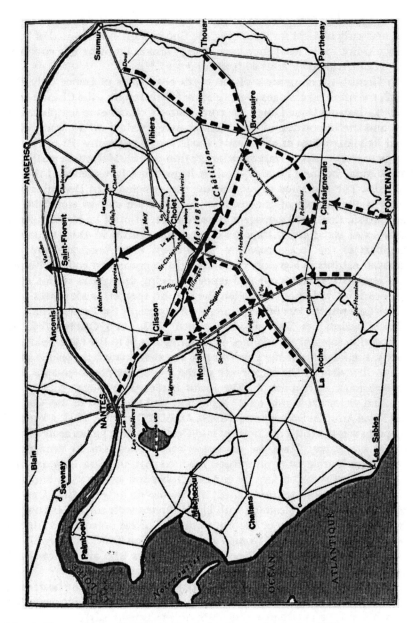

*Map 4* The war in the Vendée: the battle for Cholet, September 1793
(The unbroken line marks the insurgents' flight north after defeat; the broken line shows the republican armies' movements.)
Guerre de Vendée, 1793–1796. Sixième invasion républicaine: plan de la bataille de Cholet, 28 septembre–11 octobre 1793. RV-311533 © Collection Roger-Viollet

Vendéans and returned to Lachapelle-du-Gênet, where he lived more-or-less clandestinely until his death in 1798. He continued to preach, interpreting the course of the rising as a holy war: lost battles were the will of God to punish those who were imperfect in their conduct. In this village of 813 inhabitants, Marchais recorded that 96 had been killed in the war or its repression, 13 on one day in April 1794 in the village itself.[96]

The level of violence in the Vendée was the result of the ideological passions on both sides and the punitive fury of republican forces against people they considered traitors. Bénaben, a former teacher in a Church school and now the *commissaire* for the department of Maine-et-Loire, described a massacre of civilians that took place at Le Mans after the town was taken by Republican forces:

> I was witness to all the horror a town taken by storm can present. Soldiers spread out into the houses, and having taken the wives and girls of the brigands who had not had time to flee, took them into the squares or the streets where they were crowded together and butchered on the spot; shot, bayoneted or slashed with swords. ... Four or five leagues from Le Mans I saw on the side of the road about one hundred bodies, completely naked, piled one on top of the other, more or less like pigs ready to be salted. ... we contented ourselves with taking all the men and women who were not immediately claimed, and only killed those who could not walk, since we did not have carriages in which to transport them.[97]

Some army officers were sweeping in their approach to repression, such as General Beaufort in January 1794 who wished to 'entirely purge the soil of freedom of that cursed race'.[98] The *commission militaire* Bignon which followed the army sentenced 210 villagers from Bouguenais, on the outskirts of Nantes, to death in a collective trial.[99] The civil war resulted in extraordinary loss of life: recent estimates have suggested up to 250,000 insurgents and 200,000 republicans.[100] Reynald Secher has calculated that the 773 communes involved militarily in the war lost at a minimum nearly 15 percent of their total population (117,257 of 815,029 people), and nearly 20 percent of their housing (10,309 houses out of 53,273).[101]

This was a particularly brutal civil war in which the death toll was staggering, but violent death was not confined to the west or the battlefronts in the south and east. These were times of acute anxiety which occasionally manifested itself in raw hatred, not only of external enemies but also of all those who could be blamed for dashed hopes, hunger and the threat of death. On 26 Pluviôse Year II /14 February 1794 the Popular Society of Châteaurenard (Loiret) wrote to the Parisian section L'Homme Armé to tell them that their former seigneur Jean Fougeret lived there:

> he endlessly insulted misfortune and poverty ... he abused his despotic rights to spread his domination over the neediest class in society ... must

he survive the regeneration which is occurring? ... Comrades, be energetic against this family! The blessings of all the *sans-culottes* of our canton are guaranteed to you.

The section had Fougeret taken before the revolutionary tribunal and he was tried and executed on 23 Floréal/12 May.[102]

The deputies on mission could be uncompromising. Maignet, a supporter of Billaud-Varenne and Robespierre, was in the Vaucluse when he heard that on May Day 1794 the liberty tree had been felled, the *bonnet rouge* thrown into a well and decrees of the Convention torn and soiled in the little town of Bédoin at the foot of Mont Ventoux. Bédoin was a community of the Comtat Venaissin which had not wanted to be part of France and had rejected the Revolution. Maignet's repression was exemplary and targeted patriots he regarded as ineffectual as much as anti-revolutionaries. Sixty-three people (3 per cent of the population of 2,000) were condemned to death.[103]

Behind the statistics of repression were individual stories of personal and family tragedy. In December 1793, in a number of communities east of Paris, such as La Ferté-Gaucher, Mauperthuis and Meilleray, protesters were heard to have shouted: 'Long live religion and the Catholic army! Down with the Clubs and the Jacobins!' The primary schoolteacher Louis Prunelle was one of a number arrested, taken to Paris and condemned to death. On 12 Ventôse Year II/2 March 1794, shortly before his execution, Prunelle wrote a final letter to his wife, also a teacher:

My dear friend,
    I have taken this moment to give you and your poor children some sad news. Of all that I ask you, the one thing is not to grieve. Put your confidence in the children and in the Supreme Being who must be your force and your support. It has already been two hours since I have suffered the news of my condemnation as a result of negligence on the part of a municipal officer from the Commune of Meilleray, who did not send the documentation I asked him to. ...
    Goodbye, my friend, my dear heart, I leave you, reduced to tears, with kisses, as well as for my children, my father and mother and all my relatives whom I ask you to kiss goodbye for me. Pray to the Supreme Being for me; from the one leaving you forever.[104]

In the Year II huge numbers of French people became accustomed to the spectacle of execution, including collective killing. On 6 Nivôse Year II/ 26 December 1793 Bénaben, the *commissaire* for the department of Maine-et-Loire, described in startlingly jocular tone a mass drowning at Savenay:

it seems that more than two thousand were shot. They call that *to send to hospital*. An entirely different method is used here to get rid of this nasty lot. We put these scoundrels in boats which are then sunk to the bottom. We call that *to send to the water tower*. In truth, if the brigands have sometimes complained about dying of hunger, they at least cannot complain about dying of thirst. Today we made about twelve hundred drink. I do not know who came up with this kind of punishment, but it is much more rapid than the guillotine.[105]

Léon Dufour, just nine years of age when the Revolution began, recalled vividly how political debate in the town of St-Sever (Landes) 'did not preoccupy only men and their wives; party spirit electrified even children'. He confessed that, aged 14, he went with friends to see the execution of the elderly father of an *émigré* and a Girondin supporter.[106] Another who saw a public execution of an army officer for dereliction of duty, young Jean Massip from St-Ybars (Ariège), wrote home that, 'We were assembled around the guillotine, some twelve thousand of us, to see him beheaded, but it was soon over, both the execution and our thoughts on the matter.'[107]

\* \* \*

With the appointment of Robespierre in July 1793 and other Jacobins in September, the Committee of Public Safety had the resolve to mobilize an entire society in defence of the Revolution and to decimate its internal and external opponents. Essential to this mobilization was the creation by the Jacobin government of a rural–urban alliance by a mixture of intimidation, repression and policies aimed both to meet popular grievances and to place the entire country on a war footing. A year later the military challenge had been met. While there had been widespread resistance to requisitioning and resentment of the *armées révolutionnaires*, without the preparedness of most communities to comply with this mobilization the war would not have been won.

For the majority of the Convention, the goal of the Terror was the attainment of peace, and economic and political controls were but temporary constraints to that end. The regular extension of the powers of the committees was a recognition of their achievements during the continuing war crisis, but was not a measure of support for Jacobin ideology. In late 1793 'moderate' Jacobins such as Danton and Desmoulins urged an end to the controls of the Terror and the implementation of the Constitution of 1793. Robespierre and his closest Jacobin associates were able to paint Danton and his associates as 'indulgents', like 'enragé' militants seen as guilty of undermining republican unity. The crisis was not over: Spanish troops were still on French soil in the Pyrenees in June 1794; on 1 June France lost 5,000 men killed, wounded or taken prisoner in a naval battle with England. It was only with the battle of Fleurus (26 June) that the last of the foreign troops was expelled from northeastern French territory.

Unsurprisingly, there have long been attempts to associate the Terror ideologically with twentieth-century totalitarianism, for example, by claiming that the way the Vendée was repressed amounts to 'genocide'.[108] While this is an inaccurate use of the term, the image of the Terror as 'totalitarian' is a powerful and common one. One reason why it is unsatisfactory is that it confuses the sweeping decrees and exhortations of the committees and the Convention with how France actually was, rather than them being seen as desperate measures to deal somehow with what appeared to be an overwhelming military crisis. At the same time, many rural communities and urban neighbourhoods used a variety of strategies to sidestep or openly oppose the demands of central government and its local agents. For others, a revolution that had begun in 1789 with a humanitarian, reforming zeal seemed by 1794 to have developed into a nightmare of affronts to individual liberties and the safety of persons and property.[109]

# 8
## Settling Scores: The Thermidorian Reaction, 1794–95

Wherever they lived, the experience of French people in the years between July 1792 and July 1794 had been unimaginable. In some parts of the country, particularly the Vendée and the hinterland of 'federalist' cities such as Lyon and Marseille, these had been years of mass killing and suffering. In solidly pro-revolutionary areas, the years of military crisis had been ones of ceaseless demands for men and food for the armies at the same time as the once immutable authority of King and Pope and, at a local level, of seigneur, priest and local notable was repudiated.

Success in the mass mobilization of the nation's resources for the war by June 1794 finally exposed the divisions in the popular alliance of the Year II. The geographic incidence of executions until March 1794 had been concentrated in departments where the military threat had been greatest; but now, as the military threat receded, the number of executions for political opposition increased. A speech to the Convention by Robespierre on 8 Thermidor Year II/26 July 1794, with his vague threat to unnamed deputies, provided the motivation for reaction from those fearful that he intended to call them to account for their bloody repression of revolts in Lyon, Toulon and Marseille.

The execution of Robespierre and his associates on the twenty-eighth marked the end of a régime which had had the twin aims of saving the Revolution and creating a new society. It had achieved the former, at horrific cost, but the vision of the virtuous, self-abnegating civic warrior embodying the new society had palled for most people within the Convention and across the country. The expression 'the system of the Terror' was first used two days later.

The year of the Terror had etched divisions deep into French society. To those committed to the goals of the Revolution and mindful of the magnitude of the counter-revolution determined to crush it, it was a successful emergency military regime during which excesses were regrettable but justified. Others were horrified by what they saw as the indiscriminate and excessive use of violence against the Revolution's opponents, particularly as the military crisis receded. Whatever the case, the overthrow of Robespierre was universally welcomed at the time as symbolizing the end of large-scale executions. In Elbeuf (Seine-Inférieure), a staunchly 'patriotic' council had apparently supported the policies of the Convention at every turn; now, six weeks after the fall of Robespierre it changed the names of its sections from 'Liberty' and 'Equality' to 'North' and 'South'.[1] In Bourg (Ain), a council which had also been as resolutely Jacobin as any other in France sent a letter headed 'Liberté, Egalité, Justice, Probité' to congratulate the Convention on the arrest of those guilty of 'trying to reestablish tyranny and of killing good republicans.[2]

Shortly after the fall of Robespierre, the word 'Jacobin' became an insult, and Marat's name, which had been given to public places across the country, was effaced.[3] Others targeted those Jacobins deemed to have acquiesced in the September 1792 massacres as 'buveurs de sang' ('drinkers of blood'), 'sanguinocrates' ('aristocrats of blood') or 'septembriseurs'.[4] Gabriel Noël, a volunteer of 1791 who had fought at Valmy and Fleurus ('I had the pleasure to play my part in the important battles ... which saved the Republic') readily absorbed the news of the arrest of Robespierre and his associates. He wrote to his family on 18 Thermidor/7 August: 'May they all perish since they were traitors to the homeland ... we weren't fighting for Robespierre or for any of them, but for the *patrie* and those will always be our feelings.'[5]

Immediately after the execution of Robespierre and his closest associates, their political opponents – including some who had once been allies of Robespierre – began to reify 9 Thermidor as the moment when the Revolution passed from 'tyranny' back to 'liberty'. Historians, who appreciate chronological markers, have also seen 9 Thermidor as marking the end of Jacobin domination, even of the Revolution itself. While provincial opponents of the Revolution quickly adopted this rhetoric, the actuality of the months after Thermidor was not so clear cut. In many parts of the country, republicans who had accepted the imperatives of the Terror as the surest way to win the war, welcomed the fall of the Robespierrists without assuming that anything else would change. Along parts of the frontier, Jacobin armies were still at war with foreign troops: in the eastern Pyrenees it was only on 1 Jour Sans-Culottide Year II/17 September 1794, with the capitulation of the fort of Bellegarde at Le Perthus, that the last Spanish forces were expelled from the territory of the Republic.

Only in the most angrily divided areas did the fall of Robespierre usher in sweeping reaction against the Terror. In most places there was a good deal of continuity as people assumed that what had ended was the dominance of a small group of Jacobins and associated arrests and executions. In the district of Grenoble, a staunchly Jacobin administration continued in power and distributed *émigré* property to veterans: in the year after September 1794, 441 ha were distributed to 2,160 'défenseurs de la patrie'.[6] Similarly, in

January 1795 the surveillance Committee of Lagrasse (Aude) celebrated the end of the Terror in an address to the Convention:

> The Revolution of 9 Thermidor ... has seen the rebirth of calm and serenity in the hearts of the French, who, released from the errors into which terrorism had led them, and having broken the iron sceptre under which the scoundrel Robespierre held them subject, are enjoying the fruits of your sublime works, marching with joy along the paths of virtue. ... Formerly the men of blood slaughtered innocent victims selected by envy, and destiny led to the scaffold how many hardworking and suffering citizens, confounded with the guilty ... France is free, happy and triumphant.[7]

This was in an area where there was still a military threat from Spain. The widespread assumption here and elsewhere was that the fall of Robespierre meant that 'France is free, happy and triumphant', that the Revolution had been returned to its proper course. At the end of the year, they were still meeting daily and addressing fellow citizens as 'tu'. Their concerns were increasingly economic – the enforcement of the *Maximum* and of work on every day but the *décadi*, for villagers were still observing Sundays and feast-days – but this was couched in revolutionary terms, 'at the moment when destiny is weighing on its scales the fate of tyrants and the liberty of the world'.

Not until March 1795 did political reaction begin to touch the districts of Lagrasse and Limoux, when village councils were purged of Jacobins. Despite the extent of this purge, in many cases it may have amounted to no more than a settling of accounts or an attempt to place wealthier members of communities back in charge: in Rennes-le-Château, for example, the council 'declared that there is no one in this commune who deserves to be disarmed' (nevertheless, eight councillors were dismissed).[8] The crackdown began earlier elsewhere. When an enquiry was conducted in October 1794 into popular societies in the district of Senlis (Oise), 585 men were listed in nine of them. Only 44 were among the 4,000 inhabitants of Senlis itself; in small communities like Mello (380 inhabitants) and Ermenonville (545) there were respectively 57 and 39 members. In Acy-en-Multien (600) the 150 members must have included almost every adult male.[9] Such lists were the basis on which purges could be undertaken.

All over France, those who particularly welcomed the fall of the Robespierrists and the end of the Terror were those in rural areas and country towns who had had most to lose from the price controls, requisitioning and threats from *armées révolutionnaires*: farmers with a surplus to sell, grain merchants, millers and those involved in large-scale transport. These were men who had lived through and, in many cases, been complicit in the Terror: they had been hardened by the experience.[10] It was these men who ultimately resumed power in villages and towns across the land. The targets of their accumulated resentments were the local Jacobins who had made their livers a misery over the previous 2 years.

In politically divided areas the news of the execution of Robespierre and his associates was the signal for parallel action against the most militant Jacobins. Not surprisingly, those distinguished by their active involvement in the local face of the Terror sought to distance themselves as much as possible from Robespierre or simply decided to lie low. In the Channel port of Le Havre, a political club which had regularly had meetings of up to 300 members could attract only about 20 by late 1794, as members went to ground or simply despaired at the collapse of revolutionary hopes. Some others fled to Paris; others put up with having their windows smashed.[11]

It was not always possible to lie low. In Bourg there was a public outcry against those 'dangerous intransigents who had oppressed and harassed true patriots, exercised the most frightful tyranny over them ... and committed an infinite number of other crimes'. The council ordered 500 copies of a form to be printed in order to record all the information given to them about the suspects. The *société populaire* insisted that all official seals with the words 'Bourg Régénérée' be replaced on the grounds that 'this word dishonours the commune, the mass of whose citizens have always demonstrated devotion to liberty and equality and respect for the National Convention'. The town council agreed but, without an engraver in the commune, the costs were too high for their exhausted resources; nevertheless, they undertook to find a local artist to efface the word on all seals. The *société* was also successful in convincing the council to return to markets every Wednesday rather than the 'vicious' and 'terrorist' institution of one every ten days.[12] In the months and years after Thermidor it became commonplace for politicians and publicists to empty their anger – and, in some cases, guilt – onto Robespierre.[13] But this also happened at a local level: the Bourg council even blamed the poor state of the Church steeple on 'la règne de la tyrannie de Robespierre'.[14]

In Brittany there was a generalized passive resistance towards continuing republican festivals; in Lannion (Côtes-du-Nord) a French-language primary school run by a local republican did not admit a single student in the 6 months after its opening in August 1794.[15] The Breton face of the Thermidorian period was *chouannerie*, a punitive response by young men to what they saw as the Terror's excesses in expecting rural communities to deliver up increased taxes and conscripts for a Revolution which had delivered little of material benefit and had removed their 'good' priests. For the next two years until mid-1796, the *chouans* were to dominate local life.[16] This was accompanied by discriminate chastising of individuals. In Fleurigné (Ille-et-Vilaine) *chouans* forced the 'patriot' Jean Chalmel to climb to the top of the village steeple, to wave a white flag and to shout 'Long live Louis

XVII'.[17] People in the small town of Vic-le-Comte (Puy-de-Dôme) created a similar form of popular leisure and festival early in 1795:

> Every evening there is a joyful celebration; we tie up a Jacobin and parade him through the streets to the accompaniment of fife and drum; we sing and dance; we stop for a moment in front of the Jacobins' houses and frighten them; it's their turn to be strung up.[18]

Elsewhere, this was not a game. In the south, smouldering animosities were ignited by the chance to exact revenge on the persons and property of Jacobins or the local agents of the new régime. Here and in the west, up to 2,000 Jacobins were killed by 'white Terror' gangs: the victims were usually wealthy purchasers of nationalized property, and were often Protestants.[19] As Richard Cobb remarked, 1795 was 'the great murder year': it took until then for anti-Jacobins to feel that the Jacobins had really lost power and that violent retribution would not be a fatal error.[20] In the department of the Vaucluse there was particularly bloody revenge for the executions of the Terror when, for example, 300 people were executed in Orange, and villages such as Sarrians and Bédoin were set ablaze; in the latter 63 people had been executed after the liberty tree was felled. After Thermidor the bands of Pastour and St. Christol killed at least 90 Jacobins in retribution.[21]

Stanislas Fréron, an adversary of Robespierre and one of the instigators of 9 Thermidor, was sent on a mission to the south of France to put an end to the massacre of revolutionaries by royalist gangs, but was later recalled to Paris and accused of orchestrating massacres at Toulon and Marseilles. He wrote in self-justification that the prisons of

> Aix, Arles, Tarascon, and almost all the communes of the Rhône delta, were soon crammed with prisoners, most of them detained with no charge specified on the arrest warrants. Royalism too had its 'suspects'. ... There was not one commune where, following Marseille's example, daggers were not plunged with joy into republican hearts. ... Women, children and old men were ruthlessly hacked to pieces in the name of humanity by cannibals who fought over the fragments. The department of the Vaucluse endured the same atrocities. That of the Basses-Alpes, whose people are naturally peaceful, hard-working and law-abiding, did not escape the contagion.[22]

In the southeast, it was evident that the fatal choices of individuals and communities had divided the region in violent and durable ways. This was not a simple social division for, apart from the well-to-do who were overwhelmingly anti-Jacobin, both sides were composed predominantly of peasant and artisans in similar proportions.[23]

The endemic political violence in southern France after Thermidor was commonly the result of organized groups of people rather than milling crowds. These were locals punishing people they knew and held responsible for what they had lived through. It was all the easier if Jacobins were already in prison. In Tarascon (Bouches-du-Rhône) prison massacres in May and June 1795 left 24 and 23 dead; one man was left alone because 'he's a stranger, he's none of our business'. Twenty-seven of the 64 people for whom arrest warrants were issued were on the official list of *émigrés*.[24]

The settling of scores – whether by humiliation, assault, even murder – occurred in the context of sharp and worsening economic conditions. By the time Robespierre fell, many areas of the countryside were tallying the costs of a year of military crisis: one wonders just how many farm animals and carts were left. At the same time, across much of the country 3 months of drought augured ominously for a poor harvest; in the end it was perhaps one-third thinner than usual. In the bitter winter months of 1794–95, reports flooded in from places such as Amiens, Lille and Mâcon of bands of famished farm labourers moving from farm to farm looking for or extorting food. Of course, there were winners, too: for the grain-producing farmers of the Paris basin or the Lauragais, for example, the shortages gave the opportunity to profit from exorbitant prices. The clockmaker Mâlotain of Dieppe reported that it would take him a week to describe 'the hatred the farmers have always had for the inhabitants of the towns, but what do you expect of uncultured people, who've never known anything but their own greed, and if limits aren't placed we'll see the townspeople die of misery'. The economic reaction of the large farmers was flavoured by the sweetness of retribution against men like him: as Richard Cobb described it, the moment for 'much-savoured revenge for eighteen months of humiliation and harassment' by *armées révolutionnaires* and their small-town supporters.[25]

As early as mid-October 1794 members of the Bourg town council charged with responsibility for overseeing the provisioning of markets were reporting that there were serious shortages. At the market in Bourg itself, only one-fifth of the wheat necessary had been available: 'the gravest misfortune awaits this commune if prompt emergency supplies are not found to replace the required wheat'. In mid-November there was unrest in the market place at a time of similar shortage when people saw a large food convoy making its way to Lyon. Neighbouring communes complained that the violence of the women of Bourg made it dangerous to travel there to procure food.[26]

The dearth of the Year III was not caused by the Revolution – and most people could remember those of 1774 and 1788 – but it was exacerbated by the collapse of the Church and State structures for its alleviation. Those who suffered most in this hard year December 1794–September 1795 were people in rural areas which were not self-sufficient in grains: the charcoal burners and woodcutters of forested areas, textile-workers, and those in transport or the *flotteurs de bois* on the rivers and canals. The juxtaposition of famished transport workers and artisans with movement of grain for cities along the river valleys and canals explains why food riots were most likely to flare up in places such as Mantes, Moissac, Château-Thierry or Trèbes. In the hinter-land of the cities, bands of desperate urban people scoured the countryside competing for food.[27]

With hundreds of thousands of men still at the front, rural workers in some areas could profit from the shortage of labour at harvest time to insist on higher wages. At Attichy, in the east of the department of the Oise, har-vests in August 1795 were disrupted by traditional strikes ('bacchanals') by itinerant harvesters insisting on higher payments. In most places, however, those who worked as farm labourers hired by the day or for the harvest were especially vulnerable to those on whom they had pressured the year before when harvests were abundant.[28]

The new administrations found ways of blaming Jacobins and 'terrorists' for the food rioting which was commonplace during the winter of 1794–95, as at Laon on 3 Ventôse Year III/22 February 1795, when the presence was noted in a crowd of the daughter and servant of Jacques Regnault, a former Jacobin official 'known to share the opinions of Robespierre, of whom he is a strong supporter'.[29] In March 1795 the council of Bourg received a report that a 'coalition' of 45 women had insisted that all foodstuffs held in reserve be available at the same price as under the Maximum and were unconvinced by arguments that they had been bought by the council at higher prices in case of even greater shortages. The council tried to convince itself that there must be a hidden hand behind these 'mouvements populaires', but did agree to make a regular distribution to those on the list of the indigent.[30]

The end of all fixed prices in December 1794 in the aftermath of a thin har-vest unleashed rampant inflation, and, by April 1795, the general level of prices was about 750 per cent above 1790 levels. Nevertheless, in the hard-headed atmosphere of Thermidor, the approach to the Jacobins' *Grand Livre de Bienfaisance* became increasingly desultory: on 21 Pluviôse Year III/ 10 February 1795 it was reported that less than one-fifth of the districts of France had established their local book, and the failure of the government to despatch sufficient funds to pay for the pensions soon meant that the whole scheme was abandoned in Year V. Like the schemes for hospital finances, pro-vision for poor relief was affected by the financial implications of inflation and war, and the anti-interventionist preferences of the Thermidorian period.

On the eve of the first anniversary of the overthrow of Robespierre, the council of Bourg wrote to the departmental administration complaining of the refusal of farmers to supply the town at fair prices, despite abundant har-vests: 'after all the evils that the commune of Bourg experienced from the terrorists and drinkers of blood who infected it, it is now the lot of this place to experience an even crueller tyranny', that of greedy farmers whose cup-boards were bulging with *assignats*. They had heard the poor muttering that under the Terror they had had wheat at 3 *livres* 5 *sous* whereas it was now

140 *livres*: they feared a return of the Terror in the form of a war of town against country. Bakers complained that their bread was spoiling because no one could afford it; instead, there were frequent actions by groups of women seizing carts of produce.[31]

The widespread hunger of 1794–95 fuelled the zeal with which many rural communities rushed to recommence religious life, despite the disapproval of authorities concerned to see the re-emergence of 'fanaticism'. In the Oise, for example, groups of women in many villages reopened churches and sang vespers or forced individual men to say mass. Although it was not until the clergy had taken requisite oaths that the practice of religion became formalized again, in fact many priests viewed the fall of Robespierre as the signal to start practising: immediately he was freed from prison in Besançon in August, a former priest began baptisms. Others in Alsace started saying mass in private homes.[32]

In the months immediately after Thermidor many rural communities took steps to begin the reconstruction of a shattered religious life by commandeering a recently released priest or monk to say mass, or even a devout layperson. This was sometimes coupled with new ways of remembering the recent past: in Orange (Vaucluse), a crowd estimated at up to 6,000 used All Saints Day in November to process to the mass graves of victims of the Terror.[33] There was a widespread yearning for a stability which would marry the Revolution's achievements and goals with the freedoms enjoyed after 1789. The council of Le Plessis-Brion (Oise), which had fervently opposed dechristianization, sent a petition on 28 Pluviôse Year III/17 February 1795 setting out clearly its expectations for the future, which would have resonated across much of the country:

> Equality, liberty, security, property, the public debt, the free exercise of religion, public education, social welfare, complete freedom of the press, the right to petition, the right to form political associations, the enjoyment of all the rights of man.[34]

In contrast, in regions where there had been extensive rebellion against the Convention, as in the Gévaudan around Nasbinals, the end of the Terror made little difference to sweeping measures of dechristianization, as republican forces under Alméras continued, in vain, to try to rid the region of Catholic faith as well as of its external vestiges.[35]

A citizen from Sens (Yonne) commented to the Abbé Grégoire in January 1795 that

> I think it will be difficult to restrain the countryside back within the narrow boundaries of society except by giving them back their churches and the freedom to practise the religion in which they have been brought up and nourished.[36]

In acknowledgement of the depth of such feelings, the Thermidorians sought to defuse religious tensions by enabling the reconstruction of religion and religious practice. This was to be achieved by simultaneously withdrawing all financial support for religions and their ministers (18 September), proclaiming the freedom of religion (6 December), and requiring oaths of civic obedience from ministers. The law of 3 Ventôse Year III/21 February 1795 decreed that 'communes or sections of communes cannot in the name of the collectivity acquire or hire a locale for the exercise of religious worship'. The hiring or purchase had to be conducted instead through a public auction with individuals proffering an appropriate sum of money. Other communities, because they were too poor, remote or bitter did not perceive the rationale behind the demanding of money for the reopening of a Church and chose forcible occupation instead. Either way, the law made a parish Church available to most people. On 11 Prairial Year III/30 May 1795 the régime allowed the re-opening of churches closed during the Terror. Religious observance was to be a purely private matter: bells and outward signs of religiosity were forbidden. The Church was to be sustained by the offerings of the faithful rather than direct State support. The laws separating Church and State were widely welcomed, even if its strictures banning open religious display were ignored.

The revolution had had a devastating impact on the personnel and institutional structures of the Catholic Church. In the north and east, in particular, the laity rushed to reconstruct parish life, if necessary in the absence of a priest. At St-Cyr-les-Colons (Yonne), it was reported on 2 Nivôse Year II/22 December 1794:

> Edme Barbette is the one who fills the functions of the former priests and announces all the festivals of the coming week ... and ends with the Pater and Filius intoned in the manner of a blessing by Edme Barbette, who makes the usual gestures of the former priest.[37]

It was particularly women who took the initiative in rebuilding the Church 'from below' after 1794, and their success would be the basis for a less authoritarian relationship of clergy and laity in the nineteenth century.

The Thermidorians had welcomed the end of the Terror, but they were not therefore disposed to tolerate all those who had opposed the Jacobins. The law of 25 Brumaire Year III/15 November 1794 continued to promise death to returning *émigrés*, including priests. The régime was particularly concerned about the activities of priests who had retracted earlier statements abdicating their functions or who had been released from prison, such as Claude François Réné Montrichard, who stated to the council of Bourg in March 1795 that

> when he swore the oath of loyalty and equality, he understood that he was giving an assurance of his complete respect for the constituted

authorities and of his obedience to the government; but if one wanted to draw from this consequences opposed to his religious principles, he would retract it, persisting in his wish to live and die in the body of the Catholic religion.[38]

But at times local authorities were powerless to prevent the renewed activities of emergent and recalcitrant priests: the council of the village of St-Julien (Ain) raided a house in the hamlet of Liconnas and arrested a priest but 'some ill-intentioned men disguised as women used violent means to release the prisoner and committed grave excesses on the municipal officers and guards, several of whom were seriously wounded'.[39]

The end of the Terror was the signal for the devout to repair what they saw as the sin of having registered a birth or a marriage with the civil authorities rather than having had a religious ceremony. Between December 1794 and November 1795 the priest Grillet of Bourg baptized over 150 children, some born as long ago as January 1794, others the day before, as had been the custom. He also remarried 17 couples who had had only civil ceremonies or had been married by a constitutional priest. Thus, on 23 Germinal Year III/13 April 1795, Jean Pioud, *laboureur*, and Mariego Tirand declared to him:

> that having had the misfortune to present themselves to Martine, so-called priest of the parish of St-Denis on 16 October 1792, but having subsequently understood the wrong that they had committed and being impelled to repent, they came to me to request me to bless their marriage according to the rites of the Apostolic Roman Catholic Church.[40]

The Thermidorians inherited a disastrous educational system. Only in villages and towns which had a constitutional priest who had kept the parish school open or where there was a private teacher (often a former priest) was there a continuity of instruction. Among the fortunate communities was Chelles, just to the east of Paris, where, at the festival commemorating the second anniversary of the overthrow of the monarchy, on 23 Thermidor Year II/10 August 1794, the schoolboys came with their teacher, carrying a book and a cane, and the girls with theirs, carrying a book and a crown.[41] Only in towns was there likely to have been a continuity of primary schooling. On 1 Brumaire Year III/22 October 1795 the town council of Bourg authorized three teachers to reopen the town's secondary school. While awaiting the Convention's new education law, the council also set out what should be taught and why, in the process giving an insight into the attitudes of the men who held local power after the end of the Terror. There were to be nine major areas of the syllabus:

1. The study of morality and the rights of man and of the citizen;
2. Knowledge of the laws sent by way of the Bulletin;

3. The study of history;
4. The study of geography;
5. The art of speaking and writing in French;
6. Epistolary style;
7. The principles of 'apologue' and of French versification;
8. Knowledge of mythology;
9. A course of mathematics, in the morning for its elements and in the afternoon for their application.

Members of the council would visit the school regularly to ensure that 'the purest republican principles were being professed' and that students were both assiduous and according 'the recognition which is inviolably due to their teachers'.[42]

The Lakanal Law of 27 Brumaire Year III/17 November 1794 was not implemented, like its predecessor, the Bouquier Law. While it was based on the idea of well-paid teachers of boys and girls in large communities, it would also have permitted the opening of private schools, and removed the clause on compulsory attendance at school. Had it been implemented, it would have been the one education law which sought to come to terms with linguistic diversity for, while literacy in French was to be the goal, it recognized that local languages could be an 'auxiliary medium' of instruction. In November 1794, teachers' salaries were increased to an annual 1,200 *livres* for male teachers and 1,000 *livres* for female teachers. But the shortage of teachers was chronic, so much so that the Convention recommended in January 1795 that communes be allowed just one school for each 1,500 inhabitants: the district of Château-Thierry was typical in reducing the number of its schools from 53 to 32.[43]

\* \* \*

Those who held power in the National Convention during the 'Thermidorian reaction' were the chastened deputies who had acquiesced in or been intimidated into silence by the régime of the Terror. In the towns and villages of provincial France, those who moved quickly to resume power were property owners, substantial farmers, merchants and professional men. In Artois, for example, Jean-Pierre Jessenne found that the democratization of village councils after 1792 was short-lived. By 1795 many of the same members of the élite of tenant-farmers who had dominated village politics before the Revolution and in its early years had resumed their role in this 'fermocratie', based on the great farms which dominated the region and where the farmers employed large numbers of dependent labourers.[44]

Both national and local power-holders shared a grim resolution that they would not again live through a year of privation and menace: they would do whatever was necessary to keep political power out of the hands of those with little to lose or with fierce ideas of levelling. At the same time, these were men who embraced the idea of national unity and scorned the pretensions of the clergy and others who regretted the Ancien Régime.

The combination of such values underpinned their attitude to space. On the one hand, movement of persons through territory was to be controlled in the interests of public order. A law of 23 Messidor Year III/11 July 1795 – which was to stay in place until the mid-nineteenth century – required any citizen wishing to pass from one department to another to obtain an 'internal passport' from the mayor.[45] On the other hand, movement of goods was to be facilitated. Previous systems of measuring weight, distance and volume were condemned as both bewilderingly irrational, varying as they did from district to district, and tainted by their origins in the mists of Ancien Régime time. A uniform, decimal system of weights and measures, announced the Convention on 1 August 1793, would be 'one of the greatest benefits that it can offer to all French citizens'. The 'artists' of the Academy of Science would be responsible for the design and exactitude of the measures, while 'instructions on the new measurements and their relationship to the most widely used old ones will be inserted into elementary arithmetic textbooks which will be created for national schools'. In April 1795 this new system was finally passed into law.[46] The legislation would ultimately have a profound impact on perceptions of measurement. The department of the Lot-et-Garonne, for example, encompassed an area where before 1789 there had been 65 different ways of measuring length and 26 measures of grain. In the Corbières, there had been ten different volumes for which the term *setier* was used (normally about 85 l), and no fewer than fifty different measures of area: the *sétérée* ranged from just 0.16 ha on the lowlands to 0.51 in highland areas.

As owners of significant numbers of livestock needing access to pastures, large farmers had long opposed revolutionary reforms to the use of common land. While the law of 10 June 1793 remained in force, there was now a marked hostility towards equal *partage* and a doctrinaire attempt to withdraw meadows from the ambit of *vaine pâture*. Little common land was divided up after 1794 and ways were found to forestall those divisions which had not already been implemented, or which had given rise to disputes.

One of the unresolved elements of the Rural Code of September 1791 – the balance between an individual landowner's right to make decisions about land use and collective customary rights – was now resolved. On 25 Thermidor Year III/12 August 1795 the Convention took steps to enable proprietors to restrict access to the second growth of hay (*droit au regain*) in their meadows. The Convention was responding to petitions received from farmers seeking to exclude villagers from their fields after the first cropping. This measure was fiercely resisted given that the Rural Code of 1791 had confirmed, where customary, rights of *vaine pâture, parcours* and *glanage*. In the village of

Mazeyrat (Haute-Loire), for example, a group of eight of the better-off landowners took poorer villagers to court to stop them gleaning after the first harvest on fields the landowners had acquired as *biens nationaux*, a right, said the villagers, that 'they had exercised since time immemorial'.[47]

Similar values underpinned the Thermidorians' approach to the war and its resourcing. The Jacobin rationale for war in 1792 – that this was a defensive war against tyrannical aggression which would naturally become a war of liberation joined by Europe's oppressed – now developed into a war of territorial expansion. Peace treaties were signed with Prussia and Spain in 1795 in terms recalling those of pre-revolutionary wars. Some, like the Jacobin schoolteacher Godeau from the Loir-et-Cher, looked forward to official punishment for those who had brought about the war in the first place.[48] The hopes of the conscripts of 1793 like him that this would enable them to return home were soon dashed as well.

National manufacturing of arms, uniforms and munitions was gradually transferred to private enterprise. The law of 16 Germinal Year III/6 April 1795 handed the running of the national saltpetre mines for the production of gunpowder over to private firms. Only in footwear was there a need for government control: in Brumaire Year II, it was stipulated that every shoemaker in the country was to supply his town council or section with five pairs of boots every ten days for each journeyman and apprentice in his employ. The boots would be paid for, and the leather for them supplied, at the price established by the Maximum.

The majority in the Convention sought a political settlement which would stabilize the Revolution and end popular upheaval. To that end the Constitution of the Year III (August 1795) restricted participation in electoral assemblies by wealth, age and education as well as by sex. Popular sovereignty was to be limited to the act of voting: petitions, political clubs and even unarmed demonstrations were banned. The social rights promised in the Jacobin Constitution of 1793 were removed; property ownership was again to be the basis of the social order and political power, as in 1789–92. Gone now was the optimism of 1789–91, the belief that with the liberation of human creativity all could aspire to the 'active' exercise of their capabilities. Instead, the Constitution of 1795 included a declaration of 'duties', exhorting respect for the law, the family and property. It was plain that only those with an adequate stake in society could be trusted to govern, that is, wealthy, educated, middle-aged and married males:

3.  Equality is a circumstance in which the law is the same for all ...
8.  The cultivation of land, all production, every means of labour, and the entire social order are dependent on the maintenance of property.[49]

The explicit statement of the centrality of marriage and property as the social fibre of the nation led the Thermidorians to re-examine the divorce laws. On 15 Thermidor Year III/2 August 1795 the amendments of 1793 and 1794 were suspended on the grounds that they allowed for an excessive rate of divorce, particularly initiated by women using it to divorce their husbands who were separated from them by the exigencies of the revolutionary wars. The original provisions of the 1792 law were reapplied. In its essentials, however, the law continued to enable women in particular to leave an unhappy marriage, for example, on the grounds expressed by the *citoyenne* Jacquette of the commune of Fervaques (Calvados):

> To save my life from the fury of my spouse; to keep me from sharing his infamy when he is condemned for a criminal act; to shield me from his cruelty, crimes, and harsh insults; to avoid witnessing his derangement; to punish him for his ingratitude when he has been cruel enough to abandon me; finally, to keep me from being blamed as the accomplice of his emigration or tyrannized when his crime is turned against me; I find salvation only in the law of divorce.[50]

In the socially conservative atmosphere after Thermidor, however, women would find the courts increasingly reluctant to accept all but the most incontrovertible evidence in both divorce and inheritance cases.[51] In the district of Oloron, in the Basque country, four or five cases a month were being taken by younger children taking advantage of the Nivôse Year II application of retrospectivity to July 1789. So the five children of Marie Lesquère, who had died before 1789, and Jean-Clair Lareu had their claims ruled upon so that their mother's property was distributed according to the custom of Béarn and their father's according to strict equality.[52] But this retrospectivity was suspended on 5 Floréal Year II/24 April 1795 and legal decisions under it were annulled on 9 Vendémiaire Year II/25 September 1795.

*       *       *

In its essentials, the constitution of 1795 was a return to the provisions of the constitution of 1791: France was again to be governed by representative, parliamentary government based on a property qualification and the safeguarding of economic and civil liberties. Certainly, there were differences between the constitutions of 1791 and 1795: the new régime of the 'Directory' was to be republican, not monarchical, and religious divisions were to be resolved by separating Church and State. But by excluding the poor from active participation in the political process, the Directory sought to create a republican régime based on 'capacity' and a stake in society. To avoid a strong executive with its Jacobin connotations, there were to be frequent partial elections to the Council of Five Hundred and rotation of executive authority through five Directors. The rule of the wartime committees was over.

The Constitution was put to the electorate: perhaps 1.3 million men voted in favour and 50,000 against, considerably fewer than for its predecessor in 1793. Subsequent decrees on 5 and 13 Fructidor/23 and 31 August required that two-thirds of the incoming legislature were to be chosen from the men of the Convention. Only 208,000 bothered to vote in favour of this decree. Anger was expressed that the price of social order was to limit democracy. Voters in Triel (Seine-et-Oise) insisted that '[t]he deputies should not be called Representatives of the Nation ... they are merely mandatories of the section which has elected them and can recall them if necessary'.[53] In Elbeuf, where 195 voters (out of 1,095) had unanimously accepted the Constitution of 1793, now 163 (with 10 against) voted for the Constitution of the Year III. But the two-thirds decrees were rejected by 85 to 25 with the resolution that '[t]his article [is] contrary to the rights of the people and will obviously have the effect of compromising its sovereignty'.[54] Even at the height of the Revolution most men in Elbeuf had been prepared to leave politics in the hands of the militants; now many of the latter had joined those for whom the Thermidorian outcomes were irrelevant or unattractive.

French people had wanted nothing so much in mid-1794 as the opportunity to enjoy the fruits of a successful if bloody defence of the revolutionary gains so that they might rebuild the shattered patterns of community life, particularly its religious rituals, in a climate of civil liberty and peace. The post-Thermidorian regime would be republican, but driven above all else by the imperative to end the Revolution, most obviously by suppressing the sources of instability represented by the Jacobins and their supporters. The Thermidorians were hard men, many of them former Girondins, who had lived through the Terror in resentful and fearful opposition, and were determined that the terrifying experience would not be repeated. While there was a widespread longing for a return to democratic freedoms, a bitter social reaction was also unleashed by the removal of wartime restrictions. The Thermidorian Convention had not only brought peace – but only temporarily – but had also acted to ensure that never again would people of substance be vulnerable to threats to individual liberties and private property.

# 9
# A New Régime and
# Its Discontents, 1795–99

The years of the Directory have commonly been understood as the increasingly unstable rule of a narrow élite of propertied conservatives who reduced popular participation in politics and embarked on territorial expansion, opening the way for military dictatorship. In the process, it is argued, vast numbers of working people in town and country retreated into sullen withdrawal from the Revolution or even into outright opposition. More recently, however, historians have seen these years as an integral part of a revolutionary decade which further embedded the assumptions of a new 'political culture' of popular sovereignty and citizenship. James Livesey, for one, has discerned in the language of the market in land and produce across rural France a 'commercial republicanism' which was fundamental to the shift towards a democratic public culture. In debates about common lands, for example, rural producers articulated their views in ways which suggested new attitudes towards the market and landed resources.[1]

Such arguments have reopened debate on whether the foundation of the Directory in 1795 represented the 'end' of the Revolution, or whether the years 1795–99 were one phase of a revolution which was only ended by Napoleon's coup d'Etat of 1799. Donald Sutherland has instead stressed the way the Directory acted to close down independent political practice; even though the period was of importance in engraining the practice of electoral politics, this was of little significance compared with the restrictions. For example, the regime established the 5,250 cantons rather than the 41,000 communes as the key element in the local administrative structure, sharply curtailing the bold democracy of 1792–94. In the words of Georges Fournier, referring to rural political life in Languedoc, 'petty notables dominated soulless cantons'.[2]

Each commune within the canton would now elect an *agent municipal* and his deputy to the cantonal administration, headed by an elected president and monitored by a government-appointed commissioner. From Brumaire Year IV/November 1796, village assemblies met only once each year to elect their two members of the cantonal body: there was a sharp decline, too, in the volume of information being received at the level of the commune.[3] Only the cantonal *chef-lieu* needed to have a school; it alone needed to observe the revolutionary festivals. Municipal agents were required to take an oath: 'I swear hatred for royalty and anarchy, I swear fidelity and devotion to the Republic and the Constitution of the Year III'. They had an unenviable job, imposing orders from Paris about new taxes, conscription levies and the republican calendar on a population deliberately excluded from participation.[4]

The location of cantonal centres renewed the energetic scuffles for recognition evident in 1789–91. Rieux (Haute-Garonne), once an important ecclesiastical and administrative centre, now found even its cantonal status contested in Prairial Year VI/June 1798 by people from Salès, who complained that

> everything calls us to Carbonne, which is our common centre. All our affairs bring us to that place, whether for the market or by virtue of its river commerce ... whereas nature has placed often insurmountable obstacles in the way of going to Rieux.[5]

The restriction of political life at the communal level makes it very difficult to gauge popular responses to the régime beyond occasional expressions of conflict. When, for example, the voters of the canton of Neffiès (Hérault) gathered to elect their justice of the peace and canton president in the 'ci-devant église', those from Gabian were furious that 'the royalists of Roujan, Alignan and Margon surrounded the desk and obstructed it so that republicans couldn't get near. ... The republicans of Gabian want to exercise their rights'. The matter was settled outside in a fight.[6]

We cannot usually recover the informal ways in which such divisions were generated and resolved. Does the silence of most communities in the archival record suggest that, with seigneurialism abolished and the nation apparently safe, people acceded to the withering of the institutions of participation they had known in 1792–94? Certainly, however, political life itself was not dead. In Allan (Drôme), the village notables simply continued to meet as in nothing had changed, recognizing the new 'official' canton of Donzère only for matters such as taxes. On 3 Prairial Year V/22 May 1797 they planted a thirty-foot pine painted in the 'three national colours', as was the liberty cap which crowned it. Elsewhere, improvised festivals recalled pleasure at the demise of the Jacobins: at Beaumont-de-Périgord on 26 Thermidor V/13 August 1797 young people burned 'a straw man, to whom they gave the name Robespierre'; at Blois (Loir-et-Cher), the commemoration of 10 August 1792 in the Year VI also involved burning an effigy of Robespierre.[7] In such ways Robespierre served to personify the bloody images of the Terror for moderate republicans as much as for royalists.

The forced withdrawal of peasants and artisans from formal political life did not represent a hiatus in popular politics. At times, a mixture of anger and despair at the apparent outcomes of the Revolution could result in reactions which were openly counter-revolutionary. At Beaupuy (Gers), a crowd of 1,500 people overwhelmed a squad of 15 gendarmes seeking deserters and draft-evaders to shouts of 'To hell with the Republic and *la nation* ... We want our priests and a king!' People from the neighbouring villages of Encausse, Cassemartin and Monbrun then invaded the small town of L'Isle-Jourdain to seize back Church bells confiscated in 1793.[8] On 27 Prairial Year IV/15 June 1796 the garrison commander at Privas (Ardèche) wrote to the Minister of the Interior of the murder of a wealthy Protestant farmer near Florac:

> Attacks on individuals in the department of Lozère are multiplying in alarming fashion, and always ... on patriots, patriots of 89, the good and virtuous, and above all, wealthy Protestants. The fanatics ... want to recreate the old wars of fanaticism in the Cévennes.[9]

For the authorities, such dissidence was indistinguishable from other forms of 'brigandage', even when it had no discernible purpose other than the violent repudiation of the claims of the State and a marked taste for horror. The most frightening of the bands that roamed many parts of the countryside was the Barbets of the region around Nice, who killed and decapitated their victims and relished the claims that they practised cannibalism.[10] In the Beauce south of Paris in 1796–97 travellers were terrified by the 'bande d'Orgères', an organized, violent group of perhaps 150 men and women of all ages whose 95 forays resulted in 75 murders.[11] Stories of the band's humiliation and violation of their victims and of their subsequent orgies horrified polite society (as did those of the 'chauffeurs' of the south, so-called because they roasted their victims' feet to extract information). When finally arrested in 1798, 22 of the band were executed. On the Franco-Belgian frontier the 'Bande à Salambier' committed a series of murders and thefts in 1795–96. Salambier and 21 accomplices were ultimately caught and executed.[12]

In Germinal Year V 'a horde of scoundrels', over forty in number, were tried for a series of about fifty crimes around Alençon and in the neighbouring departments of the Mayenne and Sarthe, including attacks on mail coaches, several homicides and political crimes such as forcing a priest to call out 'Vive le Roi!' in the middle of mass. The tribunal alleged that 'it was with the name of the royal pretender, with that of religion, that they coloured their crimes. Refractory priests supported them, accompanied them and were their accomplices'.[13] The embattled republican administrators of the Orne were convinced that those on the move through the department, whether travellers or beggars, were spies in the service of the counter-revolution. Innkeepers were directed to provide the police with details of all guests.[14]

The régime's unpopularity and the cynicism with which it had excluded the great majority of people from an effective political voice resulted in a resistance of a different type, that of a refusal to participate: in the national by-elections of October 1795, only about 15 per cent of the 30,000 wealthy voters went to the polls (and elected royalists almost exclusively). The wider electorate for local elections often boycotted polls as a sign of their opposition to the bourgeois Republic.[15] In towns of 5,000–10,000 people, too, participation was both broadened – with all men above 21 years on the tax register eligible to vote – and sharply restricted, with just five municipal officers being elected for two years under the tutelage of a *commissaire du directoire*.

In some places, the coincidence of a new political system so obviously in the interests of the well-to-do with ongoing problems of subsistence, particularly in towns, had the effect of arousing positive memories of the Terror. The town council of Bourg began the new Year IV (22 September 1796) with a desperate appeal to its citizens to set aside the political differences now so bitterly dividing the community. There had been armed gatherings in the streets for several nights; revolutionary songs were frightening people when what was needed was the language of friendship and fraternity.[16] The régime had thoroughly alienated masses of people, especially young men who could not see why they should, for example, volunteer for service in the national guard. By this time brawls between the young men of Bourg and soldiers from the garrison were a nightly occurrence, and dance halls were ordered to close at sunset. At the 'festival de la jeunesse' held in Bourg on 10 Germinal Year IV/31 March 1796 the authorities sang patriotic hymns, made the requisite speeches and then invited young men of 16–21 years to come forward and sign the national guard register on the altar of the homeland. Not one did so. By May 1796 the council had despaired of the young men who had failed to register, who delighted in the 'murderous words' of the Thermidorian song 'Le Réveil du Peuple' while whistling and cat-calling when the 'Marseillaise' was sung, who refused to wear the tricolour cockade, who assaulted army officers and who, they believed, had felled the liberty tree. Despite the council's measures, a fortnight later it was further alarmed by the sight of guillotines drawn in red on several houses.[17] As in many other towns across the country, the combination of inflation and shortages, resurgent non-juring clergy and disaffected youth made the work of the council impossible: the stylized invocations to participate in the new festivals on the tenth of each month (those of youth, old age, victory and so on) were no solution.

The revolutionary calendar continued to lose in its confrontation with ancient cycles of agriculture, religious observance and popular entertainments. The unwelcome challenge to hitherto unquestioned assumptions about the rhythms of the week, month and year affected people in both town and country. The administrators of the department of the Isère castigated their colleagues in the little market town of Le Pont de Beauvoisin on 15 Brumaire Year VII/6 November 1798 for turning a blind eye to shops staying open on the *décadi* but closing on the former All Saints Day. A detachment of 14 soldiers had been powerless to stop the huge crowds in attendance. Rural people were using the dispensation allowing indispensable agricultural tasks to be carried out on the *décadi* to define all their work that way, and how could they then be prevented from doing no farmwork on the old Sundays?[18]

In rural areas, the challenge was all the more disconcerting because Church year and agricultural year were entwined. In Brumaire Year VI/November 1797 the minister of the interior stressed to departmental administrations the necessity of finding ways for the *décadi* to become accepted as the day of rest: 'under the gaze of their parents, young people should devote themselves to exercises to develop and strengthen their bodies. Locate and prepare large and suitable places for these exercises and games'. The minister of police wrote further to departments in Frimaire Year VII/December 1797 suggesting that edifying entertainments might be organized rather than the torturing and killing of animals:

remove from the sight of your fellow citizens, especially the young, these barbaric amusements, and may inanimate objects replace these bloody victims; remember the law of an ancient republic which it was a crime to be cruel to animals.[19]

Strongly pro-revolutionary areas had accepted the *décadi* under the Terror as a symbol of their patriotism, but there was a general return to rhythms of the Gregorian calendar under the Directory, despite the official use made of the republican calendar and the government's exhortations. This coincided with the return of significant numbers of priests, which created a confusing coincidence in republican communities of priests wanting to celebrate mass while municipal authorities insisted on having republican ceremonies on the *décadi*. At times it was resolved by having both every 10 days, as just south of Paris at Sucy-en-Brie, where the 'republican cult' had the Church from 6 to 9 in the morning and the 'Catholic cult' then used it from 9 to 12. Even there, however, there were complaints against those caught working on Sundays. From the Year VI, nearby Choisy celebrated at the same time the fall of Robespierre, the patron-saint's feast-day, and the feast of the Virgin Mary.[20]

These years were remarkable for a construction from below of a new Catholicism. This renaissance testifies to the widespread resilience of religious faith, but is no less significant for what it revealed of regional and gender variations. This great surge in populist religiosity was above all the work of women and was at its strongest in certain rural areas (such as parts of the west, Normandy and the southwest) where huge proportions of priests had emigrated and in provincial towns (Bayeux, Arles, Mende, Laon) where the collapse of the institutions of the Ancien Régime had left women particularly vulnerable to unemployment and destitution. For example, in Bayeux in April 1796, a crowd of furious women invaded the cathedral – converted into a 'temple of reason' during the Terror – and dashed a bust of Rousseau to the floor to cries of 'When the good Lord was there we had bread!' In Normandy more generally, the religious confraternities which had gone underground or adapted to the religious policies of successive governments, had re-emerged openly by 1797.[21] On 5 Germinal Year III/26 March 1796 an 'immense concourse' of citizens in the town of Elbeuf presented a petition signed by 88 women requesting the opening of the Church and, when officials demurred, forced them to give them the keys after six hours of 'a stormy meeting'. At nearby Oissel the tricolour was removed from the town hall, and the liberty tree uprooted and replaced by a calvary.[22]

Whatever the reasons for female religiosity, men in general were far less likely to return so passionately to the Church: boys born after 1785 would not have attended parish schools, hundreds of thousands of men born after 1770 had served in secular military units and the republican calendar itself legitimized an attitude to Sunday as a day like any other. In these ways, a gender-based difference in religiosity, already apparent before the Revolution, was widened. Women, often mistrustful of constitutional clergy and tired of waiting for *émigré* priests to overcome their scruples, expressed a populist religiosity which was profound and self-reliant. Communal authorities were forced to reopen Churches, as were those who had bought them as national property, venerable lay people said 'messes blanches', as at Les Rotours (Orne) where the former seigneur Angot conducted the service. Midwives baptized the new born and emptied Church treasuries were filled with salvaged relics and venerated non-Christian objects of devotion. There were unprecedented scenes of collective rejoicing and forced penitence, as at Carpentras (Vaucluse) in the Year IV, when an estimated 4,000 people gathered to hear a former constitutional priest retract his oath.[23]

The régime allowed *émigré* priests to return under the decree of 7 Fructidor Year IV/24 August 1796, but on condition that they took a civic oath. The separation of Church and State had not resolved the religious problem, for large numbers of priests refused to take the requisite oath. Some continued to say mass in defiance of the law. In the old religious centre of Blesle (Haute-Loire), two infirm, elderly refractory clergy were freed from house arrest in the Year V so that they could say mass.[24] A temporary resurgence of more 'Jacobin' policies in Fructidor Year V/September 1797 tightened the oath for religious, including now 'hatred of royalty', and encouraged local administrations to be more exacting. On 22 Messidor Year VI/11 July 1798, for example, the departmental administration of the Aisne closed the Church of Notre-Dame-de-Liesse, for centuries a place of mass pilgrimage, because

> it is a daily assembly point for a crowd of vagabonds and people from elsewhere who, using the pretext of religion and pilgrimage, stir up dangerous trouble in this commune, threatening public calm and aggravating fanaticism and superstitious beliefs.[25]

Another wave of repression and persecution of non-juring clergy was unleashed in Vendémiaire Year VI/October 1798. Often referred to as the Second Terror, this period saw many non-juring clergy driven once again into hiding and many were deported or killed. Once again, the feeling was that religion and religious practice was closely associated with royalism.

For non-juring priests, the new oath was as restrictive as the old one. For Blondel, *curé* of Banneville-la-Campagne to the east of Caen, it smacked of a time during the Terror when '100 livres was offered for a priest's head, just as for wolves in Scotland'. The Revolution, for Blondel, had been a time

> when we saw the apotheosis of Marat, bended knees before the idol of reason, our churches profaned, our altars broken … when we still have in our hands the bizarre republican calendar, where poisonous plants and base animals have taken the place, deliberately, … of the great saints and the great men who honour the annals of religion.[26]

The most militant non-jurors simply sidestepped restrictions on their activities. In the Gévaudan region of the southern Massif Central there were, according to the local administration on 14 Vendémiaire Year VI/6 October 1797, 'whole cantons entirely in the hands of the priests, where the republican régime is completely ignored'; if constitutional priests tried to say mass they would be stoned.[27]

There were many priests resolute in their rejection of any oath to secular authority. On 27 Brumaire Year VII/17 November 1798, François-Joseph Levrat was arrested by two gendarmes on a road leading out of St-André, in the Ain southeast of Mâcon. Levrat was suspected of being a non-juror, roaming the countryside to give clandestine masses. A native of Charix, near Nantua in the east of the department, he had been a non-juror in 1791 while priest of Izenave. On 6 Frimaire/26 November, when asked by the president of the criminal tribunal of the Ain whether he had taken the oath, Levrat dissembled that he had done so 'with religious feeling', code for a conditional and unacceptable oath. He was deported on 8 Floréal. Other priests were arrested and deported in the same department for saying clandestine masses without the requisite oath. On 9 Germinal Year VII/30 March 1799, for example, gendarmes in Ruffiex entered the home of the widow Bruinet and discovered her extinguishing the Church candles – which they could still smell – and the priest François Bourret throwing his silver chalice out the window into the snow. Bourret refused to cooperate, saying that, as Bruinet was his servant, it was a purely private matter. The house was found to contain Bourret's vestments and other objects necessary for mass.[28]

But people enjoyed bucking the system, whatever its policies. At Lain, near Auxerre (Yonne), just as locals ostentatiously took Sunday off in defiance of the *décadi*, now the reintroduction of Sunday worship was also mocked. The mayor reported that '[p]eople stay in the tavern; they play cards during mass and vespers; they scythe, they plough'.[29] The politics of resistance to the new régime could result in a syncretism of revolutionary language and popular culture and religiosity. On 17 Floréal Year VI/7 May 1798, a Sunday, on an open space in Laon long used for public dances on Sundays and feast-days, a drummer suddenly appeared beating his drum and shouting 'Ça ira!' A crowd then chased the police from the square and drowned out the president of the municipal administration with shouts of 'You have your *décades* but we want Sundays and dancing!'[30]

Everywhere there were tensions between clergy who had remained in France and the 'pure' who had now returned from exile: in Colmar, Marc-Antoine Berdolet, the new constitutional bishop of the Haut-Rhin, insisted on living in his own home rather than have to share accommodation with former non-jurors. Twenty-nine of his 157 priests had abdicated during the Terror: there was palpable tension between them and returned *émigrés*. The constitutional clergy's experience of these years was often lonely and humiliating.[31]

There was, however, no necessary correlation between this yearning for familiar religious rituals and antipathy to the Republic: in the departments of the Yonne and Nord, for example, the devout insisted that they were republicans exercising constitutional guarantees of religious freedom. Petitioners from Chablis (Yonne) claimed that 'we wish to be Catholics and republicans, and we can be both one and the other'. A petition from 900 'Catholics and republicans' in the district of Bousbecque in the department of the Nord demanded the opening of their Church in March 1795 with a menacing reference to the Constitution of 1793:

> We declare to you ... We will celebrate our divine mysteries in our church on the first of Germinal if our priest does not flee, and if he does flee, we will find another one. Remember that insurrection is a duty for the people when their rights are violated.[32]

The schoolteacher of Souday (Loir-et-Cher) resigned because his attempt to replace religious with republican texts led parents to retort that 'we find our children educated enough and we are taking them from you straight away'; Sister Duffan, on the other hand, wanted her Catholic school to form 'good Christians and good republicans ... for I am far from thinking these two titles incompatible. ... I find in the Gospel the purest maxims of the republican code'.[33]

The separation of Church and State and the attempt to placate non-juring clergy permitted parents to turn to 'good' clergy for the blessing of births, deaths and marriages. Almost 900 of these registers exist in the department of the Ain. Charles-Aimé Bouveyron had been the priest at Péronnas for 25 years when, as a refractory, he decided to bury the sacred vessels of his Church; he subsequently spent a year in prison in Bourg. During that time, the steeple and the walls of the sanctuary and sacristy were demolished. In March 1796 he undertook a mission to his native village of Treffort-Cuisiat to baptize and marry those who had not received a Church blessing.[34]

The resilience of Catholic practice is evident too in the registers kept clandestinely by the priest Claude Marre in the village of Montaut (Ariège) between 1793 and 1801. Despite the introduction of civil marriages, Marre gave a religious ceremony to 90 per cent of spouses, and 33 per cent had this ceremony alone: only 10 per cent had the civil ceremony alone.[35] Similarly, the *curé* of the small Pyrenean border town of St-Laurent-de-Cerdans Joseph Sicre had fled to Spain on 24 September 1792 in what he called 'las circumstancias calamitosas de la Iglesia de la frança'; although he probably returned to his parish with the invading Spanish army in 1793–94, his movements from then until 1796 are unknown. But, from 11 September 1796, the date of the benediction of the little chapel of Sant-Cornélis, he once again began to play a vital role in the lives of his parishioners. Built in a field just across the border at the River Muga, which at that point is no more than a stream, the chapel was to become a sacred place for hundreds of Laurentins who walked for an hour and a half along the rough tracks over the Pyrenees to marry or to bring a baby for baptism. Before his return to St-Laurent in December 1800, Sicre baptized 331 Laurentins, many of them brought by their fathers on the day of their birth, as was the practice before the Revolution, and performed 158 marriages involving Laurentins. His presence there was widely known: he also performed 124 other marriages and 281 baptisms of people from as far away as the lowlands around Perpignan 60 km to the northeast.[36]

Women were prominent in repeated actions to force individuals or municipalities which had bought chapels or churches as *biens nationaux* to return them to religious worship. In Pecquencourt (Nord), women forced one such purchaser to surrender his keys, then celebrated the reopening of the chapel by improvising a procession through the little town.[37] In Collioure (Pyrénées-Orientales) on 13 Germinal An V/2 April 1797, a huge crowd of women returning from mass in a nearby village threatened the officer in charge of a grain store located in a former Dominican chapel, demanding both bread and the reopening of the chapel. According to the mayor, Jacques Xinxet Lanquine, 'fanaticism, the primary source of all our problems', was to blame: 'let's cut the evil at the roots if we want to have internal calm'. The women, poor, devout and hungry, were manifesting the identification of worship and bread in popular attitudes: 'Give us this day our daily bread'. At the same time, they were expressing their hostility the bourgeois élite, whose contempt for their 'fanaticism' was obvious.[38]

Xinxet Lanquine was the archetypal man of the Directory. Thirty-five years old in 1789, he was the third in a line of royal notaries in Collioure since 1711. He was linked to the major Catalan families of merchants and officials in the bustling little port; his brother-in-law was a constitutional

priest. Xinxet was an enthusiastic supporter of the Revolution from the outset and was at the forefront of local and departmental politics for 30 years
from 1789, as much from his commitment to a Revolution which had
removed privilege from his town as from a sense of obligation to provide
direction in the interests of social order. He was made justice of the peace of
his canton, and led local resistance to the Spanish invasion in 1793; his
wife's family emigrated. By 1795 he was mayor of Collioure. The municipal
archives for the Directory bulge with the ceaseless exhortations, instructions
and reports from this talented, irascible, intensely patriotic small-town
notable. He was dismissive of religion, yet had led the protests against the
impact of the Civil Constitution of the Clergy in 1791; he was the major purchaser of Church property, but resold the prime lot – the hermitage of Notre
Dame de Consolation – to a group of 80 Colliourencs in 1804, including
himself, for the same price he had paid. In the years 1797–99, however, he
was the lonely and deeply unpopular face of a régime far removed in space
and affection.[39]

Men of the Directory like Xinxet shared with the Jacobins the belief that
people of the countryside, more so than of towns, were prey to the 'supersti-
tious' and 'fanatical' practices of the Ancien Régime. What was required, it
was believed, was a national system of festivals to break down ignorance: if
this had been done earlier, urged the Breton deputy Lequinio, 'you would not
have had the Chouans nor the war in the Vendée'. The basis of such festivals,
he argued, needed to be the civilized indicators of social maturity: respect for
the elderly, a love of modesty rather than vanity among girls, a greater
courage and devotion to duty among boys, mutual responsibility between
rich and poor. Under the Directory there would be five national festivals, to
commemorate 14 July, 10 August, 22 September (the proclamation of the
Republic), 21 January and 9 Thermidor. A decree of 3 Brumaire Year IV/
24 October 1795 added to these five 'moral' festivals: Youth, Old Age,
Spouses, Thanksgiving and Agriculture.[40]

Typical of the 'Fêtes de l'Agriculture' was that celebrated at Wassigny
(Aisne) in the Year V, when

> the citizen Augustin Boulogne, a farmer in the commune of Venerolles
> (responsible for a family of thirteen children, one of whom has died for
> the Republic), because of his intelligence, good conduct and activity was
> proposed as a good example, his name was announced, and he sat next to
> the president throughout the ceremony.[41]

In general, however, the festivals of the Directory lacked the resonance of
religious rituals and the spontaneity of the celebrations of the early years of
the Revolution. The frequency and detail of instructions from Paris on how
they were to be organized and the breathless exhortations to civic duty are
testimony to their lack of popularity. Speakers were chosen to sing the praises

188

Figures 11 and 12: In a vain attempt to shore up dwindling support for its internal politics and external wars, the Directory resorted to celebrating the virtues of loyalty, courage and patriotism, such as an act of bravery by a cook in saving a 'defender of the homeland' in March 1797. Probably from this period is a plate proclaiming its owner 'Jaque Guillon' (from Faremoutier – see no. 10) 'a good farmer and a good republican'.

of the Directory as the consummation of the goals of 1789; people were expected (improbably) to shout 'Eternal hatred for royalism and anarchism!'

One senses the pleasure taken by Claude Bailly, a saddle-maker from Chinon (Indre-et-Loire), in recording in his diary for 28 April 1796 (he kept to the Christian calendar):

> A festival took place called the festival of spouses. You go with your wife to the temple of Reason to listen to a speech, give wreaths to the newly married and to sing songs. But the only people there were the municipal officers and a detachment of soldiers.

Festivals celebrating citizens and farmers in succeeding months met with the same disdain.[42] The 'Fête de l'Agriculture' of 9 Messidor Year VI/28 June 1798 was timed to replace the great festival of Saint-John. In Châtillon-sur-Chalaronne (Ain), the captain of the National Guard refused to convoke his men to participate on the grounds that 'these people have no time to lose; they have to work to pay their taxes!'. When ordered to call them to arms, not one responded.[43]

In his repeated speeches to those assembled at the Directory's festivals, landowners such as Bourdon-Badoire in Alençon and others like him across the country articulated a narrative of a revolution they believed to have concluded. Over two days on 9–10 Thermidor Year IV/28–29 July 1796 he gave his audience a history of the Revolution. 'The most odious feudal tyranny' and 'arbitrary authority' had in 1789 confronted French citizens 'in whose hearts liberty had germinated'. After long struggles with internal and external enemies, 'it was only at the moment when the monarchy was overthrown that France re-conquered its independence and freedom'. But at the moment of the Republic's triumph, 'misconstrued patriotism, demagogic ignorance and anarchy' delivered France to factionalism. Only when the Convention overthrew 'a tyranny which was particularly dangerous because it wore the mantle of popularity' could France have a social pact which now protected it against both royalism and anarchy. Finally France had reached its repose as a fraternal people practising the social and civic virtues.[44]

At the same time that political power at the local level was hardening in the hands of local notables like Bourdon-Badoire, the remaining *émigré* land came onto the market. Earlier sales of such land had often been to the less wealthy, favoured by Jacobin policies allowing subdivision and long-term repayments. Now, a return to larger-scale sales advantaged those with ready savings. Tenant farmers and better-off peasants were also able to take advantage of the escalating prices paid for their produce to buy land, clear taxes and pay off leases. In contrast, subsistence-oriented leasers of small plots faced rising rents as landowners began to re-impose the 'bourgeois tithe', adding the value of the old tithe paid to the Church to the rents they charged.[45] Resolutely committed to a *laissez-faire* economy, the régime also sought to impose agrarian individualism and legal hegemony for the rights of private property. No government since 1789 had been willing to confront directly the ancient mesh of communal controls over forest resources, gleaning, commons, use of uncultivated land and rights of access across private land. Now the Directory acted to legislate for the priority of the rights of the individual owner of private property in forests and on harvested or uncultivated land and encouraged the sale of common lands by auction.

In mid-1795 François de Neufchâteau, one of the authors of the decree on common land of 14 August 1792, expressed his delight at seeing across more than 300 km in northeastern France, 'a vast and superb garden formed, the length of my journey, of the parts of the commons that had been divided, and which were covered with the most beautiful produce! I admit that my heart swelled at the sight'.[46] On 21 Prairial Year IV/9 June 1796 and 2 Prairial Year V/21 May 1797, however, two laws were passed that suspended indefinitely the alienation of the commons which the decrees of 1792 and 1793 had made possible. On 19 Thermidor IV/6 August 1796 free access to grazing on harvested land was banned altogether.

On other issues which divided the rural community the Directory consistently upheld the rights of substantial property owners. The regime of *domaine congéable* had rankled with the tenant farmers of Lower Brittany since long before the Revolution, and the failure of the National Assembly to address their grievances was, with the Civil Constitution of the Clergy, a major cause of their disaffection against the Revolution. A law of 27 August 1792 had given them the means to buy the property provided they compensated the owner; now, on 9 Brumaire Year VI, *domaine congéable* was re-established.[47] Similarly, the decree of 1 Brumaire Year II/22 October 1793 which had stipulated that sharecroppers with verbal leases were no longer required to pay the 'neo-tithe' had been ambiguous about whether the decree applied to cases where rents were simply increased; now, under the Directory, the landowners of the southwest succeeded in prosecuting those who had refused to pay full rents in 1794.[48]

The régime had no more success than its predecessors in regularizing access to forests. Forty-five laws and 50 decrees concerning forests had been passed in 1790–95, but with little impact. People continued to cut wood illegally, like the 65-year-old charcoal-burner Vincent Treille, who dissembled to the court in Limoux (Aude) on 23 Brumaire Year V/13 November 1796 that

> [a]s he is poor and it was a question of such a minor thing that he didn't think he was committing a crime, that it's the first time that's happened to him, and from the moment he was warned by the forest guard Bonnet he had not returned.[49]

By 1795 the evidence of clearances and woodcutting, especially in the south, had become of national importance. In a series of reports, the Jacobin agronomist and former priest Coupé de l'Oise argued that southern France was now as denuded as other parts of the Mediterranean coast from Spain to the Near East. He reported that the Narbonnais, 'which the Romans called their province and Italy itself, no longer offers anything but arid mountains for the most part':

> Even in living memory, people believe that the climate has changed; vines and olives suffer from frosts now, they perish in places where they used to flourish, and people give the reason: the hillsides and peaks were formerly covered with clumps of woods, bushes, greenery ... the greedy fury of clearances arrived; everything has been cut down without consideration; people have destroyed the physical conditions which conserved the temperature of the region.[50]

Coupé was one of many who overstated the responsibility of revolutionary 'licence' for the sad state of France's forests. Indeed, the Directory on 4 Messidor Year VI/23 June 1798 guaranteed as private property land in Languedoc cleared in response to Louis XV's decrees of the 1760s on tax relief for 'défrichements' which had resulted in massive hillside clearances, and in November the same year offered incentives of its own for those who would clear 'wastelands'.

The Directory's search for a viable social basis of support led it to vacillate in its political direction; however, its social policies reveal a far more consistent set of assumptions, for example, regarding education. Schools were in a parlous state in 1795. Most primary schools had closed with the departure of non-juring clergy and it is likely that only a minority of villages and urban neighbourhoods had a priest or lay teacher in the late 1790s. The Daunou Law of 3 Brumaire IV/25 October 1795 abandoned the revolutionary project of seeking to educate all citizens in new ways of envisaging the world as well as in basic skills. It decreed that teachers would be paid from pupils' fees, that girls would be taught 'useful skills' in separate schools and that there need only be a school in each canton rather than in every commune. The school established in Chalais (Charente), for example, drew its students from six other villages from up to 5 km away: in none of them was more than 3 per cent of the population attending school in the Year VI. In Ste-Colombe (Seine-et-Marne), in contrast, 15 per cent – almost all boys of 5–12 – seem to have been attending.[51] As before the Revolution, in any case, the incidence of schooling varied with local understandings of what level of education was necessary and at what age, and in time with the annual cycles of the agricultural year.

The régime's reliance on fees rather than State funding to support primary education restricted the number of children attending State schools and ensured that Church schools were more common. The rich educational projects of revolutionary legislators and pedagogues had come to nought until the Daunou law. Since this law did not provide salaries for teachers, it encouraged a proliferation of private schools: it is estimated that two-thirds of all primary schools were private in 1798. In the Year VI, for example, private schools outnumbered State schools by 99 to 11 in the Charente and by 138 to 23 in the Bas-Rhin, and communes without either were in a majority. (However, a study of 259 of these private schools has found that 44 per cent of them, whether run by lay teachers or constitutional clergy, were overtly republican in pedagogical content.[52])

Perhaps only 25 of the almost 350 secondary schools open in 1789 were still operating five years later. Now more substantial change came to secondary schooling. Central schools were established in all departments, and the École Polytechique developed to cater for the State's needs in public works. Even though students from artisan and shopkeeping backgrounds were present in these schools, the total number attending secondary schools by 1799 was only about 10,000, one-tenth the number of 1789.[53]

There were no laws governing the employment of children (in this regard, nothing had changed). The 60,000 children in orphanages and hospices were particularly sought after for work in textile factories. In Frimaire Year III/December 1795, a textile manufacturer from Bourges named Butel successfully sought permission from the Convention's Committee for Agri-culture and Crafts to employ 500 girls of 10–15 years of age. Several other firms followed suit in the Year IV. Despite the assumption in the Revolution's economic legislation of the 'liberty of the work place', the Directory felt impelled to issue minimum regulations, including a limit of 12 hours work per day and a requirement that the girls be paid the same wages as local workers, be cared for under 'paternal authority', have schoolteachers and be no more than two to a bed. These requirements do not seem to have been strictly imposed. In return the girls would wear uniform to make escape more difficult. The girls were only free to leave, with their accrued payments, at age 21.[54]

The Jacobins' law guaranteeing to children born outside wedlock the right to inherit equally had always been difficult to interpret with precision: just what constituted proof of paternity? The requirement in the Constitution of the Year III that deputies be married men or widowers over 40 years of age exemplified a new, conservative revision of notions of maternity and paternity. On 9 Ventôse Year IV/28 February 1796 the *tribunaux de famille* were abolished, six years after being established, on the basis that cases before them dragged on interminably. Henceforth, all divorce proceedings other than those by mutual consent or on the ground of incompatibility would be heard by regularly constituted courts, first by the Tribunal de District and subsequently by the Tribunal Civil. Cases were now heard by the regular judiciary and were more expensive.

The Directory reversed the Convention's policy of nationalized hospitals and State responsibilities for welfare. The legislation of 23 Messidor Year II/11 July 1794 was annulled by the law of 3 Brumaire Year IV/25 October 1795, which ordered that all sales of hospital property be temporarily halted and that individual hospitals should be allowed to enjoy the fruits of their possessions. On 16 Vendémiaire Year V the Jacobin initiative was finally overturned when the Convention ordered that hospital boards were to have responsibility for hospital administration and welfare again became based on private charity, despite the pleas of hospitals that they needed state aid because they had lost their pre-revolutionary rights to levy dues on local communities. The government undertook that, where sales of hospital property had already been carried out, *biens nationaux* of equal value to the lands alienated would be given to the hospitals so that their independent income could be guaranteed. In reality, however, all that many hospitals received was a promise that lands would be found, whereas their real need was for short-term advances of money to deal with urgent crises. On 5 Ventôse Year VIII/ 24 February 1800 local councils were ordered to help finance their hospitals by establishing *octrois de bienfaisance* on foodstuffs entering their communes – in effect a return to the system of levies and tolls which had been abandoned by the Revolution as being random and inequitable.

The régime's philosophy of individual responsibility underscored class antipathies more sharply than at any other period of the Revolution. In sharp contrast to such *laissez-faire* attitudes, however, it reintroduced Ancien Régime controls over prostitution, as always a last resort for young women migrants to towns. Prostitutes were placed outside the law but were required to register with police and to work in closed and discreet brothels to control the spread of syphilis and to make public thoroughfares more 'respectable'. No controls were placed on their clients.[55]

In Year IV, the régime settled on a strict, legalistic definition of *enfants trouvés* because too often departments were including in their quotas of children babies whose mothers and fathers were known to authorities, partly because the *fille mère's* right to a State pension to help her raise her child was risibly small (a Maximum of 80 *livres* per annum). Single mothers without resources were in a miserable situation. The civil registers of deaths are witness to their desperate hopes of preventing their child's death. Mothers who abandoned children often did so with notes – sometimes in the shape of a heart – requesting the religious order or local authority to take good care of the child in the hope that her lot would improve to the point where she could reclaim her infant. It was observed by Citizeness Faget of a child abandoned to the Sisters of Charity in Bourg-en-Bresse on 1 Floréal Year V/ 20 April 1797 that 'this infant had around its left leg a shoddy ribbon which appears to have once been pink, and behind its back between the wrap and the linen a scrap of paper containing a little pinch of salt'. A few days later Faget found a label on an abandoned child stating 'this infant has been baptized'.[56]

In the exercise of justice, too, the Directory chose the path of efficacy and firmness. The parlous state of judicial control in much of France under the

Directory was a major reason for the erosion of the jury system among magistrates and notables: juries were seen as simply too lenient towards locals.[57] The jurisdiction of the *police correctionnelle* was limited to misdemeanours for which the punishment did not exceed three days in prison or the value of three days of labour. For offences liable to a longer prison sentence, the Directory created *tribunaux correctionnels* at the level of the *arrondissement* consisting of the president (a judge from a civil tribunal), a commissioner named by the Directory, a clerk and two justices of the peace whose cantons fell within the *arrondissement*.

Underpinning the interlocking tensions of religious resurgence and ecclesiastical disorganization, desertion and *insoumission*, political abstention and bitter feuds, were the Directory's economic policies. In an economy still on a war-footing, the abandonment of price controls in December 1794 had unleashed a massive spurt of inflation. By October 1795, the *assignat's* purchasing power stood at just 0.75 per cent of its face value; by the following February, when the paper currency was abandoned, it was just 0.25 per cent. The difficulties for urban wage-earners created by unchecked price rises were worsened by the harvest failure in autumn 1795. Arguably the worst harvest of the century, and followed by a severe winter, the great subsistence crisis of 1795–96 intensified the volatility of popular responses to the Directory.

The years 1795 and 1796 were probably the hardest years of the revolutionary decade, if not of the century. Figures from the civil registers are stark. In Bourg there were 273 deaths in 1795, compared with 166 in 1794; 75 of them were infants under one year of age. In 1796 there were 250 deaths, 24 of them soldiers and 69 of them were children under one year: 30 of these infants had died at the Charité.[58] The grave shortages of all necessities served to focus belated attention on conditions in prisons. As the winter of 1795–96 approached, the town council of Bourg reported on the necessity of procuring coal for prisoners, 'both for protection against the extreme cold and the damp of the approaching winter, and for making soup, the only food they have to sustain their unhappy existence'. The prisoners' effects 'are constantly wet, exposing the detainees to pain and all sorts of catarrhs'.[59] Country towns across France had similarly harrowing tales to tell.

By early 1796 inflation was at such a level that the Directory decided to dispense with the *assignats*: in March the printing plates were ceremoniously destroyed, and a new system – the *mandat territorial* – was introduced, but suffered from the same problems and was withdrawn the following February. The benefits of high inflation to those on long-term leases and those paying off debts were offset to some extent by the increased capacity of the State to collect direct taxes: by 1797 it was collecting about as much as in 1789. Those needing to borrow or to rent land, in contrast, found themselves up against ruinous interest rates or requirements of repayment in kind.[60]

While rapidly devaluing paper currency had been a boon for rural producers, particularly those renting land or paying off purchases of *biens nationaux*, a new initiative, to reintroduce indirect taxes (on doors and windows, and on essentials, levied at town gates), was bound to be as unpopular as it was effective. In 1797 the Finance Minister Ramel succeeded in implementing a sharp deflation with a return to metallic currency for taxes; by late 1798 the economy had stabilized significantly, and was again based on cash.

Despite a good harvest in 1798, the French economy was in tatters: the Bas-Rhin had only 146 master-weavers operating compared with 1,800 in 1790, and the Basses-Pyrénées had only 1,200 people employed in the woollens industry compared with 6,000 a decade earlier. The Directory was a period of rapid change in manufacturing, as Paris and the northeast in particular imported raw cotton from North America to supply textiles to the national and continental markets and to the army. In contrast, the woolen textile industries of southern towns like Carcassonne and Lodève found army orders inadequate recompense for the ending of their trade with the Middle East: the English naval blockades had a devastating effect. At the northern extremity of the country, in Montigny and its region of Cambrésis, the period saw the collapse of a distinctive rural textile economy. The free trade treaty with England in 1786 had been a body blow to the textile industry; now the revolutionary wars after 1792, which swept back and forth across the region, would destroy the market for linen. When the vast Church lands (the cathedral chapter of Cambrai was the seigneur and the Church owned 46 per cent of land) were sold as national property after 1790, the merchant-weavers who had thrived before the Revolution rushed to buy them as a refuge from a collapsing industry. The poorer peasantry often managed to purchase a small plot. The countryside was becoming as agricultural as it had been a century earlier, and a reconstructed textile industry was centred in towns.[61]

For the better-off, the régime of the Directory represented much of what they wanted: the guarantee of the major revolutionary achievements of 1789–92 without the threat from popular politics. The years of the Directory were often characterized, however, by bitter tensions occasioned by religious divisions, desertion from the army and avoidance of conscription, political abstention and violent revenge for the deadly politics of the Year II. Underpinning all these tensions were the Directory's economic policies, which ultimately alienated the great mass of people. As it trod its narrow path the Directory had to protect the régime against resurgent political forces on either side. The elections of 1797 returned a majority of royalists of various nuances, resulting in the Directors annulling of the elections of 177 deputies and calling in troops on 17–18 Fructidor Year V/3–4 September 1797. Then, on 22 Floréal Year VI/11 May 1798 another coup was effected to prevent a resurgence of Jacobinism: this time 127 deputies were prevented from taking their seats.

Since 1794 the war had lost any real similarity to that launched in 1792 as a matter of revolutionary survival and as a platform for the liberation of 'sister republics'. It was now a war of territorial expansion and defence in which increasingly reluctant conscripts fared as best they might. Gabriel Noël, a veteran of Valmy and Fleurus, was disgusted by a new preparedness to pillage. At Mayence, he wrote home to Sommerviller, near Nancy, on 3 Frimaire Year III/29 November 1795 of 'the most frightful pillage. Several officers who tried to prevent it were killed ... The infantry is barefoot, there are no shoes.' Disillusioned by the way in which the war had become one of territorial expansion, he resigned in December 1797.[62]

In 1798 the Directory established 'sister republics' in Switzerland and the Papal States; the left bank of the Rhine was incorporated into the 'natural boundaries' of what was increasingly referred to as 'la grande nation'. Conflict with Britain and Austria continued. A peace with the latter was signed at Campo-Formio on 27 Vendémiaire Year VI /18 October 1797, but hostilities recommenced in Italy in 1798. This, together with the extension of war with Britain into Ireland and Egypt, and the massive desertion rates in the army, convinced the Directory that irregular army levies had to be replaced by annual conscription levies of young single men.

The Jourdan Law (19 Fructidor Year VI/5 September 1798) introduced conscription on a systematic basis for the first time. The continuing state of war meant that, once again, new recruits were urgently needed to swell the ranks. This new law obliged young men between the ages of 20 and 25 to sign on locally in whichever of the five annual *classes* they belonged on the first day of Vendémiaire each year. The maximum length of service prescribed was five years. Since the youngest would in principle march first, the 20 year olds who formed the *première classe*, this implied that any conscript who reached his twenty-fifth birthday, and who had worked his way through to the fifth *classe* without being conscripted, would automatically receive his *congé absolu*. Some form of *remplacement* was again available to conscripts, whereby wealthy conscripts could buy a substitute from the poor or unemployed who had escaped the ballot. Those who volunteered for seven years of service at least had a choice of the regiment in which they would serve, but their wounds would not be as generously compensated as under the 6 June 1793 law making severely wounded veterans honorary officers and cutting the link between benefits and rank and seniority.[63]

The Jourdan Law was a striking failure: the department of the Puy-de-Dôme, for example, was able to provide only 18 per cent, 15 per cent and 5.8 per cent of its quota in the first three levies. Much of this massive rejection of the Directory's military demands must be put down to resentment towards the changes wrought by the Revolution in the religious and family structures of the area. A similar story is evident through much of the southwest.[64] It is impossible to know, however, whether the unwillingness of young men to answer the call-up – and the willingness of their families and communities to support them – was the reflection of a counter-revolutionary stance or, more likely, a longstanding resentment of the claims of the State.

The law sharply intensified resentment of military service because it increased the numbers of healthy young men removed from the pool of household labour to fight on foreign, often distant, soil and because it reintroduced the system of 'replacements'. Again, those regions where the hold of the Royal State before 1789 had been weakest (such as parts of the Massif Central, Brittany and the west) or which had been incorporated more recently into the State (the Pyrenees, parts of the southeast), particularly resented the deeper intrusion of the State's exactions. Resistance to conscription often became part of a complex of refusal involving religious and ethnic antipathies: in Brittany and the west violent opposition known as *chouannerie* proved to be ineradicable. In areas far from Paris, *insoumission* (refusal of conscripts to join the army) became endemic, often with the tacit approval of most of the community: *insoumis* continued to live and work as before, disappearing only when police appeared. Young men also sought to avoid conscription by self-mutilation or by arranged marriages (for elderly women, the new availability of labour could be an adequate compensation). Occasionally, attempts were made to thwart military bureaucracy by destroying birth records, as on the night of 5 Nivôse An VII (Christmas 1799), when the town hall of St-Girons (Ariège) was destroyed by fire, and with it the district's civil registers. Resistance was most durable when it had general community support. In rural areas, where officials and the dwindling number of supporters of the régime were likely to be involved in agriculture, the use of threats, arson and other destruction of property could intimidate officials into inaction.[65]

By 1799, parts of the west, Massif Central and Pyrenees were virtually ungovernable. From these areas came an endless flood of despairing reports. So a *commissaire* in Tarn in Prairial Year VI reported that 'the four detachments that we have furnished come only from those cantons which have constantly been in support of the Revolution'; his counterpart from the Allier noted that, of the twenty-three conscripts from Ygrande, 'twenty-two have come back and are peacefully at home'.[66] Such peacefulness was always temporary: deserters lived in a constant state of watchfulness and suspicion. In Vendémiaire Year VIII/October 1799 Louis Godeau, a patriotic schoolteacher from the Loir-et-Cher who had been in the army for eight years, rebuffed his parents' urgings to come home:

> Each letter that you write breaks my heart. You cite the example of several boys who have returned to their homes by fleeing from their units, living in fear of recapture. As soon as they return home, they are continually harassed and forced to hide in the forests.[67]

Following a major reorganization in 1798, the gendarmerie became the most visible face of the Directory in the countryside as the régime sought to minimize the capacity of deserters and *insoumis* to avoid arrest.[68] When they succeeded in arresting miscreants, the punishments were severe, though not so much as to deter others. On 24 Pluviôse Year VII/13 February 1799, for example, a military court sentenced ten deserters, all under 21 years of age, from the department of the Orne to five years in prison.[69] Claude Bailly, from the little town of Chinon between Tours and Saumur, noted in his diary that the sweeping conscription of the Year VII 'is very hard for the young men and for fathers and mothers who need their children. That has plunged us into a great sadness'. Their departure 'causes a lot of tears when it is time to quit family and friends'. His town of Chinon was divided, with 'patriots' guarding the liberty tree day and night in case 'chouans' should try to cut it down as they had in nearby towns.[70]

Donald Sutherland, Nigel Aston and others have concluded from such evidence, and much more besides, that most French people were engaged in some form of rebellion against the Republic in these years, that the anti-revolutionary sentiment evident in devout areas in the early years of the Revolution had hardened into support for Counter-Revolution, especially among women.[71] It was not the Republic as such that was being spurned, however, but rather the class politics of its self-perpetuating élite. There is certainly abundant evidence of popular disaffection in these years, but this should not be generalized as representing attitudes in those regions which are 'silent' in the historical record. There is little evidence in any case that – outside the northwest and the royalist insurrection in the Haute-Garonne – that this disaffection was counter-revolutionary rather than opposition to the policies of the Directory. And there is no evidence that the working people of town and country wished a return to the complete edifice of an imagined Ancien Régime.

The experience of small town and village inhabitants in these years cannot be reduced to withering evidence of formal participation in public life. The years after 1795 were instead the occasion of novel forms of public behaviour mixed with longstanding beliefs and practices, ranging from illegal religious practice to large-scale crime. Nor was there a common theme: certainly an imputation of 'Counter-Revolution' would be too sweeping a generalization. These were hard years of poor harvest and escalating inflation when people made their own politics in defiance of increasingly desperate exhortations of the régime to appropriate behaviour.

Certainly, the Directory's military ambitions were increasingly resented by rural populations liable to conscription and requisitioning at a time of economic difficulty. Resentments climaxed in the summer of 1799 in large scale but uncoordinated royalist risings in the west and southwest. By that time, too, the requisitioning, anticlericalism and repression practiced by French armies was provoking discontent and insurrection in all of the 'sister republics'. This and the initial successes of the second coalition formed between Russia, Austria and England provided a pretext for a challenge to the Directory, led by Napoleon, the army officer who had dispersed royalist insurgents in Paris in 1795 and who now abandoned his shattered forces in Egypt.

In this he was supported by Sieyès and Talleyrand, two of the architects of revolutionary change in 1789–91. On 18–19 Brumaire VIII/9–10 November 1799, the furious members of the Five Hundred were driven out by troops and a decade of parliamentary dominance was over. On 24 Frimaire VIII/ 15 December 1799, three new 'consuls' (Bonaparte, Sieyès and Ducos) announced that a new Constitution would terminate uncertainty while being based on 'the sacred rights of property, equality, and liberty':

> The powers which it institutes will be strong and stable, as they must be in order to guarantee the rights of citizens and the interests of the State. Citizens, the Revolution is established upon the principles which began it: it is ended.[72]

# Conclusion – A Revolution for the People?

Towards the end of the revolutionary decade the nonagenarian Marquise de Créquy made a trip into the countryside. She was contemptuous:

> The châteaux have been demolished, the large farms devastated and the upkeep of the main roads left to the communes, which are crushed by taxes. In the towns you see only insolent or evil people. You are spoken to only in a tone which is brusque, demanding or defiant. Every face has a sinister look; even children have a hostile, depraved demeanour. One would say that there is hatred in every heart. Envy has not been satisfied, and misery is everywhere. That is the punishment for making a revolution.[1]

By that time the first of the histories of the Revolution had appeared. One of them estimated the total loss of life at 2,022,903, including 800,000 dead on the field of battle, 184,000 Europeans and slaves in the colonies and 900,000 in the Vendée. It claimed that 4,790 people had committed suicide 'out of terror' and that 3,400 women had died in premature labour, not to mention the 1,550 'driven mad' by the Revolution.[2] Like that of the Marquise de Créquy, this perspective was jaundiced, again for understandable reasons. Certainly the figures of deaths were fanciful: those for war losses and the Vendée must be halved, at least. But there was indeed the reality of massive numbers of premature deaths and wrecked lives: it has been estimated, for example, that half of the 30,000 volunteers and conscripts from the department of the Aisne were dead by 1799.[3] Across the revolutionary decade some two million men were to serve in the army: some 7 per cent of the population and about one-third of all adult men. About one-third of families were directly affected by the departure of a son or husband for the army.

These grim conclusions might suggest that the major changes wrought by the French Revolution in the lives of the rural and urban masses were premature death for many and sullen disappointment for the rest. A Revolution which had begun in 1789 with boundless hopes for a golden era of political liberty and social change had ended in 1799 with a military seizure of power. In the process, French people had had to endure a decade of political instability, civil war and armed conflict with the rest of Europe, at the cost of many hundreds of thousands of lives. For the people who inhabited France's country towns and villages, was life in 1799 essentially the same as in 1789, except for the 'punishment' that the Marquise felt was so well merited? How 'revolutionary' had been the experience of a decade of Revolution?

François Furet and others have argued that, well into the nineteenth century, French society and the economy remained much as it had under the Ancien Régime. In Furet's words, 'nothing resembled French society under Louis XVI more than French society under Louis-Philippe [1830–48]'. These historians have argued that the essentials of daily life emerged largely unchanged: especially patterns of work, the position of the poor, social inequalities and the inferior status of women. France remained a land dominated in every way by an élite of noble and bourgeois landowners.[4]

Such a view of the significance of the French Revolution cannot do justice to the social importance of this protracted upheaval. No French adult alive in 1799 was in any doubt that they had lived through a revolutionary upheaval, willingly or resentfully, and that the society in which they lived was fundamentally different. A consideration of the social significance of the Revolution from a longer-term perspective suggests that this was no illusion.

This was, in the first place, a revolution in perceptions of identity. By the end of the decade, French people made sense of the world around them in radically different ways. The most revolutionary transformation of the French Revolution – indeed, of any revolution – was that from subject to citizen. The assumption that the sovereign will lay in a body politic of citizens rather than in a hierarchy of appointment speaks of an irreversible transformation of political culture. The evaporation by 1792 of the mystique of divine-right monarchy was the most fundamental shift in popular understandings of power. Even the seizure of power by Napoleon in 1799 and the restoration of monarchy in 1814 could not reverse assumptions of citizenship, even if democratic republicanism could be outlawed.[5] Henceforth the place of monarchy within a political structure was to be a matter for political debate and division, not – as before 1789 – an element of *mentalité*.

Collective practices in thousands of clubs, section meetings and 41,000 local councils introduced millions of people to the language and forms of popular sovereignty. Of course, it may be countered that this was mere verbiage, that people had picked up the new vocabulary as verbal fashion, that the words were devoid of substance. This assumes that language is no more than the words in which thoughts are made verbal, rather than defining how people think. If the latter is the case, then the language of rights, freedom, sovereignty and equality expressed a change in consciousness.

Not only had the democratization of politics introduced unprecedented numbers of people to the practice also of popular sovereignty, but this practice also underpinned a shift in identity, to self-definition through 'horizontal' links with people whom one would never meet. The *société populaire* of Chauny, a town of about 3,000 people in the Aisne, met three or four times weekly between July 1791 and November 1794. In that time it had written contact with 31 other societies, seven in its own department, but including others as far away as Niort, Bayonne, Perpignan and Toulon.[6] Whether they were 'patriotic', anti-revolutionary or counter-revolutionary, all French people now lived within radically changed structures and understandings of political power and its administration.

Voting was another way of implanting a new geographical map in people's consciousness, as cantons, districts and departments were not only new in name but also commonly did not respond closely to Ancien Régime boundaries. Malcolm Crook has estimated that about three million men were involved in voting across the revolutionary decade. Participation in elections varied according to how important and relevant they were seen to be to local concerns, and should not be read as a gauge of levels of 'political consciousness'. Significantly, electoral participation was consistently highest in small rural communities. In the Aube, for example, participation rates were 50 per cent for the Estates-General, and up to 75 per cent for the first municipal elections and cantonal elections in 1790. After levels of 40 per cent for the 1793 referendum, they started to decline and under the Directory averaged less than 20 per cent.[7] Only a minority of voters participated in most national elections but, rather than this being interpreted simply as a gauge of lack of interest, the reasons for abstention included hostility to the Revolution and the impracticalities of participating in often lengthy voting procedures. In addition, there were so many elections (several per year) that a certain lassitude developed. In referenda, too, only those in favour bothered to vote.[8]

Linked to this essential transformation in perceptions of the basis of legitimacy and authority was a reordering of the way people experienced the structures which administered, judged, taxed and instructed them, and valued, weighed and measured what they produced. The revolts which erupted in the spring and summer of 1789, and which came to be known as the Revolution of 1789, occurred in a society characterized by a striking regional diversity within a State system and territory over which the monarchy had limited hold. Economic structures which sought to meet the needs of the household within a regional or micro-regional market underpinned the vibrancy of regional cultures and minority languages and dialects. The gradual extension of Capetian and Bourbon control over the territory of France since the eleventh century had not eroded loyalties of region and ethnicity: indeed, the cost to the royal state of establishing institutional hegemony had been a patchwork of regional and local immunities, exemptions and prerogatives. Across the kingdom privilege – especially of the First and Second Estates – was embedded in the practices of daily life. The institutional structures of public life – in administration, customs and measures, the law, taxation and the Church – everywhere bore the imprint of these privileges and of historical accretion.

In 1789–91, revolutionaries sought to reshape every aspect of institutional and public life according to assumptions of popular sovereignty, rationality, uniformity and efficiency. Underpinning this sweeping transformation was an administrative system of departments, districts, cantons and communes. These departments were henceforth to be administered in precisely the same way within an identical structure of responsibilities, personnel and powers. Diocesan boundaries coincided with departmental limits, and cathedrals were almost always located in departmental capitals. This uniformity was reflected in the introduction of a national, decimal system of weights, measures and currency. These evident benefits to business and commerce were accentuated by the abolition of tolls and internal customs: henceforth, too, governments legislated on the basis of free trade within this national market. All French citizens, whatever their social background and residence, were to be judged according to a single uniform legal code, and taxed by the same obligatory proportional taxes on wealth, especially landed property, one of the meanings of 'fraternity' and 'national unity'.

The corollary of the revolutionary concept of popular sovereignty and of uniformity of institutions across the country was the greater presence of central government and ultimately of bureaucratic control. This would find its most developed expression under Napoleon, when municipal councils were narrowly restricted in function as well as personnel, but the seeds of greater centralism had been sown with reforms to municipal government from Calonne through the Revolution, heightened by the imperatives of mass mobilization for war after 1792. Perhaps as many as 30,000 laws had been passed during the revolutionary decade.

Central to the revolutionary project as conceived by successive regimes was the civic education of the new citizenry through edifying commemorations which would celebrate the new virtues and, from 1792, seek to replace the rituals which had underpinned monarchy and Catholicism. The commissioners sent out from Paris under the Directory to report on public spirit were horrified by the tenacity of traditional festivals and minority languages. 'How weak the links must have been between the Revolutionary festival and popular life', concludes Mona Ozouf; the Revolutionary festival was 'an impossible, absurd grafting'.[9] Michel Vovelle, in his study of festivals in Provence, was forced to conclude similarly that the Revolution's impact had been ephemeral by the time the Restoration reintroduced traditional festivals.[10] Both Ozouf and Vovelle insist, however, that the spontaneous celebrations which surged from below were a different matter, for they were a syncretic, resonant bonding of seasonal rituals with revolutionary values, most obviously in the planting of the revolutionary maypoles (*mais sauvages*) and the liberty trees. For Ozouf, the revolutionary decade saw the transfer of sacrality from a Catholic Church in crisis onto the social and political virtues of rights, liberty and the homeland. 'How can it be said that the Revolutionary festival failed in that? It was exactly what it wanted to be: the beginning of a new era'.[11]

The meanings of this new political culture varied by class, gender and region; they also left a legacy of contrasting ideologies, none of which could claim to represent the aspirations of a majority of French people. Political upheaval and division left a legacy of memories, both bitter and sweet, and of conflicting ideologies which has lasted until our own times: from communism to authoritarian royalism via liberal constitutionalism and social democracy. Memories of the Terror, and of mass conscription and war were etched deep into the memories of every individual and community.[12] French people were to remain divided about the political system best able to reconcile authority, liberty and equality. Was economic freedom a necessary corollary of – or inimical to – civil liberties? Could these liberties be reconciled with social equality? And how was 'equality' to be understood: as equality before the law, of political rights, of social status, of economic well-being, of the races, of the sexes?

The next time that all French men would have the right to elect their representatives would be a half-century later, in the elections of May 1849, seen by historians as the first democratic elections offering a genuine choice between 'right' and 'left'. These were to reveal regional loyalties which would underpin voting patterns until the 1980s. Historians have often analysed the reasons for the outcomes in 1848–49 and have agreed on one thing: the importance of memory. For the privileged orders of the Ancien Régime the decade after 1789 had been politically and personally traumatic: long after the Revolution, the Catalan noble Jaubert de Passa was haunted by 'memories which swirl round in my head like a leaden nightmare'. In contrast, a local State attorney claimed that for left-wing Catalans, 'the Republic of 93 has left memories which are handed down from father to son, which will never disappear from the spirit of the people and against which it is useless to struggle'.[13] As an Occitan, a Protestant and a rural labourer, it is not surprising that the young Jean Fontane from the village of Anduze (Gard) should have been a *démoc-soc* in 1849, though, significantly, he himself imputed it to history: 'If a majority of us were republicans, it was in memory of our beautiful Revolution of 1793, of which our fathers had inculcated the principles which still survive in our hearts. Above all, we were children of the Revolution.'[14]

In sharp contrast, in the Comtadin or Comtat-Venaissin area in the west of Vaucluse, as in many other places, political divisions had been so bitter and experiences so unforgettable that they would inform political choice well into the nineteenth century.[15] Negative memories of 1793 and the heroism of the Vendéan insurrection remain the central element in the collective identity of the region. For example, the discovery of masses of bones in Les Lucs by the parish priest in 1860 was to result in a myth, still potent today, of the 'Bethlehem of the Vendée', according to which 564 women, 107 children and many men were massacred on a single day, on 28 February 1794.[16] Both at the time, and especially in nineteenth-century memoirs, abundant testimony was recorded of atrocities real or imagined. In Clisson (Loire-Inférieure), it was claimed that people who were still alive were thrown into the well of a castle; 150 women were allegedly burned to make fat. In Angers, the skin of the victims was tanned, to make riding breeches for superior officers. The same thing was said to have been done in Nantes and La Flèche.[17]

The Revolution was not only a turning point in the uniformity of State institutions, but, for the first time, the State was also understood as representing a more emotional entity, 'the nation', based on citizenship. It is for this reason that the French Revolution is so often seen by historians as the seed-bed of modern nationalism, the classic example of Benedict Anderson's concept of 'imagined community' as the basis of national identity.[18] This was especially the case for the millions of young men conscripted to fight for the Republic, glory or their own survival. Mixed with other young citizens within a French national military bureaucracy, such men were exposed to the language of France, *patrie* and nation. Just as 'patriot' was a political term of pride or denigration, so 'patriotism' pointed to the tension between the 'pays' or region and the 'patrie' or nation. In the Year III, General Kléber asked that his Alsacien compatriot Ney accompany him in the Army of the Rhine 'so that … I can at least speak immediately with someone who knows my language'.

The French Revolution was a critical period in the forging and contesting of collective identities among the linguistic and ethnic minorities who together made up the majority of French people.[19] National unity was not only at the expense of the exemptions and prerogatives possessed by privileged social orders, occupations and localities, but also superimposed an assumption of centralized uniformity on the complex ethnic reality of France. Ever since 1330 French rulers had sought to make their language that of public administration; now, however, the French language was assumed to be intrinsic to citizenship, even to be at the core of the Revolution itself. From early in the Revolution political élites expressed the view that French was the language of liberty and equality. The national language bore the name of its nation. When the majority of the King's subjects who spoke other languages became citizens of the new nation, this was to be an imagined community defined in a language in which they were incompetent but which was the sole source of linguistic unity. This is why, on 10 September 1791, Talleyrand expressed his surprise to the National Assembly that

the national language … remains inaccessible to such a large number of inhabitants … Elementary education will put an end to this strange inequality. In school all will be taught in the language of the Constitution and the Law and this mass of corrupt dialects, these last vestiges of feudalism, will be forced to disappear.[20]

For successive governments in the years after 1789, effective citizenship was to be predicated on French as the national language. Politicians, officials and army officers from French-speaking areas, and their counterparts from among ethnic minorities – those most likely to have needed a facility in French under the Ancien Régime – shared this prejudice. The collaboration of some non-French speakers, especially priests, in border areas with invading foreign armies increased the suspicion in the capital that good patriots spoke French. Indeed, from 1792 there were repeated calls in Paris for other languages to be banned.[21]

We know an enormous amount about the ways in which regional populations participated in and responded to the French Revolution,[22] but far less about shifts in self-definition, about the ways in which people defined themselves individually and collectively. For only rarely do we hear members of linguistic minorities without the intermediary of a lawyer, a police officer, an official or a priest. While popular attitudes to the Revolution among the linguistic minorities who together made up a majority of the population varied from enthusiasm to outright hostility across time and place, the Revolution and Empire everywhere had a profound impact on collective identity, on the 'francisation' of the citizens of a new society. This shift in mental universe was apparent when the criminal band of Occitan speakers in Gabian (see Chapter 6) taunted the revolutionary officials who attempted to arrest them that 'things are going well in the Vendée'.

In Collioure, similarly, longstanding competition with fishing and trading ports south of the border had deeply ingrained an assumption that their fellow Catalans to the south were 'Spaniards'. But nor did they see themselves simply as 'French', just as they referred to people from the region to the north as *gavatx*. After the appalling experience of the Spanish occupation in 1793–94 the *société populaire* of Collioure appealed to Paris in August 1794:

> For too long the soil of this commune has been infected by the impure presence of the slaves of the Castillian despot, but finally three months ago it was returned to our dear homeland. Many thanks be given to the genius of the French who seconded and supported the energy of our brave brothers in arms.[23]

This 'francisation' was underpinned by the presence in 1793–94 in the department of the Pyrénées-Orientales of an estimated 100,000 soldiers (more than half the resident population) from 27 other departments. While a majority of French Catalans welcomed the victory of the Jacobin armies, a considerable minority did not and was forced to emigrate. Similar division marked the revolutionary experiences of Basques, Flamands and Alsaciens.

This cultural shift is of profound importance, since it involves the way people understand who they are. Imagining the world in part in terms of 'nation' and 'popular sovereignty' was not a natural or inevitable part of becoming citizens. People were taught, and learnt to be, members of a nation. This came from below as well as above. It was a process which had begun long before, under the monarchy and was incomplete long after the Revolution. Competing discourses about the nation and the *pays* continued to resonate, especially in Brittany, the Basque country and the Roussillon, where there was a more durable sense of ethnic distinctiveness. For all ethnic and linguistic minorities, this 'double identity' was limited to an acceptance of national institutions and the vocabulary of a new, French politics. There is little evidence that minority languages and popular cultures were undermined: the passing clothing fashions of the cities, for example, seem to have had no impact on the great diversity of regional costume.[25] French remained the daily language of a minority of people and France a land of great cultural and linguistic diversity throughout the nineteenth century.

In Alsace-Lorraine, francophone peasants had long come to define their identity in opposition to the 'other', in this case German speakers, whatever side of the border they were from: they did not need the State or the army to teach them about national identity. David Hopkin has found a remarkable absence of the *patrie* in popular attitudes to the army in this eastern frontier region, incorporated into France only in 1766. In this region there were some rare examples of pro-revolutionary papers not in French, such as the *Argos* and *Rheinische Chronik*. In general, however, few people were fully literate in most minority languages: their participation and understandings were not primarily expressed through the written word.[24]

Whether they spoke French or German, the people of Alsace, like the ethnic minorities of the Basque country, Flanders and the Roussillon, had borne the full brunt of the international wars for the survival or destruction of the Revolution. It had been a horrific experience. This was true of all departments which were invaded in 1792–94 and those contiguous with them which bore the heaviest demands of requisitioning. The northeastern department of the Aisne was typical in this regard, but far from typical in that there were 375 priests and 642 nobles among its 1,189 *émigrés*: across France, the bulk of the *émigrés*, like most of those who went to the guillotine during the Terror, were members of the old Third Estate.[26] According to Donald Greer, 13,925 noble males over 12 years had emigrated; in all, 1,158 noble men and women were executed during the Terror. Even if one accepts Chaussinand-Nogaret's low estimate of a total of some 125,000 nobles in the 1780s, it is clear that the Revolution was not a holocaust of nobles.[27]

The continued economic prominence of the old nobility is remarkable: despite the loss of seigneurial rights and, for *émigrés*, land, nobles remained at the pinnacle of landholding, and landholding remained the major source of wealth in France. France in 1799 remained a sharply inegalitarian, hierarchical society, one in which most Ancien Régime nobles continued to be eminent. Across half of the country, a majority of the wealthiest landowners surveyed in 1802 were nobles, and they dominated the wealthiest areas, such as the Paris basin, the valley of the Rhône, Burgundy, Picardy and Normandy.[28] The rhythm of the Revolution may be encapsulated in the struggle over the meaning of 'equality', and in the end was restricted to equality before the law, but the source of economic power, social eminence and political legitimacy had changed radically. The wealthy survivors of the landholding élite of the Ancien Régime were now only part of a far broader élite which included all of the wealthy, whatever their social background, and embraced notables in agriculture, business and administration drawing their wealth from a combination of State employment and business.

The abolition of seigneurialism and the shift in the nobles' relation with the land underpinned a revolutionary change in rural social relations, articulated in political practice after 1789. Social authority in the rural community was now based on personal esteem and direct economic power rather than on claims to deference due to a superior order of society. Even when a noble survived the Revolution with landholdings intact, social relations underwent a major change. In the Provençal village of Lourmarin, Jean-Baptiste Jérôme de Bruny, a former councillor in the *parlement* at Aix, retained his extensive property but became the largest taxpayer, assessed for 14 per cent of all taxes payable by the community. His *tasque* (one-eighth of harvested grain and olive oil), *banalités* and other dues were gone. The estimated annual value of his *seigneurie* had been about 16,000 *livres*, but by 1791 the taxable revenue from his lands was estimated at only 4,696 *livres*, a fall of about 70 per cent. Relations between him and the village were henceforth those of property, labour and rent, suggested by the speed with which locals began litigation with 'citizen Bruny' after 1789. In the decades after 1800, they fought a protracted, successful battle with Bruny over his attempts to ignore ancient collective rights in his woods, 'dealing not with their seigneur but simply with another French citizen.'[29]

While most nobles were pragmatic enough to withdraw from public life and accept, however begrudgingly, the institutional changes of the Revolution, their losses were massive. Robert Forster's judgement, though based on scattered and contrasting case studies, is that, in real terms, an average provincial noble family's income fell from 8,000 to 5,200 francs. Seigneurial dues had represented as little as 5 per cent of noble income near Bordeaux, while immediately to the north, in Aunis and Saintonge, they had amounted to 63 per cent. While many noble families survived with their lands intact, some 12,500 – up to one-half – lost some land, and a few virtually all. To an extent, the losses of lands and dues were compensated for by charging higher rents to tenants and sharecroppers but, whereas 5 per cent at most of noble wealth was taken by State taxes before 1789, thereafter the uniform land tax was levied at approximately 16 per cent.[30] Moreover, nothing could compensate for the loss of judicial rights and power – ranging from seigneurial courts to the *parlements* – or the incalculable loss of prestige and deference generated by the practice of legal equality. The *émigré* noble returned to a transformed world, of litigation by creditors and peasants, the collapse of mystique and the exigencies of running an estate as a business.

The decision by César de Marens to emigrate from his estates at Varennes on the Vienne river in Poitou ruined his family, and most of his estate was sold to a merchant before some relief was accorded by the Restoration's compensation in 1825.[31] Unlike Marens, most nobles kept their lands intact (Robert Forster estimates that about one-fifth of noble holdings were seized and sold), but their method of surplus extraction of necessity changed fundamentally. The final abolition of feudal dues in 1793 implied that nobles' income from property would henceforth be based on rents charged to tenants and sharecroppers or on direct exploitation of noble holdings by farm managers employing labourers. Accordingly, rents charged by nobles increased by an average of 50 per cent in the years 1800–20 as they sought to compensate for the loss of seigneurial rights.

The Marquise de la Tour du Pin was born in 1770 as Henrietta-Lucy Dillon, the descendent of English and Irish Jacobites who had been exiled to France after the defeat of James II in 1691. Her husband was an army officer from an ancient and wealthy family. Her liberal father-in-law was Minister for War in 1789–90, but his support for Louis XVI during his trial led to his execution. Lucy and her husband emigrated to Boston in 1793, returning in 1796. Reflecting in later life on the impact of the Revolution, she focused primarily on the decrees of 4–11 August, which

> ruined my father-in-law and our family fortunes never recovered from the effect of that night's session. It was a veritable orgy of iniquities. The value of the property at La Roche-Chalais [Dordogne] lay entirely in feudal dues, income from invested money and leases or from the mills. There was also a toll river-crossing. The total income from all these sources was 30,000 francs per year ... We also lost the toll crossing at Cubzac on the Dordogne, which was worth 12,000 francs, and the income from Le Bouilh, Ambleville, Tesson and Cénévrières, a fine property in the Quercy which my father-in-law was forced to sell the following year. And that was how we were ruined by the stroke of a pen ... When I married, my father-in-law was understood to have an income of eighty thousand francs. Since the Revolution, our losses have amounted to at least fifty-eight thousand francs a year.[32]

Those peasants who owned their own land were direct and substantial beneficiaries of such losses. This is the single most important 'social fact' of the French Revolution. About 40 per cent of the land of France belonged to peasants who worked it directly: that land was now free of seigneurial charges and tithes. As Arthur Young commented at the start of 1792, 'small proprietors, who farm their own lands, are in a very improved and easy situation'.[33] With the sales of *biens nationaux*, the total of peasant holdings increased from perhaps one-third to two-fifths of the total (from 31 to 42 per cent in the Nord). In broad terms, there was a difference between the south – where peasants owned more than 50 per cent in the Auvergne, Dauphiné, Béarn and Haute-Provence – and the north, where they owned less than one-quarter in the Beauce, Brie and much of Normandy. Here those who owned little other than a garden or perhaps a cottage were commonly 20–25 per cent of the population.[34]

The weight of the tithe and seigneurial exactions had varied enormously, but a total weight of 20–25 per cent of the produce of peasant proprietors (not to mention the *corvée*, seigneurial monopolies and irregular payments) was common outside the west of France. Producers retained an extra portion of their output which was often directly consumed by a better-fed population: in 1792, only one in seven of the army recruits from the impoverished mountain village of Pont-de-Montvert (Lozère) had been 1.63 metres (5'4") or taller; by 1830, that was the average height of conscripts.

Apart from those able to take advantage of the rampant inflation of 1795–97 to buy their way out of leases or to purchase land, tenants and sharecroppers experienced limited material improvements from the Revolution. In regions like the Vannetais in Lower Brittany, the failure to reform the *domaine congéable* in favour of tenants soured the countryside against the Revolution very early.[35] Like every other group in the rural community, however, tenants and sharecroppers had been affected by seigneurial *banalités* (monopolies of mills, ovens, wine- and oilpresses) and, with rural labourers, had been those most vulnerable to the often arbitrary justice of the seigneur's court. The introduction of the system of elected justices of the peace was one of most valued innovations of the revolutionary period, providing villagers and townspeople with a way of resolving minor grievances that was prompt, cheap, less partial and accessible.[36] One important implication is that the success of the justices of the peace may be one of the reasons for the decline in spectacular, collective violence in rural France in the nineteenth century.

One of the few early histories that considered the social outcomes of the Revolution was that published by the Count de Lezay in 1797. His brief history concluded by arguing that among the chief outcomes of the Revolution was the way in which internal free trade encouraged greater productivity in town and country and at the same time the shortage of labour led to an increase in wages: 'the greater ease with which [workers] could leave an unfavourable position enabled them to be less dependent on entrepreneurs, and forced the latter to pay more to those they wished to keep'.[37] Of course, this was the direct result of the absence of so many able-bodied single men in the army at the time that he wrote.

Historians' estimates of the increase in the purchasing power of wages 1790–1810 have ranged from 10 to 20 per cent but, as Donald Sutherland has concluded, 'there was very little in the revolutionary settlement for people with little or no property'. The 'penniless', he argues, accounted for 40 per cent of the population; even for landed peasants, feudal dues were no more than 1–3 per cent of their income: little wonder then that the most massive peasant participation was in Counter-Revolution. These figures seem inaccurate: even the local reports to the national survey on indigence, which had every reason to inflate the number of beggars in order to secure financial aid, put the number of the very poor at about one in seven, not one in two or three.[38] Certainly, feudal exactions were light in areas of Brittany and the west, and this was a major reason for mass disaffection from the Revolution throughout the northwest. Elsewhere, however, the proportion of produce taken by the tithe and seigneurial dues was far higher, together representing generally over one-fifth of all production.[39] Though rural communities protested loud and long that the new tax régime put in place from the start of 1791 had substantially increased State taxes, there is no question that they were significantly better off.

Research on the extent and social incidence of land sales during the Revolution remains piecemeal, but it was significant in most areas. The most detailed estimate is that over 10 per cent of land changed hands as a result of the expropriation of the Church (about 6.5 per cent) and *émigrés*.[40] Church land in particular was usually of prime quality, sold in large lots by auction and purchased by urban and rural bourgeois – and more than a few nobles – with the capital to thus expand pre-existing holdings. Anne Jollet's close study of Amboise and its surrounding villages in Touraine reveals that the impact of land sales was to intensify existing markets for property, for in all about 15 per cent of the land in the region was sold as *biens nationaux* by 1811. In Amboise itself, the Church had owned about 15 per cent of property, and its availability provided the opportunity for local bourgeois to acquire more.[41] In all, there were up to 700,000 purchasers: about one family in six bought some land.

Donald Sutherland has argued that the changes wrought by the Revolution were attenuated, then smothered by, 'the vast weight of ancient peasant France', which was beyond fundamental, rapid change. This book has instead argued that the Revolution affected even the intimate dimensions of daily life. It is, however, difficult to disagree with Sutherland's conclusion, that support for the Revolution in the countryside was strongest in areas of substantial small property, where the Revolution brought tangible benefits; elsewhere, the refusal of successive governments to address the complaints of renters of land provoked resentment and even rebellion.[42]

With few exceptions, such as wine, agricultural production remained at similar levels in 1800 or 1820 as in 1780. There is no doubt that, in the words of Le Goff and Sutherland, for the vast majority of rural people, 'the

Revolution was long and hard'.[43] Most French people in 1799 remained, like their parents, owners of small plots, tenants and sharecroppers. Decisions taken by successive assemblies, under massive peasant pressure in 1792–93, to finally abolish compensation due to nobles for the end of feudal dues and to make *émigré* land available in small plots at low rates of repayment, encouraged small owners to stay on the land. The 1790 and 1793 partible inheritance laws, further codified by Napoleon, ensured that farms would be constantly threatened by subdivision (*morcellement*).[44]

For these reasons the French Revolution has generally been understood as retarding agrarian capitalism. Across much of the country, the polycultural and subsistence orientation of agriculture would persist well into the nineteenth century. Farming techniques were unchanged by the Revolution, and the household basis of rural production would dominate French rural society for many decades to come. Nevertheless, profit-oriented farm enterprise was facilitated by a series of legislative changes and the relative consistency with which successive régimes after 1789 upheld the primacy of private ownership and control over collective usages and community decisions. Only the strength of the attachment to communal lands by the poorer members of rural communities (although in some areas wealthier peasants also valued such lands for grazing animals) prevented a thoroughgoing change to total private control of rural land. More specialized agriculture became possible with the abolition of the collection of tithes and dues in kind, especially grains; now landowners were able to use their land for their own purposes. This was particularly the case in parts of Normandy and Languedoc. In the countryside around Bayeux, the heavy, damp soils were quickly converted to cattle-raising once the Church ceased exacting a fixed tithe in grain.

An alternative view, that of 'la voie paysanne', of the 'peasant route' to market specialization and capitalism, has been supported by studies of particular communities and regions which have identified small and medium producers as the initiators of change.[45] Gilles Postel-Vinay, for example, has emphasized those factors which stimulated demand for wine, especially the incentive offered by supplying cheap wines to the army as part of soldiers' rations and by the abolition of indirect taxes on wine until 1804. He has estimated that, despite the absence of able-bodied men drafted into the army, rural producers responded to these incentives by slightly increasing wheat production and producing one-third more wine by 1812 compared with the years before the Revolution.[46]

Where small peasants felt greater security about producing for the market, the results could be dramatic, particularly in winegrowing. In the Gard, more than 70 per cent of the land which had been seized and cultivated in villages such as Tavel, Pujat, Orsan and St-Victor-la-Coste was planted in vines.[47] Land sales in Balazuc (Ardèche) were dominated by smallholders who used their purchases to create a new economy based on wine and silk.[48] In the

Aude, similarly, the ending of seigneurial and Church exactions in grain, coupled with the collapse of the textile industry, encouraged peasants to turn to wine as a cash crop. For example, at Ribaute, the seigneur, the abbey of Lagrasse, had taken a *setier* of wheat for every 13 ha of land, cultivated or not, necessitating the growing of grain on almost all cultivable land. The community also needed the abbey's permission to clear new land. With the end of these constraints, the area under vines at Ribaute increased from 83 to 186 ha in the four decades after 1789. Across the 30 years after 1789, the estimates provided by mayors for the area under vines in the department showed an increase of 75 per cent, from 29,300 to 51,100 ha. The volume of wine produced in the department may have trebled to 900,000 hl across these years. As the mayor of neighbouring Lagrasse put it in 1828, a pastoral economy had largely been replaced by viticulture: 'since 1789, this land has gone from being a place of a nomadic people to one of an agricultural people'.[49] The *cultivateur* David Nicolas from near Béziers (Hérault) agreed: his fellow farmers 'have embraced changes and innovations which may be fruitful for them. They have abandoned the routine practices of our grandfathers'.[50]

This 'peasant route' to capitalism was only one of the ways in which the Revolution facilitated agrarian economic change. There are many examples, particularly in northern France, of the ways in which the political economy of successive revolutionary assemblies facilitated capitalist agriculture, based on large-scale ownership or renting of land and the employment of labour. For example, the Chartier family of Gonesse, just north of Paris, had been tenant farmers but took advantage of the sale of Church lands in 1791 to buy up a large holding: a Chartier became mayor in 1802, beginning a line that would last until 1940. Similarly, in 1786 the Thomassin family of Puiseux-Pontoise (Seine-et-Oise, today Val-d'Oise) owned 3.86 ha and rented 180 more from the seigneur, the Marquis de Girardin. They then bought up large amounts of nationalized property from the abbey of St-Martin-de-Pontoise, the Sisters of Charity and eight other ecclesiastical landowners: by 1822 they owned 150.64 ha, 27.5 per cent of the land in the commune, including much of the Marquis' estate. This land was used for commercial grain-growing and, finally, for sugar-beet and a sugar distillery.[51]

In urban areas work continued to be concentrated in small workplaces, where masters worked side by side with three or four skilled journeymen and apprentices. There had been a withering in the role of the guilds, one of whose functions had been to inspect and approve apprenticeship contracts. After the abolition of the guilds by the law of 2 May 1791, these contracts were simply registered by a notary: it was assumed that they were the result of negotiation. Apprenticeships certainly continued: there were, for example, 123 in Bourg in 1789–99, but the number fell from an annual average of 16 in 1789–93 to just six in 1794–99. In certain trades – such as wigmaking and, more surprisingly, printing and building trades – their numbers declined sharply. In terms of trades, however, there was great continuity: boys sought above all positions in watchmaking, food preparation and tanning, girls in tailoring, laundering or textiles.[52]

It could be argued that life for the urban *menu peuple* had changed little. A major grievance in 1789, indirect taxation, had been reintroduced and customs houses ringing cities and towns had been re-erected. The *laissez-faire, laissez-passer* legislation of the Revolution, notably the Le Chapelier law of June 1791, had if anything left them more vulnerable to the oscillations of a 'free' market. Memories of 1792–94 were to be cold comfort for dashed expectations of real social change. The descendants of the *sans-culottes* of the 1790s had to wait many decades for the realization of such hopes: until 1848 for the implementation of manhood suffrage (for women not until 1944); until 1864 for the right to strike and 20 years more for the right to form trade unions; until the 1880s for free, secular and compulsory education; and until the early twentieth century for an income tax and social welfare provisions for the sick, the elderly and the unemployed.

There is abundant evidence of the ways in which the Revolution and pro-tracted wars had a crippling effect on the economy of coastal cities and towns, and their hinterlands. East of Bordeaux in the Lot-et-Garonne, the small town of Tonneins had had 1,000 rope-makers in 1789: there were 200 in 1800. It had had 1,200 workers in the tobacco industry; there were fewer than 200 in 1800. Certain branches of the textile industry fared far better. Despite their polarized politics, Bédarieux and Lodève were two small south-ern textile towns which survived and at times prospered through army con-tracts, despite the loss of trade with the Levant.[53] Other textile towns such as Troyes or St-Quentin in northeastern France were not so fortunate: the num-bers of looms fell from 2,000 to 800 and from 12,000–14,000 to 3,000 respec-tively.[54] One reason why the land-clearers of Languedoc were desperate in their desire for an arable plot, particularly to plant grapevines, was because of the collapse of Carcassonne's textile trade with the Middle East after 1783 and especially after 1792. In the words of Serge Chassagne, the state of the textile industry in 1810 'must be read as the end of a commercial era, that of the export of the famous Levantine cloth through Marseille, then in a com-plete slump'.[55] That is, the desperate pressure of the peasantry to clear new land was above all a response to the decline of the local pastoral economy. There were many men like Claude Bonnet de Paillerets, in the southern Massif Central, much of whose fortune had come from the trade in wool and textiles, but who hankered after noble status and abandoned commerce for landowning during the Revolution. He succeeded in entering the world of the nineteenth-century notable.[56]

In inland cities, however, the effects were not always as dramatic, and it is estimated that industrial output was about 60 per cent of its 1789 levels a decade later. The cotton, iron and coal industries were stimulated by France's role in the continental system and protection from British imports.

The manufacturers of the small Norman textile town of Elbeuf had complained bluntly in their *cahier* of 1789 about the 'impediments to commerce' created by internal customs barriers and the maze of different weights and measures, and the lack of attention paid by government to the views of people like themselves.[57] This budding industrial bourgeoisie achieved its goals, including the recognition of their own importance: in the Year V, it was asked for the first time its opinion on a number of commercial treaties, and in the Year IX the advisory role of Chambers of Commerce was formally institutionalized. While Elbeuf felt the full brunt of trade blockades and food shortages, the revolutionary period was an important phase in the mechanization and concentration of the textile industry in the town rather than in rural piecework. Power remained throughout in the hands of manufacturers adept at protecting their control from challenges from workers as well as from Ancien Régime élites.

While it is impossible to generalize about the impact of the Revolution on standards of living, it seems clear that one class of people who were significantly better off were the élite of farmers – *laboureurs, fermiers* and large *métayers* – who under the Directory were able to pay off their rents or loans in *assignats* and sell their produce for hard currency. English visitors to France were struck by the change. Helen-Maria Williams, for example, noted in 1798:

> this class of wealthy peasants, hitherto unknown in France, and their wives and daughters, who formerly used to go bare-footed, who now are proud of their good shoes, their lace, their earrings and, above all, their gold crosses, witness to their vanity more than to their faith.[58]

Her comments were applied more broadly across rural society by Charles-Joseph Trouvé, a highly intelligent and politically adaptable man from an artisan family to whom the Revolution offered opportunities which would have been unthinkable under the Ancien Régime. In 1794, when just 26 years old, Trouvé had become editor of the *Moniteur*. He was stridently anti-Jacobin, but no less hostile to Ancien Régime élites and the Church. As Baron Trouvé, he was prefect of the department of the Aude in 1803–16 and recognized the improvement in the peasants' standard of living:

> The suppression of feudal dues and the tithe, the high price of foodstuffs, the division of the large estates, the sale in small lots of nationalized lands, the ending of indebtedness by [the inflation in the value of] paper currency, gave a great impulse to the industry of the peasantry. ... Although the Revolution had an impact on the diet of the people of the countryside, this impact was even more marked on clothing. ... In the old days, rough woollen cloth, or homespun linen, was their finest apparel; they disdain that today, cotton and velveteen cloth are the fabrics they desire, and the

large landholder is often confused with his sharecroppers because of the simplicity of his clothing.[59]

The Revolution was a watershed in rural–urban relations. In many ways the provincial centres of Ancien Régime institutions had been parasitic on the countryside: cathedral chapters, religious orders and resident nobles extracted 'surplus' from peasants which was expended in provincial towns such as Bayeux, Bourg and Laon through direct employment of domestic servants, indirect maintenance of skilled trades, especially in luxury goods, and in provision of charity. In the countryside around Angers, the Benedictine abbey of Ronceray had formerly owned 5 manors, 12 barns and winepresses, 6 mills, 46 farms and 6 houses, bringing into the town 27,000 *livres* annually. Some of it employed and was collected by lawyers in the 53 courts and tribunals charged with ensuring that the countryside met its obligations.

As a direct result of the Revolution, the countryside largely liberated itself from towns, leaving marketing and administration as the remaining links. It was this which aggravated the suffering of the destitute in such towns after 1789 and the impoverishment of those directly or indirectly dependent on expenditure by clerical and noble élites. This was the case, for example, in Bayeux, where the Sisters of Charity were no longer in a position to shelter the hundreds of poor rural girls in their lace-making workshops. The population of Bayeux declined by 15 per cent by 1830, leaving administrators, those involved in the rich cattle and dairy industries, farm suppliers and an impoverished artisanate who could never hope to return to the days when they serviced a numerous and wealthy noble and clerical élite.[60]

Another of the bonds tying the countryside to cities was loosened by the Revolution: the practice of wet-nursing. A precious resource for rural women in the hinterland of Paris and Lyon was the money earned from suckling the babies both of the urban wealthy and of wage-earning women whose work rendered breast feeding impracticable. Before the Revolution, about 85 per cent of the 20,000 babies born in Paris each year were sent to *nourrices* in the villages around Paris or to Normandy, Picardy and the Champagne (one-third would die before their mothers saw them again). While the practice would remain common into the nineteenth century, the Revolution marked the period when middle-class women accepted the Enlightenment critique of the practice as inhumane and unhealthy. By the Year X fewer than half of Parisian babies were sent to the countryside.[61]

Whatever the grand schemes and principles of the Jacobins, the destitute continued to constitute a large urban and rural underclass swollen in times of crisis by poorer labourers and workers. The realization by the National Assembly that poverty was not simply the result of the Church's charity, and that local government could simply not cope with poor relief, had generated a series of work schemes and temporary relief measures which were always piecemeal and never adequately financed by governments preoccupied with war. The revolutionary ideals of providing welfare to all French citizens who were unable to sustain themselves and their families were ended under the Directory. Only in the care of abandoned children was there an ongoing assumption of responsibility by the State.

The hungry years after 1794, when the collapse of economic regulation coincided with harvest failure, exposed the poor to a starvation against which the charity of parish clergy with fewer resources could never be adequate protection. The archives of provincial France are studded with stories such as that recounted by Alan Forrest of Guillaume Laurent of the village of Bully in the Rhône who in January 1793 despaired to the administration of his nine starving children after the death of his two cows.[62] Artisans could respond to threats posed by free enterprise by new organizations – in 1803 the glove-workers of Grenoble created the first mutual-aid society in France – but the poor remained particularly vulnerable.[63] In Forrest's words, 'never had so many measures been passed in the name of the people and supposedly in their interests; yet for these poor the reforms had brought little direct benefit'. Political reform and the abolition of seigneurialism were irrelevant to the landless and malnourished.[64]

One way in which the rural poor – particularly in the south, parts of the Massif Central and the mountains of the east – sought to take advantage of the Revolution was by seizing and clearing uncultivated land belonging to the commune as commons or to former seigneurs. Previously used for grazing livestock, these 'wastelands' or *vacants* were placed under extreme pressure as the rural poor cleared them for cultivation. This was a continuing and major concern to successive assemblies, and one of the most significant elements of the revolutionary experience for the rural poor was a struggle – often violent, and certainly not resolved by 1799 – over the ownership and use of this marginal land.

Between 1789 and 1799 successive governments issued a maze of legislation pertaining to land use, from a reformed Forest Code to a general Rural Code, laws on the subdivision of commons and on illegal land clearances. Of particular importance were decrees seeking to protect forests, decrees outlawing unauthorized clearing of common and State-owned land and others authorizing the subdivision and sale of Church and common land. Much of this legislation was predicated on the assumption of the unqualified rights of individual owners to use their property as they wished. Inevitably, such agrarian individualism conflicted with a concern to protect the environment, and it is this tension which generated much of the debate about private rights and public good, economic individualism and environmental protection.

In 1799–1801 a series of decrees issued by the Consulate placed all forests within State control, requiring illegally seized land to be returned, and outlawing unauthorized land-clearing. But not until Napoleon's restructuring of the forests administration was there an effective reassertion of State control over forest resources. Such was the extent of post-1789 land clearances and

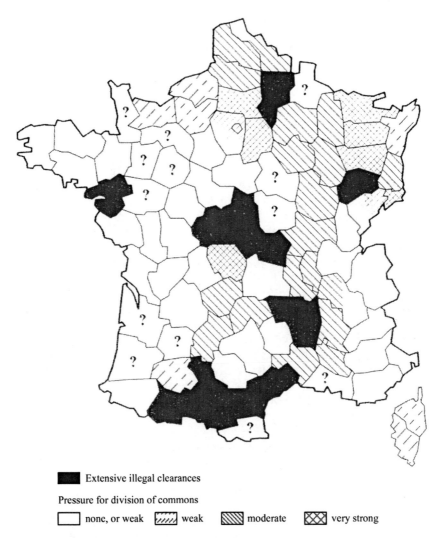

Extensive illegal clearances

Pressure for division of commons

none, or weak    weak    moderate    very strong

*Map 5*   Extent of illegal clearances of common land
Reproduced with permission from Nadine Vivier, *Propriété collective et identité communale: les biens communaux en France, 1750–1914*. Paris: Publications de la Sorbonne, 1998. Histoire de la France aux XIXe et XXe siècles: 46

tree-felling that a durable view quickly took hold that the Revolution had unleashed the essentially rapacious attitudes of peasants towards their environment, that the Revolution was an ecological disaster. Historians have agreed: the Revolution of 1789, claims Pierre Gresser, unleashed 'an onslaught on the forests;' revolutionary governments were unable to contain 'cette anarchie dévastatrice.'[65] Jean-Pierre Pitte agrees: 'The forest ... underwent new outrages during the Revolution and Empire. It was the massacre of the goose which laid the golden eggs. Peasant abuses were now rarely repressed.'[66]

Not surprisingly, officials of the French forests administration reconstituted in the early nineteenth century have also lent their weight to the perpetuation of this *légende noire* of the peasant revolution, that the revolutionary period was an unmitigated disaster for the natural environment until the re-emergence of effective authority under Napoleon.[67] During the Napoleonic Empire – 'the golden age of French statistics' – prefects were several times required to report on the condition of their department: its resources, production, character and public opinion. Not surprisingly, the prefects assured the Emperor that everything was improving, and they used the 'excesses' of the Revolution as the backdrop to Napoleon's achievements in ending forest depredation and illegal land clearances.

From the Loire-Inférieure Jean-Baptiste Huet de Coetlizan claimed that tree-felling had reduced rainfall and increased silt in rivers, both of which were ruinous for the Loire. The only animals which had increased in numbers were wolves; there were fewer deer. The prefect of the Bas-Rhin noted that, along the river, the killing of birds (especially magpies and pigeons) had had the effect of allowing the increase of weeds, caterpillars, bugs and bats, as had the population of rats multiplied with the killing of foxes, wildcats and other hunting animals. Here as elsewhere, there had been a proliferation of goats, 'the resource of the poor'.[68] Amans-Alexis Monteil, in his brilliant report on the Aveyron, noted that people were in general better off than before the Revolution, but bemoaned the environmental impact:

> People were already complaining about the degradation of forests before the Revolution: since that time, most of them have been razed. What little is left will soon accede to the pillagers' axes, the murderous teeth of animals, and the greed of the new owners.[69]

The comments of the prefect of the Vaucluse were echoed everywhere along the Mediterranean: 'After having cleared the plain, the hillsides were cleared, then even parts of the mountains were cleared; the remainder of the woods perished later under the axes of crime and greed, or under the teeth of flocks.'[70] Perhaps one-fifth of the surface of the Department of the Aude had been cleared, mostly illegally, after 1789. During the widespread, often violent battles over the ownership of the rough hillside pastures which covered most of the region, the poorer sections of the rural population illegally seized and cleared huge areas, uprooting the dominant tree cover, the ilex or green oaks, to extract tannic acid for the leather industry and to make charcoal.[71] The prefect, Baron Trouvé, claimed that unchecked land clearances had wreaked environmental damage:

> In this region, people have always complained about the fury of land seizures and clearances. Decrees and laws were made to repress it. The storms of the Revolution having released this brake, now powerless against anarchy, seizures multiplied, clearances became an almost general calamity; and a region, formerly covered with pastures and flocks, suddenly found itself threatened with losing the raw material for its manufactures, the principal source of its wealth. ... bushes and trees have been uprooted; and the fields on the hillsides, formerly so fertile and useful, were no long held together by the tree-roots and were washed into the streams which they have blocked and forced to overflow on to the river-flats, and to cover them with the gravel and stones with which their beds were obstructed.[72]

A less powerful counter-narrative has sought to nuance this bleak picture of unchecked pillage. More recently, some historians have instead placed stress on the Ancien Régime's encouragement of land-clearing and have highlighted an environmental consciousness among sections of rural society.[73] In particular, Louis XV's decrees encouraging clearances had exposed hundreds of thousands of hectares of hillsides to the effects of erosion. Some of the prefects had this longer-term perspective. From the Creuse, the baron Jean-Joseph de Verneilh-Puyraseau noted that the Revolution had only struck the final blows to a long process of deforestation. From the Tarn the prefect reported that the land clearances and deforestation went back a half-century. More specific was the report from Aix: 'the decree of 12 April 1767 devastated our forests, ruined the soil, blocked springs, at the same time as it led to the most destructive floods'.[74]

While there is no question that the Revolution of 1789 had unleashed a dramatic, prolonged period of human stress on the environment, the imputation that the battered landscape the administrators and legislators lamented in 1799 or 1815 was the result of revolutionary excess alone was therefore wide of the mark. Rougier de la Bergerie insisted that degradation, which was worst 'in the highlands and in the Midi,' had initially been unleashed by the monarchy's encouragement of land clearances in the 1760s and the interest the Church and seigneurs had had in seeing land come into production of crops and hence of tithes and harvest dues.[75]

The burgeoning demands of wood-fuelled industry and the royal navy were at least as responsible for depletion of forest resources as was the peasantry. For example, an average-sized navy vessel of 74 cannon required

2,800 century-old oaks for its construction, and 47 such vessels (as well as 37 frigates) were built in the 1780s.[76] Well before 1789 the administration and conservation of forests was under great strain because of increased pressure from rising population and wood prices and more commercial attitudes from owners of forest resources.[77] In any case, while forests may have been placed under severe stress by unchecked tree-felling after 1789, they were hardly 'devastated' by the time stricter legislation was reimposed by the law of 16 Nivôse Year IX/6 January 1801. Across France as a whole, the forested area lost by 1820 was about one-quarter of the total, extensive but hardly 'pillage.'[78]

One *légende noire* of the popular revolution has therefore been that the revolutionary period was a disaster for the environment, that the collapse of authority in 1789 removed constraints on peasants' atavistic impulses, ushering in a decade of unchecked destruction. As we have seen, the reality was far more complex. A second *légende noire* is that the French Revolution was similarly destructive of the family.[79] By instituting liberal divorce provisions, abolishing the testamentary power of parents and making marriage a purely civil act, it was soon argued that the Revolution had undermined parental authority and debased the institution of marriage.

Again, the reality is far more complex. Revolutionaries themselves argued that the intent of the reforms was in fact to 'regenerate' the family, seen to have been corrupted by the inequality of the Ancien Régime. The social practices of family life have rarely been studied: most analyses of 'private life' during the Revolution have gone no further than literary and visual representations and political discourse. The nature of family life and demographic practices in the early nineteenth century suggest that the Revolution did in fact accelerate significant change in family relationships, but there is no evidence that the value placed on the family or the institution of marriage had been eroded.

Added to the losses of life during the revolutionary decade – for which there are no reliable figures, but which were in the order of 1 million – the birth rate plummeted towards the end of the decade and in the early years of the new century: the total number of births in 1804 (933,700) was the lowest since 1748.[80] Nevertheless, it is estimated that the population increased by about 1.3 million, and by 2.5 million by 1814, the result of an increase in the marriage rate and a decline in the mortality rate. Using the massive data base of the Institut National d'Études Démographiques, Paul Spagnoli has demonstrated that there was a decisive decline in mortality and an increase in life expectancy from the 1780s to the 1820s: for women from 28.1 to 39.3 years and for men from 27.5 to 38.3 years. In searching for an explanation of a phenomenon unique in Europe, he concludes that it was directly linked to the consequences of the Revolution in the countryside: land sales, fiscal equity, the removal of seigneurial dues and the tithe, higher wages for agricultural labourers and greater incentives to increase production.[81]

The collapse or absence of clerical authority over birth control facilitated the response of the peasantry to the Revolution's inheritance laws of 1790 and 1793 requiring children to inherit equally. Given the desire and need to keep small family holdings intact, rural people responded not only by deliberately limiting family size, usually by *coïtus interruptus*, but also by using knowledge of the fertility cycle, abortion, douching, abstinence and occasionally infanticide.[82] The people of Lourmarin (Vaucluse) had long practised sexual relations before marriage, but the number of first-born children conceived before marriage escalated from 19.1 per cent in 1781–90 to no fewer than 34.4 per cent in 1791–1800; but they also practised birth control, and fewer children overall were born in the 1790s.

Lourmarin was by no means typical of rural communities: in the devout Norman parish of Crulai (Orne), only 3 per cent of children were born before their parents had been married for eight months. Even there, however, a startling demographic change points to one of the clearest indications of the impact of the Revolution on daily life: an unprecedented – and permanent – decline in the birth rate, from 42.5 per thousand in the 1780s to 36.6 in the following decade. Nationally the decline was from 38.8 per thousand in 1789 to 32.9 in 1804; the average interval between births increased from 19–30 to 31–48 months, a further indication of deliberate limitation of family size. In 1789–1824 there was a 22.6 per cent fall in female fecundity.

The legal status of women changed significantly in specific areas. In 1791 the law on inheritance guaranteed daughters equal inheritance rights to their brothers; only the addition in 1801 of a share of property set aside for parental discretion altered a law essentially in force to this day.[83] The Constitution of September 1791 defined civil majority in identical terms for men and women. In 1792 women were also acknowledged to possess sufficient reason and independence to serve as witnesses to public documents and to enter contracts. They were also allowed to share in the division of communal property in 1793. The important laws of September 1792, concerning civil status and divorce, treated husband and wife in symmetrical terms. In the words of Elisabeth Sledziewski:

> They acquired the stature, if not the rights, of complete citizens, in the sense that they were now looked upon as free, rational individuals capable of self-government. Of course, this acquisition of civil liberties did not include civic, that is, political rights, but it was a necessary condition of such rights and made their absence that much more unacceptable.[84]

Some things did not change. The divorce law was restricted in 1804, then abolished in 1816. In the first version of a new Civil Code proposed to the Convention by Cambacérès in 1793, mothers enjoyed the same prerogatives as fathers in the exercise of parental authority, but this was never implemented. A decade after the legislation of 1793, the Civil Code was careful to reassert paternal authority as the natural order of things: as Portalis put it on 5 Vendémiaire Year X/27 September 1801, the obedience of wives and daughters was not a matter of political subjugation but rather the outcome of a law of nature. Nor could the exhortation of revolutionaries to a harmonious and peaceful family life erode a tradition of domestic violence (*correction modérée*) to which men resorted.[85]

Indeed, few generalizations about the French Revolution have been echoed with such certainty than that it was a thoroughly negative experience for women, a turning point in the rhetoric and practice of domesticity and the private sphere. Lynn Hunt, Joan Landes and others have argued that, despite the political claims made by radical women in 1789–93, the transition from absolutism, under which all were subjects of the King, to a republican fraternity of male citizens ultimately served to reinforce the subordinate political position of women.[86]

In contrast, a recent analysis by Suzanne Desan of family law and its consequences has argued that a 'revolutionary challenge to domestic practices took place not just in the cultural and political imagination, but also in the texture of interpersonal relations and in the very partition of family goods'.[87] Men who made laws about the family, and peasant women who used or sidestepped them, were part of a central debate of the Revolution, how the new State would interact with its citizenry about suffrage, property and the embodiment of a new order: 'the family became a practical terrain for wrestling with the most fundamental questions of the French Revolution'.[88]

In Normandy, the area of Desan's case study, parents had complete testamentary freedom before the Revolution, but could not endow daughters with more than one-third of their property. 'A father can dower his daughter with a bouquet of roses', went one adage; 'he owes his daughter a husband and nothing more'.[89] Rural women as well as their urban sisters welcomed revolutionary legislation on inheritance in Normandy. Of 83 court cases in Caen over wills contested between siblings between 1790 and 1796, 45 were won by sisters. The citizeness Montfreulle stated to the court in 1795: 'I was married in 1773 "for a bouquet of roses", to use the Norman expression. That was how girls were married then. Greed was in the air and one often sacrificed the daughters for the happiness of one son'. Forty women from Falaise claimed in 1795 that 'from birth nature gave us equal rights to the succession of our fathers'.[90] For Basque and Catalan peasants in the Pyrenees, in contrast, the principle of equal inheritance undermined the central element of the continuity of the extended family and its house.

Between 70,000 and 100,000 people were divorced in 1792–1803, mainly in cities such as Paris and Rouen and in country towns like Vire, Bayeux and Honfleur. It was overwhelmingly women who initiated the divorce, to escape marriages that had ended in desertion, violence or misery. The incidence of divorce varied by social class and locale: in general, the smaller the community, the lower the divorce rate. In the department of Meuse, the

413 of 586 communes which had no divorce were mostly small. But there were specific factors, too: Orbec, a town of about 3,000 people in the Pays d'Auge, had 24 divorces and a remarkably high divorce/marriage ratio of about 1 to 10. The comparably sized town of Vassy in the Bocage Virois, in contrast, did not have a single divorce during the revolutionary period.[91] Many devout rural women found divorce a profoundly disturbing prospect. They had, after all, sworn before God and their parish that this was a union for life. Everywhere, however, the divorce law represented an opportunity and a challenge.

The effects of the new inheritance law and the abolition of seigneurialism may well have meant that women were both better nourished and in a stronger position within the family. In countless households after 1790, the rights of daughters became a family issue, just as the divorce law empowered wives – this was the most significant shift in the status of women in these years. Even though in the Basque country, for example, parents sought ways to sidestep revolutionary legislation, 'the wind of equality got up', in the words of Jacques Poumarède, 'and would never die down'.[92]

In many areas, such as the southern Massif Central and the Pyrenees, inheritance patterns continued, whereby sons ultimately received the family holding, so that daughters must have either been cajoled into renouncing their share or were compensated in other ways.[93] In Marlhes (Haute-Loire), for example, parents adopted a strategy to ensure that every child was provided for while preserving the household's wealth intact. This was done most commonly by agreement between the children after their parents' death, on whether to divide the farm or whether some siblings should leave and be materially compensated. The historian of Marlhes, James Lehning, has concluded that the revolutionary and Napoleonic legislation marked 'an important shift of control towards heirs', including daughters. On the other hand, because parents were able to transfer their property at any time, they retained an important measure of control over their offspring, even if they could no longer threaten to disinherit them, for example, over the choice of a marriage partner. Whatever the case, the social consequence of this legislation was to focus attention on children's rights as well as on the family estate.[94] In and around Montauban, the inheritance law did not abruptly change patterns of passing on the family holding to the eldest son, but there was a perceptible – and requisite – concern to meet the rights of his siblings, and a shift in values which saw the material needs of widows being expressly met in wills.[95]

The *légende noire* of the Revolution's attack on the family was particularly powerful among those for whom these years represented a protracted nightmare of violent assault on the Catholic Church. The Church emerged from Revolution without its extensive property, internally divided, and with several thousand of its clergy prematurely dead. It had lost its privileges and – because of its role in the emigration, Counter-Revolution and wars – much of its authority and prestige. The Revolution marks the end of the near-universal practice of Church-going in France, especially among men who had experienced life in the army and years free of Church education and the presence of a priest. This decline in the social authority of the Church was reflected in changes to the seasonality of marriages. During the eighteenth century, only about 3 per cent of marriages occurred in the months of December (Advent) and March (Lent). There was a sharp increase during the Revolution (to 12.4 per cent in 1793–99), and while pre-revolutionary patterns re-emerged thereafter, they were never so marked: in 1820–29 7.5 per cent of marriages occurred in these two months (in towns the figures were a few percentages higher).[96]

The Catholic Church's claims to a monopoly of worship and morality, so vigorously expressed in its *cahiers* in 1789, could not be realized: for virtually all the 169,500 priests, monks and nuns the revolutionary decade was a turbulent, terrifying and, for many, a tragic experience. What was experienced as an attack on the Church is still visible today in the disfigured statues around Church doorways or in cloisters that have never been repaired. Even in parts of the west, the experience of civil war and deep political divisions may have disrupted the beliefs of a significant minority. In 1785 95.5 per cent of children in Alençon were baptized on the day of their birth or the morrow; this slowly declined across the 1790s to 86 per cent in 1800.[97]

Yet the laity – especially women – had proved their religious commitment in large areas of the countryside; from women, too, would come a widening stream of recruits to religious orders. Cultural practices continued to express deeply engrained Catholic morality. Like revolutionaries before and since, moreover, Jacobins were to find that the attempt to forge a new, revolutionary culture that would replace the religious dimensions of the Ancien Régime as surely as the Republic had replaced the monarchy would founder on popular attachment to the rituals of belief. Despite the richness of the revolutionary culture, it could not replace a Catholicism that seemed to many deeper in substance and promise. This was to be a key cause of the violence of the revolutionary decade.

For France's 700,000 Protestants and 40,000 Jews, in marked contrast, the legislation of 1789–91 represented legal emancipation, civil equality and the freedom to worship. Protestant communities such as Pont-de-Montvert (Lozère) and Lourmarin (Vaucluse) were enthusiastic in their support for the Revolution. Though there seems to have been a decline in religiosity during the eighteenth century, oral memories of earlier religious atrocities were kept alive within the community. The construction of a Protestant Church in Lourmarin in 1805 and in Pont-de-Montvert in 1818 was to be a tangible reminder of the significance of the Revolution for their descendants. Despite the tardy and reluctant extension of civic equality to the Ashkenazim Jews of the east, emancipation facilitated the Dreyfus family's rise from itinerant pedlars in Alsace in the 1780s to wealthy, confident textile magnates in the

1860s, and imbued in them an ineradicable love of a France which symbol-ized civil liberty, equality of opportunity and fraternity between Jews and Christians.[98]

The path to emancipation was not a straightforward or pleasant one for members of either minority. Protestants in the south had been implicated in horrific bloodshed in Nîmes and Montauban and fears that militant Catholics had not accepted their civic equality were realized in the bloodlet-ting after Thermidor. Jews had similar stories to tell; unlike Protestants, moreover, they could never be confident that their fellow citizens had accepted their beliefs as a religion like any other rather than marking them as members of a 'nation' or 'race'. For Jews thereafter, acceptance as a citizen often meant complete assimilation.

*   *   *

David Andress concluded an overview of popular participation by entitling his final chapter 'Revolution against the People?' His answer is that this was never the people's revolution. 'The common people of France had made the Revolution, even if its meaning and course had been taken from them': what the people won they had had to fight for by violent insurrection. In the end, he argues, the only significant gain for the common people was the abolition of feudalism.[99]

In contrast, Peter Jones has compared six villages from very different regions: Lorraine, the Ile-de-France, Brittany, the Gévaudan region of Lang-uedoc, the Rhône valley and Gascony. His conclusions reinforce the findings of Lefebvre, Markoff and others about the social impact of the Revolution: while the weight of seigneurialism varied widely, the abolition of seigneurial dues and other rights, and of the tithe, then the introduction of justices of the peace and widespread land sales had a direct, material impact on every village. The abolition of privilege and the call to participation in national elections underpinned the central cultural and political change: the assump-tion by villagers that they were equal in the eyes of the law and ultimately the sovereign people.[100] This book has highlighted the value of such closely observed social history for an understanding of the extraordinary shift in cultural meanings and social behaviours that was the French Revolution.

It is true that, whatever the importance of these changes to government, political ideas and memories, many of the essential characteristics of daily life emerged largely unchanged. Much of daily life and the deepest assump-tions about why the world is as it is were beyond the reach of revolutionary reformers. As understood by Fernand Braudel and others of the *Annales* school, real change to daily life was a matter of the *longue durée*, not of short-term upheaval. If human history were likened to a day in the life of an ocean, then the few really transforming structural changes to the way humans have used the environment and technology could be imagined as the irresistible force of the tides. Less powerful by far, if more spectacular, have been the variety of human social systems which could be likened to a series of waves crashing on the shore. In this view, the French Revolution was but one of these waves. As for the history of politics – the mere history of events, as the scholars of the *Annales* school dismissed it – it has been no more than the froth on those waves, and as fleeting and inconsequential. In Philippe Ariés' classic study of the history of childhood, the French Revolution is accordingly subsumed into general comments on the rise of liberal individualism and industrialism.[101]

Except in places where the rural economy had changed abruptly, for example, to more market-oriented winegrowing, or where a branch of urban work had collapsed, most people worked in 1799 as they had in 1789. The nature of their work – manual, skilled, repetitive – remained the same. The production of wine, wheat and cloth involved the same techniques: only the scale of production had changed in particular areas. As in 1700, the countryside in 1800 was a busy, crowded landscape of manual labour. Even in areas where land use remained unchanged, however, the Revolution went to the heart of community and family life: this was a revolutionary experience. Certainly, some of the changes may have been ephemeral: under the Directory, the practice of giving revolutionary names to one's children or to one's community largely disappeared; 'regenerated' towns and villages reverted to their Ancien Régime nomenclature; and children with revolutionary names were rebaptized or simply took on another name. The Napoleonic Code sharply restricted grounds for divorce. A resurgent Church was soon as present in the countryside as before 1789. In other ways, however, the practices of daily life were changed forever, as were the markers in the mental universe which gave meanings to people about who they were and how the world might be.

The conclusion of this book reminds us, finally, of the fundamental – if necessarily illusory – goal of the historian: to understand the past as the present to those who lived through it. All people live with insecurities and fears as well as dreams, but the revolutionary decade after 1789 was for most French people a time of unprecedented hopes and anxieties, a time when the most fundamental elements of daily life were improved, threatened and laid bare. The single most important characteristic of daily life after 1789 was uncertainty about when the most profound aspirations of 1789 and the basic needs of survival might be enjoyed in peace. The legislative impulses of revolution originated in national assemblies in Paris, but it was in small towns and villages that the Revolution was lived.

# Notes

## Introduction

1. Peter McPhee, *Revolution and Environment in Southern France: Peasants, Lords, and Murder in the Corbières, 1780–1830* (Oxford, 1999), 60.
2. Richard Cobb, *The Police and the People: French Popular Protest 1789–1820* (Oxford, 1970), part I: a brilliant discussion of the nature and limitations of these archival sources.
3. See, for example, Georges Bordenove, *La vie quotidienne en Vendée pendant la Révolution* (Paris, 1974), which, despite its title, is essentially a history of the insurrection in the Vendée through the words of its élite supporters.
4. Alain Corbin, *The Life of an Unknown: The Rediscovered World of a Clog Maker in Nineteenth-Century France* (New York, 2001).
5. Cobb, *The People's Armies*, trans. Marianne Elliott (New Haven, CT, 1987).
6. Cobb, *Police and the People*; *Reactions to the French Revolution* (London, 1972); *Paris and Its Provinces* (Oxford, 1975).
7. Cobb, *Police and the People*, 224–5, 294.
8. *Ibid.*, especially part III; *Reactions to the French Revolution*, especially 128–80. See Martyn Lyons, 'Cobb and the Historians', in Gwynne Lewis and Colin Lucas (eds), *Beyond the Terror: Essays in French Regional and Social History, 1794–1815* (Cambridge and New York, 1983).
9. Albert Soboul, *Les sans-culottes parisiens en l'an II: histoire politique et sociale des sections de Paris, 2 juin 1793–9 Thermidor An II* (La Roche-sur-Yon, 1958), trans. Gwynne Lewis as *The Parisian Sans-Culottes and the French Revolution, 1793–4* (Oxford, 1964).
10. Cobb, *Police and the People*, 296.
11. *Ibid.*
12. See, for example, David Garrioch, *The Making of Revolutionary Paris* (Berkeley and London, 2002); Gail Bossenga, *The Politics of Privilege: Old Regime and Revolution in Lille* (Cambridge, 1991); Alan Forrest, *Society and Politics in Revolutionary Bordeaux* (1975); Bill Edmonds, *Jacobinism and the Revolt of Lyon, 1789–1793* (1990); William Scott, *Terror and Repression in Revolutionary Marseilles* (1973); Paul Hanson, *Provincial Politics in the French Revolution: Caen and Limoges, 1789–1794* (1989).
13. Georges Lefebvre, 'La Révolution française et les paysans', *AHRF* 10 (1933), 97–128.
14. Anatolï Ado, *Paysans en Révolution. Terre, pouvoir et jacquerie 1789–1794*, trans. Serge Aberdam, Marcel Dorigny *et al.* (Paris, 1996); Peter Jones, *The Peasantry in the French Revolution* (Cambridge, 1988); John Markoff, *The Abolition of Feudalism: Peasants, Lords, and Legislators in the French Revolution* (University Park, PA, 1996).
15. Sutherland, *The French Revolution and Empire: The Quest for a Civic Order* (Oxford, 2003), 387.
16. Cobb, *Reactions to the French Revolution*, 125; Eugen Weber, *Peasants into Frenchmen: The Modernization of Rural France, 1870–1914* (Stanford, CA, 1976), 247, 255; Sutherland, *France, 1789–1815: Revolution and Counterrevolution* (Oxford and New York, 1986), 439, 440; Le Goff's comment was made in an acerbic review of P.M. Jones, *The Peasantry in the French Revolution* (Cambridge, 1988).

17. David Andress, *French Society in Revolution, 1789–1799* (Manchester and New York, 1999), 6; *The French Revolution and the People* (London, 2004), conclusion.
18. Georges Lefebvre, *Questions agraires au temps de la Terreur. Documents publiés et annotés* (La Roche-sur-Yon, 1954); Albert Soboul, *Problèmes paysans de la Révolution, 1789–1848* (Paris, 1976); Ado, *Paysans en Révolution*; Andress, *The French Revolution and the People*; Jones, *The Peasantry in the French Revolution*; Markoff, *The Abolition of Feudalism*; Sutherland, *The French Revolution and Empire*; Michel Vovelle, *La découverte de la politique. Géopolitique de la Révolution française* (Paris, 1993).
19. Andress, *The French Revolution and the People*.
20. Different 'calendars' are described in Cobb, *Reactions to the French Revolution*.
21. Excellent general overviews of rural France are Daniel Roche, *France in the Enlightenment*, trans. Arthur Goldhammer (Cambridge, MA, 1998), ch. 4; Jones, *The Peasantry in the French Revolution*, chs 1, 2; Georges Duby and Armand Wallon (eds), *Histoire de la France rurale*, vol. iii (Paris, 1976). Population figures are in Jacques Dupâquier, *Histoire de la population française*, vol. 3 (Paris, 1988).
22. See, for example, Georges Lefebvre, 'The Place of the Revolution in the Agrarian History of France', in Robert Forster and Orest Ranum (eds), *Rural Society in France: Selections from the Annales* (Baltimore, MD, 1977), 31–49; Alfred Cobban, *The Social Interpretation of the French Revolution* (Cambridge, 1964); Cobb, *Paris and Its Provinces*. Note the comments of Alan Forrest and Peter Jones in *Reshaping France: Town, Country and Region during the French Revolution* (Manchester, 1991), 2–4.
23. Peter Jones, *Liberty and Locality in Revolutionary France: Six Villages Compared, 1760–1820* (Cambridge and New York, 2003). See also Serge Bianchi and M. Chancelier, *Draveil et Montgeron, deux villages en Révolution* (Le Mée-sur-Seine, 1989).
24. Jean-Pierre Jessenne, *Pouvoir au village et révolution: Artois 1760–1848* (Lille, 1987); Liana Vardi, *The Land and the Loom: Peasants and Profit in Northern France 1680–1800* (Durham, NC, and London, 1993).
25. *Poètes audois dans la tourmente: André Chénier, Venance Dougados, Fabre d'Églantine* (Carcassonne, 1993), 17; Jean Sagnes (ed.), *Le Pays catalan* (Pau, 1983), 571.
26. Jean Robiquet, *Daily Life in the French Revolution* (New York, 1965).
27. Jean-Paul Bertaud, *La vie quotidienne en France au temps de la Révolution (1789–1795)* (Paris, 1983); Michel Vovelle, *La mentalité révolutionnaire: société et mentalité sous la Révolution française* (Paris, 1985).
28. Serge Bianchi, *La Révolution culturelle de l'An II* (Paris, 1982); Alan Forrest, *Paris, the Provinces and the French Revolution* (London, 2004); Isser Woloch, *The New Regime: Transformations of the French Civic Order, 1789–1820s* (New York, 1994), 18.
29. Alan Forrest, *Soldiers of the French Revolution* (Durham, NC, 1990); Jean-Paul Bertaud, *The Army of the French Revolution: From Citizen-Soldiers to Instruments of Power*, trans. R.R. Palmer (Princeton, NJ, 1988).
30. Malcolm Crook, *Elections in the French Revolution: An Apprenticeship in Democracy, 1789–1799* (Cambridge, 1996); Mona Ozouf, *Festivals and the French Revolution*, trans. Alan Sheridan (Cambridge, MA, 1988).

# 1   Describing the old regime

1. *La Révolution vue de l'Aisne, en 200 documents* (Laon, 1990), 18.
2. Jones, *The Peasantry in the French Revolution*, 27–9.

3. Note the comments on this issue by Gilbert Shapiro and John Markoff, *Revolutionary Demands: A Content Analysis of the Cahiers de Doléances of 1789* (Stanford, CA, 1998), 140–7; Jones, *The Peasantry in the French Revolution*, 63.
4. Gilbert Larguier *et al.* (eds), *Cahiers de doléances audois* (Carcassonne, 1989); McPhee, *Revolution and Environment in Southern France*, 42.
5. Edward A. Allen, 'L'influence des cahiers modèles en 1789: l'expérience du Gard', *AHRF* 291 (1993), 13–31.
6. *Cahiers de doléances du bailliage d'Amont*, vol. 1 (Besançon, 1918); vol. 2 (Auxerre, 1927). This analysis is based on several thousand parish *cahiers* which were published in the first half of the twentieth century under the auspices of the Ministère de l'Instruction Publique as the *Collection de Documents Inédits sur l'Histoire Économique de la Révolution Française*. This series is outlined in Shapiro and Markoff, *Revolutionary Demands*, 117–19.
7. Larguier *et al.* (eds), *Cahiers audois*, 20–1, annexes IV and V. See the comments of Shapiro and Markoff, *Revolutionary Demands*, 147–60.
8. Gilbert Larguier *et al.*, 'Les Assemblées primaires de la sénéchaussée de Carcassonne (8–16 mars 1789): typologie et composition sociale', *Bulletin de la Société des Études Scientifiques de l'Aude* 89 (1989), 101–20. See also Shapiro and Markoff, *Revolutionary Demands*, 136–40.
9. Jones, *The Peasantry in the French Revolution*, ch. 2; Sutherland, *The Chouans: The Social Origins of Popular Counter-Revolution in Upper Brittany, 1770–1796* (Oxford, 1982), 70.
10. Robert Forster, *The Nobility of Toulouse in the Eighteenth Century: A Social and Economic Study* (Baltimore, MD, 1960), especially chs 2–3, and 'Obstacles to Agricultural Growth in Eighteenth-Century France', *AHR* 75 (1970), 1600–15. On the size and internal hierarchy of the nobility, see Guy Chaussinand-Nogaret, *The French Nobility in the Eighteenth Century: From Feudalism to Enlightenment*, trans. W. Doyle (Cambridge, 1985), chs 2, 4.
11. Annie Antoine, 'La seigneurie en France à la fin de l'Ancien Régime. État des connaissances et nouvelles perspectives de recherches', in Gérard Béaur *et al.* (eds), *Les sociétés rurales en Allemagne et en France (XVIIIe et XIXe siècles). Actes de colloque international de Göttingen (23–25 novembre 2000)* (Rennes, 2004), 47–64.
12. Markoff, *The Abolition of Feudalism*; Shapiro and Markoff, *Revolutionary Demands*.
13. On the limitations to the usefulness of the *cahiers*, see Jones, *The Peasantry in the French Revolution*, 58–67; Markoff, *The Abolition of Feudalism*, 25–9.
14. Jacques Bernet (ed.), *Le journal d'un maître d'école d'Île-de-France (1771–1792): Silly-en-Multien de l'Ancien Régime à la Révolution* (Villeneuve-d'Asq, 2000), 181–3. The commune is today Silly-le-Long.
15. Ado, *Paysans en Révolution*, 114.
16. *Cahiers de doléances du bailliage d'Amont*, vol. 2, 199. I owe this reference to Kieko Matteson.
17. Étienne Frénay (ed.), *Cahiers de doléances de la province de Roussillon (1789)* (Perpignan, 1979), 163–4.
18. Markoff, *The Abolition of Feudalism*, ch. 2.
19. Denise, Maurice and Robert Bréant, *Menucourt. Un village du Vexin français pendant la Révolution 1789–1799* (Menucourt, 1989), 45–6.
20. Abel Poitrineau, 'Les assemblées primaries du bailliage de Salers en 1789', *RHMC* 25 (1978), 441.
21. See Jean-Claude Hocquet, 'Une révolution dans la Révolution. Quelques motifs de la creation du système métrique décimal', *L'Espace et le temps reconstruits: la*

*Révolution française, une revolution des mentalités et cultures?* (Aix-en-Provence, 1990), 97–108.

22. Alfred Gandilhon, *Cahiers de doléances du bailliage de Bourges et des bailliages secondaires de Vierzon et d'Henrichement pour les Etats-Généraux de 1789* (Bourges, 1910), 170–84, 187–91. Translated in Philip Dwyer and Peter McPhee (eds), *The French Revolution and Napoleon. A Sourcebook* (London and New York, 2002).

23. Peter McPhee, *Une communauté languedocienne dans l'histoire: Gabian 1760–1960* (Nîmes, 2001), ch. 1; Albert Fabre, *Histoire des communes du canton de Roujan* (Mâcon, 1894), 145–55.

24. Anthony Crubaugh, *Balancing the Scales of Justice. Local Courts and Rural Society in Southwest France, 1750–1800* (University Park, PA, 2001).

25. *Ibid.*; Nicole Castan, *Justice et répression en Languedoc* (Paris, 1980), 54–82; Jeremy D. Hayhoe, 'Neighbours before the Court: Crime, Village Communities and Seigneurial Justice in Northern Burgundy, 1750–1790', *FH* 17 (2003), 127–48; Sutherland, *The Chouans*, 182–4; Jonathan Dewald, *Pont-St.-Pierre, 1378–1789: Lordship, Community and Capitalism in Early Modern France* (Berkeley and Los Angeles, CA, 1987), 254–5; Steven G. Reinhardt, *Justice in the Sarladais, 1770–1790* (Baton Rouge, 1991).

26. Jones, *The Peasantry in the French Revolution*, 94–8.

27. Paul Beik (ed.), *The French Revolution* (London, 1971), 56–63.

28. Larguier *et al.* (eds), *Cahiers de doléances audois*, 120–1.

29. Shapiro and Markoff, *Revolutionary Demands*, especially ch. 14 and appendix I; Markoff, *The Abolition of Feudalism*, ch. 2. Virtually all of these environmental grievances ranked higher in parish concerns than in general Third Estate *cahiers* and well above noble concerns.

30. *Cahiers de doléances du bailliage de Mirecourt* (Epinal, 1928), 34.

31. *Cahiers de doléances du bailliage de Troyes et du bailliage de Bar-sur-Seine pour les États-Généraux de 1789*, 3 vols (Troyes, 1909–11), vol. 1, 423. This was also voiced at Fay and Provency et Genouilly, vol. 2, 102, 444; *Cahiers de doléances de la sénéchaussée de Rennes pour les Etats-Généraux de 1789*, 4 vols (Rennes, 1909–12), vol. 2, 745. For the frequency of this complaint, see Shapiro and Markoff, *Revolutionary Demands*, 450.

32. *Cahiers de doléances du bailliage d'Orléans pour les États-Généraux de 1789*, 2 vols (Orléans, 1906–07), vol. 1, 761; *Cahiers de doléances des sénéchaussées de Niort et de Saint-Maixent et des communautés et corporations de Niort et Saint-Maixent pour les États-Généraux de 1789* (Niort, 1912), 87.

33. In general on anti-industrial grievances in the *cahiers*, see Andrée Corvol, *L'homme aux bois. Histoire des relations de l'homme et de la forêt, XVIIe-XXe siècle* (Paris, 1987), 71–78.

34. *Cahiers de doléances du bailliage d'Amont*, vol. 1, 286; vol. 2, 75. A similiar complaint came from Gros-Chêne (Loir-et-Cher): *Cahiers de doléances du bailliage de Blois et du bailliage secondaire de Romorantin pour les États-Généraux de 1789*, 2 vols (Blois, 1907–08), vol. 1, 475. On the environmental impact of rural industry in eastern France, see Jean-Marie Schmitt, 'De la proto-industrie à la révolution industrielle: la vallée de Saint-Amarin, région pionnière au XVIIIe siècle', *Historiens et géographes* 86 (1995), 207–10; Jean-Paul Jacob and Michel Mangin (eds), *De la mine à la forge en Franche-Comté, des origines au XIXe siècle: approche archéologique et historique* (Besançon, 1990); François Vion-Delphin, 'Forêts et cahiers de doléances: l'exemple de la Franche-Comté', in Denis Woronoff (ed.), *Révolution et espaces forestiers. Colloque des 3 & 4 juin 1987, Groupe d'histoire des forêts françaises* (Paris, 1988), 11–22.

35. *Cahiers de doléances du bailliage de Mirecourt*, 30.
36. *Cahiers de doléances pour les États-Généraux de 1789: département de la Marne*, vol. 1 (Epernay, 1906–11), 74. See also, among many others, Brizeaux: 108, Charmontois-l'Abbé: 136.
37. *Cahiers de doléances des bailliages des généralités de Metz et de Nancy pour les États-Généraux de 1789*, vol. 1 (Nancy, 1907–30), 13, 43. See Jean-Pierre Husson, 'Les paysages forestiers lorrains, rôle et impact de l'épisode révolutionnaire (étude de géographie historique)', in Woronoff (ed.), *Révolution et espaces forestiers*, 63–70.
38. *Cahiers de doléances des bailliages des généralités de Metz et de Nancy*, vol. 1, 66.
39. *Ibid.*, 130–1.
40. *Ibid.*, 175.
41. *Cahiers de doléances du bailliage de Bourges et des bailliages secondaires de Vierzon et d'Henrichement pour les États-Généraux de 1789* (Bourges, 1910), 383.
42. *Cahiers des doléances des corporations de la ville d'Angers et des paroisses de la sénéchaussée particulière d'Angers pour les États-Généraux de 1789*, vol. 2 (Angers, 1916), 744. For Lower Normandy it has been estimated that in the 1780s forges were consuming 57,000–62,000 *cordes* of timber (a *corde* was approximately 3 m$^3$) annually from forests capable of producing 30,000–35,000: G. Houzard, 'Les grosses forges ont-elles mangé la forêt?', *Annales de Normandie* 30 (1980), 245–69.
43. Alain Le Bloas, 'La question du domaine congéable', *AHRF* 331 (2003), 1–27.
44. *Cahiers de doléances des sénéchaussées de Quimper et de Concarneau pour les États-Généraux de 1789* (Rennes, 1927), 37. See Michel Duval, 'Besoins de guerres et forêts bretonnes', in Woronoff (ed.), *Révolution et espaces forestiers*, 119–26.
45. *Cahiers de doléances des sénéchaussées de Quimper et de Concarneau pour les États-Généraux de 1789*, 100; *Cahiers de doléances de la sénéchaussée de Rennes pour les États-Généraux de 1789*, vol. 4 (Ploumogoar), 152.
46. *Cahiers de doléances du bailliage de Troyes et du bailliage de Bar-sur-Seine pour les États-Généraux de 1789*, vol. 2, 32.
47. *Cahiers de doléances du bailliage de Mirecourt*, 133.
48. Georges and Hubert Bourgin, *L'industrie sidérurgique en France au début de la Révolution* (Paris, 1920), 277.
49. Corvol, *L'Homme aux bois*, ch. 8.
50. *Cahiers de doléances pour les États-Généraux de 1789: département de la Marne*, vol. 1, 642.
51. *Cahiers de doléances du bailliage d'Orléans pour les États-Généraux de 1789*, vol. 1, 43; *Cahiers de doléances de la sénéchaussée de Rennes pour les États-Généraux de 1789*, vol. 1, 136; *Cahiers de doléances du bailliage de Sens pour les États-Généraux de 1789* (Auxerre, 1908), 197.
52. *Cahiers de doléances des bailliages des généralités de Metz et de Nancy pour les États-Généraux de 1789*, vol. 1, 639.
53. *Ibid.*, vol. 3, 142. For the consumption of wood in Lorraine, see baron de Dietrich, *Description des gîtes de minérai, forges, salines, verreries, tréfileries, fabriques de fer-blanc, porcelaine, faïence, etc., de la Lorraine méridionale* (Paris, 1799–1800); Loysel, *Observations sur les salines du département de la Meurthe ...* (Paris, an III).
54. Some 66 of Shapiro and Markoff's sample of 748 parish *cahiers* expressed their concerns about wild or 'destructive animals'. Gilbert Shapiro, FRAS: The French Revolution Analysis System. A Portable Data Archive, Version 1. I am grateful to Gilbert Shapiro for making available this rich resource.
55. *Cahiers de doléances de la sénéchaussée de Cahors pour les États-Généraux de 1789* (Cahors, 1908), 327–8.

56. *Ibid.*, 95. On the vulnerability of the Lot to flooding, see Philippe Delvit, 'Construire en rivière au XVIIIe siècle: les continuateurs de Colbert sur le Lot', *Annales du Midi* 95 (1983), 429–47.

57. *Cahiers de doléances de la sénéchaussée de Cahors pour les États-Généraux de 1789*, 21, 72.

58. *Ibid.*, 198.

59. *Ibid.*, 285, 297.

60. *Cahiers de doléances de la sénéchaussée de Bigorre pour les États-Généraux de 1789* (Tarbes, 1925), 403.

61. *Ibid.*, 455, 500.

62. However, Lacassagne and Lafitole asserted the direct contrary, 'however often they might have need': *Ibid.*, 135, 156, 326, 331.

63. For example, from St-Pierre-de-Coutances, Hauteville-près-la-Mer and Nicorps: *Cahiers de doléances du bailliage de Cotentin (Coutances et secondaires) pour les États-Généraux de 1789*, vol. 1 (Paris, 1907), 107, 346, 484.

64. *Ibid.*, vol. 1, 631.

65. Larguier *et al.* (eds), *Cahiers de doléances audois*.

66. *Cahiers des doléances des corporations de la ville d'Angers et des paroisses de la sénéchaussée particulière d'Angers pour les États-Généraux de 1789*, vol. 2, 530, 558.

67. *Cahiers de doléances du bailliage de Blois et du bailliage secondaire de Romorantin pour les États-Généraux de 1789*, vol. 1, 51.

68. *Cahiers de doléances du bailliage d'Arques (secondaire de Caudebec) pour les États-Généraux de 1789* (Lille, 1922), 34, 532.

69. *Cahiers de doléances de la sénéchaussée de Civray pour les États-Généraux de 1789* (Niort, 1925), 180–1.

70. This anticipates the argument of McPhee, *Revolution and Environment in Southern France*, 47–48, 141–47; Fréréric Ogé, 'Héritage révolutionnaire: les forêts pyrénéennes, enjeux de conflis États-communautés', in Andrée Corvol (ed.), *La Nature en Révolution, 1750–1800* (Paris, 1993), 156; Denis Woronoff, 'La "dévastation révolutionnaire" des forêts', in Denis Woronoff (ed.), *Révolution et espaces forestiers. Colloque des 3 & 4 juin 1987* (Paris, 1988), 52.

71. Marquis de Turbilly, *Mémoire sur les défrichemens* (Paris, 1760); Archives Nationales (hereafter AN), Procès-verbaux des Comités d'Agriculture. Turbilly's own experience was, however, confined to Anjou, and his recommendations had as much to do with reforestation as with burning scrub.

72. AN Recueil général des anciennes lois, AD IV, 4; Archives Départementales (hereafter AD) Aude 10C 22, 23; Léon Dutil, *L'État économique du Languedoc à la fin de l'Ancien Régime* (Paris, 1911), 106–30; Jones, *Peasantry*, 11, 144. On Colbert's ordinance, see Simon Schama, *Landscape and Memory* (New York, 1995); Andrée Corvol (ed.), *La Forêt. Actes du 113e Congrès national des sociétés savantes, Strasbourg 1988* (Paris, 1991).

73. Albert Soboul, *Les campagnes montpelliéraines à la fin de l'ancien régime: propriété et culture après les compoix* (Paris, 1958); E.A. Allen, 'Deforestation and Fuel Crisis in Pre-Revolutionary Languedoc', *FHS* 13 (1984), 466; Gilbert Larguier, 'Le drap et le grain en Languedoc. Recherches sur Narbonne et le Narbonnais (1300–1789)', Doctorat d'État, 3 vols (Université de Paris-VII, 1992), 560–63; McPhee, *Revolution and Environment in Southern France*, 21–4. In a July 1790 debate on 'défrichements' in the Comité d'Agriculture, reference was made to a debate in 1787 between Cheyssac and Lavoisier, when the former claimed that far more land had been cleared following Louis XV's decrees than had been declared: AN Procès-verbaux

du Comité d'Agriculture. For two examples of the extent of *défrichements*, see AD Aude 4E 144 1D 2, Délibérations, Fitou; 435 1D 1, Délibérations, Villerouge-Termenès, 1770–89.

74. McPhee, *Revolution and Environment in Southern France*, 122–26, 182–84. In general, see Michel Noël, *L'Homme et la forêt en Languedoc-Roussillon. Histoire et économie des espaces boisés* (Perpignan, 1996), especially 61–9.

75. *Cahiers de doléances de la sénéchaussée de Nîmes pour les États-Généraux de 1789*, 2 vols (Nîmes, 1908–09), vol. 1, 131.

76. *Cahiers de doléances du bailliage de Troyes et du bailliage de Bar-sur-Seine pour les États-Généraux de 1789*, vol. 3, 348.

77. *Ibid.*, vol. 1, 618. See the similar views of Bengy-sur-Craon: *Cahiers de doléances du bailliage de Bourges et des bailliages secondaires de Vierzon et d'Henrichement pour les États-Généraux de 1789*, 51.

78. *Cahiers de doléances du bailliage de Mirecourt*, 147. Also Rouvres-en-Xaintois: 204.

79. Larguier *et al.* (eds), *Cahiers de doléances audois*, 182–4.

80. Steven L. Kaplan, *La fin des corporations* (Paris, 2001).

81. Gilbert Larguier, *1789 dans la sénéchaussée de Limoux* (Limoux, 1989), 52–6; Larguier *et al.* (eds), *Cahiers de doléances audois*, 260–75.

82. André Abbiatéci and Paul Perdrix, *Les débuts de la Révolution dans les pays de l'Ain (1787–1790)* (Bourg-en-Bresse, 1989), 154–5.

83. Steven L. Kaplan and Cynthia J. Koepp (eds), *Work in France: Representations, Meaning, Organization and Practice* (Ithaca, NY, 1986), chs 2–9; William H. Sewell, *Work and Revolution in France: The Language of Labor from the Old Régime to 1848* (Cambridge, 1980), chs 2–3; Michael Sonenscher, *Work and Wages: Natural Law, Politics and the Eighteenth-Century French Trades* (Cambridge, 1989).

84. Jeffry Kaplow (ed.), *France on the Eve of Revolution* (New York, 1971), 161–67; Michel Morineau, 'Budgets populaires en France au XVIIIe siècle', *Revue d'histoire économique et sociale* 1 (1972), 203–37.

85. Kaplow (ed.), *France on the Eve of Revolution*, 161–7; Richard Cobb and Colin Jones (eds), *Voices of the French Revolution* (Topsfield, MA, 1988), 42. The village in question may be Vaudrimesnil.

86. Jeffry Kaplow, *Elbeuf during the Revolutionary Period: History and Social Structure* (Baltimore, MD, 1964), 192–205.

87. The difficulties of reconciling noble 'reformism' with the intransigence of their deputies in 1789 is reflected in the tension between the 'afterword' and chapters 5, 7 and 8 in Chaussinand-Nogaret, *French Nobility*. The *cahier* of Dourdan is reproduced in John Hall Stewart (ed.), *A Documentary Survey of the French Revolution* (New York, 1951), 76–84.

88. *Pétition des femmes du tiers-état au Roi, 1 janvier 1789, passim.*

89. 'Cahier des doléances et réclamations des femmes par Mme. B ... B ..., 1789', in *Cahiers des doléances des femmes et autres textes* (Paris, 1981), 47–59.

90. John W. Shaffer, *Family and Farm: Agrarian Change and Household Organization in the Loire Valley 1500–1900* (Albany, NY, 1982), 48–49. On the household economy, see Olwen Hufton, 'Women and the Family Economy in Eighteenth-Century France', *FHS* 9 (1975), 1–22; and *The Prospect Before Her: A History of Women in Western Europe, 1500–1800* (New York, 1996), especially ch. 4; David Troyansky, *Old Age in the Old Régime: Image and Experience in Eighteenth-Century France* (Ithaca, NY, 1989), ch. 6.

91. Frénay (ed.), *Cahiers de doléances de la province de Roussillon*; Larguier *et al.* (eds), *Cahiers de doléances audois*; McPhee, *Revolution and Environment in Southern France*, 42. In general, see Forrest, *Paris, the Provinces and the French Revolution*, chs 2–3.

92. McPhee, *Revolution and Environment in Southern France*, 47.
93. Emily Chester, 'Identité régionale et identité nationale: 1789 dans le Roussillon et le Bas-Languedoc', MA thesis, University of Melbourne, 1995, 44.
94. Peter McPhee, 'Counter-Revolution in the Pyrenees: Spirituality, Class and Ethnicity in the Haut-Vallespir, 1793–1794', *FH* 7 (1993), 313–43.
95. Michel Vovelle, 'La représentation populaire de la monarchie', in Keith Baker (ed.), *The Political Culture of the Old Régime* (Oxford, 1987), 77–96.
96. Vardi, *The Land and the Loom*, 205.
97. Olwen Hufton, 'Attitudes towards Authority in Eighteenth-Century Languedoc', *SH* 3 (1978), 281–302; Georges Fournier, *Démocratie et vie municipale en Languedoc du milieu du XVIIIe au début du XIXe siècle*, 2 vols (Toulouse, 1994); McPhee, *Revolution and Environment*, 36–9.
98. On this point see Jones, *Liberty and Locality in Revolutionary France*, ch. 3 and 266–7.
99. This calls into question the title of 'La Bresse invente la concorde. Le cahier commun des doléances', special issue of *Les Nouvelles Annales de l'Ain*, 1990. On the spirit of compromise in 1789, see Kenneth Margerison, *Pamphlets and Public Opinion: The Campaign for a Union of Orders in the Early French Revolution* (West Lafayette, 1998).

## 2  Elation and anxiety: The revolutionary year

1. McPhee, *Revolution and Environment in Southern France*, 40.
2. Guy Lemarchand, 'La féodalité et la Révolution française: seigneurie et communauté paysanne (1780–1799)', *AHRF* 242 (1980), 536–58; 'Troubles populaires au XVIIIe siècle et conscience de classe: une préface à la Révolution française', *AHRF* 279 (1990), 32–48; Jones, *The Peasantry in the French Revolution*, 53–8.
3. James C. Scott, *Weapons of the Weak: Everyday Forms of Peasant Resistance* (New Haven, CT, 1985); *Domination and the Arts of Resistance: Hidden Transcripts* (New Haven, CT, 1990).
4. Markoff, *The Abolition of Feudalism*, 226.
5. T.J.A. Le Goff, *Vannes and Its Region: A Study of Town and Country in Eighteenth-Century France* (Oxford, 1981), 340.
6. Jean Boutier, 'Jacqueries en pays croquant: les révoltes paysannes en Aquitaine (décembre 1789–mars 1790)', *Annales* 34 (1979), 765. See, too, Boutier's *Campagnes en émoi. Révoltes et Révolution en Bas-Limousin, 1789–1800* (Treignac, 1987), on the endemic violence in the Bas-Limousin region.
7. Nicole Castan, *Les criminels du Languedoc: les exigences d'ordre et les voies du ressentiment dans une société pré-révolutionnaire (1750–1790)* (Toulouse, 1980), 159 and chs 3–4; Yves Castan, *Honnêteté et relations sociales en Languedoc, 1715–1780* (Paris, 1974); Olwen Hufton, 'Attitudes towards authority in eighteenth–century Languedoc', *SH* 3 (1978), 281–302.
8. On the elections of 1789, see Crook, *Elections in the French Revolution*, ch. 1; Jones, *The Peasantry in the French Revolution*, 28, 62–4.
9. Jones, *The Peasantry in the French Revolution*, 65–7; Georges Lefevbre, *The Great Fear of 1789: Rural Panic in Revolutionary France* [1932], trans. Joan White (New York, 1973), 39.
10. Forrest, *Paris, the Provinces and the French Revolution*, 49.
11. Larguier, *Limoux*, especially ch. 6.

12. Arthur Young, *Travels in France during the Years 1787, 1788 and 1789* (Cambridge, 1929), 169, 173.

13. Eugène Dubois, *Histoire de la Révolution dans l'Ain*, vol. 1, *La Constituante (1789–1791)* (Bourg, 1931), 60–8; Louis Trenard, 'Le "vandalisme révolutionnaire" dans les pays de l'Ain: faits matériels et motivations', in Simone Bernard-Griffiths, Marie-Claude Chemin and Jean Ehrard, (eds), *Révolution française et 'vandalisme révolutionnaire'. Actes du colloque international de Clermont-Ferrand 15–17 décembre 1988* (Paris, 1992), 252–3.

14. Abbiatéci and Perdrix, *Les débuts de la Révolution dans les pays de l'Ain*, 194.

15. Ted W. Margadant, 'Summary Justice and the Crisis of the Old Regime in 1789', *Historical Reflections/Réflections historiques*, 29 (2003), 495–528.

16. Clay Ramsay, *The Ideology of the Great Fear: The Soissonnais in 1789* (Baltimore, MD and London, 1992), ch. 4.

17. *Ibid.*, 7.

18. Henri Texier *et al.* (eds), *La Révolution française 1789–1799 à Saintes* (Poitiers, 1988), 48–50.

19. McPhee, *Revolution and Environment in Southern France*, 50.

20. Bernet (ed.), *Le journal d'un maître d'école*, 189, 195–6.

21. Claude Muller, 'Religion et Révolution en Alsace', *AHRF* 337 (2004), 70; Timothy Tackett, 'Collective Panics in the Early French Revolution', *FH* 17 (2003), 149–58.

22. Christian Bonnet, 'Les pillages d'abbayes dans le Nord et leur signification (1789–1793)', in Bernard-Griffiths et al. (eds), *Révolution française et 'vandalisme révolutionnaire'*, 169–73.

23. Markoff, *The Abolition of Feudalism*, 238.

24. *AHRF*, 1955, 161–62. Translated in Dwyer and McPhee (eds), *The French Revolution and Napoleon*, 22–3.

25. Ramsay, *The Ideology of the Great Fear*, ch. 8.

26. *Ibid.*, conclusion.

27. McPhee, *Gabian*, ch. 1.

28. Jones, *The Peasantry in the French Revolution*, 81–5; Michael P. Fitzsimmons, *The Night the Old Regime Ended: August 4, 1789 and the French Revolution* (University Park, PA, 2003).

29. Hans-Jürgen Lüsebrink and Rolf Reichardt, *The Bastille: A History of a Symbol of Despotism and Freedom*, trans Norbert Schurer (Durham, NC and London, 1997).

30. Ozouf, *Festivals and the French Revolution*, 33.

31. *Ibid.*, 38.

32. Gilbert Shapiro and John Markoff, *Revolutionary Demands: A Content Analysis of the Cahiers de Doléances of 1789* (Stanford, CA, 1998).

33. E.J. Hobsbawm, 'Peasants and Politics', *Journal of Peasant Studies* 1 (1973), 13.

34. Abbiatéci and Perdrix, *Les débuts de la Révolution dans les pays de l'Ain*, 205.

35. Young, *Travels in France*, 227.

36. *Archives parlementaires*, 11 December 1789.

37. Young, *Travels in France*, 226.

38. McPhee, *Revolution and Environment in Southern France*, 126. See Geoffroy de Gislain, 'Chasse et nuisibles dans les cahiers de doléances,' in Corvol (ed.), *La Nature en Révolution*, 86–93.

39. Bernet (ed.), *Le journal d'un maître d'école*, 194.

40. *Ibid.*, 199–207.

41. Comte de Courchamps, *Souvenirs de la marquise de Créquy de 1710 à 1803*, vol. 9 (Paris, 1865), 107–8.

42. Peter McPhee, *Collioure 1780–1815. The French Revolution in a Mediterranean Community* (Melbourne, 1989), 24. A year later the seigneur successfully prosecuted the fishermen.
43. Steven G. Reinhardt, 'The Revolution in the Countryside: Peasant Unrest in the Périgord, 1789–90', in Reinhardt and Elisabeth A. Cawthorn (eds), *Essays on the French Revolution: Paris and the Provinces* (Arlington, TX, 1992), 12–37.
44. Jones, *The Peasantry in the French Revolution*, 105–17.
45. Boutier, 'Jacqueries en pays croquant', 761–2.
46. Boutier, *Campagnes en émoi*, 276–8.
47. Jones, *The Peasantry in the French Revolution*, 70–4; Procès-verbal of AN 2 February, 17–18 June, 3 August, 16 September 1790. Bryant T. Ragan 'Rural Political Equality and Fiscal Activism in the Revolutionary Somme', in Ragan and Elizabeth A. Williams (eds), *Re-creating Authority in Revolutionary France* (New Brunswick, NJ, 1992), 46; Ozouf, *Festivals and the French Revolution*, 37–9. The continuing revolution in the countryside is studied by Jones, *The Peasantry in the French Revolution*, 67–85; Markoff, *The Abolition of Feudalism*, chs 5–7; Ado, *Paysans en Révolution*, chs 4–6; Sutherland, *The French Revolution and Empire*, 87–91.
48. Jones, *The Peasantry in the French Revolution*, 67–85; Boutier, 'Jacqueries en pays croquant', 760–86; Anatoli Ado, ' "Les Propos incendiaires" du curé Jacques Benoît', *AHRF* 39 (1967), 399–401.
49. Ado, *Paysans en Révolution*, 233.
50. Madame Vigée Lebrun, *Memoirs of Mme Vigée Lebrun*, tanslated by Lionel Strachey (New York, 1989), 55–6.
51. Alexandre de Tilly, *Memoirs of the Comte Alexandre de Tilly*, trans. Françoise Delisle (London, 1933), 401–2.
52. AN D XXIX 83. A family history written in 1907 reported that Jean-Baptiste fled to Spain after he had killed 'a revolutionary' at Leuc: see Claude Marquié, *L'Industrie textile carcassonnaise au XVIIIe siècle. Étude d'un groupe social: les marchands-fabricants* (Carcassonne, 1993), 376–80.
53. Roger Dupuy, 'Les émeutes anti–féodales de Haute–Bretagne (janvier 1790 et janvier 1791): meneurs improvisés ou agitateurs politisés?' in Jean Nicolas (ed.), *Mouvements populaires et conscience sociale, XVI-XIXe siècles. Actes du colloque de Paris 24–26 mai 1984* (Paris, 1985), 453–4.
54. François Lebrun (ed.), *Parole de Dieu et Révolution. Les sermons d'un curé angevin avant et pendant la guerre de Vendée* (Paris, 1988), 69.
55. *Ibid.*, 102–3.
56. AD Aude, 4E 359 St-Michel-de-Lanes, Registre des délibérations du Conseil municipal, 1790-an VIII; 4E 418 Villasavary, Registre des délibérations du Conseil municipal, 1778–93.
57. McPhee, *Revolution and Environment in Southern France*, 54.
58. Jill Maciak, 'Of News and Networks: The Communication of Political Information in the Rural South-West during the French Revolution', *FH* 15 (2001), 273–306; Vivian R. Gruder, 'Can We Hear the Voices of Peasants? France, 1788', *History of European Ideas* 17 (1993), 167–90.

## 3   Reimagining space and power, 1789–91

1. See William Doyle, *The Ancien Regime* (Houndmills, Macmillan, 1986).
2. Jones, *The Peasantry in the French Revolution*, 167–80; Charles Tilly, 'The Emergence of Citizenship in France and Elsewhere', *International Review of French History* 40

(1995), 223–36. On the provincial support for the 'regeneration' of France, see Michael P. Fitzsimmons, *The Remaking of France: The National Assembly, the Constitution of 1791 and the Reorganization of the French Polity* (Cambridge and New York, 1994); and Philip Dawson, *Provincial Magistrates and Revolutionary Politics in France, 1789–1795* (Cambridge, MA, 1972).

3. Woloch, *The New Régime*, 34.
4. Dale Van Kley (ed.), *The French Idea of Freedom: The Old Regime and the Declaration of Rights of 1789* (Stanford, CA, 1994); Lynn Hunt (ed.), *The French Revolution and Human Rights: A Brief Documentary History* (Boston, 1996), intro.
5. Jones, *Liberty and Locality in Revolutionary France*, 130.
6. Jones, *The Peasantry in the French Revolution*, 27–9.
7. Jessenne, *Pouvoir au village*, 61–9.
8. Bernet (ed.), *Le journal d'un maître d'école*, 214–5.
9. Jones, *The Peasantry in the French Revolution*, ch. 6; Lawrence Wylie, *Chanzeaux: A Village in Anjou* (Cambridge, MA, 1966), 27–31; Alison Patrick, 'The Approach of French Revolutionary Officials to Social Problems, 1790–1792', *AJFS* 18 (1981), 248–63.
10. Maciak, 'Of News and Networks', 285n.
11. On venality, see William Doyle, *Venality: The Sale of Offices in Eighteenth-Century France* (Oxford, 1996).
12. Ted W. Margadant, *Urban Rivalries in the French Revolution* (Princeton, NJ, 1992); Marie-Vic Ozouf-Marignier, *La formation des départements: la représentation du territoire français à la fin du 18e siècle* (Paris, 1989); Alan Forrest, 'Le découpage administrative de la France révolutionnaire', in *L'Espace et le temps reconstruits: la Révolution française, une révolution des mentalités et cultures?* (Aix-en-Provence, 1990), 3–12; *Paris, the Provinces and the French Revolution*, ch. 5.
13. Courchamps, *Souvenirs de la marquise de Créquy*, vol. 9, 145.
14. Ferdinand Brunot, *Histoire de la langue française des origines à 1900*, t. IX, 1ère partie (Paris, 1927), chs 2, 4; Jones, *The Peasantry in the French Revolution*, 209; Maciak, 'Of News and Networks', *passim*. Grégoire's inquiry is discussed in J.-Y. Lartichaux, 'Linguistic Politics during the French Revolution', *Diogenes* 97 (1977), 65–84; Martyn Lyons, 'Politics and Patois: The Linguistic Policy of the French Revolution', *AJFS* 18 (1981), 264–81; Michel de Certeau, Dominique Julia and Jacques Revel, *Une politique de la langue: la Révolution française et les patois. L'enquête de Grégoire* (Paris, 1975).
15. Gérard Cholvy, 'Société, genres de vie et mentalités dans les campagnes françaises de 1815 à 1880', *Information Historique* 36 (1974), 161; Brunot, *Histoire de la langue française*, 19.
16. Thomas Sheppard, *Lourmarin in the Eighteenth Century: A Study of a French Village* (Baltimore, MD, 1971), 180.
17. Brunot, *Histoire de la langue française*, 27.
18. Gary Kates, 'Jews into Frenchmen: Nationality and Representation in Revolutionary France', in Ferenc Fehér (ed.), *The French Revolution and the Birth of Modernity* (Berkeley, CA), 103–16; Richard Ayoun, *Les juifs de France. De l'émancipation à l'intégration (1787–1812)* (Paris and Montreal, 1997); Patrick Girard, *Les juifs en France de 1789 à 1869* (Paris, 1976); David Feuerwerker, *L'émancipation des juifs en France de la fin de l'Ancien Régime à la fin du Second Empire* (Paris, 1976); Nigel Aston, *The French Revolution 1789–1804. Authority, Liberty and the Search for Stability* (Basingstoke and New York, 2004), 120–1; and the special issue of *AHRF* 235 (1979).
19. Ronald Schechter, *Obstinate Hebrews: Representations of Jews in France, 1715–1815* (Berkeley and London, 2003).

20. Alyssa Goldstein Sepinwall, 'Eliminating Race, Eliminating Difference: Blacks, Jews, and the Abbé Grégoire,' in Sue Peabody and Tyler Stovall (eds), *The Color of Liberty: Histories of Race in France* (Durham, NC and London, 2003); *The Abbé Grégoire and the French Revolution: The Making of Modern Universalism* (Berkeley, CA and London, 2005).
21. Comte Stanislas de Clermont-Tonnerre, député de Paris, *Opinion* (Paris, 1789).
22. Crubaugh, *Balancing the Scales of Justice*, ch. 5.
23. Boutier, 'Jacqueries en pays croquant'; *Campagnes en émoi*; Ozouf, *Festivals and the French Revolution*, 37–8, 232–43; Reinhardt, 'The Revolution in the Countryside'.
24. Markoff, *The Abolition of Feudalism*, 426. Ado, *Paysans en Révolution*, 253, outlines three waves of 'jacqueries' in 1789–91.
25. Two studies of such areas are Jean-Noël Luc, *Paysans et droits féodaux en Charente-Inférieure pendant la Révolution française* (Paris, 1984); McPhee, *Revolution and Environment in Southern France*. On the legislation and its outcomes see Fitzsimmons, *The Night the Old Regime Ended*.
26. These features are characteristic of peasant rebellions from eighteenth-century France to twentieth-century Russia. See Daniel Field, *Rebels in the Name of the Tsar* (Boston, 1976); George Rudé, *The Crowd in History* (New York, 1964).
27. AD Charente-Maritime L 147, 739. See also Crubaugh, *Balancing the Scales of Justice*, 55–6.
28. The analysis which follows is from McPhee, *Revolution and Environment in Southern France*, chs 2–3.
29. Bernet (ed.), *Le journal d'un maître d'école*, 213–14, 223–4.
30. Serge Aberdam, 'La Révolution et la lutte des métayers', *Études rurales* 59 (1975), 73–91; Sutherland, 'Peasants, Lords, and Leviathan: Winners and Losers from the Abolition of French Feudalism, 1780–1820', *Journal of Economic History* 62 (2002), 1–24.
31. Ado, *Paysans en Révolution*, 225.
32. *Instruction de l'Assemblée Nationale concernant les fonctions des assemblées administratives* 12–20 août 1790, 297.
33. AN AD IV 19.
34. Nadine Vivier, *Propriété collective et identité communale. Les biens communaux en France 1750–1914* (Paris, 1998), 97–8 and chs 3–4.
35. Georges Bourgin, *Le partage des biens communaux; documents sur la préparation de la loi du 10 juin 1793* (Paris, 1908), 22–3.
36. Fernand Gerbaux and Charles Schmidt, *Procès-verbaux des comités d'agriculture et de commerce de la constituante, de la Législative et de la Convention*, 5 vols (Paris, 1906–37), vol. 2, 171.
37. Jones, *Liberty and Locality in Revolutionary France*, 100.
38. Gerbaux and Schmidt, *Procès-verbaux des comités d'agriculture et de commerce*, vol. 1, 686.
39. AD Ain, Archives Communales (hereafter AC) de Bourg, Registre des délibérations du Conseil Municipal, 2 décembre 1790.
40. McPhee, *Revolution and Environment in Southern France*, 84–5.
41. *Ibid.*, 122–3.
42. Xavier de Massary, 'Les usages de l'arrondissement de Château-Thierry: l'époque révolutionnaire', *Fédération des sociétés d'histoire et d'archéologie de l'Aisne. Mémoires*, 34 (1989), 21–43.
43. Procès-verbal de l'Assemblée nationale.

44. AD Ain, AC Bourg, Registre des délibérations du conseil municipal de Bourg, 1 juin 1790.

45. AD Aisne, L 603, 'Insurrections dans les districts de Chauny, St-Quentin, Soissons et Château-Thierry, février-octobre 1791'; G. Dumas, 'Les "émotions populaires" dans le département de l'Aisne de la fin de 1790 à l'an IV (1795–1796)', *Société d'histoire et d'archéologie de Senlis* 22 (1977), 41.

46. Alan Forrest, *The French Revolution and the Poor* (Oxford, 1981).

47. AD Ain 6L 142 Mendicité, canton of Oyannax. I am grateful to Alison Patrick for this reference.

48. Forrest, *The French Revolution and the Poor*, 107.

49. AD Ain, AC de Belley, Régistre des délibérations du Conseil Général de la Commune de Belley, 3 mars 1790.

50. Olwen Hufton, *Bayeux in the Late Eighteenth Century: A Social Study* (Oxford, 1967).

51. *Pétition des entreposeurs du tabac à l'Assemblée nationale.*

52. Christopher H. Johnson, *The Life and Death of Industrial Languedoc, 1700–1920* (New York and Oxford, 1995), 13–14.

53. Liana Vardi, 'The Abolition of the Guilds during the French Revolution', *FHS* 15 (1988), 704–17.

54. AN AD IV 23; Jones, *The Peasantry in the French Revolution*, 183–5.

55. See, for example, Le Goff, *Vannes andI Its Region*, 343.

56. Jones, *The Peasantry in the French Revolution*, 181–91.

57. Ado, *Paysans en Révolution*, 206–7.

58. Georges Lefebvre, *Les paysans du Nord pendant la Révolution française* (Bari, 1959), 514–21.

59. Scattered research on the sales of *biens nationaux* is synthesized in Bernard Bodinier and Eric Teyssier, *L'événement le plus important de la Révolution: la vente des biens nationaux en France et dans les territoires annexés, 1789–1867* (Paris, 2000); Bernard Bodinier, 'La vente des biens nationaux: essai de synthèse', *AHRF* 315 (1999), 7–19; Jones, *The Peasantry in the French Revolution*, 154–61.

60. McPhee, *Revolution and Environment in Southern France*, ch. 3.

61. Michel Péronnet, Robert Attal and Jean Bobin, *La Révolution dans l'Aisne, 1789–1799* (Le Coteau, 1988), 109; *Histoire de Laon*, 199.

62. Aimé Coiffard, *La vente des biens nationaux dans le district de Grasse (1790–1815)* (Paris, 1973), 94–103.

63. Colin Lucas, 'Aux sources du comportement politique de la paysannerie beaujolaise', in *La Révolution française et le monde rural. Actes du colloque tenu en Sorbonne les 23, 24 et 25 octobre 1987* (Paris, 1989), 345–65.

64. AD Haute-Garonne, 1L 116–18, Registre des délibérations du Conseil général, 30 September 1790.

65. Ozouf, *Festivals and the French Revolution*, 51.

66. Bernet (ed.), *Le journal d'un maître d'école*, 222.

67. Michel Vovelle, *Les métamorphoses de la fête en Provence de 1750 à 1820* (Paris, 1976), 71, 103.

68. Pierre Massé, *Varennes et ses maitres. Un domaine rural, de l'Ancien Régime à la Monarchie de Juillet (1779–1842)* (Paris, 1956), 69–72.

69. This 'political culture' is explored in the four volumes of *The French Revolution and the Creation of Modern Political Culture* (Oxford, 1987–94); Michael Kennedy, *The Jacobin Clubs in the French Revolution: The First Years* (Princeton, NJ, 1982); Ozouf, *Festivals and the French Revolution*; Vovelle, *Métamorphoses de la fête*; Lynn Hunt, *Politics, Culture, and Class in the French Revolution* (Berkeley, CA, 1984); Timothy

Tackett, *Becoming a Revolutionary: The Deputies of the French National Assembly and the Emergence of a Revolutionary Culture (1789–1790)* (Princeton, NJ, 1996); and Woloch, *The New Regime*.

70. Kennedy, *The Jacobin Clubs in the French Revolution: The First Years*, passim.
71. Crook, *Elections in the French Revolution* passim; Patrice Gueniffey, *Le nombre et la raison. La Révolution française et les élections* (Paris, 1993); Woloch, *The New Regime*, 60–8.
72. Anne-Henri Cabot, marquis de Dampmartin, *Mémoires sur divers événemens de la Révolution et de l'émigration* (Paris, 1825), 185–200.
73. Jacques Poumarède, 'La législation successorale de la Révolution entre l'idéologie et la pratique', in Irène Thery and Christian Biet (eds), *La Famille, la loi, l'État. De la Révolution au Code Civil* (Paris, 1989), 167–82.
74. Élisabeth Claverie and Pierre Lamaison, *L'impossible marriage: violence et parenté en Gévaudan, XVIIe, XVIIIe et XIXe siècles* (Paris, 1982); Suzanne Desan, *The Family on Trial in Revolutionary France* (Berkeley and London, 2004).
75. Nicole Pellegrin, *Les vêtements de la Liberté: Abécédaire des pratiques vestimentaires en France de 1780 à 1800* (Aix-en-Provence, 1989), 159.
76. McPhee, *Revolution and Environment in Southern France*, 60.
77. Bernard Vinot, 'La Révolution au village, avec Saint-Just, d'après le registre des délibérations communales de Blérancourt', *AHRF* 335 (2004), 97–110.

## 4  Without Christ or King, 1791

1. Madame de la Tour du Pin, *Memoirs: Laughing and Dancing Our Way to the Precipice*, trans. Felice Harcourt (London, 1999), 145, 153–5.
2. Pierre-Louis-Auguste de Crusy, marquis de Marcillac, *Souvenirs de l'émigration à l'usage de l'époque actuelle* (Paris, 1825), 8.
3. Alexandre de Tilly, *Memoirs of the Comte Alexandre de Tilly*, trans. by Françoise Delisle (London, 1933), 231.
4. Marie-Victoire Monnard, *Souvenirs d'une femme du peuple, 1777–1802* (Creil, 1989), 62–96, trans. in Dwyer and McPhee (eds), *The French Revolution and Napoleon*, 204–5.
5. Hufton, 'Women in Revolution 1789–1796', 98.
6. *Procès-verbal de la municipalité de Montauban envoyé à l'Assemblée nationale, 12 mai 1790*; Clarke Garrett, 'Religion and Revolution in the Midi-Toulousain, 1789–90', in Reinhardt and Cawthorn (eds), *Paris and the Provinces*, 38–63.
7. Gwynne Lewis, *The Second Vendée: The Continuity of Counter-Revolution in the Department of the Gard, 1789–1815* (Oxford, 1978), 31–37 and *passim*; James N. Hood, 'Protestant-Catholic Relations and the Roots of the First Popular Counterrevolutionary Movement in France', *JMH* 43 (1971), 245–75; 'Patterns of Popular Protest in the French Revolution: The Conceptual Contribution of the Gard', *JMH* 48 (1976) 259–93; François de Jouvenel, 'Les camps de Jalès (1790–1792), épisodes contre-révolutionnaires?', *AHRF* 337 (2004), 1–20.
8. AD Aisne, L 1503, Affaires ecclésiastiques: correspondence générale, novembre 1790–février 1791; Martine Plouvier, 'L'abbaye de Prémontré au XVIIe et XVIIIe siècles'. Thèse de troisième cycle, Paris I, 1982. There had been a serious division in the abbey on the eve of the Revolution: L 1508, 'Querelle entre l'abbé de Prémontré et les religieux de l'abbaye, août-octobre 1790'.
9. André Vacherand, 'Les biens et revenus de l'abbaye royale d'Origny-Sainte-Benoîte en 1790', *Fédération des sociétés d'histoire et d'archéologie de l'Aisne. Memoires*, 34 (1989), 153–77.
10. Augustin Theiner, *Documents inédits rélatifs aux affaires religieuses de la France* (Paris, 1857), 88.

11. Timothy Tackett, *Religion, Revolution, and Regional Culture in Eighteenth-Century France* (Princeton, NJ, 1986); Nigel Aston, *Religion and Revolution in France, 1780–1804* (Basingstoke, 2000), ch. 7; Jones, *The Peasantry in the French Revolution*, 191–204. A study of a region of high oath-taking is Tackett, *Priest and Parish in Eighteenth–Century France: A Social and Political Study of the Curés in a Diocese of Dauphiné, 1750–1791* (Princeton, NJ, 1977).

12. AD Aisne, L 1502, 1505, 'Affaires ecclésiastiques: correspondance générale', juin-novembre 1790; mai–décembre 1791; Archives municipales de Laon, SRL 99, Culte catholique; Péronnet, Attal and Bobin, *La Révolution dans l'Aisne*, 88.

13. Archives municipales (hereafter AM) de Laon, SRL 1, Délibérations de la commune de Laon, juin–décembre 1790.

14. AD Ain, AC Bourg, Registre des délibérations du conseil municipal, 13 Avril, 1 Juin 1791, 5 mars 1792.

15. Robert Attal and Alain Blanchard, 'Le clergé du Soissonnais pendant la Révolution, 1789–1791', *Fédération des sociétés d'histoire et d'archéologie de l'Aisne. Mémoires*, 34 (1989), 203.

16. Michel Péronnet and Gérard Bourdin, *La Révolution dans L'Orne, 1789–1799* (Le Coteau, 1988), 109.

17. AD Aisne, L 1505, Affaires ecclésiastiques: correspondence générale, mai-décembre 1791.

18. Alison Patrick, 'French Revolutionary Local Government, 1789–1792', in Colin Lucas (ed.), *The Political Culture of the French Revolution* (London, 1988), 412–17; Jones, *The Peasantry in the French Revolution*, 191–204; John McManners, *French Ecclesiastical Society under the Ancien Régime* (Manchester, 1960), chs 12–15.

19. Jean–Marie Carbasse, 'Un des premiers cas de résistance populaire à la Révolution: l'émeute du 25 janvier 1791 à Millau', *Bulletin d'histoire économique et sociale* (1984–85), 57–72; Timothy Tackett, 'Women and Men in Counterrevolution: The Sommières Riot of 1791', *JMH* 59 (1987), 680–704.

20. Gilbert-Jacques Martinant de Préneuf, *Huit années d'émigration. Souvenirs de l'abbé ... curé de Vaugirard, de Sceaux et de Saint-Leu (1792–1801)* (Paris, 1908), 290–3. On 14 September 1792, following the law of 26 August, he left the country.

21. McPhee, *Revolution and Environment*, 77–8.

22. Simon Gruget, *Mémoires et journal de l'abbé Gruget, curé de la Trinité d'Angers* (Angers, 1902), 187–8.

23. *Protestation de cent cinq curés de la Bretagne contre la nouvelle organisation civile du clergé, addressée à l'Assemblée nationale*, 11, 18.

24. T.J.A. Le Goff and D.M.G. Sutherland, 'The Revolution and the Rural Community in Brittany', *P&P* 62 (1974), 96–119.

25. Martyn Lyons, 'Regionalism and Linguistic Conformity in the French Revolution', in Forrest and Jones (eds), *Reshaping France*, 187–8.

26. Claude Muller, 'Religion et Révolution en Alsace', *AHRF* 337 (2004), 66–71.

27. McPhee, *Gabian*, ch. 2.

28. Paris, 1791.

29. J.F. Nusse, *Lettre à un curé patriote, qui a des doutes sur son serment, d'après deux brefs attributes au pape* (Laon, 1791); Édouard Fleury, *Le clergé du department de l'Aisne pendant la Révolution. Études révolutionnaires* (Paris and Laon, 1853), vol. 1, 90.

30. Martinant de Préneuf, *Huit années d'émigration*, 148–151, 190. See also François-Dominique Reynaud, comte de Montlosier, *Souvenirs d'un émigré (1791–1798)* (Paris, 1951); Joseph de Pradel de Lamasse, *Notes intimes d'un émigré ... officier à l'armée de Condé, Les campagnes de l'émigration* (Paris, 1913); Joseph de Pradel de

Lamasse, *Nouvelles notes intimes d'un émigré ... officer à l'armée de Condé, Les grandes journées révolutionnaires* (Paris, 1914–20); Charlotte Louise Eléonore Adélaïde d'Osmond Boigne, *Mémoires de la Comtesse de Boigne, née d'Osmond*, vol. 1 (Paris, 1908), 137–8.

31. Jeremy Whiteman, *Reform, Revolution and French Global Policy, 1787–1791* (Aldershot, 2003); Orville T. Murphy, *The Diplomatic Retreat of France and Public Opinion on the Eve of the French Revolution, 1783–1789* (Washington, DC, 1998).

32. Joseph-Louis-Gabriel Noël, *Au temps des volontaires: lettres d'un volontaire de 1792* (Paris, 1912), 23–4.

33. *Ibid.*, 110.

34. Timothy Tackett, *When the King took Flight* (Cambridge, MA, 2003), 152–3; Henri Texier *et al.* (eds), *La Révolution française 1789–1799 à Saintes* (Poitiers, 1988), 88.

35. Georges Lefebvre, 'The Murder of the Comte de Dampierre (June 22, 1791)', in Jeffry Kaplow (ed.), *New Perspectives on the French Revolution: Readings in Historical Sociology* (New York, 1965), 279.

36. AD Aisne, L 605, 'Retour de Louis XVI à Paris: incidents survenus lors de son passage dans le département, juin 1791'; Raymond Josse, 'En 1791, la fuite de la famille royale. L'événement dans le département de l'Aisne' (Laon, 1966).

37. Timothy Tackett, 'Collective Panics in the Early French Revolution', *FH* 17 (2003), 149–50, 159–71; *When the King took Flight*, ch. 6; Ado, *Paysans en Révolution*, 248.

38. Tackett, *When the King took Flight*, 190–1.

39. AD Ain, AC Belley, Registre des délibérations du Conseil Général, 14 juillet 1790, 7 et 14 juillet 1791.

40. William Murray, *The Right–Wing Press in the French Revolution: 1789–92* (London, 1986), 126–28, 289; Sheppard, *Lourmarin*, 186.

41. Ado, *Paysans en Révolution*, 241–3; Jacques Bernet, 'Les grèves de moissonneurs ou "bacchanals" dans les campagnes d'Ile-de-France et de Picardie au XVIIIe siècle', *Histoire et sociétés rurales* 11 (1999), 153–86; Dumas, 'Les "émotions populaires" dans le département de l'Aisne, 51–4; AD Aisne, L 603, 'Insurrections dans les districts de Chauny, St-Quentin, Soissons et Château-Thierry, février–octobre 1791'.

42. Ado, *Paysans en Révolution*, 236–7.

43. Bernet (ed.), *Le journal d'un maître d'école*, 222.

44. *Ibid.*, 32, 245.

45. McPhee, *Revolution and Environment in Southern France*, ch. 8.

46. Le Goff, *Vannes and Its Region*, 343–6, 352–3, 366; Sutherland, *The French Revolution and Empire*, 97; 'Winners and Losers from the Abolition of French Feudalism', 1–24.

47. Alain Le Bloas, 'La question du domaine congéable', *AHRF* 331 (2003), 1–27.

48. McPhee, *Collioure*, 26–7.

49. Ferdinand Brunot, *Histoire de la langue française des origines à 1900*, t. IX, 1ère partie (Paris, 1927), 6.

## 5  Deadly divisions, 1791–92

1. *Gazette Nationale ou le Moniteur Universel* no. 271, 20 September 1791, 784–6. On the Code, see Jones, *The Peasantry in the French Revolution*, 128–37.

2. AN AD IV, 19; Marie-Noëlle Grand-Mesnil, 'La loi du 29 septembre 1791,' in Woronoff (ed.), *Révolution et espaces forestiers* (L'Harmattan), 200–5; Corvol, *L'Homme aux bois*, 64. See also the discussion of forests policy in *Opinion de*

*L. C. Cheron, député du département de Seine-et-Oise à l'Assemblée Nationale sur les dangers de l'aliénation des forêts nationales* (Paris, 1792).

3. Markoff, *The Abolition of Feudalism*, 255.
4. Pellegrin, *Les vêtements de la Liberté*, 181.
5. Vaxelaire, *Mémoires d'un vétéran*, de l'ancienne armee (1791–1800), ed. H. Gauthier-Villars (Paris, 1892), 16; Brunot, *Histoire de la langue française*, 20; Forrest, *Soldiers of the French Revolution*, 61–5.
6. Isabelle Roger-Noël, 'La Révolution aux frontières vue par un volontaire de 1792 à 1796', *Revue historique des armées* 42 (1986), 4–6; Noël, *Au Temps des volontaires*, 27, 61–3.
7. Noël, *Au Temps des volontaires*, 171, 201–2; Forrest, *Soldiers of the French Revolution*, 50.
8. Jean-Michel Deveau, *La traite rochelaise* (Paris, 1990); Daniel Roche, *France in the Enlightenment*, trans. Arthur Goldhammer (Cambridge, MA., 1998), ch. 5.
9. Paul Butel, 'Revolution and the Urban Economy: Maritime Cities and Continental Cities', in Forrest and Jones (eds), *Reshaping France*, 37–51; 'Succès et decline du commerce colonial français, de la Révolution à la Restauration', *Revue économique* 6 (1989), 1079–96.
10. See the chapters by Carolyn Fick and Pierre Boulle in Frederick Krantz (ed.), *History from Below: Studies in Popular Protest and Popular Ideology in Honour of George Rudé* (Montreal, 1985); Robert Forster, 'Who Is a Citizen? The Boundaries of "La Patrie": The French Revolution and the People of Color, 1789–91', *French Politics and Society* 7 (1989), 50–64.
11. A contrary interpretation has stressed instead the 'traditional' motivations behind the outbreak of war, that the expressions of self-defence were a smokescreen for the pursuit of longstanding strategic goals. See, for example, T.C.W. Blanning, *The Origins of the French Revolutionary Wars* (London, 1986).
12. Frédéric-Christian Laukhard, *Un Allemand en France sous la Terreur: souvenirs de Frédéric-Christian Laukhard, professeur d'université saxon et sans-culotte français, 1792–1794*, ed. W. Bauer (Paris, 1915), 61–4. Laukhard's extraordinary memoirs were written in 1795.
13. *Ibid.*, 71–2.
14. Noël, *Au temps des volontaires*, 120–1.
15. Ado, *Paysans en Révolution*, 280–2.
16. Florence Gauthier and Guy-Robert Ikni, 'Le movement paysan en Picardie: meneurs, pratiques, maturation et signification historique d'un programme (1775–1794)', in Jean Nicolas (ed.), *Mouvements populaires et conscience sociale, XVI–XIXe siècles. Actes du colloque de Paris 24–26 mai 1984* (Paris, 1985), 441.
17. Butel, 'Succès et decline du commerce colonial français', *passim.*
18. Lewis, *The Second Vendée*, chs 2–3; François de Jouvenel, 'Les camps de Jalès (1790–1792), épisodes contre-révolutionnaires?' *AHRF* 337 (2004), 1–20.
19. AM Laon, SRL 74, 'Émigrés, nobles, suspects, 1791-an II'.
20. François-Pierre Julliot, *Souvenirs d'un prêtre réfractaire du diocèse de Troyes publiés par Octave Beuve* (Arcis-sur-Aube, 1909), 49–50.
21. Muller, 'Religion et Révolution en Alsace', 78.
22. AD Aude 4E 002 Airoux, Registre des délibérations du Conseil municipal, 1751-an XII, 9 April 1792.
23. Béatrix-Étiennette Renart de Fuchsamberg, marquise de Lâge de Volude, *Souvenirs d'émigration 1792–1794* (Evreux, 1869), 47–8.
24. Gabriel-Isidore Blondin d'Abancourt, *Onze ans d'émigration. Mémoires … publiés par son petit-neveu Blondin de Saint-Hilaire … et suivis d'un historique de la Compagnie*

*des Cent-Suisses depuis Charles VIII* (Paris, 1897), 12. See too Anne-Henri Cabot, marquis de Dampmartin, *Mémoires sur divers événemens de la Révolution et de l'Émigration* (Paris, 1825), vol. 2.

25. AD Aude, Antoine de Fournas de la Brosse, 'Une famille française sous la Révolution, l'Empire et la Restauration' (n.p., n.d. [1979]); and 'Correspondance de Blaise de Fournas de la Brosse', i, '1761–1809'.

26. Ado, *Paysans en Révolution*, 264–5.

27. Eric Thierry, 'Une fête révolutionnaire à Villers-Cotterêts en 1792', *Fédération des sociétés d'histoire et d'archéologie de l'Aisne. Memoires*, 34 (1989), 276.

28. Markoff, *The Abolition of Feudalism*, especially. chs 5–7.

29. Jacques Péret, 'L'exemplaire histoire d'une famille bourgeoise poitevine, les Monnet (1660–1880)', *RHMC* 26 (1979), 114–15.

30. Markoff, *The Abolition of Feudalism*, 426, 497–8, ch. 8; Jones, *The Peasantry in the French Revolution*, 70–74; Ado, *Paysans en Révolution*, ch. 2, 306–8. According to Markoff, the August decree effectively ended anti-seigneurial protest.

31. *Gazette Nationale ou le Moniteur Universel* no. 239, 26 August 1792, vol. 13, 527–28.

32. Jones, *The Peasantry in the French Revolution*, 92–4, 114–17, 217.

33. Bourgin, *Le partage des biens communaux*, 482, 591; David Hunt, 'Peasant Movements and Communal Property during the French Revolution', *Theory and Society* 17 (1988), 269, 275.

34. AD Aisne, L 609, 'Troubles à Coucy-le-Château, septembre-décembre 1792'. Desfossés had resigned from the National Assembly in 1790. He and his wife were executed on 8 Thermidor Year II: Péronnet, Attal and Bobin, *La Révolution dans l'Aisne*, 96.

35. Michel Vovelle, *De la cave au grenier: un itinéraire en Provence au XVIIIe siècle. De l'histoire sociale à l'histoire des mentalités* (Québec, 1980).

36. Vovelle, *Les métamorphoses de la fête en Provence de 1750 à 1820* (Paris, 1976).

37. Pellegrin, *Les vêtements de la Liberté*, 161–2; Annie Geffroy 'Sans-culotte(s) – Novembre 1790–Juin 1792', *Dictionnaire des usages socio-politiques. – 1; 1985*, 59–186; R.B. Rose, *The Making of the 'sans-culottes': Democratic Ideas and Institutions in Paris*, 1789–1792 (Manchester, 1983). Richard Andrews, Michael Sonenscher and David Andress have argued that many of the *sans-culottes* were in fact bourgeois who adopted this political term through expediency: see Andrews, 'Social Structures, Political Elites and Ideology in Revolutionary Paris, 1792–1794: A Critical Evaluation of Albert Soboul's *Les sans-culottes parisiens en l'an II'*, *Journal of Social History* 19 (1985), 72–112; Andress, *The French Revolution and the People*; Michael Sonenscher, 'Artisans, sans-culottes and the French Revolution', in Forrest and Jones (eds), *Reshaping France*, 105–21.

38. McPhee, *Revolution and Environment in Southern France*, 129–31.

39. Steven L. Kaplan, *La fin des corporations* (Paris, 2001).

40. Yvonne Knibiehler, 'Femmes de Provence en Révolution', in Marie-France Brive (ed.), *Les femmes et la Révolution française Actes du colloque international 12–13–14 avril 1989* (Toulouse, 1989), 151.

41. Suzanne Desan, ' "Constitutional Amazons": Jacobin Women's Clubs in the French Revolution', in Ragan and Williams (eds), *Re-Creating Authority in Revolutionary France*, 11–35.

42. Antoine de Baecque, *The Body Politic: Corporeal Metaphor in Revolutionary France, 1770–1800* (Stanford, CA, 1997). The origins of the vituperative attacks on Marie-Antoinette are studied by Lynn Hunt, *The Family Romance of the French Revolution* (London, 1992); Chantal Thomas, *The Wicked Queen: The Origins of the Myth of*

*Marie-Antoinette*, trans. Julie Rose (New York, 2000); and Thomas E. Kaiser, 'Who's Afraid of Marie-Antoinette? Diplomacy, Austrophobia and the Queen', *French History* 14 (2000), 241–71.

43. On the September massacres, see Pierre Caron, *Les massacres de septembre* (Paris, 1935); Frédéric Bluche, *Septembre 1792: logiques d'un massacre* (Paris, 1986); and Antoine de Baecque, *Glory and Terror: Seven Deaths under the French Revolution*, trans. Charlotte Mandell (New York and London, 2001).

44. Caron, *Les massacres de septembre*; Paul Nicolle, 'Les meutres politiques d'août–septembre 1792 dans le département de l'Orne: Étude critique', *AHRF* 62 (March–April 1934): 97–118.

45. Caron, *Les massacres de septembre*; Ado, *Paysans en Révolution*, 312–19.

46. Caron. *Les massacres de septembre*; Péronnet and Bourdin, *La Révolution dans L'Orne*.

47. AD Orne L 5177.

48. AD Orne L 5336.

49. Jacques Hérissay, *Les massacres de Meaux* (Paris, 1936).

50. Bernet (ed.), *Le journal d'un maître d'école*, 15, 255. A volume of the diary covering 1792–1803 has been lost.

51. AD Aisne, 'Mémoires de Nicolas-Joseph Grain', 156–57; also in *La Révolution vue de l'Aisne*, 153–4; Péronnet, Attal and Bobin, *La Révolution dans l'Aisne*, 128.

52. AD Aisne, L 1081, also in *La Révolution vue de l'Aisne*, 157. Tensions may have been heightened by the arrival in Soissons of nuns whose orders had been closed on the sixth: L 1506, 'Affaires ecclésiastiques: correspondance générale, 1792-an VI'.

53. Simon Schama, *Citizens: A Chronicle of the French Revolution* (New York, 1989), 637; J.F. Bosher, *The French Revolution* (New York, 1988); François Furet, *The French Revolution 1774–1884* (Oxford, 1992). Note the acerbic remarks of Richard Cobb on the 'sanitizing' approach to violence and protest of George Rudé and others in *Police and the People*, 89–90.

54. Jeffrey Larrabee Short, 'The Lantern and the Scaffold: The Debate on Violence in Revolutionary France', April–October 1789', PhD thesis, State University of New York at Binghamton, 1990, 14, 29.

55. Brian Singer, 'Violence in the French Revolution: Forms of Ingestion/Forms of Expulsion', in Ferenc Fehér (ed.), *The French Revolution and the Birth of Modernity* (Berkeley, CA and Oxford, 1990).

56. Lucas' remarks concern the common mutilation of bodies of political enemies, although none of his Parisian examples involve decapitation. Colin Lucas, 'Themes in Southern Violence after 9 Thermidor', in Lewis and Lucas (eds), *Beyond the Terror*, 180; 'The Crowd and Politics between the Ancien Régime and Revolution in France', in Timothy Blanning (ed.), *The Rise and Fall of the French Revolution*, 199–235.

57. Roger-Noël, 'La Révolution aux frontières vue par un volontaire'.

# 6 In the fires of war, 1792–93

1. McPhee, *Revolution and Environment*, 92.

2. Noël, *Au temps des volontaires*, 233–44, 299.

3. Jean-Paul Bertaud, 'The Volunteers of 1792', in Forrest and Jones (eds), *Reshaping France*, 168–78.

4. Félix Mourlot (ed.), *Recueil des documents d'ordre économique contenus dans les registres de délibérations des municipalités du district d'Alençon*, vol. 2 (Alençon, 1908), 368–72.

5. See, for example, Markoff, *The Abolition of Feudalism*, 173 (table 4.14) and 406 (map 7.3); Ado, *Paysans en Révolution*, ch. 2.
6. See the discussion in David Hunt, 'Peasant Politics in the French Revolution', *SH* 9 (1984), 277–99.
7. Michel Bée, 'Dans la Normandie, entre Seine et Orne, confrères et citoyens', *AHRF* 306 (1996), 601–15.
8. Maurice Agulhon, *Pénitents et francs-maçons de l'ancienne Provence. Essai sur la sociabilité méridionale* (Paris, 1968); Régis Bertrand, 'Les confréries de Provence face à la Révolution', *AHRF* 306 (1996), 635–47.
9. Jean-Paul Rothiot, 'Comités de surveillance et Terreur dans le département des Vosges de 1793 à l'an III', *AHRF* 314 (1998), 621–68.
10. Jessenne, *Pouvoir au village*, 100–2. Two other case studies of changing political culture at the local level are Serge Bianchi, *La Révolution et la première république au village. Pouvoirs, votes et politisation dans les campagnes d'Île-de-France 1787–1800* (Paris, 2004); Jeff Horn, *Qui parle pour la nation? Les élections et les élus de la Champagne méridionale, 1765–1830* (Paris, 2004).
11. Ado, *Paysans en Révolution*, 345–8.
12. *Ibid.*, 326–34.
13. Jean-Pierre Laverrière, *Un village entre la Révolution et l'Empire. Viry en Savoie (1792–1815)* (Paris, 1980).
14. Bernet (ed.), *Le journal d'un maître d'école*, 34.
15. David M. Hopkin, *Soldier and Peasant in French Popular Culture, 1766–1870* (Woodbridge, Sussex and New York, 2003), 69.
16. Pellegrin, *Les vêtements de la Liberté*, 65.
17. Gabrielle Gauchat, *Journal d'une visitandine pendant la Terreur ou Mémoires de la Sœur Gabrielle Gauchat* (Paris, 1855), 26–7, 37.
18. Georges Fournier, 'Les femmes dans la vie politique locale en Languedoc pendant la Révolution française', in Brive (ed.), *Les femmes et la Révolution française*, 119.
19. Arend H. Huussen, 'La "crise" du mariage pendant la Révolution française', in Paul Viallaneix and Jean Ehrard (eds), *Aimer en France, 1760–1860, Actes du colloque international de Clermont-Ferrand* (Clermont-Ferrand, 1980), 331–43.
20. McPhee, *Collioure*, 30.
21. AD Ain 110 J 345 BM 'Actes de Mr Grillet, Prêtre Chanoine de Bourg'.
22. See Cobb, *Reactions to the French Revolution*, 142–8, *A Sense of Place* (London, 1975), 77–135; Roderick Phillips, *Family Breakdown in Late-Eighteenth Century France: Divorces in Rouen, 1792–1803* (Oxford, 1980), especially 108–24, 161–2; Vovelle, *La mentalité révolutionnaire*, ch. 13.
23. *Gazette Nationale ou le Moniteur Universel*, no. 284, 10 October 1792, vol. 14, 158–9.
24. Roderick Phillips, 'Remaking the Family: The Reception of Family Law and Policy during the French Revolution', in Reinhardt and Cawthorn (eds), *Essays on the French Revolution*, 64–89.
25. AD Ain, Registres d'Etat Civil, Bourg-en-Bresse, 2E 46224, 46225, 46226.
26. McPhee, *Gabian*, ch. 2, 44; *Collioure*, ch. 6; AD Aisne, L 2629, Tribunal de famille et tribunal d'arbitrage de Laon, 7 Fructidor Year II.
27. Margaret Darrow, *Revolution in the House: Family, Class and Inheritance in Southern France, 1775–1825* (Princeton, NJ, 1989), ch. 7.
28. Kennedy, Michael, *The Jacobin Clubs in the French Revolution: The Middle Years* (Princeton, NJ, 1988).
29. Kaplow, *Elbeuf during the Revolutionary Period*, 173.

30. Max Frey, *Les Transformations du vocabulaire français à l'époque de la Révolution (1789–1800)* (Paris, 1925); Laukhard, *Un Allemand en France*, 141, 177–8n.
31. Hopkin, *Soldier and Peasant*, 33, 55.
32. Alison Patrick, *The Men of the First French Republic: Political Alignments in the National Convention of 1792* (Baltimore, MD, 1972); Michael Sydenham, *The Girondins* (London, 1961); David Jordan, *The King's Trial: The French Revolution versus Louis XVI* (Berkeley, CA, 1979); Michael Walzer (ed.), *Regicide and Revolution: Speeches at the Trial of Louis XVI* (Cambridge, 1974).
33. Edward Duyker, *Citizen Labillardière: A French Naturalist in New Holland and the South Pacific* (Melbourne, 2003).
34. On this behaviour, see Cobb, *The People's Armies*, 471–9.
35. Pellegrin, *Les vêtements de la Liberté*, 186–7.
36. Peter Sahlins, *Unnaturally French: Foreign Citizens in the Old Regime and After* (Ithaca, NY and London, 2004).
37. Hopkin, *Soldier and Peasant*, 246.
38. McPhee, *Revolution and Environment*, 97.
39. *Ibid.*, 97–101.
40. Forrest, *Soldiers of the French Revolution*, 68–74.
41. Jones, *The Peasantry in the French Revolution*, 225; on this region, see Colin Lucas, *The Structure of the Terror: The Example of Javogues and the Loire* (Oxford, 1973). On rural political tendencies, see Hunt, 'Peasant Politics in the French Revolution', 277–99; Jones, *The Peasantry in the French Revolution*, 206–40; R.B. Rose, 'The "Red Scare" of the 1790s: The French Revolution and the "Agrarian Law"', *P&P* 103 (1984), 113–30.
42. AD de l'Aude, 4E 181 Labécède-Lauragais, Registre des délibérations du Conseil municipal, 1790–1807, 26 April 1793.
43. Tilly, 'The Emergence of Citizenship in France and Elsewhere', 224–5.
44. Forrest, *Soldiers of the French Revolution*, 73–4.
45. McPhee, *Gabian*, ch. 2.
46. André Bendjebbar, 'Propriété et contre-révolution dans l'Ouest', in *La Révolution française et le monde rural*, 287–300.
47. Jean-Clément Martin, 'Histoire et polémique, les massacres de Machecoul', *AHRF* 291 (1993), 33–60.
48. Claude Petitfrère, 'Les grandes composantes sociales des armées vendéennes d'Anjou', *AHRF* 45 (1973), 1–20.
49. *Mémoires pour servir à l'Histoire de la Guerre de la Vendée par le Général Turreau* (Paris, 1824), 26–8.
50. Peter McPhee, 'Counter-Revolution in the Pyrenees: Spirituality, Class and Ethnicity in the Haut-Vallespir, 1793–1794', *FH* 7 (1993), 313–43.
51. Michel Biard, *Missionnaires de la République* (Paris, 2002), ch. 2.
52. Soboul, *French Revolution*, 309. On this *journée*, see Rudé, *The Crowd in the French Revolution* (Oxford, 1959), ch. 8; Morris Slavin, *The Making of an Insurrection: Parisian Sections and the Gironde* (Cambridge, MA, 1986).
53. Sheppard, *Lourmarin*, 196–203. Among the many studies of 'Federalism', see Forrest, *Paris, the Provinces and the French Revolution*, ch. 8; William Scott, *Terror and Repression in Revolutionary Marseilles* (London, 1973); Paul Hanson, *Provincial Politics in the French Revolution: Caen and Limoges, 1789–1794* (Baton Rouge, LA, 1989); Bill Edmonds, '"Federalism" and Urban Revolt in France in 1793', *JMH* 55 (1983), 22–53; Malcolm Crook, ' "Federalism" and the French Revolution: The Revolt of Toulon in 1793', *History* 65 (1980), 383–97; David Longfellow, 'Silk

Weavers and the Social Struggle in Lyon during the French Revolution', *FHS* 12 (1981), 1–40.

54. McPhee, *Revolution and Environment*, ch. 4.
55. *Archives parlementaires*, 24 June 1793, vol. 67, 143–50.
56. Crook, *Elections in the French Revolution*, ch. 5.
57. Fournier, 'Les femmes dans la vie politique locale en Languedoc', 117.
58. McPhee, *Collioure*, 33.
59. Serge Aberdam, 'Délibérations en assemblées de citoyens et *portions de souveraineté en 1793*', in Michel Pertué (ed.), *Suffrage, citoyenneté et révolutions 1789–1848. Collections études révolutionnaires*, no. 3 (Paris, 2002), ch. 1; 'Deux occasions de participation féminine en 1793: le vote sur la constitution et le partage des biens communaux', *AHRF* 339 (2005), 17–34.
60. See Anne Verjus, *Le Cens de la famille. Les femmes et le vote, 1789–1848* (Paris, 2002). More conventionally feminist in its contributions is Evelyne Morin-Rotureau (ed.), *1789–1799: combat de femmes. La Révolution exclut les citoyennes* (Paris, 2003).

## 7 The experience of terror, 1793–94

1. Olwen Hufton, 'Women in Revolution', *French Politics and Society* 7 (1989), 77.
2. Forrest, *Soldiers of the French Revolution*, 75–8, ch. 5; Hopkin, *Soldier and Peasant*, 126–30.
3. Forrest, *Soldiers of the French Revolution*, 143.
4. McPhee, *Revolution and Environment*, 103.
5. Brunot, *Histoire de la langue française*, livre II, chs 1–2.
6. Marcel Reinhard, 'Nostalgie et service militaire pendant la Révolution', *AHRF* 30 (1958), 1–15; Forrest, *Soldiers of the French Revolution*, 150.
7. Alan Forrest, *Conscripts and Deserters: The Army and French Society during the Revolution and Empire* (Oxford, 1989), 94–5.
8. Peter McPhee, *A Social History of France, 1780–1914*, 2nd edn (London and New York, 2004), 58. Soldiers' experiences are well captured in Jean-Paul Bertaud, *The Army of the French Revolution: From Citizen Soldiers to Instruments of Power*, trans. R.R. Palmer (Princeton, NJ, 1988); Forrest, *Soldiers of the French Revolution*, ch. 6.
9. Bruno Ciotti, *Du volontaire au conscrit, les levées d'hommes dans le Puy-de-Dôme pendant la Révolution française*, 2 vols (Clermont-Ferrand, 2001).
10. AD Aude, 4E 181 Labécède-Lauragais, Registre des délibérations du Conseil municipal, 1790–1807, 11 Septembre 1793.
11. John A. Lynn, *The Bayonets of the Republic: Motivation and Tactics in the Army of Revolutionary France, 1791–1794* (Champaign, IL, 1984).
12. Ado, *Paysans en Révolution*, 355–70.
13. *Ibid.*, 370–3.
14. Serge Aberdam, 'La Révolution et la lutte des métayers', *Études rurales* 59 (1975), 73–91; Jones, *The Peasantry in the French Revolution*, 102–3.
15. Éric Teyssier, 'Appliquer une loi sociale en France sous la Convention. La mise en oeuvre de la loi du 13 septembre 1793', *AHRF* 312 (1998), 265–83.
16. Peter Jones, 'Agrarian Radicalism during the French Revolution', in Forrest and Jones (eds), *Reshaping France*, 137–51.
17. Aberdam, 'Deux occasions de participation féminine en 1793', 31.
18. Noelle L. Plack, 'Agrarian Individualism, Collective Practices and the French Revolution: The Law of 10 June 1793 and the Partition of Common Land in the Department of the Gard', *EHQ* 35 (2005), 39–62.

19. Bourgin, *Le partage des biens communaux*, 469–72. Bourgin's work is utilized in Hunt, 'Peasant Movements and Communal Property', 255–83.
20. Bourgin, *Le partage des biens communaux*, 481–2.
21. Jones, *The Peasantry in the French Revolution*, 137–54; Plack, 'Agrarian Individualism, Collective Practices and the French Revolution', 45–7.
22. Ado, *Paysans en Révolution*, 373–9; McPhee, *Revolution and Environment*, 129–31.
23. A law of 9 Brumaire XIII/31 October 1804 reversed the principle of the 1794 reform to common woodland, and the rights of *affouage* (wood-cutting) were once more graded according to custom.
24. Gerbaux and Schmidt, *Procès-verbaux des comités d'agriculture et de commerce*, 130–1.
25. Pierre Caron (ed.), *Rapports des agents du Ministre de l'Intérieur dans les départements (1793 – an II)*, 2 vols (Paris, 1913–51), vol. 1, 27–8.
26. Félix Mourlot, *Recueil des documents d'ordre économique contenus dans les registres de délibérations des municipalitiés du district d'Alençon, 1788-An IV* (Alençon, 1907), 404.
27. *Ibid.*, 138–9, 165–6.
28. Jean-Michel Derex, 'Le décret du 14 frimaire an II sur l'assèchement des étangs: folles espérances et piètres résultats. L'application du décret en Brie', *AHRF* 325 (juillet/septembre 2001), 77–97.
29. Mona Ozouf, 'War and Terror in French Revolutionary Discourse (1792–1794)', in Blanning (ed.), *The Rise and Fall of the French Revolution*, 266–84.
30. Ado, *Paysans en Révolution*, 405–15.
31. AD Aisne, L 1541, 'Secours divers: correspondance générale'.
32. AD Aisne, 5M1 73, État civil, Laon; Archives municipales de Laon, SRL 34, 'Subsistences'.
33. Jean-Pierre Gross, *Fair Shares for All: Jacobin Egalitarianism in Practice* (Cambridge and New York, 1997), 85–7.
34. AD Orne L 4601.
35. Péronnet and Bourdin, *La Révolution dans L'Orne*, 123–4.
36. AD Ain, AC Bourg, Registre des délibérations du Conseil Général, 13 Pluviôse An 2.
37. AD Ain, État civil de Bourg-en-Bresse.
38. Ado, *Paysans en Révolution*, 416–23; R. Legrand, *La Révolution dans la Somme* (Abbeville, 1988), 262. The argument that the Terror was designed to contain this popular protest and fury as much as to crush counter-revolution is put, unconvincingly, by Sophie Wahnich, *La liberté ou la mort: essai sur la Terreur et le terrorisme* (Paris, 2003).
39. McPhee, *Revolution and Environment*, 116.
40. Yvonne Crebouw, 'La salariés agricoles face au maximum des salaires', in *La Révolution française et le monde rural*, 120–1.
41. AD Ain, AC Bourg, Registre des délibérations du Conseil Général, 17, 22 Pluviôse An 2.
42. AD Ain, AC Belley, Registre des délibérations du Conseil Général, 20 Nivôse Year II.
43. Ozouf, *Festivals and the French Revolution*, 115.
44. Bernet (ed.), *Le journal d'un maître d'école*, 34.
45. Yves Tripier, ' "Vandalisme révolutionnaire" en Bretagne ou imposition par le pouvoir républicain d'une nouvelle culture, 1793–1795', in Simone Bernard-Griffiths, Marie-Claude Chemin and Jean Ehrard (eds), *Révolution française et*

'*vandalisme révolutionnaire*'. *Actes du colloque international de Clermont-Ferrand 15–17 décembre 1988* (Paris, 1992), 149.

46. Nicole Bossut, 'Terreur à Clamecy. Quelques réflexions', *AHRF* 311 (1998), 49–77.
47. Serge Bianchi, 'Le "vandalisme" anti-féodal et le "vandalisme" anti-religieux dans le sud de l'Île-de-France', in Bernard-Griffiths *et al.* (eds), *Révolution française et 'vandalisme révolutionnaire*', 161.
48. AD Aude 4E 359 St-Michel-de-Lanes, Registre des délibérations du Conseil municipal, 1790-an VIII, 21 Germinal Year II.
49. François Lebrun (ed.), *Histoire des Catholiques en France du XVe siècle à nos jours* (Toulouse, 1980), 260–1. On 'dechristianization' in general, see the provocative Daniel Guérin, *Class Struggle in the First French Republic: Bourgeois and Bras Nus 1793–1795*, trans. I. Patterson (London, 1977), chs 5–6; Michel Vovelle, *Religion et révolution. La déchristianisation de l'An II* (Paris, 1976); the debate between Vovelle and Gérard Cholvy in *AHRF* 233 (1978), 451–70.
50. Bianchi, *La Révolution culturelle*, 119; Ozouf, *Festivals and the French Revolution*, 89–91. General discussions of the effects on the church are Aston, *Religion and Revolution*, part III; Michel Vovelle, *The Revolution against the Church: From Reason to the Supreme Being*, trans. Alan Jose (Cambridge, 1991).
51. Jean Michel, *Journal de la déportation des ecclésiastiques du département de la Meurthe dans la rade de l'Ile d'Aix, près Rochefort, en 1794 et 1795, par un de ces déportés* (Nancy, 1840), 37.
52. *Ibid.*, 25–6.
53. Donald Greer, *The Incidence of the Emigration during the French Revolution* (Cambridge, MA, 1951); *The Incidence of the Terror during the French Revolution: A Statistical Interpretation* (Cambridge, MA, 1935).
54. Plouvier, 'L'abbaye de Prémontré', 358–9.
55. Cobb, *The People's Armies*, 159–205; Laukhard, *Un Allemand en France sous la Terreur*, 264–9.
56. Cobb, *The People's Armies*, 508.
57. *Ibid.*, 272–6, 471, 728.
58. *Ibid.*, 433, 697.
59. Cobb, *Paris and Its Provinces*, 123–32; Raymonde Monnier, 'La politisation des paroisses rurales de la banlieue parisienne', in *La Révolution française et le monde rural*, 436.
60. Jacques-François le Bourguignon du Perré, *Notes d'un détenu de la maison de réclusion des ci-devant Carmélites de Caen pendant la Terreur* (Écreux, 1903), 11–12.
61. Jacques Bernet, 'Les limites de la déchristianisation de la l'an II éclairées par le retour au culte de l'an III', *AHRF* 312 (1998), 287; see too Serge Bianchi, 'La bataille du calendrier ou le décadi contre le dimanche. Nouvelles approaches pour la reception du calendrier républicain en milieu rural', *AHRF* 312 (1998), 245–64.
62. Danièle Pingue, 'Qui étaient les "Jacobins" Haut-Normands? Objectifs, sources, methods d'une enquête prosopographique', *AHRF* 297 (1994), 413–23.
63. Philippe Bourdin, 'Le recrutement des sociétés populaires du Puy-de-Dôme', *AHRF* 290 (1992), 491–516.
64. Lucas, *The Structure of the Terror*, 96.
65. McPhee, *Revolution and Environment*, 106–7. See Jean Boutier *et al.*, *Atlas de la Révolution française*, vol. 6, *Les sociétés politiques* (Paris, 1992).
66. Cobb, *Paris and Its Provinces*, 33–4, 221–2.
67. Jones, *The Peasantry in the French Revolution*, 231; Georges Fournier, 'La vie politique au village en l'an II', *AHRF* 300 (1995), 271–82.

68. Sutherland, *The French Revolution and Empire*, 179–80.
69. Emmet Kennedy, *A Cultural History of the French Revolution* (New Haven, CT, 1989), 304. See Melvin Edelstein, *'La Feuille villageoise': communication et modernisation dans les régions rurales pendant la Révolution* (Paris, 1977); Jones, *The Peasantry in the French Revolution*, 207–17; Colin Lucas, 'The Problem of the Midi in the French Revolution', *Transactions of the Royal Historical Society* 28 (1978), 1–25.
70. AD Ain, AC Bourg, Registre des délibérations du Conseil Général, 5 Pluviôse An 2.
71. Colin Lucas, 'The Theory and Practice of Denunciation in the French Revolution', *JMH* 68 (1996), 781.
72. Nathalie Alzas, 'Don, patriotisme et sociétés populaires en l'an II', *AHRF* 329 (2002), 41–65.
73. Andress, *The French Revolution and the People*, 213, 216, 220.
74. Jean-Claude Malsy, *Les noms de lieu du département de l'Aisne*, 3 vols (Paris, 1999); Édouard Fleury, *Le clergé du département de l'Aisne pendant la Révolution. Études révolutionnaires* (Paris and Laon, 1853), vol. 2, 16–17; Lucas, *The Structure of the Terror*, xiv–xv. On revolutionary place and given names in general, see the special issue of *AHRF* 322 (2000); Bianchi, *Révolution culturelle*, ch. 6.
75. Péronnet and Bourdin, *La Révolution dans L'Orne*, 128.
76. AD Ain, AC Bourg, Registre des délibérations du Conseil Général, 6 germinal An 2, 30 Vendémiaire An 3.
77. AD Aisne, 5M1 73, État civil, Laon.
78. AD Aisne, 5M1 150, État civil, Coucy-le-Château; 5M1 534, État civil, Notre-Dame-de-Liesse.
79. McPhee, *Gabian*, ch. 2.
80. Frey, *Les transformations du vocabulaire, passim*; Laukhard, *Un Allemand en France sous la Terreur*, 332; Prudhomme, *Histoire générale et impartiale des erreurs, des fautes et des crimes commis pendant la Révolution française* (Paris: Year V – 1797), vol. VI, 522.
81. Kennedy, *Cultural History of the French Revolution*, 353–62; R.R. Palmer, *The Improvement of Humanity: Education and the French Revolution* (Princeton, NJ, 1985), chs 4–5; Marie-Françoise Lévy (ed.), *L'Enfant, la famille et la Révolution* (Paris, 1989).
82. *Rapport et projet de décret, formant un plan général d'instruction publique, par G. Bouquier, membre de la Convention nationale et du Comité d'instruction.*
83. Dominique Julia, 'L'institution du citoyen. Instruction publique et éducation nationale dans les projets de la période révolutionnaire (1789–1795)', in Lenoël and Lévy (eds), *L'enfant, la famille et la Révolution française*, 164–8.
84. Huussen, 'La "crise" du mariage pendant la Révolution française', 337.
85. Jacques Poumarède, 'La législation successorale de la Révolution entre l'idéologie et la pratique', in Irène Thery and Christian Biet (eds), *La Famille, la loi, l'État. De la Révolution au Code Civil* (Paris, 1989), 167–82.
86. *Ibid.*, 176–7.
87. AD Ain Registre du tribunal de famille, 4 Nivôse, 3 Prairial Year II.
88. This most significant episode in the history of women's political participation is discussed by Suzanne Desan, ' "Constitutional Amazons": Jacobin Women's Clubs in the French Revolution', in Ragan and Williams (eds), *Re-Creating Authority in Revolutionary France*, 30–5; Scott H. Lytle, 'The Second Sex (September, 1793)', *JMH* 26 (1955), 14–26; Marie Cerati, *Le club des citoyennes républicaines révolutionnaires* (Paris, 1966); R.B. Rose, *The Enragés: Socialists of the French Revolution?* (Melbourne, 1965), chs 5–6.
89. Alan Forrest, *The Revolution in Provincial France: Aquitaine 1789–1799* (Oxford and New York, 1996), 234–5.

90. Peter McPhee, 'Social Change and Political Conflict in Mediterranean France: Canet in the Nineteenth Century', *FHS* 22 (1981), 80; Pierre Vidal, *Histoire de la Révolution française dans le département des Pyrénées-Orientales* (Perpignan, 1889), vol. 1, 260–3.
91. McPhee, *Collioure*, 39–40. For an example of a collaborator who fled with the Spanish and whose only motive seems to have been religious, see Alain Ayats *et al.* (eds), *Entre Révolution et guerres. mémoires de Pierre Comellas, apothicaire de Perpignan 1789–1813* (Perpignan, 2005).
92. Muller, 'Religion et Révolution en Alsace', 63–83.
93. Maciak, 'Of News and Networks', 281; Roger Dupuy, *De la Révolution à la chouannerie: paysans en Bretagne* (Paris, 1988), 7–8. See, too, Lyons, 'Politics and Patois', 264–81; Patrice Higonnet, 'The Politics of Linguistic Terrorism and Grammatical Hegemony during the French Revolution', *SH* 5 (1980), 41–69.
94. Christian Bonnet, 'Un cas de résistance à la nouvelle organisation du temps et de l'espace: la Flandre maritime (1792–1794)', in *L'espace et le temps reconstruits: la Révolution française, une révolution des mentalités et cultures?* (Aix-en-Provence, 1990), 197–205; Forrest, *Soldiers of the French Revolution*, 110.
95. Claude Petitfrère, 'La Vendée en l'an II: défaite et répression', *AHRF* 300 (1995), 178–9.
96. François Lebrun (ed.), *Parole de Dieu et Révolution. Les sermons d'un curé angevin avant et pendant la guerre de Vendée* (Paris, 1988), 31–44.
97. Claude Petitfrère, *La Vendée et les Vendéens* (Paris, 1981), 58–60. Translated in Dwyer and McPhee (eds), *The French Revolution and Napoleon*, 100.
98. Reynald Secher, *A French Genocide: The Vendée*, trans. George Holoch (Notre Dame, IN, 2003), 250. It is evidence such as this which enabled Secher to make his assertion that the repression in the Vendée amounted to 'genocide'.
99. Sutherland, *The French Revolution and Empire*, 203.
100. See Jean-Clément Martin, *La Vendée et la France* (Paris, 1986); Aston, *The French Revolution*, 168–81; Michel Ragon, *1793: l'insurrection vendéenne et les malentendus de la liberté* (Paris, 1992); Paul Tallonneau, *Les Lucs et le génocide vendéen: comment on a manipulé les textes* (Paris, 1993); Alain Gérard, *La Vendée: 1789–1793* (Paris, 1992).
101. Secher, *A French Genocide*, 251, 253. See, too, *La Chapelle-Basse-Mer, village vendéen: révolution et contre-révolution* (Paris, 1986).
102. Ado, *Paysans en Révolution*, 366.
103. Jacques Guilhaumou and Martine Lapied, 'La mission Maignet', *AHRF* 300 (1995), 283–94.
104. Olivier Blanc, *La dernière Lettre. Prisons et condamnés de la Révolution, 1793–1794* (Paris, 1984), 209–10.
105. Emphasis in the Original, Petitfrère, *La Vendée et les Vendéens*, 58–60; see also his *Les Vendéens d'Anjou (1793)* (Paris, 1981).
106. Léon Dufour, *A travers un siècle (1780–1865), science et histoire: souvenirs d'un savant français* (Paris, 1888), 1, 8–9.
107. Forrest, *Soldiers of the French Revolution*, 163.
108. For example, by Eli Sagan, *Citizens and Cannibals: The French Revolution, the Struggle for Modernity, and the Origins of Ideological Terror* (Lanham, MD, 2001. Sagan's polemic recalls Jacob L. Talmon, *The Origins of Totalitarian Democracy* (Boulder, CO, 1985 [1952]). Note, too, the comments of Hugh Gough, 'Genocide and the Bicentenary: The French Revolution and the Revenge of the Vendée', *Historical Journal* 30 (1987), 978; Sutherland, *The French Revolution and Empire*, 223–5.

109. Schama, *Citizens*, 447; Patrice Gueniffey, *La politique de la Terreur: essai sur la violence révolutionnaire* (Paris, 2000); the special issue of *AHRF* 57 (2002); Ozouf, 'War and Terror in French Revolutionary Discourse', 266–84.

## 8  Settling scores: The Thermidorian Reaction, 1794–95

1. Kaplow, *Elbeuf during the Revolutionary Period*, 25.
2. AD Ain, AC Bourg, Registre des délibérations du Conseil Général, 15 Thermidor An 2.
3. Laukhard, *Un Allemand en France sous la Terreur*, 328–9.
4. Frey, *Les transformations du vocabulaire, passim*.
5. Roger-Noël, 'La Révolution aux frontières vue par un volontaire', 6–7.
6. Teyssier, 'La mise en oeuvre de la loi du 13 septembre 1793', 279–81.
7. McPhee, *Revolution and Environment*, 120.
8. *Ibid.*, 117–18.
9. Jacques Bernet, 'L'organisation du movement populaire sous la Révolution française: les sociétés populaires dans les districts de Senlis et Crépy-en-Valois en 1793–1795', in Nicolas (ed.), *Mouvements populaires et conscience sociale*, 465–71.
10. Bronislaw Baczko, *Ending the Terror. The French Revolution After Robespierre* (Cambridge, 1994).
11. Forrest, *Paris, the Provinces and the French Revolution*, 188; Cobb, *Police and the People*, 132.
12. AD Ain, AC Bourg, Registre des délibérations du Conseil Général, 3 Fructidor An 2; 27 Fructidor, 24 Pluviôse, 6 Messidor An 3.
13. Among many examples of published anti-Robespierrist hyperbole, see J.F.N. Dusaulchoy, *Agonie de Saint-Lazare, sous la tyrannie de Robespierre* (Paris, 1797).
14. AD Ain, AC Bourg, Registre des délibérations du Conseil Général, 8 Messidor An 3.
15. Yves Tripier, ' "Vandalisme révolutionnaire" en Bretagne ou imposition par le pouvoir républicain d'une nouvelle culture, 1793–1795', in Bernard-Griffiths *et al.* (eds), *Révolution française et 'vandalisme révolutionnaire'*, 152.
16. Sutherland, *The Chouans, passim*.
17. Le Goff and Sutherland, 'The Revolution and the Rural Community in Brittany', 118.
18. Ozouf, *Festivals and the French Revolution*, 96.
19. Michel Péronnet and Georges Fournier, *La Révolution dans l'Aude* (Le Coteau, 1989), 113, 127. Popular politics in the countryside are studied by Lewis, *Second Vendée*, ch. 3; Lucas, 'Themes in Southern Violence After 9 Thermidor', ch. 6; Cobb, *Reactions to the French Revolution*, 19–62; Jones, *The Peasantry in the French Revolution*, 240–7.
20. Cobb, *The Police and the People*, 109, 143.
21. Jonathan Skinner, 'The Revolutionary and Royalist Traditions in Southern Village Society: The Vaucluse Comtadin, 1789–1851', in Forrest and Jones (eds), *Reshaping France*, 206–20.
22. Richard Cobb and Colin Jones (eds), *The French Revolution: Voices from a Momentous Epoch, 1789–1795* (London, 1988), 236.
23. Colin Lucas, 'Résistances populaires à la Révolution dans le sud-est', in Nicolas (ed.), *Mouvements populaires et conscience sociale*, 473–85.
24. Lucas, 'Themes in Southern Violence After 9 Thermidor', ch. 6.
25. Cobb, *The Police and the People*, 299–300.

26. AD Ain, AC Bourg, Registre des délibérations du Conseil Général, 27 Fructidor An 2; 27 Brumaire, 27 Pluviose An 3.
27. On the famine of 1794–96 see Cobb, *The Police and the People*, part III.
28. Bernet, 'Les grèves de moissonneurs', 153–86.
29. Archives municipales de Laon, SRL 34, 'Subsistences'; also in *La Révolution vue de l'Aisne*, 284–5.
30. AD Ain, AC Bourg, Registre des délibérations du Conseil Général, 17 Ventôse An 3.
31. AD Ain, AC Bourg, Registre des délibérations du Conseil Général, 7 Thermidor An 3.
32. Bernet, 'Les limites de la déchristianisation de l'an II', 285–99; Muller, 'Religion et Révolution en Alsace', 77.
33. Sutherland, *The French Revolution and Empire*, 242.
34. Bernet, 'Les limites de la déchristianisation de l'an II', 291–2.
35. Etienne Andrieu, *La Contre-Révolution en Gévaudan (Aveyron et Lozère); Marc-Antoine Charrier et l'insurrection de l'Armée chrétienne du Midi en 1793* (Paris, 2000).
36. Suzanne Desan, *Reclaiming the Sacred: Lay Religion and Popular Politics in Revolutionary France* (Ithaca, NY, 1990), 225.
37. Olwen Hufton, 'The Reconstruction of a Church 1796–1801', in Lewis and Lucas (eds), *Beyond the Terror*, 48–9.
38. AD Ain, AC Bourg, Registre des délibérations du Conseil Général, 21 Ventose An 3.
39. *Ibid.*, 6 Pluviose An 3.
40. AD Ain, 110 J 345 BM, 'Actes de Mr Grillet, Prêtre Chanoine de Bourg'. Also 110 J 887, 888.
41. Ozouf, *Festivals and the French Revolution*, 202.
42. AD Ain, AC Bourg, Registre des délibérations du Conseil Général, 1 Brumaire An 3.
43. Woloch, *The New Regime*, 183–4.
44. Jessenne, *Pouvoir au village*. See, too, Bianchi, *La première république au village*; Horn, *Qui parle pour la nation?*
45. Gérard Noiriel, *Réfugiés et sans-papiers. La République face au droit d'asile XIXe–XXe siècle* (Paris, 1998), 51.
46. *Gazette Nationale ou le Moniteur Universel*, 214 (2 August 1793), vol. 17, 287.
47. Gwynne Lewis, 'Political Brigandage and Popular Disaffection in the South-East of France, 1795–1804', in Lewis and Lucas (eds), *Beyond the Terror*, 226.
48. Forrest, *Soldiers of the French Revolution*, 159.
49. Stewart (ed.), *Documentary Survey*, 572–612.
50. Desan, *The Family on Trial*, 103–4.
51. Suzanne Desan, 'Qu'est-ce qui fait un père? Illégitimité et paternité de l'an II au Code civil', *Annales* 57 (2002), 935–64.
52. Poumarède, 'La législation successorale', 173–7.
53. Crook, *Elections in the French Revolution*, 124–8.
54. Kaplow, *Elbeuf during the Revolutionary Period*, 252–4.

## 9 A new régime and its discontents, 1795–99

1. James Livesey, *Making Democracy in the French Revolution* (Cambridge, MA and London, 2001). On the Directory in general, see Georges Lefebvre, *The Directory*, trans. R. Baldick (London, 1964); Denis Woronoff, *The Thermidorian Regime and the Directory, 1794–1799*, trans. J. Jackson (Cambridge, 1984); Martyn Lyons, *France Under the Directory* (Cambridge, 1975); Michael Sydenham, *The First French Republic, 1792–1804* (London, 1974), part II.

2. Sutherland, *The French Revolution and Empire*, ch. 9; Georges Fournier, 'Entre vallée de l'Hérault et vallée de la Garonne: les bastions fermement républicains sous le Directoire', in Jean Sentou (ed.), *Révolution et contre-révolution dans la France du Midi (1789–1799)* (Toulouse, 1991), 181–204.
3. Woloch, *The New Regime*, 113–27.
4. Isser Woloch, 'The State and the Villages in Revolutionary France', in Forrest and Jones (eds), *Reshaping France*, 221–42.
5. Woloch, *The New Regime*, 119.
6. McPhee, *Gabian*, ch. 2.
7. Jones, *Liberty and Locality*, 125–6; Ozouf, *Festivals and the French Revolution*, 96.
8. Sutherland, *The French Revolution and Empire*, 273.
9. Cobb, *The Police and the People*, 350.
10. Sutherland, *The French Revolution and Empire*, 274.
11. This violence is examined by Sutherland, *France 1789–1815*, ch. 8; Cobb, *Reactions*, ch. 5; Michel Vovelle, 'From Beggary to Brigandage: The Wanderers in the Beauce during the French Revolution', in Kaplow (ed.), *New Perspectives on the French Revolution*, 287–304.
12. Cobb, *Paris and Its Provinces*, 194–207.
13. AD Orne L 5415.
14. AD Orne L 3052, 3054.
15. Cobb, *Reactions to the French Revolution*, 19–62, and *Police and the People*, 85–117; Jones, *The Peasantry in the French Revolution*, 240–7.
16. AD Ain, AC Bourg, Registre des délibérations du Conseil Général, 2 Vendémiaire, 4 Brumaire An IV.
17. AD Ain, AC Bourg, Registre des délibérations du Conseil Général, 10 Germinal, 30 Floréal, 11 Prairial An IV.
18. AD Isère L 254, 'Calendrier républicain'.
19. Le Ministre de l'intérieur aux administrations centrales des départements, 18 Brumaire Year VI; AD Isère, L 254, 'Calendrier républicain'.
20. Serge Bianchi, 'La bataille du calendrier ou le décadi contre le dimanche. Nouvelles approches pour la réception du calendrier républicain en milieu rural', *AHRF* 312 (1998), 245–64.
21. Bée, 'Dans la Normandie, entre Seine et Orne, confrères et citoyens'.
22. Kaplow, *Elbeuf during the Revolutionary Period*, 246.
23. Sutherland, *The French Revolution and Empire*, 267–8.
24. *Ibid.*, 267.
25. Bruno Maës, 'Le pèlerinage de Notre-Dame-de-Liesse de 1780 à la Restauration', in *La Religion et la Révolution française. Actes du Colloque international de Chantilly, 1986*, 612–17.
26. Blondel, *Adresse des bons prêtres du département du Calvados à la Convention, juste et sage*, 8, 17.
27. Elisabeth Claverie and Pierre Lamaison, *L'impossible marriage: violence et parenté en Gévaudan, XVIIe, XVIIIe et XIXe siècles* (Paris, 1982), 171.
28. AD Ain Série L, Documents non-classés, 'Dossiers de prêtres réfractaires'; 'Prêtres déportés ou déportables'.
29. Olwen Hufton, 'The Reconstruction of a Church 1796–1801', in Lewis and Lucas (eds), *Beyond the Terror*, ch. 2. On the correlation of priestly attitudes and local views, see Vovelle, *The Revolution Against the Church*, and the debate with Gérard Cholvy in *AHRF* 233 (1978), 451–70.
30. AD Aisne, L 606, 'Police générale du département, 1792-an VIII'.

31. Muller, 'Religion et Révolution en Alsace', 78–9; Claude Langlois and Timothy Le Goff, 'Les vaincus de la Révolution: jalons pour une sociologie des prêtres mariés', in Albert Soboul (ed.), *Voies nouvelles pour l'histoire de la Révolution française* (Paris, 1978).
32. Desan, *Reclaiming the Sacred*, 146, 162.
33. Suzanne Desan, 'The Rhetoric of Religious Revival during the French Revolution', *JMH* 60 (1988), 1–27; Jean Vassort, 'L'enseignement primaire en Vendômois à l'époque révolutionnaire', *RHMC* 25 (1978), 625–55; Kennedy, *Cultural History*, 360.
34. Brigitte Ladde, *Inventaire de la sous-série 110J, Régistres des baptêmes mariages et sépultures tenus par les prêtres réfractaires de l'Ain 1790–1801* (Bourg-en-Bresse, 1999); AD Ain 110 J 187 BMS.
35. Suzanne Grezaud, 'Un cas de registres paroissiaux tenus par un prêtre réfractaire', *AHRF* 200 (1970), 346–9.
36. McPhee, 'Counter-Revolution in the Pyrenees', 339–40.
37. Sutherland, *The French Revolution and Empire*, 268.
38. McPhee, *Collioure*, 72–3. The argument that such popular contestation represented deliberate Catalan resistance to the French state is put, not always convincingly, by Michel Brunet, *Le Roussillon: une société contre l'Etat, 1780–1820* (Toulouse, 1986).
39. McPhee, *Collioure*, ch. 4.
40. Ozouf, *Festivals and the French Revolution*, 120–1; Sherri Klassen, 'The Domestic Virtues of Old Age: Gendered Rites in the Fête de la Vieillesse', *Canadian Journal of History* 32 (1997), 393–403; *Des fêtes nationales, par Lequinio, député du Morbihan, 16 Nivôse Year III*.
41. AD Aisne, L 588, 'Procès-verbaux de célébration des fêtes nationales, an V-an VIII'.
42. Claude Bailly, *Journal d'un artisan tourangeau 1789–1830* (Chinon, 1989), 51–3.
43. Adrien Favre, *Histoire de Châtillon sur Chalaronne* (n.p., 1972), 70.
44. Pergamon Press French Revolution Research Collection 6.2/2760.
45. On this important, understudied period of rural social relations, see Jones, *The Peasantry in the French Revolution*, 103, 122–3, 134–7; Lewis, 'Political Brigandage and Popular Disaffection in the Southeast of France, 1795–1804'; Aberdam, 'La Révolution et la lutte des métayers', *passim*.
46. François de Neufchâteau, *Les Vosges*, 1796, 37.
47. Alain Le Bloas, 'La question du domaine congéable', *AHRF* 331 (2003), 1–27.
48. Aberdam, 'La Révolution et la lutte des métayers'; Jones, *The Peasantry in the French Revolution*, 98–103, 134–7.
49. Noël, *L'homme et la forêt en Languedoc-Roussillon*, 121.
50. AN AD IV 19. Coupé may have been referring to the comments in Pliny, *Natural History*, trans. H. Rackham (London, 1942), book III. iv. See, too, J.-B. Rougier de la Bergerie, *Mémoire et observations sur les abus des défrichemens et la destruction des bois et forêts; avec un projet d'organisation forestière* (Auxerre, An IX), 3.
51. Dominique Julia *et al.*, *Atlas de la Révolution française*, 2, *L'enseignement 1760–1815* (Paris, 1987), 22.
52. Kennedy, *Cultural History*, 360.
53. Palmer, *The Improvement of Humanity*, 242–57.
54. Schmidt, *Notes sur le travail des enfants*, 198–213; Serge Chassagne, 'L'enfant au travail dans les manufactures pendant la Révolution', in Lenoël and Lévy (eds), *L'enfant, la famille et la Révolution française*, 97–103.
55. Cobb, *Police and the People*, 234–9; Colin Jones, 'Picking up the pieces: the politics and the personnel of social welfare from the Convention to the Consulate', in Lewis and Lucas (eds), *Beyond the Terror*, 53–91.

56. AD Ain, Etat Civil de Bourg-en-Bresse, 1 Floréal, 7 Floréal An VI.
57. James M. Donovan, 'Magistrates and Juries in France, 1791–1952', *FHS* 22 (1999), 379–81.
58. AD Ain, Etat Civil de Bourg-en-Bresse.
59. AD Ain, AC Bourg, Registre des délibérations du Conseil Général, 4 jour supplementaire An 2, 11 Vendemiare An 3.
60. Le Goff and Sutherland, 'The Revolution and the Rural Economy', 71–2.
61. Vardi, *The Land and the Loom*, ch. 11.
62. Roger-Noël, 'La Révolution aux frontières vue par un volontaire', 13. From 1806 to 1850 Noël would be mayor of his village of Sommerviller in the department of the Meurthe.
63. Isser Woloch, *The French Veteran from the Revolution to the Restoration* (Chapel Hill, NC, 1979); Forrest, *Soldiers of the French Revolution*, 83–8.
64. Ciotti, *Du volontaire au conscrit*; Louis Bergès, *Résister à la conscription, 1798–1814. Le cas des départements aquitains* (Paris, 2002).
65. Alan Forrest, 'Conscription and Crime in rural France during the Directory and Consulate', in Lewis and Lucas (eds.), *Beyond the Terror*, 92–120; Sutherland, *The Chouans, passim.*
66. Cobb, *The Police and the People*, 101–2.
67. Forrest, *Soldiers of the French Revolution*, 170.
68. Jean-Noël Luc (ed.), *Gendarmerie, état et société au XIXe siècle* (Paris, 2002); Howard G. Brown, 'From Organic Society to Security State: The War on Brigandage in Revolutionary France, 1797–1802', *JMH* 69 (1997), 661–95.
69. AD Orne L 3113.
70. Claude Bailly, *Journal d'un artisan tourangeau 1789–1830* (Chinon, 1989), 73, 78.
71. Sutherland, *France 1789–1815*, ch. 8; Aston, *The French Revolution*, 124, 139–41. See, too, Woloch, *The New Regime*, 95–108; Lynn Hunt, David Lansky and Paul Hanson, 'The Failure of the Liberal Republic in France, 1795–1799: The Road to Brumaire', *JMH* 51 (1979), 734–59; Colin Lucas, 'Résistances populaires à la Révolution dans le sud-est', in Nicolas (ed.), *Mouvements populaires et conscience sociale.*
72. Stewart, *Documentary Survey*, 780.

## Conclusion – a revolution for the people?

1. Courchamps, *Souvenirs de la marquise de Créquy*, vol. 9, 144–5.
2. Prudhomme, *Histoire générale et impartiale des erreurs, des fautes et des crimes commis pendant la Révolution française* (Paris, Year V–1797), vol. VI, 522.
3. Péronnet, Attal and Bobin, *La Révolution dans l'Aisne*, 138; Jacques Houdaille, 'Le problème des pertes de guerre', *RHMC* xvii (1970), 418. In general see Forrest, *Soldiers of the French Revolution*; Woloch, *The New Regime*, ch. 13.
4. François Furet, *Interpreting the French Revolution*, trans. E. Forster (Cambridge, 1981), 24. See too William Doyle, *The Oxford History of the French Revolution* (Oxford, 1989), ch. 17; Roger Price, *A Social History of Nineteenth-Century France* (London, 1987); Schama, *Citizens*, epilogue.
5. See the important book by Sheryl Kroen, *Politics and Theater: The Crisis of Legitimacy in Restoration France, 1815–1830* (Berkeley, CA, 2000).
6. Bernard Degonville, 'De la société populaire de Chauny pendant la Révolution', *Fédération des sociétés d'histoire et d'archéologie de l'Aisne. Memoires*, 34 (1989), 61. More generally on the place of the Revolution in creating the bases for new types

and arenas for voluntary associations, see William H. Sewell, 'Collective Violence and Collective Loyalties in France: Why the French Revolution Made a Difference', *Politics & Society* 18 (1990), 527–52; Renée Waldinger, Philip Dawson and Isser Woloch (eds), *The French Revolution and the Meaning of Citizenship* (Westport, CT, 1993).

7. Jeff Horn, 'Toute politique est locale', *AHRF* 311 (1998), 89–109.
8. Crook, *Elections in the French Revolution, passim*. Different views of the meaning of elections and voting underpin Gueniffey, *Le Nombre et la raison*; Melvin Edelstein, 'La place de la Révolution française dans la politisation des paysans', *AHRF* 280 (1993), 135–44; Peter McPhee, 'Electoral Democracy and Direct Democracy in France, 1789–1851', *EHQ* 16 (1986), 77–96.
9. Ozouf, *Festivals and the French Revolution*, 217 and ch. IX.
10. Vovelle, *Métamorphoses de la fête, conclusion*.
11. Ozouf, *Festivals and the French Revolution*, 282 and ch. X.
12. Outside the Vendée, there has been surprisingly little analysis of the importance of collective memories of the Revolution. The outstanding study is Agulhon, *Marianne into Battle*; see also Raymond Huard, 'La Révolution française, événement fondateur: le travail de l'histoire sur l'héritage et la tradition', *Cahiers d'histoire de l'Institut de recherches marxistes* 32 (1988), 54–71.
13. Peter McPhee, *Les Semailles de la République dans les Pyrénées-Orientales, 1846–1852: classes sociales, culture et politique* (Perpignan, 1995), 187–8. See, too, Edward Berenson, 'Politics and the French Peasantry: The Debate Continues', *SH* 12 (1987), 219–29; McPhee, *The Politics of Rural Life: Political Mobilization in the French Countryside 1846–1852* (Oxford, 1992), ch. 5; Maciak, 'Of News and Networks'; Jones, *The Peasantry in the French Revolution*, 207–17.
14. Raymond Huard, 'Souvenir et tradition révolutionnaires: le Gard (1848–1851)', *AHRF* 258 (1984), 565–87.
15. Skinner, 'The Vaucluse Comtadin', 206–20.
16. Steven Laurence Kaplan, *Farewell Revolution: Disputed Legacies, France 1789/1989* (Ithaca, NY, 1995), 84–111. A more recent estimate is that between 300 and 500 of Les Lucs' 2,320 people were killed in all the fighting during the Vendéen insurrection: Jean-Clément Martin and Xavier Lardière, *Le Massacre des Lucs-Vendée 1794* (Vouillé, 1992); Paul Tallonneau, *Les Lucs et le génocide vendéen. Comment on a manipulé les textes* (Luçon, 1993).
17. Secher, *A French Genocide*, 134.
18. Benedict Anderson, *Imagined Communities: Reflections on the Origin and Spread of Nationalism* (London, 1983).
19. See Forrest, *Paris, the Provinces and the French Revolution*, and the essays in Pierre Nora (ed.) *Rethinking France: Les Lieux de mémoire*, vol. 1, *The State*, trans. Mary Trouille (Chicago, 2001). The brilliant study by David A. Bell, *The Cult of the Nation in France: Inventing Nationalism, 1680–1800* (Cambridge, MA, 2001), emphasizes the pre-revolutionary roots of nationalism, but sees nation-building to have been an élite project alone.
20. Brunot, *Histoire de la langue française*, 13–14. Brunot's classic text also epitomizes this view of the place of the French language as 'the language of liberty'.
21. Ibid., 159; Lartichaux, 'Linguistic Politics during the French Revolution', 65–84; Martyn Lyons, 'Politics and Patois'; Lyons, 'Regionalism and Linguistic Conformity in the French Revolution', 187–8; Certeau, Julia, and Revel, *Une politique de la langue*.
22. Much of this information is synthesized by Vovelle, *Découverte de la politique, passim*.
23. McPhee, *Collioure*, 86.

24. Hopkin, *Soldier and Peasant*; Hugh Gough, 'The Provincial Press in the French Revolution', in Forrest and Jones (eds), *Reshaping France*, 201.

25. Daniel Roche, 'Apparences révolutionnaires ou révolution des apparances?', in Pellegrin, *Les vêtements de la Liberté*, preface.

26. Péronnet, Attal and Bobin, *La Révolution dans l'Aisne*, 147.

27. Greer, *Terror*, chs 2, 5, and *Emigration*, chs 2, 4; Guy Chaussinand-Nogaret, *The French Nobility in the Eighteenth Century: From Feudalism to Enlightenment*, trans. W. Doyle (Cambridge, 1985), ch. 2; Robert Forster, 'The Survival of the Nobility during the French Revolution', *P&P* 37 (1967), 71–86; Thomas Beck, 'The French Revolution and the Nobility: A Reconsideration', *JSH* 15 (1981), 219–34.

28. Louis Bergeron, Guy Chaussinand-Nogaret and Robert Forster, 'Les notables du 'Grand Empire' en 1810', *Annales* 26 (1971), 1052–75.

29. Sheppard, *Lourmarin*, 211 and ch. 8. Sheppard himself preferred to emphasize the continuities of daily life in Lourmarin.

30. Forster, 'Survival of the Nobility'. Forster later formulated a more 'minimalist' view: see 'The French Revolution and the "New" Elite, 1800–1850', in Jaroslow Pelenski (ed.), *The American and European Revolutions, 1776–1848* (Iowa City, 1980), 182–207.

31. Massé, *Varennes et ses maitres*, 69–72.

32. Felice Harcourt (ed. and trans.), *Escape from the Terror: The Journal of Madame de la Tour du Pin* (London, 1979), 93–4, 243–4.

33. Young, *Travels in France*, 351.

34. Jones, *The Peasantry in the French Revolution*, 7–9; *Liberty and Locality*, 245–50.

35. Le Goff, *Vannes and Its Region*, 343–6, 352–3, 366.

36. Ibid., ch. 8; McManners, *Ecclesiastical Society*, 251–2; Crubaugh, *Balancing the Scales of Justice*, Part II, ch. 5.

37. Adrien Lezay, *Des causes de la Révolution et de ses résultats* (Paris, Year V – 1797), 73–4.

38. Sutherland, *The French Revolution and Empire*, 46, 64, 385.

39. Jones, *The Peasantry in the French Revolution*, 259.

40. Bodinier and Teyssier, *La vente des biens nationaux*, conclusion; Bodinier, 'La vente des biens nationaux', *passim*.

41. Anne Jollet, *Terre et société en Révolution: approche du lien social dans la région d'Amboise* (Paris, 2000).

42. Sutherland, *Revolution and Counterrevolution*, 440–2.

43. Le Goff and Sutherland, 'The Revolution and the Rural Economy', 52–85.

44. See, for example, Lefebvre, 'The Place of the Revolution in the Agrarian History of France'; Alfred Cobban, *The Social Interpretation of the French Revolution* (Cambridge, 1964), chs 7, 12, 14; Peter McPhee, 'The French Revolution, Peasants, and Capitalism', *AHR* 94 (1989), 1265–80; Peter Jones, 'Agricultural Modernization and the French Revolution', *Journal of Historical Geography* 16 (1990), 38–50.

45. Ado, *Paysans en Révolution*. See, too, McPhee, *Revolution and Environment in Southern France*; Plack, 'Agrarian Individualism, Collective Practices and the French Revolution'; James Livesey, 'Material Culture, Economic Institutions and Peasant Revolution in Lower Languedoc 1770–1840', *P&P* 182 (2004), 143–73; Jean-Michel Boehler, 'Routine ou innovation agraires? Les pays de "petite culture" au XVIIIe siècle', in Béaur *et al.* (eds), *Les sociétés rurales en Allemagne et en France*, 83–101. Peter Jones is sceptical of this argument in *The Peasantry in the French Revolution*, 124–8.

46. Postel-Vinay, 'Révolution économique dans les campagnes', 1028. Postel-Vinay appears to miss the significance of the end of tithes.
47. Plack, 'Agrarian Individualism, Collective Practices and the French Revolution, 57.
48. John Merriman, *The Stones of Balazuc: A French Village in Time* (New York, 2002), 68–9.
49. McPhee, *Revolution and Environment*, ch. 7. A superb recent case study is Jollet, *Terre et société en Révolution*.
50. 25 Floréal Year VII: Livesey, 'Material Culture, Economic Institutions and Peasant Revolution', 164.
51. Albert Soboul, 'Concentration agraire en pays de grande culture: Puiseux-Pontoise (Seine-et-Oise) et la propriété Thomassin', in *Problèmes paysans*, ch. 11.
52. Georges Subreville, 'L'apprentissage à Bourg sous la Révolution', *Les Nouvelles Annales de l'Ain*, 1982, 127–62.
53. Johnson, *Life and Death of Industrial Languedoc*, 13–15.
54. Butel, 'Revolution and the Urban Economy', 40–2, and Le Goff and Sutherland, 'The Revolution and the Rural Economy', 71–5.
55. Marquié, *L'industrie textile carcassonnaise au XVIIIe siècle* (Carcassonne, 1993); Serge Chassagne, 'L'industrie lainière en France à l'époque révolutionnaire et impériale, 1790–1810', *Voies nouvelles pour l'histoire de la Révolution française* (Paris, 1978), 143–67; Butel, 'Revolution and the Urban Economy', 50; Kaplow, *Elbeuf during the Revolutionary Period*, conclusion.
56. Thomas Castaing, 'Histoire d'un patrimoine en révolution: Claude Bonnet de Paillerets, robin de Marvejols en Lozère de 1766 à 1815', *AHRF* 290 (1992), 517–37.
57. Kaplow, *Elbeuf during the Revolutionary Period*, especially chs 3, 5.
58. H.-M. Williams, *Nouveau voyage en Suisse*, trans. J.-B. Say, 1798, 72, cited in Pellegrin, *Les vêtements de la Liberté*, 100.
59. Charles-Joseph Trouvé, *États de Languedoc et département de l'Aude*, 2 vols (Paris, 1818), vol. 1, 452–3, 563.
60. McManners, *Ecclesiastical Society*, chs 1, 6; Hufton, *Bayeux*; Hufton, conclusion, 'Women in Revolution 1789–1796', *passim*. Despite its title, Hufton's article essentially concerns women in provincial cities, those who suffered most from economic dislocation during the Revolution. While the Revolution destroyed the charity networks of the Ancien Régime, these had not always been effective: 80–90 per cent of abandoned children in Paris and Rouen died before their first birthday.
61. George D. Sussman, *Selling Mothers' Milk: The Wet-Nursing Business in France 1715–1914* (Urbana, Il, 1982), ch. 5. For the recollections of a middle-class Breton boy placed with a wet-nurse for five years, see Émile Souvestre, *Mémoires d'un sansculotte bas-Breton* (Bruxelles, 1843).
62. Forrest, *French Revolution and the Poor*, 84.
63. Kathryn Norberg, *Rich and Poor in Grenoble, 1600–1814* (Stanford, CA, 1985), 294; Cissie Fairchilds, *Poverty and Charity in Aix-en-Provence, 1640–1789* (Baltimore, MD, 1976), ch. 7, conclusion.
64. Forrest, *French Revolution and the Poor*, conclusion; Woloch, *The New Regime*, chs 8–9.
65. Pierre Gresser et al, *Les hommes et la forêt en Franche-Comté* (Paris, 1990), 103.
66. Jean-Robert Pitte, *Histoire du paysage français*, vol. ii, *Le profane: du XVIe siècle à nos jours*, 2nd edn (Paris, 1983), 86. See, too, John F. Freeman, 'Forest Conservancy in the Alps of Dauphiné', *Forest & Conservation History* 38 (1994), 171–80.
67. See, for example, Raymond Viney, 'L'ordonnance forestière de Colbert et les législateurs de la Révolution française', *Revue forestière française* 21 (1969), 607–10;

P. Fourchy, 'Déboisement et reboisement. Les débuts de la lutte contre l'érosion au XIXe siècle dans les Alpes françaises', *Revue forestière française* 18 (1966), 469. On the *légende noire*, see Fréréric Ogé, 'Héritage révolutionnaire: les forêts pyrénéennes, enjeux de conflis États-communautés,' in Corvol (ed.), *La nature en Révolution*, 156; Denis Woronoff, 'La 'dévastation révolutionnaire' des forêts', in Woronoff (ed.), *Revolution et espaces forestiers*, 52.

68. Jean-Baptiste Huet de Coetlizan, *Recherches économiques ... sur le département de la Loire-Inférieure* (Nantes, 1804), 22, 89; Jean Charles Joseph Laumond, *Statistique du département du Bas-Rhin* (Paris, An X), 29; Jacques Peuchet and Pierre Grégoire Chanlaire, *Description topographique de la France* (1810), 23–4.

69. Amans-Alexis Monteil, *Description du département de l'Aveyron* (Rodez, An X), 32. Note the comments on Monteil by Peter Jones in *The Peasantry in the French Revolution*, 248–51.

70. Abbé Maxime Seguin de Pazzis, *Mémoire statistique sur le département du Vaucluse* (Carpentras, 1808), 236.

71. McPhee, *Revolution and Environment*, ch. 7.

72. Trouvé, *États de Languedoc*, vol. 1, 530–1.

73. Corvol (ed.), *La Nature en Révolution*; Denis Woronoff, 'La 'dévastation révolution-naire' des forêts'; McPhee, *Revolution and Environment*, ch. 5; and 'Popular Attitudes to the Environment in the Revolution of 1789', *passim*.

74. Jean-Joseph de Verneilh-Puyraseau, *Mémoire sur le département de la Corrèze* (Tulle, An IX), 9; Comité des Travaux historiques et scientifiques, Section d'histoire moderne (depuis 1715) et d'histoire contemporaine, *Statistique agricole de 1814* (Paris, 1914), 536; Deverneilh, *Observations des Commissions consultatives sur le Projet de Code Rural* (Paris, 1810–14).

75. Rougier de la Bergerie, *Mémoire et observations*, 6–11.

76. Martine Acerra, 'Marine militaire et bois de construction. Essai d'evalution (1779–1789)', in Woronoff (ed.), *Révolution et espaces forestiers*, 114.

77. Corvol, *L'homme aux bois*, 232–3.

78. Pierre Chevallier and Marie-José Couailhac, 'Sauvegarde des forêts de montagne en France au XIXe siècle (l'exemple du Dauphiné)', in Corvol, *La Forêt*, 334; Guillaume de Bertier de Sauvigny, *The Bourbon Restoration*, trans. Lynn Case (Philadelphia, 1966), 214. See also David Bruce Young, 'A Wood Famine? The Question of Deforestation in Old Regime France', *Forestry* 49 (1976), 45–56; Paul Walden Bamford, 'French Forest Legislation and Administration, 1660–1789', *Agricultural History* 29 (1955), 101.

79. Huussen, 'La "crise" du mariage pendant la Révolution française', 331–43.

80. See the comments by Peter Jones in *The Peasantry in the French Revolution*, 5–6.

81. Paul Spagnoli, 'The Unique Decline of Mortality in Revolutionary France', *JFH* 22 (1997), 425–61.

82. Etienne Gautier and Louis Henry, *La population de Crulai, paroisse normande: étude historique* (Paris, 1958), 119; Dupâquier *et al.* (eds), *Population française*, ch. 7; Jones, *The Peasantry in the French Revolution*, 252–3; Alain Bideau, 'A Demographic and Social Analysis of Widowhood and Remarriage: The Example of the Castellany of Thoissey-en-Dombes, 1670–1840', *JFH* 5 (1980), 28–43. Reasons for the change in fertility patterns are discussed by Marcel Reinhard, 'Demography, the Economy, and the French Revolution', in Evelyn M. Acomb and Marvin L. Brown (eds), *French Society and Culture since the Old Régime* (New York, 1966), 20–42; Angus McLaren, *Sexuality and Social Order: The Debate over the Fertility of Women and Workers in France, 1770–1820* (New York, 1983), ch. 1; Étienne van de

Walle, 'Motivations and Technology in the Decline of French Fertility', in Robert Wheaton and Tamara K. Hareven (eds), *Family and Sexuality in French History* (Philadelphia, 1980), 135–78.

83. Antoinette Fauve-Chamoux, 'Transmission des biens, pouvoirs familiaux et rôle des femmes en France, XVIIIe-XIXe siècles', in Béaur *et al.* (eds), *Les sociétés rurales en Allemagne et en France*, 141–56.

84. Élisabeth G. Sledziewski, 'The French Revolution as the Turning Point', in Geneviève Fraisse and Michelle Perrot (eds), *A History of Women in the West: Emerging Feminism from Revolution to World War*, trans. Arthur Goldhammer (London and Cambridge, 1993), 37. See also Martine Lapied, 'La place des femmes dans la sociabilité et la vie politique locale en Provence et dans le Comtat Venaissin pendant la Révolution', *Provence historique* 46 (1996), 457–69. Sledziewski's argument may be compared with, for example, James F. McMillan, *France and Women, 1789–1914: Gender, Society and Politics* (London and New York, 2000), 31.

85. Sledziewski, 'The French Revolution as the Turning Point', 37–9. On the continuity of family relations and violence in a region of the Massif Central, see Claverie and Lamaison, *L'impossible marriage*, especially chs 4, 11.

86. Lynn Hunt, *The Family Romance of the French Revolution* (Berkeley, CA, 1992); Joan Landes, *Women and the Public Sphere in the Age of the French Revolution* (Ithaca, NY, 1988); Christine Fauré, *Democracy Without Women: Feminism and the Rise of Liberal Individualism in France*, trans. Claudia Gorbman and John Berks (Bloomington, IN, 1991); Madelyn Gutwirth, *The Twilight of the Goddesses: Women and Representation in the French Revolutionary Era* (New Brunswick, NJ, 1992); Dorinda Outram, *The Body and the French Revolution: Sex, Class and Political Culture* (New Haven, CT, 1989). A contrary argument is put by Carla Hesse, 'The Cultural Contradictions of Feminism in the French Revolution', in Colin Jones and Dror Wahrman (eds), *The Age of Cultural Revolutions: Britain and France, 1750–1820* (Berkeley and Los Angeles, 2002).

87. Desan, *The Family on Trial*, 174.

88. *Ibid.*, 3.

89. *Ibid.*, 151.

90. Suzanne Desan, ' "War between Brothers and Sisters": Inheritance Law and Gender Politics in Revolutionary France', *FHS* 20 (1997), 624, 628.

91. Desan, *The Family on Trial*, 124, 377.

92. Poumarède, 'La legislation successorale', 177.

93. Claverie and Lamaison, *L'impossible marriage*, ch. 4.

94. James R. Lehning, *The Peasants of Marlhes. Economic Development and Family Organization in Nineteenth-Century France* (London, 1980), ch. 8.

95. Desan, 'Inheritance Law and Gender Politics in Revolutionary France', 633; Darrow, *Revolution in the House*. See, too, Jones, *Southern Massif Central*, 101–4; Louis Assier-Andrieu, 'Custom and Law in the Social Order: Some Reflections upon French Catalan Peasant Communities', *Law and History Review* 1 (1984), 86–94.

96. Jacques Houdaille, 'Un indicateur de pratique religieuse: la célébration saisonnière des mariages avant, pendant et après la Révolution française', *Population* 2 (1978), 367–80.

97. AD Orne, Etat civil d'Alençon.

98. Michael Burns, *Dreyfus: A Family Affair, 1789–1945* (London, 1992), ch. 1.

99. Andress, *The French Revolution and the People*, 257.

100. Jones, *Liberty and Locality in Revolutionary France*, ch. 7, conclusion.

101. Philippe Ariès, *Centuries of Childhood* (London, 1962).

# Bibliography

## Archives Nationales, Paris

*AD – Archives imprimées*
AD IV: Agriculture: eaux et forêts: 4, 14, 19–20, 22–4
*D – Missions des représentants du peuple et Comités des Assemblées*
D III: Comité de législation: 24–6
D XIV: Comité des droits féodaux: 2, 12
D XXIX: Comité des rapports: 17, 22, 34, 43, 83–4
*F – Versements des ministères et des administrations qui en dépendent*
F$^7$: Police générale:
3656: Police générale. Aude 1790–1820

## Archives départementales de l'Ain, Bourg-en-Bresse

Série L Administration et tribunaux de la période révolutionnaire
6L 142 Mendicité
Documents non-classés, 'Prêtres déportés ou déportables'

Registres d'État Civil, Bourg-en-Bresse

Sous-série 110J, Registres des baptêmes mariages et sépultures tenus par les prêtres
réfractaires de l'Ain 1790–1801

Registre des délibérations du Conseil Général de la Commune de Belley

Registre des délibérations du Conseil Général de la Commune de Bourg-en-Bresse

## Archives départementales de l'Aisne, Laon

Série L Administration et tribunaux de la période révolutionnaire
L 588 Procès-verbaux de célébration des fêtes nationales, an V–an VIII
L 603 Insurrections dans les districts de Chauny, St-Quentin, Soissons et Château-
Thierry, février–octobre 1791
L 605 Retour de Louis XVI à Paris: incidents survenus lors de son passage dans le
département, juin 1791
L 606 Police générale du département, 1792-an VIII
L 607 Désordres à Champs par suite d'hostilité entre le curé et les habitants, mars–
avril 1792
L 608 Arrestation d'individus soupçonnés de contre-révolution et se disant commis de
la loterie de Cologne, avril–mai 1792
L 609 Troubles à Coucy-le-Château, septembre–décembre 1792
L 1136 Procès-verbaux d'arrestation de conscrits ou de réquisitionnaires par les
gendarmes des brigades, an VI
L 1502–6 Affaires ecclésiastiques: correspondance générale, juin 1790-an VIII
L 1508 Querelle entre l'abbé de Prémontré et les religieux de l'abbaye, août–octobre 1790

L 1538–9 Enfants trouvés: correspondance générale, 1790-an VIII
L 1540 Sourds-muets, correspondance générale
L 1541–2 Secours divers: correspondance générale, 1790-an VIII
L 1999 Délibérations des administrations municipales des cantons. Coucy, an IV-an V
L 2116 Délibérations du comité de surveillance de Coucy-le-Château, 1793-an II
L 2669–72 Bureau de paix et de conciliation de tribunal du district de Chauny siégant à Coucy-le-Château. Délibérations, 1790-an X
L 2628–39 Tribunal de famille et tribunal d'arbitrage de Laon
L 2848–9 Tribunal de famille et tribunal d'arbitrage de Vervins
5M1 73 État civil, Laon
5M1 150 État civil, Coucy-le-Château
5M1 487 État civil, Autremencourt
5M1 534 État civil, Notre-Dame-de-Liesse
Q 1238 Registre récapitulatif des ventes de biens nationaux: district de Laon, 1791-an IV

### Archives municipales de Laon

SRL 1–2 Délibérations de la commune de Laon, 1790–91
SRL 34 Subsistences
SRL 74 Émigrés, nobles, suspects, 1791-an II
SRL 99 Culte catholique

### Archives départementales de l'Aude, Carcassonne

*Série B – Cours et jurisdictions*
240, 532, 540, 542, 551, 590: Sénéchausée de Carcassonne
1229, 1237, 1239–42: Cour royale et viguerie de Termenès et Fenouillèdes
1431, 1447, 1486, 1491–2, 1521, 1542, 1560, 1570, 1573, 1577, 1579–80: Temporalité de l'Abbaye de Lagrasse
1613–17: Viguerie de la baronnie de Capendu
1618–20: Viguerie de la baronnie de Cascastel
1653–69: Viguerie de la baronnie de Fabrezan
1670–80: Viguerie de la baronnie de Talairan
1681–93: Viguerie de la baronnie de Villerouge
1694–1712: Viguerie de la commanderie de Douzens
1713–14: Viguerie de Mouthoumet
1753–62: Justice de la baronnie de Moux
1813–16: Justice et gruyerie de Durfort
1817–21: Justice et gruyerie de Fontiès-Rive d'Aude
1891–8: Justice d'Auriac
1899–1900: Justice de Barbairan
1936–8: Justice de Montirat
*Série C – Administrations provinciales avant 1790*
5C – États généraux et provinciaux, municipalités
9: Diocèse de Carcassonne: noms de seigneurs justiciers et mode d'élection consulaire, 1788
36: Subdélégation de Carcassonne: Correspondance relative aux affaires des communautés, 1780–2

10C – Agriculture et élevage XVII-XVIIIe s.
22: Subdélégation de Carcassonne: défrichements 1770–82

23: Diocèse de Narbonne: défrichements 1770–82
62C – Papiers des officiers des États
6: Comptabilité des syndics généraux, 1780
7: Compte-rendu des impositions et de la province, 1789
*Série E – Féodalité, familles, notaires, communes, état civil*
2E – Familles et sociétés
119–23: Papiers de la famille Pailhoux de Cascastel
3E – Notaires
2636–7: Actes notariaux: Majorel – Limoux.

4E – Archives Communales
Airoux, Arquettes-en-Val, Camplong, Duilhac, Ferrals, Fitou, Granès, Labécède-Lauragais, Ladern-sur-Lauquet, Ornaisons, St Hilaire, St-Michel-de-Lanes, Valmigère, Villasavary, Villerouge-Termenès, Villesèque-des-Corbières

*Série H – Clergé régulier avant 1789*
95, 190: Abbaye de Lagrasse
458: Abbaye de Fontfroide

*Série 3J – Documents d'archives*
3J 255: Montlaur, 1777–1807
3J 161: Papiers de la famille Pailhoux de Cascastel
3J 164: Archives de la seigneurie de Portel
3J 193: Vente de la seigneurie du Val-de-Dagne, 1588
3J 194: États-Généraux de 1789
3J 232: St-Ferriol, 1774
3J 613: Lettre du lieutenant général commandant le 10e division militaire au ministre de la guerre au sujet de l'assassinat du marquis de Gléon et de son fils.
7J 2–4, 32–3, 40, 42–3, 49–50: Archives Montesquieu-Roquefort
8J 10–14: Archives de la famille de Mage
13J 26, 43, 47, 50: Fonds Girard

*Série K – Lois, ordonnances, arrêtés*
33K – Arrêtés du Préfet
43–7: Défrichements. Arrêtés an XIV-1816
53–4: Biens communaux, 1818–20

47K – Dossiers des affaires portées devant le Conseil de préfecture, an XI-1914
17, 179, 195, 199, 223, 238, 373, 472, 512, 544–5: Arquettes, Duilhac, Ferrals, Fitou, Granès, Ladern, Ornaisons, St Hilaire, Valmigère, Villerouge-Termenès, Villesèque-des-Corbières
*Série L Administration et tribunaux de la période révolutionnaire*
97–103: Délibérations du directoire du département de l'Aude, 1790–3
110–18, 124–4: Arrêtés du directoire du département, 1790-an IV
247–50: Correspondance du Procureur-général-syndic avec les districts, 1790-2
343: Destitution des fonctionnaires publics, an III
395–6, 399–402: Crimes et délits, procès-verbaux, rapports, 1790-an VII
405: Émigrés et prêtres déportés, visites domiciliaires, an VI
419: Fêtes, district de Carcassonne, 1790-an VI
498: Dénombrements, 1790-an VIII
513: Eaux et forêts: lois, circulaires, instructions
514–18: Délits forestiers et coupes de bois, 1791-an VII
585, 587–92: Impositions, 1790

609–12: Contributions 1791-an II
747, 751–2: Listes des volontaires, 1791–3
754: Bataillon des braconniers montagnards et des chasseurs des Corbières
857–60: Déserteurs, an II-an VIII
866–88: Gendarmerie nationale
1071–2: Clergé constitutionnelle. Évêque, clergé district de Lagrasse
1076–8: Procès-verbaux de prestations de serment, 1790–2
1082: Listes des prêtres émigrés

Districts
1088: Prêtres insermentés et prêtres réfractaires
1187: Sommier des affaires contentieuses, district de Carcassonne, 1790
1188: District de Carcassonne: registre rélatif aux liquidations des prestations ci-devant seigneuriales, 1790–3
1199–1202: Correspondance avec le procureur-général-syndic et avec le directoire du district de Carcassonne, 1790-an II
1248: Registres pour les déclarations rélatives aux défrichements, Carcassonne, 1791
1408–20: Registre des délibérations du directoire du district de Lagrasse, 1790-an III
1431: Registre des avis du directoire du district de Lagrasse, 10 mars-21 juin 1792
1454–60: Correspondance, procureur-syndic de Lagrasse, 1790-an II
1466–90: Correspondance, procureur-syndic Lagrasse, 1790–3
1538: Délibérations du tribunal du district de Lagrasse
1637: Dégradations aux églises, district de Limoux
1638: District de Limoux: Arrestation, désarmement des citoyens ayant participé aux horreurs commises sous la tyrannie qui a précédé le 9 thermidor
1650: District de Limoux: bois de Crausse et de Rieunettes, délits et litiges, 1791-an II
1671: Inscription des anciens droits supprimés en précompte du montant des contributions foncières et immobilières de 1793. Cantons de St-Hilaire et Villardebelle, an II
1725–8: Correspondance, procureur-syndic du district de Narbonne, 1790-an III
1777: District de Narbonne: dénonces, troubles, dévastations, 1792-an III
1781: District de Narbonne: analyse des délibérations et correspondance des comités de surveillance et des communes, an II–III
1787: District de Narbonne. Registre pour les déclarations à faire par les propriétaires avant de commencer des … défrichements, etc., 1790–3
1788: District de Narbonne. Enregistrement des procès-verbaux de visite des terrains défrichés, etc, 1791-an IV
1901: Délibérations du Directoire du district de Quillan, 1790-an II
2185–9: Délibérations du Comité de surveillance du canton de Lagrasse, an II-an III
2190–1: Délibérations du Comité de surveillance régénéré, Lagrasse, an II-an III
2192–3: Correspondance, Comité de surveillance, Lagrasse, an II-an III
2194: Procès-verbaux du Comité de surveillance, Lagrasse, an II-an III
2260: Comité de surveillance des cantons de Capendu et Trèbes, an II-an III
2262: Comité de surveillance du canton de Tuchan, an II
2507: Procédures du Tribunal du district de Lagrasse, 1790
2526: Affaires portées devant le Juge de paix du canton de Fabrezan, 1791
2530: Affaires portées devant le Juge de paix du canton de Serviès, an VII

*Série 1Q – Domaines*
Biens de première origine
25: Clergé séculier 1790–1
26: Clergé régulier, 1790–1
27: Procès-verbaux d'estimations des biens

30: District de Limoux, biens de première origine: Ordre régulier
36: District de Narbonne, biens de première origine: Ordre régulier
56: District de Lagrasse, Clergés séculier et régulier
68: Biens de première origine, district de Carcassonne
70: Biens de première origine, districts de Lagrasse, Limoux, Narbonne, Quillan

Biens de seconde origine
83–4: Inventaire, séquestration et estimation des biens, dossiers par noms de familles, 1792-an VIII
102, 107: États des émigrés dont les biens ont été sequestrés, 1792–3
140: Liste générale des émigrés, an II-an X

Affiches des ventes, soumissions, adjudications
394: États récapitulatifs par districts des ventes de biens nationaux, 1791-an IV
395: Tableau des ventes effectuées dans le département, an IV-an V
458: Vente des biens de 2e origine, Quillan, prairial II-floréal III
490: Biens communaux: partage en exécution de la loi du 10 juin 1793

Liquidation
624: Enregistrement d'actes de rachat des droits féodaux, 1791–2

Régie et contentieux des domaines
710: Sommier des biens et revenus des émigrés, 1792-an III
Fonds de l'administration des domaines
1001: Sommier des ventes des biens nationaux de seconde origine, an II-an III
1103: Biens communaux. Tableaux des biens des communes, 1813
1173: Sommier des baux à ferme des biens des émigrés, 1793–1824
1178: Sommier des revenus des émigrés, an VII-an VIII
1331: Sommier des biens et revenus des émigrés, 1792-an VI
1353: Registre des rachats des droits féodaux, tasques, censives, 1791

## Archives départementales de la Charente-Maritime, La Rochelle

L1085–7 Dépositions

## Archives Municipales de La Rochelle

1D 1/3, 1/4 Délibérations du conseil general

## Archives départementales de la Haute-Garonne

Série L Administration et tribunaux de la période révolutionnaire
1L 116–18 Registre des délibérations du Conseil général, 1790–1792

## Archives départementales de l'Hérault, Montpellier

Série B Cour et juridictions
B 2358, 9700, 9701

Série C Intendance, subdélégations, États de Languedoc
C 73, 523, 2725, 2957, 4988, 6698, 6702

45–6: Mémoires des diocèses de Carcassonne, Limoux

2827–40: Défrichements: états de déclarations, 1771–89
5405: Défrichements et dessèchements: ordonnances, 1718–87
5157: Biens nobles, Villesèque-des-Corbières, 1757
6694–5: Plaintes et placets, diocèse d'Alet, 1781–9
6723–35: Plaintes et placets, diocèse de Carcassonne, 1750–88
6800–7: Plaintes et placets, diocèse de Narbonne, 1747–89
Série L Administration et tribunaux de la période révolutionnaire
L 765, 792, 1109, 1523, 1627, 1629, 2763, 4164, 4210, 4298, 4332, 4334, 4364, 4365,
    4366, 4367, 4436, 5533, 5703, 6117, 6126, 6140, 6950, 7584, 8882
Série Q Biens nationaux
Q 219

## Archives départementales de l'Indre, Châtearoux

Série L Administration et tribunaux de la période révolutionnaire
L8 Procès-verbal du Conseil général, 1790–1791

## Archives départementales de l'Isère, Grenoble

Série L Administration et tribunaux de la période révolutionnaire
L 254 Calendrier républicain

## Archives départementales de l'Orne, Alençon

Série L Administration et tribunaux de la période révolutionnaire
L 3052 Arrêtés de l'administration municipale du canton, frimaire an VI-messidor an VII
L 3054 Police générale et administrative: enquêtes; mesures de police urbaine; régle-
    ment des marchés de la ville; recherches; requête d'un déporté pour l'Espagne, prair-
    ial an II-thermidor an VII
L 3055 Fêtes révolutionnaires (plan d'un autel de la Patrie), thermidor an III-floréal
    an VII
L 3069 Cultes: prêtres insermentés connus dans le canton; pensions ecclésiastiques,
    brumaire an VI-messidor an VII
L 3086 Fonctionnaires publics: serment de haine à la royauté et de soumission à la
    Constitution de l'an III (Thomas Louisfert, agent municipal à St-Nicholas-des-Bois);
    Certificat de civisme du secrétaire en chef, fructidor an V-prairial an VIII
L 3113 Conscription militaire: instructions, frimaire an IV-ventôse an VIII
L 3115 Conscription militaire: bons à partir; exemptés temporaires ou définitifs,
    fructidor an VII-germinal an VIII
L 3117 Déserteurs: amnistie en leur faveur, thermidor an VII
L 3128 Réquisitions de chevaux pour l'armée, prairial an IV-floréal an VIII
L 4601 Circulaires et correspondance des Comités de la Convention nationale: Comité
    de Salut public et de et de Sûreté générale, Commission des dépêches, frimaire an
    II-pluviôse an III
L 4605 Lettres des représentants du peuple aux membres du Comité de Surveillance du
    district et de la commune d'Alençon, frimaire an II-pluviôse an III
L 4609 Lettres officielles et privées adressés au Comité de Surveillance d'Alençon, mars
    1793-nivôse an III

L 4635 Tableau des personnes détenues en la maison d'arrestation de la commune d'Alençon, pluviôse-germinal an II

L 5177 Quatre prêtres ont été assassiné à Gacé le 9 septembre 1792, reprise de l'enquête par un commissaire député de l'Aigle: François Bonhomme est condamné à mort et son pourvoi rejeté; amnistié, fevrier 1793-messidor an III

L 5196 Jean-Baptiste Segaux, curé constitutionnel de St-Aubin-d'Appenai, et Charles Duneugermain, neveu de Philippe Hébert, ex-curé réfractaire de la même commune, sont en conflit: Segaux est condamné à un mois de prison pour injures et propos sanguinaires, juin 1793-nivôse an II

L 5242 Jacques Vienne d'Alençon, prevenu d'avoir écrit des propos contre-révolutionnaires: emprisonné Nivôse an II

L 5336 Le 6 septembre 1792, le capucin Valframbert, condamné à la deportation, est massacré par la foule, Floréal-fructidor an III

L 5415 'Assassinats et brigandages ont été commis par une horde de scélérats dans les environs d'Alençon et les départements voisins (Mayenne et Sarthe),' Germinal an V-floréal an VI

## Archives départementales des Pyrénées-Orientales, Perpignan

Sous-série 2 B 1546
3 B – *Amirauté de Collioure*
3 B 1, 3, 8, 11, 14, 15, 16, 19, 20, 25, 26, 28
Série C – *Administration provinciale (jusqu'à la Révolution)*
C 820, 1132, 1133, 1155, 1162, 1163, 1164, 1195, 1706, 1718, 1719, 2103, 2114
IC 1068
Série 1E 271, 373, 594, 835
Série J – *Achats, don, dépôts*
1 J 63, 160, 273/3, 408, 419/3
2 J 35/1 [AN Flc III P.-O. 8], 59, 65 [AN F19 2560], 81, 82 [AN F17* 139 (P.-O.)]
11 J 35, 36, 37, 38
Série L – *Administration et tribunaux de la période révolutionnaire*
36–9: Lettres des administrations du canton d'Estagel à l'administration centrale du département
65–8: Arrêtés du département, district de Perpignan, 1790–2
685, 764, 789: Affaires communales, 1790–an VIII (Opoul-Périllos, Tautavel, Vingrau)
1157, 1161: Curés, déclarations des biens, prestations de serment
L364, 365, 428, 430, 431, 432, 433, 434, 435, 436, 437, 466, 467, 468, 469, 469bis, 602, 1149, 1151, 1281, 1382, 1434, 1435, 1441, 1461L
Série M – *Administration générale et économique (depuis 1800)*
2 M' 10
3 M' 5, 10, 18, 22, 31, 33
Mnc. 3773/2
Série O – *Administration et comptabilité communales*
O – Collioure 1, Collioure 2
Série Q – *Domaines, enrigistrement, hypothéques*
Q 119, 124, 149, 207, 208, 209, 210, 211, 293, 294, 296, 298, 459, 472, 596, 598, 600, 604, 623, 666, 734, 736, 750, 794, 795, 796, 798, 799, 800, 801, 802, 803

Série 1Q – *Domaines nationaux*
720: Tableaux des émigrés du département des Pyrénées-Orientales

Série R – *Affaires militaries*
1R 34, 313
2R 181, 206, 207, 208, 227

Série T – *Enseignement*
1T 37, 82, 186, 253, 283, 402, 407, 423, 425, 447

Série U – *Justice*
U2427, 2428, 2429, 2430, 2431, 2432

Série V – *Cultes*
1V 3, 29, 33, 47
2V 37, 56, 64
5V 5, 7
6V 17

15X 5

1Z 1, 2

Fêtes et cérémonies 4, 5

Série EDT – *Archives communales déposées*
Collioure
St Laurent-de-Cerdans
Vingrau

Série 1025W – *Cadastres*
133: Opoul
141: Périllos
214: Tautavel
240: Vingrau

## Printed sources

### French Revolution Research Collection

*Newspapers*

*La Feuille villageoise*, 1790–95
*La Vedette, ou journal du département du Doubs, par une société de gens de lettres, amis de
    la constitution*, 1791–1795
*Journal de Lyon et du département du Rhône et Loire*, 1790–91
*Archives parlementaires*
*Réimpression de l'ancien Moniteur*, 1789–1799

*Other printed sources*

Alphonse, Francois Jean-Baptiste d', *Mémoire statistique du département de l'Indre*, Paris,
    Imp. de la Republique, An XII.
*Les Amis de la Constitution aux sociétés affiliées, Caen, le 15 février 1792*, Caen, 1792.
*Annales de statistique*, Tome II, 1802, État de situation de la République; extrait de la corre-
    spondance du ministre de l'Intérieur, avec les préfets des départements.
*Annales de statistique*, Tome II, 1802, Observations ... d'Auvergne.

Anon., *Description abrégé du département du Morbihan*, Paris, Imp. de la République, An VII.

Anon. [Dubuisson], *Restauration de l'agriculture en France et moyen de prévenir toute disette. Par un cultivateur, député de l'Assemblée Nationale*, Paris, Baudouin, 1790.

Auvray, Louis Marie, *Statistique du département de la Sarthe*, Paris, Imp. des Sourds-muets, an X.

Aveline, Jean-Baptiste, *Rapport et projet de décret sur le partage et le défrichement des biens communaux, faits et présentés au nom du comité d'agriculture*, Paris, Imp. Nationale, 1792.

Ayats, Alain et al. (eds), *Entre Révolution et guerres. Les mémoires de Pierre Comellas, apothicaire de Perpignan 1789–1813*, Perpignan, 2005.

Bailly, Claude, *Journal d'un artisan tourangeau 1789–1830*, Chinon, Amis du vieux Chinon, 1989.

Balguerie, préfet, *Tableau statistique du département de Gers*, Paris, Imp. des Sourds-muets, An 10.

Barante, Claude Ignace Brugière de, *Observations sur les États de situation du département de l'Aude*, Carcassonne, G. Gareng, An XI.

Barère de Vieuzac, *Rapport des comités réunis des domaines …*, Paris, 1790.

Barrère [sic], *Rapport des comités réunis des domaines, des finances, de l'aliénation des biens nationaux, de la marine, du commerce et d'agriculture sur les bois et forêts nationales*, Paris, Imprimerie Nationale, 1790.

Beauvau, Marie-Charlotte de Rohan-Chabot, princesse de, *Souvenirs*, Paris, 1872.

Bernet, Jacques (ed.), *Le journal d'un maître d'école d'Île-de-France (1771–1792): Silly-en-Multien de l'Ancien Régime à la Révolution*, Villeneuve-d'Asq, Presses universitaires du Septentrion, 2000.

Billecocq, Jean-Baptiste, *Souvenirs de Jean-Baptiste Billecocq 1765–1829. En prison sous la Terreur*, Paris, 1981.

Blondin d'Abancourt, Gabriel-Isidore, *Onze ans d'émigration. Mémoires*, Paris, 1897.

Boigne, Charlotte Louise Eléonore Adélaïde d'Osmond, *Mémoires de la Comtesse de Boigne, née d'Osmond*, vols 1–4, Paris, 1908.

Bonnaire, baron Félix, *Mémoire au Ministre de l'Intérieur sur la situation du département des Hautes-Alpes*, Paris, Imp. des Sourds-muets, An IX.

Bonnemain, Antoine-Jean-Thomas, *Les Chemises rouges, ou, Mémoires pour servir à l'histoire du règne des anarchistes*, Paris, 1799.

Borie, Nicolas Yves, *Statistique du département d'Ille-et-Vilaine*, Paris, Imp. des Sourds-muets, An IX.

Bossi, Giuseppe, *Statistique générale de la France …*, Paris, Tastu, 1808.

Boucqueceau, Philippe, *Mémoire statstque du département de Rhin-et-Moselle …*, Paris, Imp. de la République, An XII.

Bouillé, François-Claude-Aman, marquis de, *Mémoires sur la Révolution française*, Londres, 1797.

Bourguignon du Perré, Jacques-François Le, *Notes d'un détenu de la maison de réclusion des ci-devant Carmélites de Caen pendant la Terreur*, Evreux, 1903.

Bourguin, Georges, *Le partage des biens communaux; documents sur la préparation de la loi du 10 juin 1793*, Paris, 1908.

Brun, *Archives statistiques de la France*, tome I, An XI.

Bruslé de Valsuzenay, baron Claude Louis, *Tableau statistique du department de l'Aube*, Paris, Imp. des Sourds-muets, an X.

Bry, Jean Antoine Joseph, baron de, *Mémoire statistique du département du Doubs*, Paris, Imp. Impériale, An XII.

*Cahiers de doléances de la sénéchaussée d'Angoulême et du siège royal de Cognac pour les États-Généraux de 1789*, Paris, P. Boissonnade, 1907.

*Cahiers de doléances de la sénéchaussée de Bigorre pour les États-Généraux de 1789,* Ministère de l'Instruction Publique, Tarbes, 1925.

*Cahiers de doléances de la sénéchaussée de Cahors pour les États-Généraux de 1789,* Cahors, Ministère de l'Instruction Publique, 1908.

*Cahiers de doléances de la sénéchaussée de Civray pour les États-Généraux de 1789,* Ministère de l'Instruction Publique, Niort, 1925.

*Cahiers de doléances de la sénéchaussée de Marseille pour les États-Généraux de 1789,* Marseille, Ministère de l'Instruction Publique, 1908.

*Cahiers de doléances de la sénéchaussée de Nîmes pour les États-Généraux de 1789,* 2 vols, Ministère de l'Instruction Publique, Nîmes, 1908–09.

*Cahiers de doléances de la sénéchaussée de Rennes pour les États-Généraux de 1789,* 4 vols, Rennes, Ministère de l'Instruction Publique, 1909–12.

*Cahiers de doléances des bailliages des généralités de Metz et de Nancy pour les États-Généraux de 1789,* vols 1–3, Nancy, 1907–30; vols 4–5, Paris, 1934–46.

*Cahiers de doléances des corps et corporations de la ville d'Alençon pour les États-Généraux de 1789,* Alençon, Ministère de l'Instruction Publique, 1929.

*Cahiers de doléances des sénéchaussées de Niort et de Saint-Maixent et des communautés et corporations de Niort et Saint-Maixent pour les États-Généraux de 1789,* Niort, Ministère de l'Instruction Publique, 1912.

*Cahiers de doléances des sénéchaussées de Quimper et de Concarneau pour les États-Généraux de 1789,* Rennes, Ministère de l'Instruction Publique, 1927.

*Cahiers de doléances du bailliage d'Amont,* vol. 1, Besançon, Ministère de l'Instruction Publique, 1918; vol. 2, Auxerre, Ministère de l'Instruction Publique, 1927.

*Cahiers de doléances du bailliage d'Arques (secondaire de Caudebec) pour les États-Généraux de 1789,* Lille, Ministère de l'Instruction Publique, 1922.

*Cahiers de doléances du bailliage d'Orléans pour les États-Généraux de 1789,* 2 vols, Orléans, 1906–07.

*Cahiers de doléances du bailliage de Blois et du bailliage secondaire de Romorantin pour les États-Généraux de 1789,* 2 vols, Blois, Ministère de l'Instruction Publique, 1907–08.

*Cahiers de doléances du bailliage de Bourges et des bailliages secondaires de Vierzon et d'Henrichement pour les États-Généraux de 1789,* Bourges, Ministère de l'Instruction Publique, 1910.

*Cahiers de doléances du bailliage de Cotentin (Coutances et secondaires) pour les États-Généraux de 1789,* 2 vols, Paris, Ministère de l'Instruction Publique, 3 vols, 1907–12.

*Cahiers de doléances du bailliage de Mirecourt,* Épinal, Ministère de l'Instruction Publique, 1928.

*Cahiers de doléances du bailliage de Sens pour les États-Généraux de 1789,* Auxerre, Ministère de l'Instruction Publique, 1908.

*Cahiers de doléances du bailliage de Troyes et du bailliage de Bar-sur-Seine pour les États-Généraux de 1789,* 3 vols, Troyes, Ministère de l'Instruction Publique, 1909–11.

*Cahiers de doléances du bailliage du Havre (secondaire de Caudebec) pour les États-Généraux de 1789,* Épinal, Ministère de l'Instruction Publique, 1929.

*Cahiers de doléances pour les États-Généraux de 1789: Département de la Marne,* vols 1–3, Épernay, Ministère de l'Instruction Publique, 1906–11, vol. 4, Reims, 1930.

*Cahiers des doléances des corporations de la ville d'Angers et des paroisses de la sénéchaussée particulière d'Angers pour les États-Généraux de 1789,* 2 vols, Angers, Ministère de l'Instruction Publique, 1915–16.

*Cahiers des paroisses et communautés du bailliage d'Autun pour les États-Généraux de 1789, suivis des cahiers des trois ordres et d'une iconographie de députés de Saône-et-Loire,* Autun, Dejussieu, 1895.

Cambry, Jacques, *Description du département de l'Oise*, Paris, Imp. Didot, 1803.

Cappeau, L.J.J.P., *Code rural, ou Recueil analytique des lois, règlemens et usages qui intéressent les habitans des campagnes et leurs propriétés, principalement en Provence*. Aix et Marseille, 1817.

Caron, Pierre, *Rapports des agents du Ministre de l'Intérieur dans les départements (1793 – an II)*, 2 vols, Paris, 1913–51.

Cavenne, *Statistique du Département de la Meuse-Inférieure ...*, Paris, Imp. des Sourds-Muets, An X.

Cavoleau, Jean Alexandre, *Description abrégée du Département de la Vendée*, Fontenay-le-Peuple, imp. Habert [n.d.].

Chaptal, Le comte, *De l'industrie française*, 2 vols, Paris, Renouard, 1819.

Chill, Emanuel (ed. and trans.), *Power, Property and History: Barnave's Introduction to the French Revolution and other Writings*, New York, 1971.

Cliquot de Blervache, *Mémoire sur les moyens d'améliorer en France la condition des laboureurs, des journaliers, des hommes de peine vivans dans les campagnes, et celles de leurs femmes et de leurs enfans*, Paris, Delalain l'aîné, 1783.

Cochon de Lapparent, Charles, *Description générale du département de la Vienne*, Paris, Imp. des Sourds-muets, An X.

Colchen, *Mémoire statistique du département de la Moselle*, Paris, Imp. de la République, An XI.

Colin, *Observations sur la situation du département de la Drôme*, Paris, Imp. des Sourds-muets, An IX.

Commission de recherche et de publication des documents relatifs à la vie économique de la Révolution, 'Un essai de statistique industrielle de l'An V', Paris, Ernest Leroux, 1908.

Comité des Travaux historiques et scientifiques, Section d'histoire moderne (depuis 1715) et d'histoire contemporaine, *Statistique, agricole de 1814*, Paris, 1914.

Coupé [abbé] J.M. *Rapport sur les abus des grandes exploitations rurales, et les moyens de multiplier les subsistances* [etc.]. [Paris], s.d.

Courchamps, comte de, *Souvenirs de la marquise de Créquy de 1710 à 1803*, vols 1–10, Paris, 1865.

Crebouw, Yvonne, 'La Salariés agricoles face au maximum des salaires', in *La Révolution française et le monde rural. Actes du colloque tenu en Sorbonne les 23, 24 et 25 octobre 1987*, Paris, Comité des travaux historiques et scientifiques, 1989, 113–22.

Dampmartin, Anne-Henri Cabot, marquis de, *Mémoires sur divers événemens de la Révolution et de l'Emigration*, Paris, 1825.

Danthon, Charles, *Opinion et projet de décret sur les communaux, présentés ... au comité d'agriculture*, [Paris], s.d.

Dauchy, Luc Jacques Edmond, *Statistique du département de l'Aisne*, Paris, Imp. des Sourds-muets, An X.

Delaistre, Guillaume Joseph, *Statistique du département de la Charente*, Paris, Imp. des Sourds-muets, An X.

Delfau, Guillaume, *Annuaire statistique du département de la Dordogne pour l'an XII de la République*, Périgueux, F. Dupont, An XII.

Delpierre, *Mémoire sur les moyens d'amener graduellement, et sans secousse, la suppression de la vaine pâture* [etc.].

*Des fêtes nationales, par Lequinio, député du Morbihan*, 16 Nivôse Year III.

Descolins, *Description abrégée du département de l'Aube*, Troyes, F. Mallet, Year VII.

Desgouttes, Zacharie Henri, *Tableau statistique du département des Vosges*, Paris, Imp. des Sourds-muets, An X.

Desmousseaux, Antoine François, baron, *Tableau statistique du département de l'Ourthe*, Paris, Imp. des Sourds-muets, An X.

Desodards, Antoine-Fantin, *Histoire philosophique de la Révolution de France*, Nouvelle edition, Paris, 1797.

Deverneilh, *Observations des commissions consultatives sur le projet de Code Rural* [etc], Paris, 1810–14.

Dietrich, baron de, *Description des gîtes de minérai, des forges et des salines des Pyrénées, suivie des observations sur le fer mazé et sur les mines des sards en Poitou*, Paris, Cuchet, 1786.

——, *Description des gîtes de minérai, forges, salines, verreries, tréfileries, fabriques de fer-blanc, porcelaine, faïence, etc., de la Haute et Basse-Alsace*, Paris, Didot, 1789.

——, *Description des gîtes de minérai, forges, salines, verreries, tréfileries, fabriques de fer-blanc, porcelaine, faience, etc., de la Lorraine méridionale*, Paris, Didot, 1799–1800.

Dieudonné, Christophe, *Statistique du département du Nord*, Douai, Marlier, An XII.

Dralet, *Plan détaillé de topographie, suivi de la topographie du département du Gers*, Paris, Huzard, An IX.

Du Lac de La Tour d'Aurec, Hector, *Précis historique et statistque du département de la Loire*, Le Puy, La Combe, 1807.

Dufour, Léon, *A travers un siècle (1780–1865), science et histoire: souvenirs d'un savant français*, Paris, 1888.

Dupin, Claude François Étienne, *Statistique du département des Deux-Sèvres*, Paris, Imp. des Sourds-muets, An IX; *Second Mémoire sur la statistique du département des Deux-Sèvres*, Niort, Plisson, An X.

[Dupont de Nemours], *Tableau comparatif des demandes contenus dans les cahiers des trois ordres remis a MM. les députés aux États-Généraux*, s.l., 1789.

Dusaulchoy, J.F.N., *Agonie de Saint-Lazare, sous la tyrannie de Robespierre*, Paris, De l'Imp. de Limbourg, 1797.

Duvergier, J.B., *Collection complète des lois, décrets, ordonnances, règlemens, et avis du conseil-d'État*, vol. 1, Paris, 1834.

Farnaud, Pierre Antoine, *Description abrégée du département des Hautes-Alpes*, Paris, Imp. de la République, An 8.

Fauchet, Joseph Jean Antoine, *Description abrégé du département du Var*, Paris, Imp. Des Sourds-muets, An IX.

Fouché, Jospeh, *The Memoirs of Joseph Fouché, Duke of Otranto*, London, 1896.

François de Neufchâteau, Nicolas-Louis, *Voyage agronomique dans la sénatorie de Dijon*, Paris, Huzard, 1806.

Frénay, Étienne (ed.), *Cahiers de doléances de la province de Roussillon (1789)*, Perpignan, Direction des Services d'Archives, 1979.

Froment, François, *Précis de mes opérations pour la défense de la religion et de la royauté pendant le cours de la Révolution*, 1815.

Garnier, Comte Germain, *Description géographique, physique et politique du département de Seine-et-Oise*, Paris, Imp. des Sourds-muets, An X.

Garran, J.-Ph., *Rapport sur les biens communaux fait au nom du comité de législation*, Paris, n.p., s.d., 1795.

Gauchat, Gabrielle, *Journal d'une visitandine pendant la Terreur ou Mémoires de la Sœur Gabrielle Gauchat*, Paris, 1855.

Gauthier de Brécy, Charles-Edme, *Mémoires véridiques et ingénus de la vie privée, morale et politique d'un homme de bien*, Paris, 1834.

(Géraud, Edmond), *Journal d'un étudiant pendant la Révolution 1789–1793*, Paris, 1910.

Gerbaux, Fernand and Schmidt, Charles, *Procès-verbaux des comités d'agriculture et de commerce de la Constituante, de la Législative et de la Convention*, 5 vols, Paris, 1906–37.

Grangent, Stanislas Victor, *Description abrégée du département du Gard*, Nîmes, B. Farge, An VII.

Gretre, *Mémoire sur l'État du département de l'Indre*, Chateauroux, Imp. F. Bourgeois, An VII.

Gruget, Simon, *Mémoires et journal de l'abbé Gruget, curé de la Trinité d'Angers*, Angers, 1902.

Hertault-Lamerville, *Deuxième rapport du comité d'agriculture et de commerce sur le code rural, prononcé à l'Assemblée Nationale, le 3 juin 1791*, Paris, 1791.

———, *Opinion ... sur le partage des communaux. Séance du 3 pluviôse an VII (Conseil des Cinq-Cents)*, [Paris], an VII [1709].

———, *Rapport et projet de lois rurales, au nom des comités d'agriculture et de commerce, de constitution, de féodalité, des domaines, de mendicité, des impositions, de législation criminelle, et d'aliénation*, n.p., n.d.

Huet de Coetlizan, Jean-Baptiste, *Recherches économiques ... sur le département de la Loire-Inférieure*, Nantes, 1804.

———, *Statistique du département de la Loire-Inférieure*, Paris, Imp. des Sourds-muets, An X.

Huguet, Jean Antoine, *Tableau de situation du département de l'Allier*, Paris, Imp. des Sourds-muets, An X.

Jerphanion, Gabriel Joseph, *Statistique du département de la Lozère*, Paris, Imp. des Sourds-Muets, An X.

Jessaint, Claude Laurent Bourgeis, vicomte de, *Description topographique du département de la Marne*, Paris, Imp. des Sourds-muets, An X.

Juéry, P., *Rapport fait à l'Assemblée Nationale, au nom des comités des domaines, d'agriculture, de commerce, de marine et de finances réunis, sur la question de l'aliénation des forêts nationales*, n.p., n.d.

Julliot, François-Pierre, *Souvenirs d'un prêtre réfractaire du diocèse de Troyes publiés par Octave Beuve*, Arcis-sur-Aube: Société d'histoire départementale, 1909.

Laboulinière, Pierre, *Annuaire statistique du département des Hautes-Pyrénées ...*, Tarbes, F. Lavigne, 1807.

Labretonnière, P.L.C., *Statistique du département de la Vendée*, Paris, Imp. des Sourds-muets, An IX.

Lachapelle, J., *Considérations philosophiques sur la Révolution française*. Paris: Year V.

Lacoste, D., *Observations sur la statistique du département des Basses-Pyrénées qui parut en l'année 1802, et projets d'amélioration ...* Pau, 1815.

Lâge de Volude, Béatrix-Étiennette Renart de Fuchsamberg, marquise de, *Souvenirs d'Émigration 1792–1794*, Evreux, 1869.

Lamagdelaine, *Description abrégée du département de l'Orne*, Paris, Imp. des Sourds-muets, An IX.

Lamarque, François, *Statistique du département du Tarn*, Paris, Imp. des Sourds-muets, An IX.

Laplane, Jean-Louis, *Journal d'un Marseillais 1789–1793*, Marseille, 1989.

La Tour du Pin, Madame de, *Memoirs: Laughing and dancing our way to the Precipice*, trans. Felice Harcourt, London, 1999.

Laukhard, Frédéric-Christian, *Un Allemand en France sous la Terreur: souvenirs de Frédéric-Christian Laukhard, professeur d'université saxon et sans-culotte français, 1792–1794*, ed. W. Bauer, Paris, Perrin, 1915.

Laumond, Jean Charles Joseph, *Statistique du département du Bas-Rhin*, Paris, Imp. des Sourds-Muets, An X.

Leboucher de Longchamp, *Rapport et projet de décret présentés à l'Assemblée Nationale au nom du comité des domaines, concernant les coupes des bois compris dans les échanges des biens domaniaux, non consommés*, n.p., n.d.

Lecreulx, François Michel, *Description abrégée du département de la Meurthe*, Paris, Imp. de la République, An VII.

Lejeune, Louis-François, baron, *Memoirs of Baron Lejeune*, vols 1–2, 1987.

Lenoir et Gillet-Laumont, *Rapport fait à la conférence des mines, sur la reprise des anciens travaux des mines de plomb et d'argent de la Croix, département des Vosges*, Paris, an VIII.

Lequinio de Kerblay, Joseph Marie, *Voyage dans le Jura*, Paris, Caillot. An IX.

Lezay, Adrien, *Des causes de la Révolution et de ses résultats*, Paris, Year V – 1797.

Louis-Philippe, *Memoirs 1773–1793*, trans. John Hardman, New York and London, 1977.

Loysel, *Observations sur les salines du département de la Meurthe ...*, Paris, Imp. Nationale, an III.

Lozeau, P.A., *Apperçu des travaux du comité d'aliénation et des domaines réunis, relativement à la partie des domaines*, Paris, an II.

Lucay, Jean-Baptiste Charles Legendre, comte de, *Description du département du Cher*, Paris, Imp. des Sourds-muets, An X.

Marcillac, Pierre-Louis-Auguste de Crusy, marquis de, *Souvenirs de l'émigration à l'usage de l'époque actuelle*, Paris, 1825.

Marquis, Jean Joseph, *Mémoire statistique du département de la Meurthe*, Paris, Imp. Impériale, An XIII.

Martinant de Préneuf, Gilbert-Jacques, *Huit années d'émigration. Souvenirs de l'abbé ... curé de Vaugirard, de Sceaux et de Saint-Leu (1792–1801)*, Paris, Perrin, 1908.

Masson de Saint-Amand, Amand Narcisse, *Mémoire statistique du département de l'Eure*, Paris, Imp. Impériale, An III.

Mège, Francisque, *Les Cahiers des paroisses d'Auvergne en 1789*, Clermont-Ferrand, Louis Bellet, 1899.

*Mémoire pour les quatre-vingt-quatre citoyens detenus dans la tour de Caen depuis le 5 novembre 1791*, Paris, 1792.

*Mémoire présenté par la société royale d'agriculture à l'Assemblée Nationale le 24 octobre 1789, sur les abus qui s'opposent aux progrès de l'agriculture, et sur les encouragemens qu'il est nécessaire d'accorder à ce premier des arts*, Paris, Baudouin, s.d.

*Mémoire statistique du département des Deux-Sèvres*, Paris, Imp. de la République, An XII.

*Mèmoires pour servir à l'Histoire de la Guerre de la Vendèe par le Gènèral Turreau*. Paris: Firmin Didot, 1824.

Ménétra, Jacques-Louis, *Journal of My Life*, trans. Arthur Goldhammer, New York, 1986.

Mercadier de Bélesta, Jean-Baptiste, *Ebauche d'une description abrégée du département de l'Ariège*, Foix, Imp. de Pomiès, An IX.

Michel d'Eyguieres, Joseph Etienne, *Statistique du département des Bouches du Rhône ...*, Paris, Valade, An XI.

Michel, Jean, *Journal de la déportation des ecclésiastiques du département de la Meurthe dans la rade de l'Ile d'Aix, près Rochefort, en 1794 et 1795, par un de ces déportés*, Nancy: Grimblet, Raybois et Cie, 1840.

*Le Ministre de l'intérieur aux administrations centrales des départements*, 18 Brumaire Year VI.

Molé, Louis-Mathieu, *Souvenirs de jeunesse 1793–1803*, Paris, 1991.

Monnard, Marie-Victoire, *Souvenirs d'une femme du peuple 1777–1802*, Creil, Dumerckez, 1989.

Monteil, Amans Alexis, *Description du département de l'Aveyron*, Rodez, Carrère, An X.

Montlosier, François Dominique de Reynaud, comte de, *Souvenirs d'un émigré (1791–1798)*, Paris, 1951.

Montoposé, *La vérité des oracles de l'apocalipse, ou la Révolution française predite il y a dix-huit siècles par St. Jean*, Paris, Year V – 1797.

Montvert, M. de, *De la restauration des campagnes à opérer au physique et au moral, par une division mieux étendue des possessions rurales, au plus grand avantage de tout propriétaire*, Paris, Galey, 1789.

———, *Observations sur les divers dégrés de fertilité ou de dégradation du sol du royaume suivant l'état des propriétaires dans lesquelles on indique les vrais moyens d'augmenter l'une et de diminuer l'autre, par une plus grande division des possessions rurales*, Paris, Hardouin & Galtey, 1787.

Moreau, *Statistique commérciale du département d'Indre-et-Loire et les cinq départements limitrophes, Maine et Loire, Loir et Cher, Indre et Vienne*, Tours, Imp. Mame [1811].

Mourlot, Félix (ed.), *Recueil des documents d'ordre économique contenus dans les registres de délibérations des municipalités du district d'Alençon*, 3 vols, Alençon, Ministére de l'instruction publique, 1907–10.

Necker, Jacques, *De la Révolution française*. Paris: Maret, Year V – 1797.

Neufchâteau, François de, *Les Vosges*, 1796.

Nodier, Charles, *Séraphine, Amélie, Jean-François les Bas-Bleus; souvenirs de jeunesse*, Paris, 1894.

Noël, Joseph-Louis-Gabriel, *Au temps des volontaires: lettres d'un volontaire de 1792*, ed. G. Noel, Paris, Plon, 1912.

Noel de la Morinière, Simon Barthélémy Joseph, *Premier essai [suivi de second essai] sur le département de la Seine Inférieure*, Rouen, Imp. des Arts, An III.

Nusse, J.F., *Lettre à un curé patriote, qui a des doutes sur son serment, d'après deux brefs attributes au pape*, Laon, 1791.

Paillot, Pierre-Hippolyte-Léopold, *Journal d'un émigré. Étapes d'Outre Rhin 1794–1795*, Paris, 1909.

Pasquier, Chancellor, *Memoirs (1767–1815)*, trans. Douglas Garman, London, 1967.

Perrin-Dulac, *Description générale du département de l'Isère*, Grenoble, J. Allier, 1806.

*Pétition des citoyens de la section des Lombards à la Convention nationale*, Paris, 1793.

*Pétition des femmes du tiers-état au Roi, 1 janvier 1789.*

*Pétition des propriétaires et maîtres des forges des départements de la Haute-Saône, du Doubs, du Jura, de la Côte-d'Or, de l'Aube, de la Marne, de la Haute-Marne et des Vosges, tendante à obtenir un règlement relatif aux bois*, Paris, 1791.

Peuchet, Jacques and Chanlaire, Pierre Grégoire. *Description topographique de la France*, 1810.

Pison-du-Galland, A[lexis-] F[rançois], *Rapport fait à l'Assemblee Nationale … sur le nombre, la répartition & le traitement des agens de l'administration forestière*, Paris, s.d.

*Plan d'administration des forêts nationales, et projet de décret, par un membre du comité des domaines de l'Assemblée nationale*, s.l. [1790].

Poullain-Granprey, *Projet d'un code forestier, présenté au nom des Comités de Domaines, d'Aliénation, d'Agriculture, de Commerce, des Finances et de la Guerre*, Paris, n.p., c. 1795.

———, *Rapport fait au nom des Comités des Domaines et des Finances réunis, sur la gestion, la comptabilité et l'emploi des fonds appartenans aux communes, et provenans de la vente de leurs bois*, n.p., c. 1795.

Pradel de Lamasse, Joseph de, *Notes intimes d'un émigré … officier à l'armée de Condé. Les campagnes de l'émigration*, Paris, 1913.
————, *Nouvelles notes intimes d'un émigré … officier à l'armée de Condé. Les grandes journées révolutionnaires*, Paris, 1914–20.
*Procès-verbal de la municipalité de Montauban envoyé à l'Assemblée nationale, 12 mai 1790*.
Prudhomme, *Histoire générale et impartiale des erreurs, des fautes et des crimes commis pendant la Révolution française*, Paris, Year V – 1797.
[Prudhomme, L.-M.; Mezières, Laurent de], *Résumé général, ou Extrait des cahiers de pouvoirs, instructions, demandes et doléances, remis par les divers bailliages, sénéchaussées et pays d'États du royaume* [etc.], Paris, 1789.
*Rapport et projet de décret, formant un plan général d'instruction publique, par G. Bouquier, membre de la Convention nationale et du Comité d'instruction*.
*Rapport fait au nom du comité des domaines sur la législation domaniale*, Paris, Imp. Nationale, 1790.
Rebmann, Georg Friedrich, *Coup-d'oeil sur les quatre départements de la rive gauche du Rhin*, Trêves, J.J. Linz, Coblence, Lassault, An X.
*Recherches Économiques … sur le département de la Loire-Inférieure*, Nantes, 1804.
*Réflexions d'un citoyen de Garches sur les décrets pour les chasses du Roi, rendus dans les séances du 13 et 14 septembre, sur les antécédents et sur les suites*.
*Réglement de la Société de l'harmonie sociale des deux sexes, défenseurs de la Constitution*, Paris, 1793.
*Réglement de la Société fraternelle des patriotes des deux sexes, défenseurs de la Constitution*, Paris, 1792.
*La Révolution vue de l'Aisne, en 200 documents*, Laon, 1990.
Rey, Jean Joseph, in *Archives statistiques de la France*, Tome I.
Riouffe, Honoré-Jean, *Mémoires d'un détenu, pour servir à l'histoire de la tyrannie de Robespierre*, Paris, Year III.
Roederer, Pierre-Louis, *Mémoires sur la Révolution, le Consulat et l'Empire*, Paris, 1942.
Rondonneau, L., *Code rural et forestier, ou Recueil des lois, arrêtés et décrets sur la police rurale, l'agriculture, le régime forestier et les lois relatives à l'abolition des droits féodaux, des rentes, redevances et prestations féodales, depuis 1789 jusqu'à 1810* [etc.], Paris, 1810.
Roussel, Gilles, médecin, *Topographie rurale et médicale de la partie meridionale des départements de la Manche et Calvados comme ci-devant sous le nom de Bocage …*, Paris, Huzard, An VIII.
Rudemare, Jacques-Henri, *Journal d'un prêtre parisien 1788–1792*, Paris, 1905.
Saint-Amand, Jean Florimond Boudon de, *Description abrégée du département de Lot et Garonne*, Agen, Imp. Noubel. An VIII.
Salamon, Louis-Sifrein Joseph Foncrosé, abbé de, *Mémoires inédits de l'internonce à Paris pendant la Révolution 1790–1801*, Paris, 1903.
Sales, P.-J., *Aperçu raisonné des causes et des effets de la Révolution française*, Carcassonne, Gareng, Year V.
Saulx-Tavanes, Aglaé-Marie-Louise, *Mémoires de la Duchesse de Saulx-Tavanes*, Paris, 1934.
Scott, *Essai patriotique ou Mémoire pour servir à prouver l'inutilité des communaux, l'avantage qu'il y aurait de les défricher, ainsi que toutes les terres incultes; celui que l'État retiroit de la protection accordée à l'agriculture, les causes qui en empêchent les progrès*, Genève, P. G. Simon, 1775.
Seguin de Pazzis, Abbé Maxime, *Mémoire statistique sur le département du Vaucluse*, Carpentras, Imp. Quenin, 1808.

Serviez, Emmanuel Gervais Roergas de, *Statistique du département des Basses-Pyrénées*, Paris, Imp. des Sourds-Muets, An X.

*Tableau historique et politique des pertes que la Révolution et la Guerre ont causé au peuples français, dans sa population, son agriculture, ses colonies, ses manufactures et son commerce*, London, 1799.

Texier Olivier, Louis, *Statistique générale de la France*, Paris, Tastu, 1808.

Tilly, Alexandre de, *Memoirs of the Comte Alexandre de Tilly*, trans. Françoise Delisle, London, 1933.

Tourzel, Louise-Joséphine de Croy d'Havré, duchesse de, *Mémoires de Madame la duchesse de Tourzel, Gouvernante des enfants de France pendant des années 1789, 1790, 1791, 1792, 1793, 1795*, Paris, 1883.

Vaxelaire, Jean-Claude, *Mémoires d'un vétéran de l'ancienne armée (1791–1800)*, ed. H. Gauthier-Villars, Paris, Charles Delagrave, 1892.

Vergnes, général Jacques Paul de, *Mémoire sur la statistique du département de la Haute-Saône*, Paris, Imp. des Sourds-muets, An IX.

Verneilh-Puyraseau, baron Jean Joseph de, *Mémoire sur le département de la Corrèze*, Tulle, Imp. Chirac [An IX].

———, *Statistique générale de la France ... département du Mont-Blanc*, Paris, Testu, 1807.

Vernier, Louis, *Souvenirs d'un vieux. La Terreur. L'Empire. La Restauration (1780–1815)*, publiés par Jean Charruau, Paris, 1911.

Verninac de Saint-Maur, Raymond de, *Description physique et politique du département du Rhône*, Paris, Imp. des Sourds-muets, An X.

Vigée Lebrun, Madame, *Memoirs of Mme Vigée Lebrun*, trans. Lionel Strachey, New York, 1989.

Villeneuve-Laroche-Bernaud, Louis-Gabriel de, *Mémoires sur l'expédition de Quiberon, précédés d'une notice sur l'Emigration de 1791, et sur les trois campagnes des années 1792, 1793, 1794*, Paris, 1819–22.

Vitrolles, Eugène-François-Auguste d'Armand, baron de, *Souvenirs autobiographiques d'un émigré (1790–1800)*, Paris, 1924.

Young, Arthur, *Travels in France during the Years 1787, 1788 and 1789*, Cambridge, Cambridge University Press, 1929.

## Secondary Sources

Abbiatéci, André and Paul Perdrix, *Les débuts de la Révolution dans les pays de l'Ain (1787–1790)*. Bourg-en-Bresse: Les Amis des Archives de l'Ain, 1989.

Aberdam, Serge, 'Délibérations en assemblées de citoyens et *portions de souveraineté* en 1793', in *Suffrage, citoyenneté et Révolutions 1789–1848*, ed. Michel Pertué. *Collections études Révolutionnaires*, no. 3. Paris: Société des Études Robespierristes, 2002.

———, 'Deux occasions de participation feminine en 1793: le vote sur la constitution et le partage des biens communaux', *AHRF* 339 (2005), 17–34.

Aberdam, Serge, 'La Révolution et la lutte des métayers', *Études rurales* 59 (1975), 73–91.

Ado, Anatoli, 'Bilan agraire de la Révolution française', *Cahiers d'histoire de l'Institut Maurice Thorez*, 27 (1978), 42–65.

———, *Paysans en Révolution. Terre, pouvoir et jacquerie 1789–1794*, trans. Serge Aberdam, Marcel Dorigny *et al.* Paris: Société des Études Robespierristes, 1996.

Agulhon, Maurice, *Marianne into Battle: Republican Imagery and Symbolism in France, 1789–1880*, trans. Janet Lloyd. Cambridge and New York: Cambridge University Press, 1981.

Agulhon, Maurice, Pénitents et francs-maçons de l'ancienne Provence. *Essai sur la sociabilité méridionale*. Paris: Fayard, 1968.

Allen, Edward A., 'Deforestation and Fuel Crisis in Pre-Revolutionary Languedoc', *FHS*, 13 (1984), 455–73.

———, 'L'influence des cahiers modèles en 1789: l'expérience du Gard', *AHRF* 291 (1993), 13–31.

Alzas, Nathalie, 'Don, patriotisme et sociétés populaires en l'an II', *AHRF* 329 (2002), 41–65.

Anderson, Benedict, *Imagined Communities: Reflections on the Origin and Spread of Nationalism*. London: Verso, 1983.

Andress, David, *The French Revolution and the People*. London: Hambledon and London, 2004.

———, *French Society in Revolution, 1789–1799*. Manchester and New York: Manchester University Press, 1999.

Andrews, Richard, 'Social Structures, Political Elites and Ideology in Revolutionary Paris, 1792–1794: A Critical Evaluation of Albert Soboul's *Les sans-culottes parisiens en l'an II*,' *JSH* 19 (1985), 72–112.

Andrieu, Étienne, *La Contre-Révolution en Gévaudan (Aveyron et Lozère); Marc-Antoine Charrier et l'insurrection de l'Armée chrétienne du Midi en 1793*. Paris: Guénégaud, 2000.

Ariès, Philippe, *Centuries of Childhood*. London: Penguin, 1962.

Assier-Andrieu, Louis, 'Custom and Law in the Social Order: Some Reflections upon French Catalan Peasant Communities', *Law and History Review* 1 (1984), 86–94.

Aston, Nigel, *The French Revolution 1789–1804. Authority, Liberty and the Search for Stability*. Basingstoke and New York: Macmillan, 2004.

———, *Religion and Revolution in France, 1780–1804*. Basingstoke, Hampshire: Macmillan, 2000.

Attal, Robert and Alain Blanchard, 'Le clergé du Soissonnais pendant la Révolution, 1789–1791', *Fédération des sociétés d'histoire et d'archéologie de l'Aisne. Mémoires* 34 (1989), 180–205.

Aulard, Alphonse, *La Révolution française et le régime féodal*. Paris: Alcan, 1919.

Ayoun, Richard, *Les juifs de France. De l'émancipation à l'intégration (1787–1812)*. Paris and Montreal: Harmattan, 1997.

Baczko, Bronislaw, *Ending the Terror. The French Revolution After Robespierre*. Cambridge: Cambridge University Press, 1994.

Badré, Louis, *Histoire de la forêt française*. Paris: Arthaud, 1983.

Balmes, L., 'La Vente des biens nationaux de première origine dans le district de Carcassonne', MdeM. Université de Toulouse, 1977.

Bamford, Paul W., 'French Forest Legislation and Administration, 1660–1789', *Agricultural History* 29 (1955), 101.

Bardet, Jean-Pierre *et al.* (eds), *Lorsque l'enfant grandit: entre dépendance et autonomie*. Paris: Presses de l'Université de Paris-Sorbonne, 2003.

Bart, Jean, 'Les anticipations de l'an II dans le droit de la famille', *AHRF* 300 (1995), 187–96.

Bastier, Jean, *La féodalité au siècle des lumières dans la région de Toulouse, 1730–1790*. Paris: Bibliothèque nationale, 1975.

Béaur, Gérard *et al.* (eds), *Les sociétés rurales en Allemagne et en France (XVIIIe et XIXe siècles). Actes de colloque international de Göttingen (23–25 novembre 2000)* Rennes, 2004.

Bée, Michel, 'Dans la Normandie, entre Seine et Orne, confrères et citoyens', *AHRF* 306 (1996), 601–15.

Beck, Thomas, 'The French Revolution and the Nobility: A Reconsideration', *JSH* 15 (1981), 219–34.

Bell, David A., *The Cult of the Nation in France: Inventing Nationalism, 1680–1800*. Cambridge, MA: Harvard University Press, 2001.

Bendjebbar, André, 'Propriété et contre-révolution dans l'Ouest', in *La Révolution française et le monde rural. Actes du colloque tenu en Sorbonne les 23, 24 et 25 octobre 1987*. Paris: Comité des travaux historiques et scientifiques, 1989, 287–300.

Bergès, Louis, *Résister à la conscription, 1798–1814. Le cas des départements aquitains*. Paris: Editions du Comité des travaux historiques et scientifiques, 2002.

Bernard-Griffiths, Simone, Marie-Claude Chemin and Jean Ehrard, *Révolution française et 'vandalisme révolutionnaire'. Actes du colloque international de Clermont-Ferrand 15–17 décembre 1988*. Paris: Universitas, 1992.

Bernet, Jacques, 'Les grèves de moissonneurs ou "bacchanals" dans les campagnes d'Ile-de-France et de Picardie au XVIIIe siècle', *Histoire et sociétés rurales* 11 (1999), 153–86.

———, 'Les limites de la déchristianisation de la l'an II éclairées par le retour au culte de l'an III', *AHRF* 312 (1998), 285–99.

Bertaud, Jean-Paul, *La vie quotidienne en France au temps de la Révolution (1789–1795)*. Paris: Hachette, 1983.

———, *The Army of the French Revolution: From Citizen-Soldiers to Instrument of Power*, trans. R.R. Palmer. Princeton, N.J.: Princeton University Press, 1988.

———, *et al.*, *Atlas de la Révolution française*, iii, *L'Armée et la guerre*. Paris: Editions de l'EHESS, 1989.

Bertrand, Régis, 'Les confréries de Provence face à la Révolution', *AHRF* 306 (1996), 635–47.

Bianchi, Serge, 'La bataille du calendrier ou le décadi contre le dimanche. Nouvelles approaches pour la reception du calendrier républicain en milieu rural', *AHRF* 312 (1998), 245–64.

———, *La Révolution culturelle de l'An II*. Paris: Aubier, 1982.

———, *La Révolution et la première république au village. Pouvoirs, votes et politisation dans les campagnes d'Île-de-France 1787–1800*. Paris: Comité des travaux historiques et scientifiques, 2004.

Bianchi, Serge and M. Chancelier, *Draveil et Montgeron, deux villages en Révolution*. Le Mée-sur-Seine: Amatteis, 1989.

Biard, Michel, *Missionnaires de la République*. Paris: Comité des travaux historiques et scientifiques, 2002.

Blanc, Olivier, *La Dernière Lettre. Prisons et condamnés de la Révolution, 1793–1794*. Paris: Laffont, 1984.

Blanning, T.C.W., *The Origins of the French Revolutionary Wars*. London: Longman, 1986.

Blaufarb, Rafe, *The French Army, 1750–1820: Careers, Talent, Merit*. Manchester and New York: Manchester University Press, 2002.

Bluche, Frèdèric, *Septembre 1792: logiques d'un massacre*. Paris: R. Laffont, 1986.

Bodinier, Bernard and Eric Teyssier, *L'événement le plus important de la Révolution: la vente des biens nationaux en France et dans les territoires annexés, 1789–1867*. Paris: Société des études robespierristes, 2000.

Boehler, Jean-Michel, 'Routine ou innovation agraires? Les Pays de "petite culture" au XVIIIe siècle', in Gèrard Béaur *et al.* (eds), *Les Sociétés rurales en Allemagne et en France (XVIIIe et XIXe siècles). Actes de colloque international de Göttingen (23–25 novembre 2000)*. Rennes, 2004, 83–101.

Bordenove, Georges, *La vie quotidienne en Vendée pendant la Révolution*. Paris: Hachette, 1974.

Bosher, J.F., *The French Revolution*. New York: Weidenfeld and Nicolson, 1988.

Bossenga, Gail, *The Politics of Privilege: Old Regime and Revolution in Lille*. Cambridge: Cambridge University Press, 1991.

Bossut, Nicole, 'Terreur à Clamecy. Quelques réflexions', *AHRF* 311 (1998), 49–77.

Bourgin, Georges, *Le Partage des biens communaux: documents sur la préparation de la loi du 10 juin 1793*. Paris: Imp. nationale, 1908.

Bourgin, Georges and Hubert Bourgin, *L'Industrie sidérurgique en France au début de la Révolution*. Paris: Ministère de l'Instruction Publique, 1920.

Bourdin, Philippe, 'Le recrutement des sociétés populaires du Puy-de-Dôme', *AHRF* 290 (1992), 491–516.

Boutier, Jean, *Campagnes en émoi. Révoltes et Révolution en Bas-Limousin, 1789–1800*. Treignac: Editions les Monédières, 1987.

——, 'Jacqueries en pays croquant: les révoltes paysannes en Aquitaine (décembre 1789–mars 1790)', *Annales* 34 (1979), 760–86.

Boutier, Jean, *et al. Atlas de la Révolution française*, vi, *Les Sociétés politiques*. Paris: Editions de l'EHESS, 1992.

Bréant, Denise, Maurice Bréant and Robert, Bréant, *Menucourt. Un village du Vexin français pendant la Révolution 1789–1799*. Menucourt: Mairie de Menucourt, 1989.

'La Bresse invente la concorde. Le cahier commun des doléances', special issue of *Les Nouvelles Annales de l'Ain*, 1990.

Brunet, Michel, *Le Roussillon: une société contre l'Etat, 1780–1820*. Toulouse: Privat, 1986.

Brunot, Ferdinand, *Histoire de la langue française des origins à 1900*, t. IX, 1ère partie. Paris, 1927.

Burns, Michael, *Dreyfus: A Family Affair, 1789–1945*. London: Chatto and Windus, 1992.

Butel, Paul, 'Revolution and the Urban Economy', in Alan Forrest and Peter Jones (eds), *Reshaping France: Town, Country and Region during the French Revolution*. Manchester: Manchester University Press, 1991, 221–42.

——, 'Succès et decline du commerce colonial français, de la Révolution à la Restauration', *Revue économique* 6 (1989), 1079–96.

Buttoud, G., 'Les projets forestiers de la Révolution (1789–1798)', *Revue forestière française* 35 (1983), 9–20.

Cadé, Michel, *Guerre et Révolution en Roussillon, 1793–1795*. Perpignan: Direction des Services d'Archives, 1990.

Carbasse, Jean-Marie, 'Un des premiers cas de résistance populaire à la Révolution: l'émeute du 25 janvier 1791 à Millau', *Bulletin d'histoire économique et sociale* (1984–85), 57–72.

Caron, Pierre, *Les massacres de septembre*. Paris: La Maison du Livre Français, 1935.

Castaing, Thomas, 'Histoire d'un patrimoine en revolution: Claude Bonnet de Paillerets, robin de Marvejols en Lozère de 1766 à 1815', *AHRF* 290 (1992), 517–37.

Castan, Nicole, *Les criminels du Languedoc: les exigences d'ordre et les voies du ressentiment dans une société pré-Révolutionnaire (1750–1790)*. Toulouse: Université de Toulouse-Le Mirail, 1980.

——, *Justice et répression en Languedoc*. Paris: Flammarion, 1980.

Cazals, Rémy, *Autour de la Montagne noire au temps de la Révolution*. Carcassonne: Clef, 1989.

Certeau, Michel de, Dominique Julia, and Jacques Revel, *Une politique de la langue: la Révolution française et les patois. L'enquête de Grégoire*. Paris, 1975.

Chartier, Roger, 'Figures of the "Other". Peasant Reading in the Age of Enlightenment', *Cultural History. Between Practices and Representations*. Oxford: Polity Press, 1988, 151–71.

——, *The Cultural Origins of the French Revolution*. Durham, NC: Duke University Press, 1991.

Chassagne, Serge, 'L'industrie lainière en France à l'époque révolutionnaire et impériale, 1790—1810', *Voies nouvelles pour l'histoire de la Révolution française*. Paris, 1978, 143–67.

Chaussinand-Nogaret, Guy, *The French Nobility in the Eighteenth Century: From Feudalism to Enlightenment*, trans. W. Doyle. Cambridge: Cambridge University Press, 1985.

Chester, Emily, 'Identité régionale et identité nationale: 1789 dans le Roussillon et le Bas-Languedoc', MA thesis, University of Melbourne, 1995.

Cholvy, Gérard, 'Histoires contemporaines en pays d'Oc', *Annales* 33 (1978), 863–79.

——, 'Une Révolution culturelle? Le test des prénoms', in *Pratiques religieuses, mentalités et spiritualités dans l'Europe révolutionnaire (1780–1820). Actes du colloque de Chantilly, 27–29 novembre 1986*. Paris: CNRS, 1988, 300–8.

——, 'Société, genres de vie et mentalités dans les campagnes françaises de 1815 à 1880', *Information Historique* 36 (1974), 161.

Ciotti, Bruno, *Du volontaire au conscrit, les levées d'hommes dans le Puy-de-Dôme pendant la Révolution française*, 2 vols, Clermont-Ferrand: Presses universitaires Blaise Pascal, 2001.

Claverie, Elisabeth and Pierre Lamaison, *L'impossible marriage: violence et parenté en Gévaudan, XVIIe, XVIIIe et XIXe siècles*. Paris: Hachette, 1982.

Clay, Stephen, 'Justice, vengeance et passé révolutionnaire: les crimes de la Terreur Blanche', *AHRF* 350 (2007), 109–33.

Cobb, Richard, *Paris and Its Provinces*. Oxford: Oxford University Press, 1975.

——, *Reactions to the French Revolution*, London: Oxford University Press, 1972.

——, *The People's Armies*, trans. Marianne Elliott. New Haven, CT: Yale University Press, 1987.

——, *The Police and the People: French Popular Protest 1789–1820*. Oxford: Oxford University Press, 1970.

——, *A Sense of Place*. London: Duckworth, 1975.

Cobban, Alfred, *The Social Interpretation of the French Revolution*. Cambridge: Cambridge University Press, 1964.

Corbin, Alain, *The Life of an Unknown: The Rediscovered World of a Clog Maker in Nineteenth-Century France*. New York: Columbia University Press, 2001.

Corvol, Andrée, *L'homme aux bois. Histoire des relations de l'homme et de la forêt, XVIIe-XXe siècle*. Paris: Fayard, 1987.

——, *L'homme et l'arbre sous l'Ancien Régime*. Paris: Economica, 1984.

——, 'La forêt', in Pierre Nora (ed.), *Les Lieux de Mémoire*, vol. 3, *Les France: conflits et partages*. Paris: Gallimard, 1984, 673–737.

—— (ed.), *La forêt. Actes du 113e Congrès national des sociétés savantes, Strasbourg 1988*. Paris: Editions du C.T.H.S., 1991.

——, *La forêt: perceptions et representations*. Paris, L'Harmattan, 1997.

—— (ed.), *La nature en Révolution. Colloque Révolution, nature, paysage et environnement*. Paris: Harmattan, 1993.

Crook, Malcolm, *Elections in the French Revolution: An Apprenticeship in Democracy, 1789–1799*. Cambridge and New York: Cambridge University Press, 1996.

Crook, Malcolm, 'Federalism and the French Revolution: The Revolt of Toulon in 1793', *History* 65 (1980), 383–97.

——, *Napoleon Comes to Power: Democracy and Dictatorship in Revolutionary France, 1795–1804*. Cardiff: University of Wales Press, 1998.

Crouzet, François, 'Les origines du sous-développement économique du Sud-Ouest', *Annales du Midi* 71 (1959), 3–21.

Crubaugh, Anthony, *Balancing the Scales of Justice. Local Courts and Rural Society in Southwest France, 1750–1800*. University Park: Pennsylvania State University Press, 2001.

Darrow, Margaret, *Revolution in the House: Family, Class and Inheritance in Southern France, 1775–1825*. Princeton, NJ: Princeton University Press, 1989.

de Baecque, Antoine, *The Body Politic: Corporeal Metaphor in Revolutionary France, 1770–1800*. Stanford, CA: Stanford University Press, 1997.

——, *Glory and Terror: Seven Deaths under the French Revolution*, trans. Charlotte Mandell. New York and London: Routledge, 2001.

de Jouvenel, François, 'Les camps de Jalès (1790–1792), épisodes contre-révolutionnaires?', *AHRF* 337 (2004), 1–20.

Degonville, Bernard, 'De la Société populaire de Chauny pendant la Révolution', *Fédération des sociétés d'histoire et d'archéologie de l'Aisne. Memoires* 34 (1989), 48–75.

Delpierre, Madeleine, *Dress in France in the Eighteenth Century*, trans. Caroline Beamish. New Haven and London: Yale University Press, 1997.

Delvit, Philippe, 'Construire en rivière au XVIIIe siècle: les continuateurs de Colbert sur le Lot', *Annales du Midi* 95 (1983), 429–47.

Derex, Jean-Michel, 'Le décret du 14 frimaire an II sur l'assèchement des étangs: folles espérances et piètres résultats. L'application du décret en Brie', *AHRF* 325 (2001), 77–97.

Desan, Suzanne, 'Qu'est-ce qui fait un père? Illégitimité et paternité de l'an II au Code civil', *Annales*, 57 (2002), 935–64.

——, *Reclaiming the Sacred: Lay Religion and Popular Politics in Revolutionary France*. Ithaca, NY: Cornell University Press, 1990.

——, *The Family on Trial in Revolutionary France*. Berkeley, Los Angeles and London: University of California Press, 2004.

——, 'The Rhetoric of Religious Revival during the French Revolution', *JMH* 60 (1988), 1–27.

——, ' "War between Brothers and Sisters": Inheritance Law and Gender Politics in Revolutionary France', *FHS* 20 (1997), 597–634.

Descadeillas, René, *Rennes et ses derniers seigneurs, 1730–1820. Contribution à l'étude économique et sociale de la baronnie de Rennes au XVIIIe siècle*. Toulouse: Privat, 1964.

Deveau, Jean-Michel, *La traite rochelaise*. Paris: Karthala, 1990.

DiCaprio, 'Women Workers, State-Sponsored Work, and the Right to Subsistence during the French Revolution', *JMH* 71 (1999), 519–51.

Donovan, James M., 'Magistrates and Juries in France, 1791–1952', *FHS* 22 (1999), 379–420.

Doyle, William, *The Ancien Regime* (Houndmills, Macmillan, 1986).

——, *The Oxford History of the French Revolution*, 2nd ed. Oxford and New York: Oxford University Press, 2002.

Dubois, Eugène, *Histoire de la Révolution dans l'Ain*, vol. 1, *La Constituante (1789–1791)*. Bourg: Brochot, 1931.

Duby, Georges and Armand, Wallon, *Histoire de la France rurale*, ii, *L'Age classique des paysans de 1340 à 1789*. Paris: Seuil, 1975; iii, *Apogée et crise de la civilisation paysanne de 1789 à 1914*. Paris: Seuil, 1976.

Dumas, G., 'Les "émotions populaires" dans le département de l'Aisne de la fin de 1790 à l'an IV (1795–1796)', *Société d'histoire et d'archéologie de Senlis* 22 (1977), 38–64.

Dupâquier, Jacques, *Histoire de la population française*, vol. 3. Paris: Presses Universitaires de France, 1988.

Duyker, Edward, *Citizen Labillardière: A French Naturalist in New Holland and the South Pacific*. Melbourne: Melbourne University Press, 2003.

Edelstein, Melvin, 'La Feuille villageoise': communication et modernisation dans les régions rurales pendant la Révolution. Paris, Bibliothèque Nationale, 1977.

———, 'La place de la Révolution française dans la politisation des paysans', AHRF 280 (1993), 135–44.

Edmonds, Bill, "Federalism' and Urban Revolt in France in 1793', JMH 55 (1983), 22–53.

———, Jacobinism and the Revolt of Lyon, 1789–1793. Oxford: Oxford University Press, 1990.

L'Espace et le temps reconstruits: la Révolution française, une révolution des mentalités et cultures? Aix-en-Provence: Université de Provence, 1990.

Fairchilds, Cissie, Poverty and Charity in Aix-en-Provence, 1640–1789. Baltimore, MD: Johns Hopkins University Press, 1976.

Farge, Arlette, Fragile Lives: Violence, Power, and Solidarity in Eighteenth-Century Paris, trans. Carol Shelton. Cambridge, MA: Harvard University Press, 1993.

Fauré, Christine, Democracy Without Women: Feminism and the Rise of Liberal Individualism in France, trans. Claudia Gorbman and John Berks. Bloomington, IN: Indiana University Press, 1991.

Favre, Adrien, Histoire de Châtillon sur Chalaronne, n.p., 1972.

Festy, Octave, L'agriculture pendant la Révolution française. Les conditions de production et de récolte des cereals. Paris: Gallimard, 1947.

Fitzsimmons, Michael P., The Night the Old Regime Ended: August 4, 1789 and the French Revolution. University Park: Pennsylvania State University Press, 2003.

———, The Remaking of France: The National Assembly, the Constitution of 1791 and the Reorganization of the French Polity. Cambridge and New York: Cambridge University Press, 1994.

Fleury, Édouard, Le clergé du department de l'Aisne pendant la Révolution. Études révolutionnaires, 2 vols. Paris and Laon: 1853.

Forrest, Alan, Conscripts and Deserters: The Army and French Society during the Revolution and Empire. Oxford: Oxford University Press, 1989.

———, Napoleon's Men: The Soldiers of the Revolution and Empire. London and New York: Hambledon and London, 2002.

———, Paris, the Provinces and the French Revolution. London: Arnold, 2004.

———, Soldiers of the French Revolution. Durham, NC: Duke University Press, 1990.

———, Society and Politics in Revolutionary Bordeaux. Oxford: Oxford University Press, 1975.

———, The French Revolution and the Poor. Oxford: Blackwell, 1981.

———, The Revolution in Provincial France: Aquitaine 1789–1799. Oxford and New York: Oxford University Press, 1996.

Forrest, Alan and Peter Jones (eds), Reshaping France: Town, Country and Region during the French Revolution. Manchester: Manchester University Press, 1991.

Forster, Robert, The House of Saulx-Tavanes: Versailles and Burgundy 1700–1830. Baltimore, MD: Johns Hopkins University Press, 1977.

———, The Nobility of Toulouse in the Eighteenth Century: A Social and Economic Study. Baltimore, MD: Johns Hopkins University Press, 1960.

Forster, Robert, 'The Survival of the Nobility during the French Revolution', P&P 37 (1967), 71–86.

———, 'Who is a Citizen? The Boundaries of "La Patrie": The French Revolution and the People of Color, 1789–91', French Politics and Society 7 (1989), 50–64.

Fournas de la Brosse, Antoine de, 'Une famille française sous la Révolution, l'Empire et la Restauration', n.p., c. 1979.

Fournier, Georges, *Démocratie et vie municipale en Languedoc du milieu du XVIIIe au début du XIXe siècle*, 2 vols. Toulouse: Les Amis des archives, 1994.

———, 'Entre vallée de l'Hérault et vallée de la Garonne: les bastions fermement républicains sous le Directoire', in Jean Sentou (ed.), *Révolution et contre-révolution dans la France du Midi (1789–1799)*. Toulouse: Presses universitaires du Mirail, 1991, 181–204.

———, 'Les femmes dans la vie politique locale en Languedoc pendant la Révolution française', in Marie-France Brive (ed.), *Les femmes et la Révolution française. Actes du colloque international 12–13–14 avril 1989*. Toulouse: Presses universitaires de Mirail, 1989, 115–22.

———, 'La langue des assemblées locales en Languedoc pendant la Révolution', in *La question linguistique au sud au moment de la Révolution*, i, *Lengas* 17 (1985), 157–77.

———, 'La vie politique au village en l'an II', *AHRF* 300 (1995), 271–82.

———, and Michel, Péronnet, *La Révolution dans l'Aude*. Le Coteau: Horvath, 1989.

Furet, François, *The French Revolution 1774–1884*. Oxford: Oxford University Press, 1992.

Freeman, John F., 'Forest Conservancy in the Alps of Dauphiné', *Forest & Conservation History* 38 (1994), 171–80.

Frey, Max, *Les Transformations du vocabulaire français à l'époque de la Révolution (1789–1800)*. Paris: Presses universitaires de France, 1925.

Furet, François, *Interpreting the French Revolution*, trans. E. Forster. Cambridge: Cambridge University Press, 1981.

Garrioch, David, *The Making of Revolutionary Paris*. Berkeley and London: University of California Press, 2002.

Gauthier, Florence, *La voie paysanne dans la Révolution française: l'exemple picard*. Paris: François Maspero, 1977.

Gautier, Etienne and Louis Henry, *La population de Crulai, paroisse normande: étude historique*. Paris: Les cahiers de L'INED, 1958.

Geffroy, Annie, 'Sans-culotte(s) – Novembre 1790 – Juin 1792', *Dictionnaire des usages socio-politiques – 1*. Paris: Klincksieck, 1985.

Gibson, Ralph, *A Social History of French Catholicism, 1789–1914*. London: Routledge, 1989.

Gough, Hugh, 'The Provincial Press in the French Revolution', in Alan Forrest and Peter Jones (eds), *Reshaping France: Town, Country and Region during the French Revolution*. Manchester: Manchester University Press, 1991, 201.

Graham, Hamish, 'Women and Wood: The Gender Dimensions of Timber-Gathering and Wood-Theft in the Eighteenth and Nineteenth Centuries', in Robert Aldrich and Martyn Lyons (eds), *The Sphinx in the Tuileries and Other Essays in Modern French History. Papers Presented at the Eleventh George Rudé Seminar*. Sydney: University of Sydney, 1999, 15–26.

Grand-Mesnil, Marie-Noëlle, 'La loi du 29 septembre 1791,' in Woronoff (ed.), *Rèvolution et espaces forestiers* (L'Harmattan), 200–5.

Grezaud, Suzanne, 'Un cas de registres paroissiaux tenus par un prêtre réfractaire', *AHRF* 200 (1970), 346–9.

Greer, Donald, *The Incidence of the Emigration during the French Revolution. Cambridge*, MA: Harvard University Press, 1951.

Gresser, Pierre *et al.*, *Les Hommes et la forêt en Franche-Comté*. Paris: C. Bonneton, 1990.

Gross, Jean-Pierre, *Fair Shares for All: Jacobin Egalitarianism in Practice*. Cambridge and New York: Cambridge University Press, 1997.

Gruder, Vivian R., 'Can We Hear the Voices of Peasants? France, 1788', *History of European Ideas* 17 (1993), 167–90.

Gueniffey, Patrice, *Le nombre et la raison: la Révolution française et les élections*. Paris: EHESS, 1993.

Guérin, Daniel, *Class Struggle in the First French Republic: Bourgeois and Bras Nus 1793–1795*, trans. I. Patterson. London: Pluto Press, 1977.

Guilhaumou, Jacques and Martine Lapied, 'La mission Maignet', *AHRF* 300 (1995), 283–94.

Gutwirth, Madelyn, *The Twilight of the Goddesses: Women and Representation in the French Revolutionary Era*. New Brunswick, NJ: Rutgers University Press, 1992.

Halpérin, Jean-Louis, 'Le droit prive de la Révolution: héritage legislative et héritage idéologique', *AHRF* 328 (2002), 131–51.

Hanson, Paul, *Provincial Politics in the French Revolution: Caen and Limoges, 1789–1794*. Baton Rouge, LA: Louisiana State University Press, 1989.

———, *The Jacobin Republic under Fire: The Federalist Revolt in the French Revolution*. University Park, PA: Pennsylvania State University Press, 2003.

Hayhoe, Jeremy D., 'Neighbours before the Court: Crime, Village Communities and Seigneurial Justice in Northern Burgundy, 1750–1790', *FH* 17 (2003), 127–48.

Hérrisay, Jacques, *Les massacres de Meaux*. Paris: Librairie Académique Perrin, 1935.

Hesse, Carla, 'The Cultural Contradictions of Feminism in the French Revolution', in Colin Jones and Dror Wahrman (eds), *The Age of Cultural Revolutions: Britain and France, 1750–1820*. Berkeley and Los Angeles: University of California Press, 2002.

Higonnet, Patrice, *Pont-de-Montvert: Social Structure and Politics in a French Village, 1700–1914*. Cambridge, MA: Harvard University Press, 1971.

Hobsbawm, E.J., 'Peasants and Politics', *Journal of Peasant Studies* 1 (1973), 13.

Hood, James N., 'Patterns of Popular Protest in the French Revolution: The Conceptual Contribution of the Gard', *JMH* 48 (1976), 259–93.

———, 'Protestant-Catholic Relations and the Roots of the First Popular Counterrevolutionary Movement in France', *JMH* 43 (1971), 245–75.

Hopkin, David M., *Soldier and Peasant in French Popular Culture, 1766–1870*. Woodbridge, Sussex and New York: Royal Historical Society, 2003.

Horn, Jeff, *'Qui parle pour la nation?' Les élections et les élus de la Champagne méridionale, 1765–1830*. Paris: Société des études robespierristes, 2004.

———, 'Toute politique est locale', *AHRF* 311 (1998), 89–109.

Houdaille, Jacques 'Un indicateur de pratique religieuse: la célébration saisonnière des mariages avant, pendant et après la Révolution française', *Population* 2 (1978), 367–80.

———, 'Le Problème des pertes de guerre', *Revue d'histoire moderne et contemporaine* xvii (1970), 418.

Houzard, G., 'Les grosses forges ont-elles mangé la forêt?', *Annales de Normandie* 30 (1980), 245–69.

Huard, Raymond 'Souvenir et tradition révolutionnaires: le Gard (1848–1851)', *AHRF* 258 (1984), 565–87.

Hufton, Olwen, 'Attitudes towards Authority in Eighteenth-Century Languedoc', *SH* 3 (1978), 281–302.

———, *Bayeux in the Late Eighteenth Century: A Social Study*. Oxford: Oxford University Press, 1967.

Hufton, Olwen, 'The Reconstruction of a Church 1796–1801', in Gwynne Lewis and Colin Lucas (eds), *Beyond the Terror: Essays in French Regional and Social History, 1794–1815*. Cambridge and New York: Cambridge University Press, 1983.

———, 'Women and the Family Economy in Eighteenth-Century France', *FHS* 9 (1975), 1–22.

———, 'Women in Revolution', *French Politics and Society* 7 (1989), 65–81.

———, 'Women in Revolution 1789–1796', *P&P* (1971), 90–108.

Hunt, David, 'Peasant Movements and Communal Property during the French Revolution', *Theory and Society* 17 (1988), 255–83.

——, 'Peasant Politics in the French Revolution', *SH* 9 (1984), 277–99.

Hunt, Lynn, *Politics, Culture, and Class in the French Revolution*. Berkeley, CA: University of California Press, 1984.

——, 'Presidential Address. The World We Have Gained: The Future of the French Revolution', *AHR* 108 (2003), 1–19.

——, *The Family Romance of the French Revolution*. Berkeley, CA: University of California Press, 1992.

Hunt, Lynn, David Lansky and Paul Hanson, 'The Failure of the Liberal Republic in France, 1795–1799: The Road to Brumaire', *JMH* 51 (1979), 734–59.

Husson, Jean-Pierre, *Les forêts françaises*. Nancy: Presses universitaires de Nancy, 1995.

Huussen, Arend H., 'La "crise" du mariage pendant la Révolution française', in Paul Viallaneix and Jean Ehrard (eds), *Aimer en France, 1760–1860, Actes du colloque international de Clermont-Ferrand*. Clermont-Ferrand: Faculté des Lettres et Sciences humaines, 1980, 331–43.

Ikni, Guy, 'Sur les biens communaux pendant la Révolution française', *AHFR* 247 (1982), 71–94.

Jaher, Frederic Cople, *The Jews and the Nation: Revolution, Emancipation, State Formation, and the Liberal Paradigm in America and France*. Princeton, NJ and Oxford: Princeton University Press, 2002.

Jessenne, Jean-Pierre, 'Le changement rural, l'État et l'adaptation des communautés villageoises en France et en Europe de nord-ouest à la fin du XVIIIe siècle', *AHRF* 315 (1999), 127–61.

——, *Pouvoir au village et révolution: Artois, 1760–1848*. Lille: Presses universitaires de Lille, 1987.

Johnson, Christopher H., *The Life and Death of Industrial Languedoc, 1700–1920*. New York and Oxford: Oxford University Press, 1995.

Johnson, Hubert C., *The Midi in Revolution: A Study of Regional Political Diversity, 1789–1793*. Princeton, NJ: Princeton University Press, 1986.

Jollet, Anne, *Terre et société en Révolution: approche du lien social dans la région d'Amboise*. Paris: éditions du Comité des travaux historiques et scientifiques, 2000.

Jones, Colin, *The Longman Companion to the French Revolution*. London and New York: Longman, 1988.

——, 'The Welfare of the French Foot-Soldier from Richelieu to Napoleon', *History* lxv (1980), 193–213.

Jones, P.M., 'Common Rights and Agrarian Individualism in the Southern Massif Central, 1750–1880', in Gwynne Lewis and Colin Lucas (eds), *Beyond the Terror: Essays in French Regional and Social History, 1794–1815*. Cambridge: Cambridge University Press, 1983.

——, *Liberty and Locality in Revolutionary France: Six Villages Compared, 1760–1820*. Cambridge and New York Cambridge University Press, 2003.

——, *Politics and Rural Society: The Southern Massif Central c.1750–1880*. Cambridge: Cambridge University Press, 1985.

——, *Reform and Revolution in France: The Politics of Transition, 1774–1791*. Cambridge: Cambridge University Press, 1995.

——, *The Peasantry in the French Revolution*. Cambridge: Cambridge University Press, 1988.

——, 'Agricultural Modernization and the French Revolution', *Journal of Historical Geography* 16 (1990), 38–50.

Jordan, David, *The King's Trial: The French Revolution versus Louis XVI*. Berkeley, CA: University of California Press, 1979.

Jouvenel, François de, 'Les camps de Jalès (1790–1792), épisodes contre-révolutionnaires?', *AHRF* 337 (2004), 1–20.

Julia, Dominique *et al.*, *Atlas de la Révolution française, 2, L'enseignement 1760–1815*. Paris: Éditions de l'EHESS, 1987.

Kaiser, Thomas E., 'Who's Afraid of Marie-Antoinette? Diplomacy, Austrophobia and the Queen', *FH* 14 (2000), 241–71.

Kaplan, Steven L., *Farewell Revolution: Disputed Legacies, France 1789/1989*. Ithaca, NY: Cornell University Press, 1995.

——, *La fin des corporations*. Paris: Fayard, 2001.

Kaplow, Jeffry, *Elbeuf during the Revolutionary Period: History and Social Structure*. Baltimore, MD: Johns Hopkins University Press, 1964.

Kaplow, Jeffry (ed.), *New Perspectives on the French Revolution: Readings in Historical Sociology*. New York: John Wiley, 1965.

Kennedy, Emmet, *A Cultural History of the French Revolution*. New Haven, CT: Yale University Press, 1989.

Kennedy, Michael, *The Jacobin Clubs in the French Revolution, 1793–1795*. New York: Oxford University Press, 2000.

——, *The Jacobin Clubs in the French Revolution: The First Years*. Princeton, NJ: Princeton University Press, 1982.

——, *The Jacobin Clubs in the French Revolution: The Middle Years*. Princeton, NJ: Princeton University Press, 1988.

Klassen, Sherri, 'The Domestic Virtues of Old Age: Gendered Rites in the Fête de la Vieillesse', *Canadian Journal of History* 32 (1997), 393–403.

Knibiehler, Yvonne, 'Femmes de Provence en Révolution', in Marie-France Brive (ed.), *Les femmes et la Révolution française. Actes du colloque international 12–13–14 avril 1989*. Toulouse: Presses universitaires de Mirail, 1989, 149–55.

Koubi, Geneviève (ed.), 'De l'article 2 à l'article 17 de la Declaration de 1789: la brèche dans le discours révolutionnaire', in Geneviève Koubi (ed.), *Propriété et Révolution: Actes du Colloque de Toulouse, 12–14 Octobre, 1989*. Paris: CNRS, 1990, 65–84.

Krantz, Frederick (ed.), *History from Below: Studies in Popular Protest and Popular Ideology in Honour of George Rudé*. Montreal: Concordia University Press, 1985.

Kroen, Sheryl, *Politics and Theater: The Crisis of Legitimacy in Restoration France, 1815–1830*. Berkeley, CA: University of California Press, 2000.

Ladde, Brigitte, *Inventaire de la sous-série 110J, Régistres des baptêmes mariages et sépultures tenus par les prêtres réfractaires de l'Ain 1790–1801*. Bourg-en-Bresse: Archives départementales de l'Ain, 1999.

Langlois, Claude and Timothy Le Goff, 'Les Vaincus de la Révolution: jalons pour une sociologie des prêtres mariés', in Albert Soboul (ed.), *Voies nouvelles pour l'histoire de la Révolution française*. Paris: Bibliothèque Nationale, 1978.

Lapied, Martine, 'La place des femmes dans la sociabilité et la vie politique locale en Provence et dans le Comtat Venaissin pendant la Révolution', *Provence historique* 46 (1996), 457–69.

Lardière, Martin and Xavier, *Le Massacre des Lucs-Vendée 1794*. Vouillè: Geste editions, 1992.

Larguier, Gilbert *et al.* (eds), *1789 dans la sénéchaussée de Limoux*. Limoux: Comité Limouxin du bicentenaire de la Révolution française, 1989, 52–6

——, *Cahiers de doléances audois*. Carcassonne: Association des amis des archives de l'Aude, 1989.

Larguier, Gilbert, 'Le drap et le grain en Languedoc. Recherches sur Narbonne et le Narbonnais (1300–1789)', Doctorat d'Etat, 3 vols. Université de Paris-VII, 1992.

——, 'Nation, Citoyen, Patrie. Vocabulaire et concepts des cahiers de doléances du Languedoc et du Roussillon', in *L'An I de la liberté en Languedoc et en Roussillon. Actes du colloque de Béziers (8–9 décembre 1989)*. Béziers: Comité Bitterois du bicentenaire, 1990, 50–72.

Lartichaux, J.-Y., 'Linguistic Politics during the French Revolution', *Diogenes* 97 (1977), 65–84.

Laurent, Robert and Geneviève, Gavignaud, *La Révolution française dans le Languedoc méditerranéen*. Toulouse: Privat, 1987.

Laverrière, Jean-Pierre, présenté par, *Un village entre la Révolution et l'Empire. Viry en Savoie (1792–1815)*. Paris: Éditions Albatros, 1980.

Le Bloas, Alain, 'La question du domaine congéable', *AHRF* 331 (2003), 1–27.

Le Goff, T.J.A., *Vannes and Its Region: A Study of Town and Country in Eighteenth-Century France*. Oxford: Oxford University Press, 1981.

Le Goff, T.J.A. and D.M.G. Sutherland, 'The Revolution and the Rural Community in Brittany', *P&P* 62 (1974), 96–119.

Lebrun, François, 'La guerre de Vendée: massacre ou génocide?', *Histoire* 78 (1985), 93–99.

——, (ed.), *Histoire des Catholiques en France du XVe siècle à nos jours*. Toulouse: Privat, 1980.

——, *Parole de Dieu et Révolution. Les sermons d'un cure angevin avant et pendant la guerre de Vendée*. Paris: Éditions Imago, 1988.

Lefebvre, Georges, *The Directory*, trans. R. Baldick. London: Routledge & Kegan Paul, 1964.

——, *Les Paysans du Nord pendant la Révolution française*. Bari: Laterza, 1959.

——, *Questions agraires au temps de la Terreur. Documents publiés et annotés*. La Roche-sur-Yon: Potier, 1954.

——, 'La Révolution française et les paysans', *AHRF* 10 (1933), 97–128.

——, *The Great Fear of 1789: Rural Panic in Revolutionary France* [1932], trans. Joan White. New York: Vintage Books, 1973.

——, 'The Murder of the Comte de Dampierre (June 22, 1791)', in Jeffry Kaplow (ed.), *New Perspectives on the French Revolution: Readings in Historical Sociology*. New York: John Wiley, 1965, 277–86.

——, 'The Place of the Revolution in the Agrarian History of France', in Robert Forster and Orest Ranum (eds), *Rural Society in France: Selections from the Annales*, Baltimore, MD: Johns Hopkins University, 1977, 31–49.

Lehning, James R., *The Peasants of Marlhes. Economic Development and Family Organization in Nineteenth-Century France*. London: Macmillan, 1980.

Lemarchand, Guy, 'La féodalité et la Révolution française: seigneurie et communauté paysanne (1780–1799)', *AHRF* 242 (1980), 536–58.

——, 'Troubles populaires au XVIIIe siècle et conscience de classe: une préface à la Révolution française', *AHRF* 279 (1990), 32–48.

Lenoël, Pierre and Marie-Françoise Lévy (eds), *L'enfant, la famille et la Révolution française*. Paris: Olivier Orban, 1990.

Lewis, Gwynne, *The Second Vendée: The Continuity of Counter-Revolution in the Department of the Gard, 1789–1815*. Oxford: Oxford University Press, 1978.

——, *France 1715–1804: Power and the People*. Harlow: Pearson Longman, 2004.

——, 'Political Brigandage and Popular Disaffection in the South-East of France, 1795–1804', in Gwynne Lewis and Colin Lucas, (eds), *Beyond the Terror: Essays in French Regional and Social History, 1794–1815*. Cambridge: Cambridge University Press, 1983.

————, *The Advent of Modern Capitalism in France 1770–1840: The Contribution of Pierre-François Tubeuf.* Oxford: Clarendon Press of Oxford University Press, 1993.

————, *The French Revolution: Rethinking the Debate.* London, 1993.

Livesey, James, *Making Democracy in the French Revolution.* Cambridge, MA and London: Harvard University Press, 2001.

————, 'Material Culture, Economic Institutions and Peasant Revolution in Lower Languedoc 1770–1840', *P&P* 182 (2004), 143–73.

Longfellow, David, 'Silk Weavers and the Social Struggle in Lyon during the French Revolution', *FHS* 12 (1981), 1–40.

Louisfert, Blandine, 'La vie culturelle et intellectuelle à Alençon au temps des lumières, 1750–1789', *Société Historique et Archéologique de L'Orne* 108 (1989), 29–53.

Luc, Jean-Noël, *Paysans et droits féodaux en Charente-Inférieure pendant la Révolution française.* Paris: Commission d'Histoire de la Révolution française, 1984.

———— (ed.), *Gendarmerie, état et société au XIXe siècle.* Paris: Publications de la Sorbonne, 2002.

Lucas, Colin, 'The Crowd and Politics between the Ancien Régime and Revolution in France', in Timothy Blanning (ed.), *The Rise and Fall of the French Revolution.* Chicago: University of Chicago Press, 199–235.

————, *The Structure of the Terror; the Example of Javogues and the Loire* Oxford: Oxford University Press, 1973.

————, 'Themes in Southern Violence after 9 Thermidor', in Gwynne Lewis and Colin Lucas (eds), *Beyond the Terror: Essays in French Regional and Social History, 1794–1815.* Cambridge and New York: Cambridge University Press, 1983, 180.

———— (ed.), *The French Revolution and the Creation of Modern Political Culture,* 4 vols. Oxford: Pergamon Press, 1987–94.

————, 'Aux sources du comportement politique de la paysannerie beaujolaise', in *La Révolution française et le monde rural. Actes du colloque tenu en Sorbonne les 23, 24 et 25 octobre 1987.* Paris: Comité des travaux historiques et scientifiques, 1989, 345–65.

————, 'Talking About Urban Popular Violence in 1789', in Alan Forrest and Peter Jones (eds), *Reshaping France: Town, Country and Region during the French Revolution.* Manchester: Manchester University Press, 1991.

————, 'The Theory and Practice of Denunciation in the French Revolution', *JMH* 68 (1996), 768–85.

Lyons, Martyn, 'Cobb and the Historians', in Gwynne Lewis and Colin Lucas (eds), *Beyond the Terror: Essays in French Regional and Social History, 1794–1815.* Cambridge and New York: Cambridge University Press, 1983.

————, *France Under the Directory.* Cambridge and New York: Cambridge University Press, 1975.

————, 'Politics and Patois: The Linguistic Policy of the French Revolution', *Australian Journal of French Studies* 18 (1981), 264–81.

————, *Napoleon Bonaparte and the Legacy of the French Revolution.* London: Macmillan, 1994.

Maciak, Jill, 'Of News and Networks: The Communication of Political Information in the Rural South-West during the French Revolution', *FH* 15 (2001), 273–306.

Maës, Bruno, 'Le pèlerinage de Notre-Dame-de-Liesse de 1780 à la Restauration', in *La Religion et la Révolution française. Actes du Colloque international de Chantilly, 1986,* 612–17.

Malsy, Jean-Claude, *Les noms de lieu du department de l'Aisne,* 3 vols. Paris: Société française d'onomastique, 1999.

Margadant, Ted W., *Urban Rivalries in the French Revolution.* Princeton, NJ: Princeton University Press, 1992.

————, 'Summary Justice and the Peasant Uprising of 1789 in the Mâconnais', *SFHS,* Milwaukee, 2003.

Margadant, Ted W., 'Summary Justice and the Crisis of the Old Regime in 1789', *Historical Reflections/Réflections historiques*, 29 (2003), 495–528.

Margairaz, Dominique, 'La Révolution et l'intégration des paysans à une économie marchande', in *La Révolution française et le monde rural. Actes du colloque tenu en Sorbonne les 23, 24 et 25 octobre 1987.* Paris: Comité des travaux historiques et scientifiques, 1989, 167–82.

Markoff, John, *The Abolition of Feudalism: Peasants, Lords, and Legislators in the French Revolution.* University Park, PA: Pennsylvania State University Press, 1996.

Marquié, Claude, *L'industrie textile carcassonnaise au XVIIIe siècle. Étude d'un groupe social: les marchands-fabricants.* Carcassonne: SESA, 1993.

Martin, Jean-Clément, 'Histoire et polémique, les massacres de Machecoul', *AHRF* 291 (1993), 33–60.

——, *Révolution et contre-révolution. Les Rouages de l'histoire.* Rennes, 1996.

Massary, Xavier de, 'Les usages de l'arrondissement de Château-Thierry. L'époque révolutionnaire', *Fédération des sociétés d'histoire et d'archéologie de l'Aisne. Memoires,* 34 (1989), 21–43.

Massé, Pierre, *Varennes et ses maitres. Un domaine rural, de l'Ancien Régime à la Monarchie de Juillet (1779–1842).* Paris: S.E.V.P.E.N., 1956.

Maza, Sarah, *The Myth of the French Bourgeoisie: An Essay on the Social Imaginary, 1750–1850.* Cambridge, MA: Harvard University Press, 2003.

McLaren, Angus, *Sexuality and Social Order: The Debate over the Fertility of Women and Workers in France, 1770–1820.* New York: Holmes and Meier, 1983.

McMillan, James F., *France and Women, 1789–1914: Gender, Society and Politics.* London and New York: Routledge, 2000.

——, *A Social History of France, 1780–1914*, 2nd ed. London and New York: Palgrave Macmillan, 2004.

McManners, John, *French Ecclesiastical Society under the Ancien Régime.* Manchester: Manchester University Press, 1960.

McPhee, Peter, *Collioure 1780–1815. The French Revolution in a Mediterranean Community.* Melbourne: University of Melbourne, 1989.

——, 'Counter-Revolution in the Pyrenees: Spirituality, Class and Ethnicity in the Haut-Vallespir, 1793–1794', *FH* 7 (1993), 313–43.

——, 'Electoral Democracy and Direct Democracy in France, 1789–1851', *EHQ* 16 (1986), 77–96.

——, *The French Revolution 1789–1799.* Oxford: Oxford University Press, 2002.

——, 'The French Revolution, Peasants, and Capitalism', *AHR* 94 (1989), 1265–80.

——, 'Frontier, Ethnicity and Identity in the French Revolution: Catalans and Occitans', in Ian Coller *et al* (eds), *French History and Civilization: Papers from the George Rudé Seminar* 1 (2005), 30–7.

——, ' "Il n'y a rien d'aussi horrible à voir": Reflections on Collective Killings in the French Revolution', in Greg Burgess (ed.), *Revolution, Nation and Memory. Papers from the George Rudé Seminar in French History, Hobart, July 2002.* Hobart: University of Tasmania, 2004.

——, ' "The Misguided Greed of Peasants"? Popular Attitudes to the Environment in the Revolution of 1789", *FHS* 24 (2001), 247–69.

——, *The Politics of Rural Life: Political Mobilization in the French Countryside 1846–1852.* Oxford: Oxford University Press, 1992.

——, *Revolution and Environment in Southern France: Peasants, Lords, and Murder in the Corbières, 1780–1830.* Oxford: Oxford University Press, 1999.

——, *Les Semailles de la République dans les Pyrénées-Orientales, 1846–1852: classes sociales, culture et politique.* Perpignan: Le Publicateur, 1995.

———, *A Social History of France, 1780–1914*, 2nd ed. London and New York: Palgrave Macmillan, 2004.

———, *Une communauté languedocienne dans l'histoire: Gabian 1760–1960*. Nîmes: Lacour, 2001.

Merriman, John, *The Stones of Balazuc: A French Village in Time*. New York, Norton, 2002.

Monnier, Raymonde, 'La politisation des paroisses rurales de la banlieue parisienne', in *La Révolution française et le monde rural. Actes du colloque tenu en Sorbonne les 23, 24 et 25 octobre 1987*. Paris: Comité des travaux historiques et scientifiques, 1989, 425–41.

Moran, Daniel and Arthur Waldron (eds), *The People in Arms: Military Myth and National Mobilization Since the French Revolution*. Cambridge: Cambridge University Press, 2003.

Morin-Rotureau, Évelyne (ed.), *1789–1799: combat de femmes. La Révolution exclut les citoyennes*. Paris: Éditions Autrement, 2003.

Morineau, Michel, 'Budgets populaires en France au XVIIIe siècle', *RHES* 1 (1972), 203–37.

———, 'Les moissons de la Révolution', in *La Révolution française et le monde rural. Actes du colloque tenu en Sorbonne les 23, 24 et 25 octobre 1987*. Paris: Comité des travaux historiques et scientifiques, 1989, 199–218.

Muller, Claude, 'Religion et Révolution en Alsace', *AHRF* 337 (2004), 63–83.

Murray, William, *The Right-Wing Press in the French Revolution: 1789–92*. London: Royal Historical Society, 1986.

Nadeau, Martin, 'La politique culturelle de l'an II: les infortunes de la propagande révolutionnaire au théâtre', *AHRF* 327 (Janvier/mars 2002), 57–74.

Nicod, Jean-Claude, 'Les "séditieux" en Languedoc à la fin du XVIIIe siècle', *Recueil de Mémoires et travaux de la Société d'histoire du droit et des institutions des anciens pays de droit écrit* 8 (1971), 145–65.

Nicolas, Jean (ed.), *Mouvements populaires et conscience sociale, XVI–XIXe siècles. Actes du colloque de Paris 24–26 mai 1984*. Paris: Maloine, 1985.

Nicolle, Paul, 'Les meurtres politiques d'août–septembre 1792 dans le département de l'Orne: Étude critique', *AHRF* 62 (March–April 1934), 97–118.

Noël, Michel, *L'homme et la forêt en Languedoc-Roussillon: histoire et économie des espaces boisés*. Perpignan: Presses universitaires de Perpignan, 1996.

Noiriel, Gérard, *Réfugiés et sans-papiers. La République face au droit d'asile XIXe–XXe siècle*. Paris: Hachette, 1998.

Nora, Pierre (ed.), *Rethinking France: Les Lieux de mémoire*, vol. 1, *The State*, trans. Mary Trouille. Chicago, 2001.

Norberg, Kathryn, *Rich and Poor in Grenoble, 1600–1814*. Stanford, CA: Stanford University Press, 1985.

Nordman, Daniel *et al.*, *Atlas de la Révolution française*, v, *Le territoire*. Paris: Éditions de l'EHESS, 1989.

Oge, Frédéric, 'Appropriation communautaire et/ou appropriation étatique de la forêt sous la Révolution', in Geneviève Koubi (ed.), *Propriété et Révolution: Actes du colloque de Toulouse, 1989*. Paris: CNRS, 1990, 127–33.

———, 'Héritage révolutionnaire: les forêts pyrénéennes', in Andrée Corvol (ed.), *La nature en Révolution. Colloque Révolution, nature, paysage et environnement*. Paris: Harmattan, 1993, 156–62.

Ozouf, Mona, *Festivals and the French Revolution*, trans. Alan Sheridan. Cambridge, MA: Harvard University Press, 1988.

Palmer, R.R., *The Improvement of Humanity: Education and the French Revolution*. Princeton, NJ: Princeton University Press, 1985.

Patrick, Alison, 'The Approach of French Revolutionary Officials to Social Problems, 1790-1792', *AJFS* 18 (1981), 248–63.

Patrick, Alison, 'French Revolutionary Local Government, 1789–1792', in Colin Lucas (ed.), *The Political Culture of the French Revolution*. London: Pergamon Press, 1988.

——, *The Men of the First French Republic: Political Alignments in the National Convention of 1792*. Baltimore, MD: Johns Hopkins University Press, 1972.

Pellegrin, Nicole, *Les vêtements de la Liberté: abécedaire des pratiques vestimentaires en France de 1780 à 1800*. Aix-en-Provence: Alinea, 1989.

Péret, Jacques, 'L'exemplaire histoire d'une famille bourgeoise poitevine, les Monnet (1660–1880)', *RHMC* 26 (1979), 98–124.

Péronnet, Michel and Georges Fournier, *La Révolution dans l'Aude*. Le Coteau: Horvath, 1989.

Péronnet, Michel and Gérard Bourdin, *La Révolution dans l'Orne, 1789–1799*. Le Coteau: Horvath, 1988.

Péronnet, Michel, Robert Attal and Jean Bobin, *La Révolution dans l'Aisne, 1789–1799*. Le Coteau: Horvath, 1988.

Perrot, J.-C., 'Voies nouvelles pour l'histoire économique de la Révolution', *Voies nouvelles pour l'histoire de la Révolution française*. Paris: 1978, 115–42.

Perrot, Michelle (ed.), *A History of Private Life: From the Fires of Revolution to the Great War*, trans. Arthur Goldhammer. Cambridge, MA and London: Harvard University Press, 1990.

Petitfrère, Claude, 'Les grandes composantes sociales des armées vendéennes d'Anjou', *AHRF* 45 (1973), 1–20.

——, 'The Origins of the Civil War in the Vendée', *FH* 2 (1988), 187–207.

——, 'La Vendée en l'an II: défaite et répression', *AHRF* 300 (1995), 173–87.

——, *La Vendée et les Vendéens*. Paris: Gallimard, 1981.

——, *Les Vendéens d'Anjou (1793)*. Paris: Bibliothèque nationale, 1981.

Phillips, Roderick, *Family Breakdown in Late-Eighteenth Century France: Divorces in Rouen 1792–1803*. Oxford: Oxford University Press, 1980.

——, 'Remaking the Family: The Reception of Family Law and Policy during the French Revolution', in Reinhardt and Cawthorn (eds), *Essays on the French Revolution*. Arlington, TX: Texas A&M University Press, 1992, 64–89.

Pingue, Danièle, 'Qui étaient les "Jacobins" Haut-Normands? Objectifs, sources, methods d'une enquête prosopographique', *AHRF* 297 (1994), 413–23.

Pitte, Jean-Robert, *Histoire du paysage français*, vol. ii, *Le Profane: du XVIe siècle à nos jours*, 2nd ed. Paris: Taillandier, 1983.

Plack, Noelle L., 'Agrarian Individualism, Collective Practices and the French Revolution: The Law of 10 June 1793 and the Partition of Common Land in the Department of the Gard', *EHQ* 35 (2005), 39–62.

Plouvier, Martine, 'L'abbaye de Prémontré au XVIIe et XVIIIe siècles'. Thèse de troisième cycle, Paris I, 1982.

*Poètes audois dans la tourmente: André Chénier, Venance Dougados, Fabre d'Églantine*. Carcassonne: Archives de l'Aude, 1993.

Poitrineau, Abel, 'Les assemblées primaries du bailliage de Salers en 1789', *RHMC* 25 (1978), 419–42.

Postel-Vinay, Gilles, 'À la recherche de la Révolution économique dans les campagnes (1789–1815)', *Revue économique*, 6 (1989), 1015–45.

Poumarède, Jacques, 'La legislation successorale de la Rèvolution entre l'idéologie et la pratique', in Irène Thery and Christian Biet (eds), *La Famille, la loi, l'État. De la Révolution au Code Civil*. Paris: Imp. Nationale Éditions, 1989, 167–82.

Pourcine, Pascal, 'Le département de l'Aude et la guerre avec l'Espagne, 1792–1795', Thèse de doctorat de 3e cycle. Université de Toulouse, 1985.

'Les prénoms révolutionnaires', special issue of *AHRF* 322 (2000).

Price, Roger, *A Social History of Nineteenth-Century France*. London: Hutchinson, 1987.

Ragan, Bryant T. and Elizabeth A. Williams (eds), *Re-Creating Authority in Revolutionary France*. New Brunswick, NJ: Rutgers University Press, 1992.

Ramsay, Clay, *The Ideology of the Great Fear: The Soissonnais in 1789*. Baltimore, MD and London: The Johns Hopkins University Press, 1992.

Rapport, Michael, *Nationality and Citizenship in Revolutionary France: The Treatment of Foreigners 1789–1799*. Oxford: Clarendon Press of Oxford University Press, 2000.

Reinhard, Marcel, 'Demography, the Economy, and the French Revolution', in Evelyn M. Acomb and Marvin L. Brown (eds), *French Society and Culture since the Old Régime*. New York: Holt, Rinehart and Winston, 1966, 20–42.

Reinhardt, Steven G. and Elisabeth A. Cawthorn (eds), *Essays on the French Revolution: Paris and the Provinces*. Arlington, TX: Texas A&M University Press, 1992.

*La Révolution française et le monde rural. Actes du colloque tenu en Sorbonne les 23, 24 et 25 octobre 1987*. Paris: Comité des travaux historiques et scientifiques, 1989.

Robiquet, Jean, *Daily Life in the French Revolution*. Weidenfeld and Nicolson New York, 1965.

Roche, Daniel, 'Apparences révolutionnaires ou révolution des apparances?', in Nicole Pellegrin (ed.), *Les vêtements de la Liberté: Abécédaire des pratiques vestimentaires en France de 1780 à 1800*. Aix-en-Provence: Alinéa, 1989.

——, *France in the Enlightenment*, trans. Arthur Goldhammer. Cambridge, MA: Harvard University Press, 1998.

Roger-Noël, Isabelle, 'La Révolution aux frontières vue par un volontaire de 1792 à 1796', *Revue historique des armées* 42 (1986), 3–15.

Root, Hilton, 'The Rural Community and the French Revolution', in Keith Michael Baker (ed.), *The French Revolution and the Creation of Modern Political Culture*, i, *The Political Culture of the Old Regime*. Oxford: Pergamon Press, 1987.

Rose, R.B., *The Making of the 'sans-culottes': Democratic Ideas and Institutions in Paris, 1789–1792*. Manchester: Manchester University Press, 1983.

——, 'The "Red Scare" of the 1790s: The French Revolution and the 'Agrarian Law'', *P&P* 103 (1984), 113–30.

——, *Tribunes and Amazons: Men and Women of Revolutionary France, 1789–1871*. Sydney: Macleay Press, 1998.

Rosenthal, Jean-Laurent, *The Fruits of Revolution: Property Rights, Litigation, and French Agriculture, 1700–1860*. Cambridge: Cambridge University Press, 1992.

Rothiot, Jean-Paul, 'Comités de surveillance et Terreur dans le département des Vosges de 1793 à l'an III', *AHRF* 314 (1998), 621–68.

Rudé, George, *The Crowd in the French Revolution*. Oxford: Oxford University Press, 1959.

Sagnac, Philippe and Pierre Caron, *Les comités des droits féodaux et de législation et l'abolition du régime seigneurial (1789–1793)*. Paris: Imprimerie nationale, 1907.

Sagnes, Jean (ed.), *Le Pays catalan*. Pau: Société nouvelle d'études régionales, 1983.

Sahlins, Peter, *Forest Rites: The War of the Demoiselles in Nineteenth-Century France*. Cambridge, MA and London: Harvard University Press, 1994.

——, *Unnaturally French: Foreign Citizens in the Old Regime and After*. Ithaca, NY and London: Cornell University Press, 2004.

Schama, Simon, *Citizens: A Chronicle of the French Revolution*. London: Penguin, 1989.

——, *Landscape and Memory*. New York: Harper Collins, 1995.

Schechter, Ronald, *Obstinate Hebrews: Representations of Jews in France, 1715–1815*. Berkeley, CA and London: University of California Press, 2003.

Scott, William, *Terror and Repression in Revolutionary Marseilles*. London: Macmillan, 1973.

Secher, Reynald, *A French Genocide: The Vendée*, trans. George Holoch. Notre Dame, IN: University of Notre Dame Press, 2003.

Sepinwall, Alyssa Goldstein, 'Eliminating Race, Eliminating Difference: Blacks, Jews, and the Abbé Grégoire', in Sue Peabody and Tyler Stovall (eds), *The Color of Liberty: Histories of Race in France*. Durham, NC and London: Duke University Press, 2003.

Sewell, William H., 'Collective Violence and Collective Loyalties in France: Why the French Revolution Made a Difference', *Politics & Society* 18 (1990), 527–52.

——, *Work and Revolution in France: The Language of Labor from the Old Régime to 1848*. Cambridge: Cambridge University Press, 1980.

Shapiro, Gilbert and John Markoff, *Revolutionary Demands: A Content Analysis of the Cahiers de Doléances of 1789*. Stanford, CA: Stanford University Press, 1998.

Sheppard, Thomas, *Lourmarin in the Eighteenth Century: A Study of a French Village*. Baltimore, MD: Johns Hopkins University Press, 1971.

Singer, Brian, 'Violence in the French Revolution: Forms of Ingestion/Forms of Expulsion', in Ferenc Fehèr (ed.), *The French Revolution and the Birth of Modernity*. Berkeley, CA and Oxford: University of California Press, 1990.

Sire, P., 'La Révolution française et les prénoms', *Folklore* 2 (juillet–août 1939), 286–93.

Slavin, Morris, *The Making of an Insurrection: Parisian Sections and the Gironde*. Cambridge, MA: Harvard University Press, 1986.

Sledziewski, Elisabeth G., 'The French Revolution as the Turning Point', in Geneviève Fraisse and Michelle Perrot (eds), *A History of Women in the West: Emerging Feminism from Revolution to World War*, trans. Arthur Goldhammer. London and Cambridge, MA: Harvard University Press, 1993.

Soboul, Albert, *Comprendre la Révolution: problèmes politiques de la Révolution française (1789–1797)*. Paris: F. Maspero, 1981; trans. April A. Knutson as *Understanding the French Revolution*. New York: International Publishers, 1988.

——, *The French Revolution, 1787–1799: From the Storming of the Bastille to Napoleon*, trans. Alan Forrest and Colin Jones. London: Unwin Hyman, 1989.

——, *Paysans, sans-culottes et Jacobins*. Paris: Clavreuil, 1966.

——, *Précis d'histoire de la Révolution française*. Paris: Éditions Sociales, 1962; trans. Alan Forrest and Colin Jones as *The French Revolution, 1787–1799: From the Storming of the Bastille to Napoleon*. New York: Vintage Books, 1975.

——, *Problèmes paysans de la Révolution, 1789–1848*. Paris: François Maspero, 1976.

——, *Les sans-culottes parisiens en l'an II: histoire politique et sociale des sections de Paris, 2 juin 1793–9 Thermidor An II*. La Roche-sur-Yon: H. Potier, 1958. Trans. Gwynne Lewis, *The Parisian Sans-Culottes and the French Revolution, 1793–4*. Oxford: Oxford University Press, 1964.

—— (ed.), *Contributions à l'histoire paysanne de la Révolution française, 1789–1848*. Paris, Éditions sociales, 1977.

Soboul, Albert *et al.* (eds), *Dictionnaire historique de la Révolution française*. Paris, 1989.

Soulet, Jean-François, *Les Pyrénées au XIXe siècle*, 2 vols. Toulouse: Privat, 1987.

Souvestre, Emile, *Mémoires d'un sans-culotte bas-Breton*. Bruxelles: Wouters, Raspoet, 1843.

Spagnoli, Paul, 'The Unique Decline of Mortality in Revolutionary France', *Journal of Family History* 22 (1997), 425–61.

Subreville, Georges, 'L'apprentissage à Bourg sous la Révolution', *Les Nouvelles Annales de l'Ain*, 1982, 127–62.

Sussman, George D., *Selling Mothers' Milk: The Wet-Nursing Business in France 1715–1914*, Urbana, IL: University of Illinois Press, 1982.

Sutherland, D.M.G., *The Chouans: The Social Origins of Popular Counter-Revolution in Upper Brittany, 1770–1796*. Oxford: Oxford University Press, 1982.

——, *France, 1789–1815: Revolution and Counterrevolution*. Oxford and New York: Oxford University Press, 1986.

——, 'Peasants, Lords, and Leviathan: Winners and Losers from the Abolition of French Feudalism, 1780–1820', *Journal of Economic History* 62 (2002), 1–24.

——, *The French Revolution and Empire: The Quest for a Civic Order*. Oxford: Blackwell Publishers, 2003.

Sydenham, Michael, *The Girondins*. London: Athlone Press, 1961.

——, *The First French Republic, 1792–1804*, part II. London: Batsford, 1974.

Tackett, Timothy, *Becoming a Revolutionary: The Deputies of the French National Assembly and the Emergence of a Revolutionary Culture (1789–1790)*. Princeton, NJ: Princeton University Press, 1996.

——, 'Collective Panics in the Early French Revolution', *FH* 17 (2003), 149–71.

——, *Religion, Revolution, and Regional Culture in Eighteenth-Century France: The Ecclesiastical Oath of 1791*. Princeton, NJ: Princeton University Press, 1986.

——, *When the King Took Flight*. Cambridge, MA: Harvard University Press, 2003.

——, 'Women and Men in Counterrevolution: The Sommières Riot of 1791', *JMH* 59 (1987), 680–704.

Tallonneau, Paul, *Les Lucs et le génocide vendéen. Comment on a manipulé les textes*. Luçon: Editions Hécate, 1993.

Texier, Henri *et al.* (eds), *La Révolution française 1789–1799 à Saintes*. Poitiers: Projets Éditions, 1988.

Teyssier, Éric, 'Appliquer une loi sociale en France sous la Convention. La mise en oeuvre de la loi du 13 septembre 1793', *AHRF* 312 (1998), 265–83.

Thery, Irène and Christian Biet (eds), *La famille, la loi, l'État. De la Révolution au Code Civil*. Paris: Imprimerie Nationale Éditions, 1989.

Thierry, Eric, 'Une fête révolutionnaire à Villers-Cotterêts en 1792', *Fédération des sociétés d'histoire et d'archéologie de l'Aisne. Memoires* 34 (1989), 274–88.

Thomas, Chantal, *The Wicked Queen: The Origins of the Myth of Marie-Antoinette*, trans. Julie Rose. New York: Zone Books, 2000.

Thomson, J.K.J., *Clermont-de-Lodève, 1633–1789: Fluctuations in the Prosperity of a Languedocian Cloth-Making Town*. Cambridge: Cambridge University Press, 1982.

Tilly, Charles, 'The Emergence of Citizenship in France and Elsewhere', *International Review of Social History* 40 (1995), 223–36.

——, *The Vendée*. Cambridge, MA: Harvard University Press, 1964.

Tripier, Yves, ' "Vandalisme révolutionnaire" en Bretagne ou imposition par le pouvoir républicain d'une nouvelle culture, 1793–1795', in Simone Bernard-Griffiths, Marie-Claude Chemin and Jean Ehrard (eds), *Révolution française et 'vandalisme révolutionnaire'. Actes du colloque international de Clermont-Ferrand 15-17 dècembre 1988*. Paris: Universitas, 1992, 149.

Trouvè, Charles-Joseph, *Etats de Languedoc et département de l'Aude*, 2 vols. Paris: Imprimerie nationale, 1818.

Vacherand, André, 'Les biens et revenus de l'abbaye royale d'Origny-Sainte-Benoîte en 1790', *Fédération des sociétés d'histoire et d'archéologie de l'Aisne. Memoires* 34 (1989), 153–77.

Valin, Claudy, *Autopsie d'un massacre. Les journées des 21 et 22 mars 1793 à La Rochelle* St-Jean-d'Angély: Éditions Bordessoules, 1992.

——, *La Rochelle – la Vendée 1793*. Paris: Le Croît vif, 1997.

van de Walle, Etienne, 'Motivations and Technology in the Decline of French Fertility', in Robert Wheaton and Tamara K. Hareven (eds), *Family and Sexuality in French History*. Philadelphia: University of Pennsylvania Press, 1980, 135–78.

Vardi, Liana, 'The Abolition of the Guilds during the French Revolution', *FHS* 15 (1988), 704–17.

———, *The Land and the Loom: Peasants and Profit in Northern France 1680–1800*. Durham, NC and London: Duke University Press, 1993.

Vassort, Jean, 'L'enseignement primaire en Vendômois à l'époque révolutionnaire', *RHMC* 25 (1978), 625–55.

Vaxelaire, Jean-Claude, *Mémoires d'un vétéran de l'ancienne armée (1791–1800)*, ed. H. Gauthier-Villars. Paris: Charles Delagrave, 1892.

Verjus, Anne, *Le cens de la famille. Les femmes et le vote, 1789–1848*. Paris: Belin, 2002.

Viala, Paul, 'La vente des biens nationaux de première origine dans le district de Narbonne (1791 – an IV)', MdeM. Université de Toulouse, 1974.

Viallaneix, Paul and Jean Ehrard (eds), *Aimer en France, 1760–1860, Actes du colloque international de Clermont-Ferrand*. Clermont-Ferrand: Faculté des Lettres et Sciences humaines, 1980.

Viney, Raymond, 'L'ordonnance forestière de Colbert et les législateurs de la Révolution française', *Revue forestière française* 21 (1969), 607–10.

Vinot, Bernard, 'La Révolution au village, avec Saint-Just, d'après le registre des délibérations communales de Blérancourt', *AHRF* 335 (2004), 97–110.

Vivier, Nadine, *Propriété collective et identité communale. Les biens communaux en France 1750–1914*. Paris: Publications de la Sorbonne, 1998.

Vovelle, Michel, 'From Beggary to Brigandage: The Wanderers in the Beauce during the French Revolution', in Jeffry Kaplow (ed.), *New Perspectives on the French Revolution: Readings in Historical Sociology*. New York: John Wiley, 1965, 287–304.

———, *De la cave au grenier: un itinéraire en Provence au XVIIIe siècle. De l'histoire sociale à l'histoire des mentalités*. Québec: S. Fleury, 1980.

———, *La découverte de la politique. Géopolitique de la Révolution française*. Paris: La Découverte, 1993.

———, *Religion et révolution. La Déchristianisation de l'An II*. Paris: Hachette, 1976.

———, *Idéologies et mentalités*. Paris: Maspero, 1982; trans. Eamon O'Flaherty as *Ideologies and Mentalities*. Cambridge: Polity Press, 1990.

———, *La mentalité révolutionnaire: société et mentalité sous la Révolution française*. Paris: Editions Sociales, 1985.

———, *Les métamorphoses de la fête en Provence, de 1750 à 1820*. Paris: Flammarion, 1976.

———, *Nouvelle histoire de la France contemporaine*, volume 1, *La chute de la monarchie (1787–1792)*. Paris: Seuil, 1972; trans. Susan Burke as *The Fall of the Monarchy*. Cambridge: Cambridge University Press, 1983.

———, *The Revolution against the Church: From Reason to the Supreme Being*. Cambridge: Cambridge University Press, 1991.

———, 'Le tournant des mentalités en France 1750–1789: la 'sensibilité' pré-Révolutionnaire', *SH* 5 (1977), 605–29.

———, *Ville et campagne au XVIIIe siècle: Chartres et la Beauce*. Paris: Éditions Sociales, 1980.

Wahnich, Sophie, *L'impossible citoyen: l'étranger dans le discours de la Révolution française*. Paris: Albin Michel, 1997.

———, *La liberté ou la mort: essai sur la Terreur et le terrorisme*. Paris: La Fabrique Éditions, 2003.

Waldinger, Renée, Philip Dawson and Isser Woloch (eds), *The French Revolution and the Meaning of Citizenship*. Westport, CT: Greenwood Press, 1993.

Walzer, Michael (ed.), *Regicide and Revolution: Speeches at the Trial of Louis XVI*. Cambridge: Cambridge University Press, 1974.

Weber, Eugen, *Peasants into Frenchmen: The Modernization of Rural France, 1870–1914*. Stanford, CA: Stanford University Press, 1976.

Williams, David and Maire Cross (eds), *The French Experience from Republic to Monarchy, 1792–1824: New Dawns in Politics, Knowledge and Culture*. Basingstoke: Macmillan, 2000, 12–27.

Woloch, Isser, *The French Veteran from the Revolution to the Restoration*. Chapel Hill, NC: University of North Carolina Press, 1979.

———, *The New Regime: Transformations of the French Civic Order, 1789–1820s*. New York: W.W. Norton, 1994.

———, 'The State and the Villages in Revolutionary France', in Alan Forrest and Peter Jones (eds), *Reshaping France: Town, Country and Region during the French Revolution*. Manchester: Manchester University Press, 1991, 221–42.

Woronoff, Denis, *L'Industrie sidérurgique en France pendant la Révolution et l'Empire*. Paris: Editions de l'EHESS, 1984.

——— (ed.), *Histoire de l'industrie en France. Du XVIe siècle à nos jours*. Paris, 1994.

———, *Revolution et espaces forestiers. Colloque des 3 & 4 juin 1987, Groupe d'histoire des forêts francaises*. Paris: l'Harmattan, 1988.

Woronoff, Denis, *The Thermidorian Regime and the Directory, 1794–1799*, trans. J. Jackson. Cambridge: Cambridge University Press, 1984.

Wrigley, Richard, *The Politics of Appearances: Representations of Dress in Revolutionary France*. Oxford and New York: Berg Publishers, 2002.

Wylie, Lawrence, *Chanzeaux: A Village in Anjou*. Cambridge, MA: Harvard University Press, 1966.

Young, David Bruce, 'A Wood Famine? The Question of Deforestation in Old Regime France', *Forestry* 49 (1976), 45–56.

Zink, Anne, *Azereix: la vie d'une communauté rurale à la fin du XVIIIe siècle*. Paris: S.E.V.P.E.N., 1969.

# Index

CPSIA information can be obtained at www.ICGtesting.com
Printed in the USA
LVOW101630050213

318761LV00001B/1/P